Principles of Food, Beverage, & Labor Cost Controls
for Hotels and Restaurants

Third Edition

Principles of Food, Beverage, & Labor Cost Controls

for Hotels and Restaurants

Third Edition

PAUL R. DITTMER

Hotel and Restaurant Management Department
New Hampshire College
Manchester, New Hampshire

GERALD G. GRIFFIN

Hotel and Restaurant Management Department
New York City Technical College of the
City University of New York
Brooklyn, New York

A CBI Book
Published by Van Nostrand Reinhold Company

Library of Congress Catalog Card Number 83–24111
ISBN 0–442–21973–3

Printed in the United States of America

Published by Van Nostrand Reinhold Company Inc.
135 West 50th Street
New York, New York 10020

Van Nostrand Reinhold Company Limited
Molly Millars Lane
Wokingham, Berkshire RG11 2PY, England

Van Nostrand Reinhold
480 La Trobe Street
Melbourne, Victoria 3000, Australia

Macmillan of Canada
Division of Canada Publishing Corporation
164 Commander Boulevard
Agincourt, Ontario M1S 3C7, Canada

16 15 14 13 12 11 10 9 8 7 6 5 4 3 2

Library of Congress Cataloging in Publication Data

Dittmer, Paul.
Principles of food, beverage, & labor cost controls for hotels and restaurants.

"A CBI book."
Includes index.
1. Restaurants, lunch rooms, etc.—Finance. 2. Hotels, taverns, etc.—Finance. I. Griffin, Gerald G., 1936–
II. Title.
TX911.3.F5D57 1984 647'.95'0681 83–24111
ISBN 0–442–21973–3

We dedicate this book to our wives, Barbara and Charlene, in appreciation of their faith and forbearance.

Contents

PREFACE x
INTRODUCTION xii
The Rush Hour Inn xii The Graduate Restaurant xii

PART ONE / INTRODUCTION TO FOOD, BEVERAGE, AND LABOR CONTROLS 1

1 Cost and Sales Concepts 3

Cost Concepts 4 Definition of Cost 4 Fixed and Variable Costs 4 Controllable and Noncontrollable Costs 5 Unit and Total Costs 6 Prime Cost 7 Historical and Planned Costs 7 Cost to Sales Ratio: the Cost Percentage 8 Industry-Wide Variations in Costs 12 Sales Concepts 14 Matching Costs with Sales 16 *Questions and Problems* 17

2 Control 20

Definition of Control 21 Cost Control 22 Sales Control 22 Responsibility for Control 23 Need for Control 23 Control Techniques 25 Preparing the Operating Budget 31 The Control Process 35 Cost-Benefit Ratio 36 *Questions and Problems* 37

3 Cost, Volume, and Profit Relationships 41

Cost Control and the Cost/Volume/Profit Equation 48 Calculating Average VR 53 *Questions and Problems* 59

4 Electronic Data Processing and Control 64

Historical Perspectives 65 Computers and Their Relation to Human Work 66 Computer Terminology 68 Applications of EDP for Hotels and Restaurants 69 *Questions and Problems* 73

PART TWO / FOOD CONTROL 75

5 Purchasing Control 77

Responsibility 78 Kinds of Food to be Purchased 78 Quality Purchasing 79 Quantity Purchasing 81 Sources of Supply 91 Competitive Prices 92 Centralized Purchasing 93 Standing Orders 94 Summary 94 EDP Applications 95 *Questions and Problems* 95

6 Receiving Control 97

The Receiving Clerk 98 The Invoice 99 The Invoice Stamp 100 Receiving Procedure 100 The Meat Tag 101 Receiving Clerk's Daily Report 102 EDP Applications 104 *Questions and Problems* 105

7 Control of Storing, Issuing, and Transfers 107

Storing Control 108 Dating and Pricing 111 Issuing Control 112 Food and Beverage Transfers 115 EDP Applications 118 *Questions and Problems* 119

8 Monthly Inventory and Food Cost Determinations 124

Monthly Inventory 125 Monthly Food Cost Determination 129 Adjustments to Cost of Food Issued 131 Determining Cost of Food Consumed 132 Determining Cost of Food Sold 134 Reports to Management 135 Inventory Turnovers 137 EDP Applications 139 *Questions and Problems* 140

9 Daily Food Cost Determination 144

Daily Reports 148 Book Versus Actual Inventory Comparison 152 EDP Applications 155 *Questions and Problems* 156

10 Production Standards and Portion Costs 159

Standard Costs 160 Standard Portion Sizes 161 Standard Recipes 162 Standard Portion Costs 163 Using Yield Percentages for Purchase Calculations 173 EDP Applications 174 *Questions and Problems* 175

11 Forecasting Sales and Controlling Production 177

Sales History 178 Forecasting 182 The Production Sheet 183

Par Stock Control of Preportioned Entrees 185 The Void Sheet 186 Portion Inventory and Reconciliation 187 EDP Applications 190 *Questions and Problems* 191

12 Standard Versus Actual Food Costs: Potential Savings 193

Daily Comparison 194 The Menu Pre-Cost and Abstract 196 Periodic Calculation 201 EDP Applications 203 *Questions and Problems* 204

13 Sales Control 206

Increasing the Number of Customers 207 Influencing Customer Purchases 213 Ensuring that Customer Purchases Result in Revenue 221 EDP Applications 227 *Questions and Problems* 229

PART THREE / BEVERAGE CONTROL 231

14 Beverage Control: Purchasing, Receiving, Storing, and Issuing 233

Beverage Purchasing 234 Receiving 239 Storing 240 Issuing 245 EDP Applications 249 *Questions and Problems* 250

15 Beverage Production Control 251

Quantity Control 252 Standard Recipes 257 Determining Standard Portion Costs 259 EDP Applications 267 *Questions and Problems* 267

16 Measuring the Effectiveness of Bar Controls 269

Monthly Calculation of Cost Percentage 270 Adjusting Monthly Figures 270 Daily Calculation of Cost Percentage 275 Adjusting Daily Figures 276 Ounce Control 278 Calculating Potential Sales Value 278 Adjusting Sales Values for Mixed Drinks 279 Mixed Drink Differentials based on Detailed Sales Records 280 Average Potential Sales Values 282 Standard Deviation based on Test Period 283 Sales Control 285 Sales Control Procedures at Small Bars 286 Sales Control Procedures in Larger Operations 288 EDP Applications 288 *Questions and Problems* 289

PART FOUR / LABOR CONTROL 293

17 Labor Control Determinants 295

Labor Control Determinants 298 *Questions and Problems* 307

18 Controlling Labor Costs I 309

The Purposes of Labor Control 310 Nature of Demand for Restaurant Products 310 Work Organization 312 Establishment of an Operational Plan 313 Job Descriptions 314 Analysis of Business Volume 316 Scheduling 323 Reorganization 330 End Note 332 EDP Applications 334 *Questions and Problems* 334

19 Controlling Labor Costs II 336

Standards of Performance 337 The Development of Quality Standards 337 The Development of Quantity Standards 338 Establishing Performance Standards 339 Manpower Requirements 341 EDP Applications 344 *Questions and Problems* 345

AFTERWORD 347

INDEX 349

Preface

Over the years, the authors have taught many courses whose titles have included such words as "food," "beverage," "labor," "cost," and "control" in a variety of combinations. Each teaching assignment has brought with it the responsibility for selecting an appropriate text for student use. But text selection has been a continuing problem—one we have finally solved by writing our own. In preparing this work, our objective has been to present the principles of control in a clear, direct, and logical manner. We have attempted throughout to present these principles in sufficient detail for the student whose experience in the industry may be somewhat limited.

Not surprisingly, a wealth of information about control has been available for some time, both in books and in periodicals. However, until recently, most of it has been written primarily for the practicing professional, not for the student. The amount addressed to students—the professionals of the future—has been entirely insufficient. Many educators have found it necessary to rely on these materials, even though they were not prepared primarily for student use. Valuable as they have been to the professional audience, these materials have been of limited use in the classroom. Particular articles from periodicals and certain chapters from books have been useful, especially when presented by an able instructor, but their use has tended to leave gaps, many of which have been filled chiefly by lecture—not always an entirely successful approach with students.

There has clearly been a need for a text—one that would present the principles of control in a cogent manner, and would simultaneously instill in the student an awareness of the increasing need for controls in this highly diversified industry. In our efforts to fill this need, we have tried always to keep in mind that any discussion of principles and theory must be grounded in practical, everyday terms whenever possible. To attempt such a text without this view would be to risk leaving the student ill-prepared to face the realities of the complex foodservice industry.

With these ends in mind, we have designed and written the text in four parts. Part One is a general introduction to the subjects of cost, sales, and control, the study of which will provide the student with necessary background information for mastering the topics covered in the remaining three parts: food control, beverage control, and labor control. Part One is written to be congruous with each of the other parts. Thus, the book can be used in its entirety as the text for a single course in food, beverage, and labor controls. Alternatively, by using Part One, and one or more of the other parts, it offers a suitable text for schools with some or all of the topics in two or three separate courses.

Introduction

THE RUSH HOUR INN

Until two years ago when he purchased the restaurant, Larry Rusher had been a successful salesman of heavy machinery. His annual income was substantial, and he augmented it by investing in some profitable real estate ventures with his brother. However, his job as a salesman required that he travel most of the time, and his feeling that he was a stranger to his own children made him decide to give it up in favor of operating his own business.

On the advice of his brother, he decided to go into the restaurant business, even though he lacked previous experience in the field. After all his years of travel, he felt he knew more about restaurants from the customer's point of view than most restaurateurs. So he began to look around for an appropriate property. Fortunately, he soon found a place just twelve miles from his home, located on a main road on the outskirts of a city of 75,000 people. The building and equipment were only six years old, and apparently in fine condition; and the retiring owner was anxious to sell at a very fair price. The owner's books revealed a successful operation, with a net income of approximately $40,000 per year. Larry Rusher decided to buy.

The restaurant contained 100 seats. It was open seven days a week from 6:00 A.M. to 10:00 P.M., and served a varied menu of standard American fare. Larry felt that he would be able to run it successfully with the dedicated assistance of his wife and a few loyal employees.

But after two years of operation, Larry found himself edging closer and closer to bankruptcy. The restaurant was simply not showing a profit, even though he had increased the volume of business somewhat from the time he had purchased it. The place was busy; his customers were continually complimenting him on the food and service; but he was losing his proverbial shirt. He certainly could not blame his employees; they had been loyal and helpful in every way. Somehow,

Larry Rusher found himself operating a very popular, but very unprofitable, food and beverage business. At the end of the second full year of operation, the income statement prepared by his accountant revealed a profit of $9,870 before income taxes (see figure I.1). It is apparent to Larry, his family, and his accountant, that unless something can be done to improve the profit, continued operation would not be worth the effort required.

FIGURE I.1
The Rush Hour Inn
Income Statement
For the Year Ending December 31, 19—

Sales		
Food Sales	559,300.00	
Beverage Sales	98,700.00	
Total		658,000.00
Cost of Sales		
Cost of Food Sold	223,720.00	
Cost of Beverages Sold	29,610.00	
Total		253,330.00
Gross Profit on Sales		404,670.00
Controllable Expenses		
Payroll	157,920.00	
Payroll Taxes and Employee Benefits	39,480.00	
Other Controllable Expenses	98,700.00	
Total		296,100.00
Profit Before Occupation Costs		108,570.00
Occupation Costs		65,800.00
Profit Before Depreciation		42,770.00
Depreciation		32,900.00
Profit Before Income Taxes		9,870.00

THE GRADUATE RESTAURANT

Just a few miles down the road from the Rush Hour Inn, Jim Young owns and operates the Graduate Restaurant. After spending four years in the Air Force, Jim worked for an insurance company for a few years before enrolling in a nearby college to study hotel and restaurant management. His interest in the food and beverage sector of the hospitality industry had grown steadily since his high school days. Still, it took considerable courage for him to give up a fairly promising insurance career to go back to school. He received a degree for his study and then went to work as an assistant manager of a local restaurant. Over a period of several years, he had worked in three food and beverage operations in the area (the Rush Hour Inn among them) before he decided that he was ready to try one on his own. With the help of his family and a local bank, he was able to purchase the Graduate Restaurant, a fairly popular establishment with the same type of menu as the Rush Hour Inn and comparable prices and hours of operation. In fact, the only differences to the casual observer were size and location; the Graduate Restaurant had only fifty seats and was in a somewhat less favorable location.

Under the previous owner, the restaurant had shown a profit of about $18,000 per year. But Jim felt sure he could improve that figure over a period of time by applying some of the principles he had learned in the college's hotel and restaurant management program. The employees he inherited with the restaurant were both loyal and cooperative, and he found them receptive to the few changes that he made gradually over the first year of operation. None of the changes were dramatically apparent to the customers, and at the end of the first year, most had not noticed any changes at all. In general, they were as pleased with the establishment as they had been when Jim first took it over, and they continued to return. At the end of the first full year of operation, Jim's accountant presented him with an income statement showing $37,375 profit before income taxes (see figure I.2).

The statement confirmed Jim's expectations. It proved to him that his management of the operation was effective in the ways he had anticipated. At the end of his first year, he looked to the future with confidence.

A comparison of the two restaurants' statements reveals some very important facts. As one might expect, the Rush Hour Inn, with twice as many seats as the Graduate Restaurant, as well as a comparable menu and comparable prices, shows approximately twice the dollar volume of sales. However, in spite of the favorable sales figure, the Rush Hour Inn's profit is only a small fraction of the profit generated by the Graduate Restaurant. Since the difference between sales and profit on each income statement is represented by costs of various kinds, we can infer that the difficulty in the case of the Rush Hour Inn has something to do with cost. The costs of operation are somehow in more favorable proportion to sales in the case of the Graduate Restaurant. It is to the nature of these costs, and their relations to sales, that we must look to uncover the differences between the two establishments. It is possible that the costs of operation are not as well regulated, or controlled, in the Rush Hour Inn, and that if Larry Rusher is going to save his business, he must exercise greater control over the several kinds of operating costs. The statement of income from the Graduate Restaurant suggests that Jim Young has kept his costs under control in relation to sales, and, as we shall see, this is probably a critically important factor in the success of his business. In fact, comparative investigation of the two restaurants would reveal that Jim Young had instituted various policies, routines, and reports in the Graduate Restaurant that would be found noticeably absent in Larry Rusher's business. These procedures have had the effect of enabling Jim to maintain more effective control of his

TABLE I.2
The Graduate Restaurant
Income Statement
For the Year Ending December 31, 19—

Sales		
Food Sales	276,250.00	
Beverage Sales	48,750.00	
Total		325,000.00
Cost of Sales		
Cost of Food Sold	96,687.00	
Cost of Beverages Sold	12,188.00	
Total		108,875.00
Gross Profit on Sales		216,125.00
Controllable Expenses		
Payroll	65,000.00	
Payroll Taxes and Employee Benefits	16,250.00	
Other Controllable Expenses	48,750.00	
Total		130,000.00
Profit Before Occupation Costs		86,125.00
Occupation Costs		32,500.00
Profit Before Depreciation		53,625.00
Depreciation		16,250.00
Profit Before Income Taxes		37,375.00

business. It will be important, therefore, to look very closely at the nature and effect of these procedures in the succeeding chapters. However, it will first be useful to distinguish clearly what we mean by the words **cost, sales,** and **control.** These will be the subjects of the first two chapters.

part one

Introduction to Food, Beverage, and Labor Controls

chapter 1

Cost and Sales Concepts

Learning Objectives

After reading and studying this chapter, the student should be able to:

1. Define both cost and sales.
2. Define and distinguish between the various types of costs.
3. Define the cost-to-sales ratio and cite formulas used in its calculation.
4. Perform various calculations using the cost percentage formulas.
5. List and explain factors that cause variations in cost-to-sales relationships.
6. Explain and show the importance of matching costs with sales.

COST CONCEPTS

DEFINITION OF COST

Accountants define a cost as a reduction in the value of an asset for the purpose of securing benefit or gain. That definition, while technically correct, is not very useful to a discussion of controls, so we will modify it somewhat.

As we use the term in our discussion of cost control in the food and beverage business, cost will mean *the price to the hotel or restaurant of goods or services when the goods are consumed or the services rendered.* Food and beverage items are consumed when they have been used up, wastefully or otherwise, and are no longer available for the purposes for which they were acquired. Thus, the cost of a piece of meat is incurred when the piece is sold, or thrown away because it has spoiled, or when it has been stolen and is no longer available for the purpose for which it was purchased. The cost of labor is incurred when services are rendered, whether the person rendering the service is paid at that point or at a later date.

The cost of any item may be expressed in a variety of ways—in units of weight, or volume, or total value. The cost of meat, for example, can be expressed as a value per pound or as a value per individual portion. The cost of liquor can be discussed in terms of the cost per bottle, per drink, or per ounce. Labor costs can be expressed in terms of an hourly wage or a weekly wage.

FIXED AND VARIABLE COSTS

Costs can be divided into several different categories, and it is necessary to distinguish between them.

Fixed Costs

Fixed costs are those that have little direct relationship to the volume of business. Insurance premiums, real estate taxes, and depreciation on equipment are all examples of fixed costs.

Some may increase or decrease over time, but these changes in fixed costs will be independent of changes in business volume. Insurance premiums, for example, may decrease with an increased safety record, or increase with the insurance company's experience with the restaurant industry as a whole, or their increased business costs, regardless of any increase or decrease in the business volume in any particular restaurant. Therefore, the term **fixed** should not be taken to mean static or unchanging, but merely that such changes, if they occur, are typically not related to business volume changes.

Variable Costs

Variable costs, on the other hand, have some relationship to volume of business. As business volume increases, these costs will increase; as volume decreases, so should these costs. However, accountants recognize that there are at least two different types of variable costs.

Directly variable costs are those that have a direct relationship to the volume of business, such that every increase or decrease in volume brings a corresponding increase or decrease in cost. Food and beverage costs are good examples. Every time a restaurant sells an order of roast beef, it incurs a cost for the meat sold. Each sale of a bottle of beer at the bar brings about a monetary cost for the beer sold. Directly variable costs, then, increase or decrease, or at least should do so, in direct proportion to sales volume.

Payroll costs, often referred to as **labor costs,** present an interesting contrast. Restaurant employees may be divided into two categories—first, those whose numbers will remain constant through normal fluctuations in business volume; second, those whose numbers and consequent total costs should logically, and often will, vary with normal changes in volume. The first category includes such personnel as the manager, bookkeeper, chef, and cashier. In terms of the above definition, they are fixed cost personnel. Their salaries may change, but not as a direct result of changes in business volume. The second category would include serving personnel as the most obvious example. As business volume changes, their numbers and total costs will change appropriately.

Both fixed cost and variable cost employees are included in one category on the Income Statement—"Payroll." Because payroll cost has both the fixed element and the variable element, it is categorized as a **semi-variable cost,** meaning that a portion of it should remain constant with changes in business volume, and the other portion should not.

It must be noted that each individual establishment must make its own determination of which employees shall be fixed cost employees and which variable cost. In some specialized cases, it is possible for payroll to consist entirely of either fixed cost or variable cost personnel. For example, there are restaurants whose entire staff works for an hourly wage, and whose working hours and consequent cost are almost wholly related to business volume. Conversely, in some smaller restaurants employees may all be on a regular salary, in which case labor cost would be considered fixed.

CONTROLLABLE AND NONCONTROLLABLE COSTS

Costs may also be labeled **controllable** and **noncontrollable. Controllable costs** are those that can be changed in the short term. Variable costs are normally controllable. The cost of food or beverages sold can be changed, for example, by varying portion sizes or by varying ingredients, or both, either immediately or when the supply is replenished. The cost of labor can be increased or decreased in the short run by hiring or laying off workers, or by increasing or decreasing working hours or, in some instances, by increasing or decreasing wages.

In addition, certain fixed costs are controllable, including advertising and promotion, utilities, repairs and maintenance, and administrative and general expenses, a category which includes office supplies, postage, and telephone expenses, among others.

By contrast, **noncontrollable costs** are those that cannot be changed in the short term. These are usually fixed costs, and a list of the common ones would include rent, interest on a mortgage, real estate taxes, license fees, and depreciation. Changes in any of these are normally beyond management's immediate power.

UNIT AND TOTAL COSTS

It is important to distinguish between **unit costs** and **total costs.** The units may be food or beverage portions, as in the cost of one steak or one martini, or units of work, as in the hourly rate for an employee.

On the other hand, it is sometimes useful to discuss costs in terms of totals, as in the total cost of all food served in one period—such as a week or a month, or the total cost of labor for one period. These, of course, are how costs are expressed in the income statement.

Some examples will be useful to illustrate the above. A restaurant cutting steaks from a strip loin purchases one strip loin for $52.50. If all of the strip is consumed in one day, the total cost is $52.50. However, the cost per unit, the steak, will depend on the number of steaks cut from the strip. If fifteen steaks are cut, the unit cost is an average of $3.50. However, each steak will vary in cost because it is not normally possible for a butcher to cut all steaks exactly the same weight. In the food and beverage business we usually deal with **average** unit costs, rather than **actual** unit costs. Nevertheless, it is necessary to know unit costs for purposes of pricing and determining unit profitability. Total costs, including those that appear in income statements, are normally used for broader purposes, including overall relationships between costs and sales, as will be discussed later in this chapter, and for determining overall profitability of operations.

It is significant to note that as business volume changes, the effects on various costs change. Let us assume that a restaurant has a fixed cost for rent of $2,000 per month. If 2,000 customers were served during a period of one month, the average unit rental cost to the restaurant would be $1 for each customer served. If in the succeeding month the number of customers increased to 4,000, the total fixed cost for rent would not change, but the fixed cost per unit (customer) would be reduced from $1 to 50¢.

The same analysis may be done with variable costs. The variable cost for the steak described above was $3.50 per unit. If 2,000 customers in a given month order steak, the total variable cost would be $7,000 at $3.50 average unit cost per steak. If in the following month 4,000 customers ordered steak, the variable cost per unit (the steak) should remain $3.50, while the total variable cost for 4,000 steaks increases to $14,000.

While the foregoing illustrates behavior with increase in business volume, the same relationships hold true as business volume decreases. Figure 1.1 illustrates the above behavior of fixed and variable costs per unit and in total. It is important to understand these relationships when dealing with cost-volume-profit analysis and the calculation of break-even points, which are discussed in Chapter 3.

FIGURE 1.1
Cost Behavior as Business Volume Changes*

	Unit Cost	*Total Cost*
Fixed Cost	Changes	Does not change
Variable Cost	Does not change	Changes

*It must be noted that not all will agree with this. The point must be made that actual variable costs per unit tend to decrease as volume increases. Labor becomes more productive with greater time utilization, and food purchasing at greater volume can reduce cost.

PRIME COST

Prime cost is a term our industry uses to refer to the combined total costs of food and beverages sold, plus labor payroll, payroll taxes, and employee benefits. These last three, taken together, represent the largest portion of all operating costs for virtually all food service operations. Consequently, prime cost is of the greatest interest to most owners and managers because the control of prime cost will play a large part in determining whether or not an establishment meets its financial goals. In this text, we will therefore concentrate on those controllable costs that are most important in determining profit—food cost, beverage cost, and labor cost.

HISTORICAL AND PLANNED COSTS

Two additional cost concepts are important for a deeper understanding of cost control. First, the definition of cost at the beginning of this chapter carries with it the implication that all costs are **historical,** that is, that they can be documented through such records as invoices, wage rates, and contractual agreements, such as a lease. These documents are used for various purposes, such as establishing unit costs, menu prices, and total wages for past periods. Generally, when we speak of costs we are using the term in this historical sense. However, cost control is a management tool, and it is not sensible for management merely to wait until historical costs for any period are available. Hence, **planning** is always a vital management function and in order to be effective, a manager must often use historical costs to infer what costs will be or should be for a coming period. Thus, historical costs are necessary for effective planning. Such planning is often called **budgeting,** a topic to be discussed in Chapter 2.

Costs fluctuate considerably in the food and beverage business for several reasons: (1) most food costs change seasonally, depending on supply and demand conditions; (2) inflation has been evident in the United States economy especially in the past and (3) legislated minimum wage rates and negotiated labor agreements also affect labor costs over time. Management must somehow keep these anticipated, though not necessarily accurately predictable, changes in mind when planning for future costs. For example, many banquet functions are booked substantially in advance with menus and prices agreed on. Anticipated, yet inexact, changes in cost must be factored in the agreed-on prices if adequate profits are to be derived.

COST TO SALES RATIO: THE COST PERCENTAGE

Raw dollar figures for directly variable and semivariable costs are seldom, if ever, of any particular significance for control purposes. Because these costs vary to some extent with business volume, they become significant only when expressed in relation to that volume with which they vary. We calculate costs in dollars and compare those costs to sales in dollars. This enables us to discuss the relationship between costs and sales, sometimes described as the cost per dollar of sale, but more often as the cost percentage, or the ratio of costs to sales. The formula common to the industry that we will use throughout this book is:

$$\frac{\text{Cost}}{\text{Sales}} = \text{Cost per dollar of sale}$$

The division problem implicit in the formula always results in a decimal answer, and any decimal can be converted to a percentage by moving the decimal point two places to the right and adding a % sign. For this reason, the formula is often written as:

$$\frac{\text{Cost}}{\text{Sales}} = \text{Cost \%}$$

This formula can then be extended to show the folllowing relationships:

$$\frac{\text{Food Cost}}{\text{Food Sales}} = \text{Food Cost \%}$$

$$\frac{\text{Beverage Cost}}{\text{Beverage Sales}} = \text{Beverage Cost \%}$$

$$\frac{\text{Labor Cost}}{\text{Total Sales}} = \text{Labor Cost \%}$$

Let us go back to the income statements for the Rush Hour Inn and the Graduate Restaurant in the Introduction. In the case of the Graduate Restaurant, we saw that food costing $96,687 ultimately resulted in sales of $276,250. In order to determine the percentage of sales represented by cost, we divide the cost by the sales, as in the preceding formula, and multiply the resulting decimal answer by 100 in order to convert it to a percentage.

$$\frac{\$96{,}687}{\$276{,}250} = .34999 \times 100 = 34.99\%,$$

or 35% rounded off

Thus we learn that the food cost percentage, or the cost-to-sales ratio, in the Graduate Restaurant over the past year has been 35%. This tells us that 35% of the income from food sales over the year has gone to cover the cost of the food sold. Expressed another way, the cost of food sold represents $.35 out of each $1.00 in sales. Following the same formula, we may now take the figures for food costs and food sales from the income statement of the Rush Hour Inn and calculate the food cost percentage, or cost per dollar of sale, for purposes of comparison.

$$\frac{\$223{,}720}{\$559{,}300} = .4 \times 100 = 40\%$$

So in the case of the Rush Hour Inn, the cost per dollar of sale is $.40, and the food cost percentage is 40%.

Cost percentages are useful to management in at least two ways. They provide a means of comparing costs relative to sales for two or more periods of time, and they provide a means of comparing two or more operations. When comparing cost percentages for two or more operations, it is important to note that the comparisons can only be valid if the operations are similar. Thus, comparisons are often made between two fast-food restaurants with similar products; but one could not compare a French restaurant with a local diner and expect the comparison to be meaningful.

A comparison of the figures that will reveal some useful information now can be established for our two restaurants in figure 1.2.

FIGURE 1.2

	Rush Hour Inn	*Graduate Restaurant*
Food sales	$559,300	$276,250
Cost of food sold	223,720	96,687
Cost per dollar of sale	$.40	$.35
Food cost percentage	40%	35%

It is only at this point that the figures can begin to take on some real meaning for us and that we can begin to compare them intelligently. Significantly, we learn that one of the principal differences between the two restaurants lies in the fact that the food cost per dollar of sale is $.05 higher in one. Expressed another way, we can say that the cost-to-sales ratio for food is 5% higher in the Rush Hour Inn. It is not until we have converted the raw dollar figures to this form that we have any useful way of comparing them.

Because food is a variable cost, it will increase and decrease with sales volume. It would not be possible to establish useful comparisons between operating periods for one restaurant or between comparable restaurants (as in a chain, for example) unless we were to work with the cost percentages, or the costs per dollar of sale. Since cost control figures in the hospitality industry are more commonly expressed in terms of the cost percentage, we will deal with percentage figures in this text. In addition, because dollar figures in real restaurant operations seldom result in round numbers, we will express our percentages in tenths of one percent, for example, 35.9% or 36.2%. This, too, is common to the hospitality industry, and permits a greater degree of accuracy. After all, in the case of the Rush Hour Inn, one tenth of one percent of sales is $559.30, which is a considerable quantity of real dollars.

Using the formula above, it is now possible to establish a chart comparing the two restaurants from the point of view of costs as percentages of sales (see figure 1.3).

It is both interesting and significant that with percentages as the variable, controllable costs for the Rush Hour Inn are higher in every case. The balance of controllable and noncontrollable costs, commonly referred to as overhead, are the same.

FIGURE 1.3

	Rush Hour Inn	*Graduate Restaurant*
Food cost as a % of food sales	40.0%	35.0%
Beverage cost as a % of beverage sales	30.0%	25.0%
Combined food and beverage costs as a % of total sales	38.5%	33.5%
Payroll, payroll taxes, and employee benefits as a % of sales	30.0%	25.0%
Overhead as a % of sales	30.0%	30.0%

Sometimes the formula Cost/Sales = Cost % is rearranged algebraically to facilitate other calculations—for instance, when a banquet manager has been directed by upper management to insure that all functions operate at a preestablished food cost percentage, and this manager wants to quote a sales price for a particular menu item, the cost of which is known. The calculation of sales price is simplified if the formula is rearranged in the form Cost/Cost % = Sales (or Sales Price).

If preestablished cost percentage were 30.0%, and the food cost for the item were \$3.60, the appropriate sales price would be \$12.00, as illustrated below.

$$\frac{\$3.60}{0.3} = \$12.00$$

In another instance, consider this banquet manager dealing with a group that is willing to spend \$15.00 per person for a banquet, and the same preestablished 30.0% cost percentage is to apply. Calculation of the maximum permissible cost per person is facilitated by arranging the formula as **Sales (or Sales Price) multiplied by Cost %,** so the cost per person can be calculated as \$4.50 as illustrated:

$$\$15.00 \times 0.3 = \$4.50$$

In summary, the so-called cost percentage formula is found and used in any one of three possible forms:

$$\frac{\text{Cost}}{\text{Sales}} = \text{Cost }\%$$

$$\frac{\text{Cost}}{\text{Cost }\%} = \text{Sales}$$

$$\text{Sales} \times \text{Cost }\% = \text{Cost}$$

The foregoing has assumed that costs are stable for prices quoted. However, it is often necessary to quote prices for functions to be held some months in the future. To do so with a greater degree of accuracy, one should consider both seasonal fluctuations in costs and inflation rates. For example, the price of most shellfish is highest in New England during the winter months when the catch is smaller, and this fact should be taken into account when quoting prices in July for a function to be held in January. Moreover, in times of inflation, food costs increase at various rates. These can frequently be approximated by management from published information and should be taken into account when quoting future sales prices. One possible example would be the case of an establishment quoting a banquet price for a date six months in the future when the current rate of inflation is 10% on an annual basis. If the current food cost for the function is calculated to be \$4.00, the manager could be reasonably sure that the cost would be somewhat higher in six months. While it is not possible to predict the future cost with perfect accuracy, it is possible to approximate it. One simple way would be to assume that one half of the annual rate would apply to the first six months of the upcoming year, and thus to use 5% (one half of 10%) as the approximate future cost, which in this case would be \$4.20. Assuming a preestablished food cost percentage of 30%, sales price would be increased from \$13.33 to \$14.00, as illustrated here:

$$\frac{\$4.00}{0.3} = \$13.33 \text{ versus } \frac{\$4.20}{0.3} = \$14.00$$

Mathematicians would immediately recognize that this procedure is less than wholly accurate. However, it does offer a simple system for taking inflation into some account, which is preferable to ignoring it.

INDUSTRY-WIDE VARIATIONS IN COSTS

As percentage of sales, the costs for food and beverage operations vary considerably. Some of the factors contributing to these variations would include type of service, location, price structure, and type of menu.

In very broad terms, there are two types of restaurants:

- Those that operate at a low margin of profit per item served and depend on a relatively high volume of business to make a profit.
- Those that operate at a relatively high margin of profit per item and therefore do not need to rely on such a high volume of business in order to show a profit.

It is apparent that if the two were to have any menu items in common, the menu price would tend to be lower in the first category.

The following examples of the cost structures of hypothetical restaurants in each of these two categories are intended to serve only as illustrations of relative costs. The examples should not be taken to imply either that these are standards for the industry or that any particular restaurant should have the illustrated cost structure. The cost structure for each individual restaurant must be determined for that restaurant alone, the obvious point being that as percentages of sales, costs must always total less than 100.0% if the operation is to be profitable.

Restaurants that depend principally on convenience foods—the so-called fastfood operations—are generally in the first (low margin) category above. Because of relatively lower menu prices, the food cost percentages in such establishments tend to be higher. Because they are often able to operate with less highly skilled, highly paid personnel, and often with fewer personnel, they are able to offset the high food cost percentage with a low labor cost. A typical cost analysis for such a restaurant might be as seen in figure 1.4.

Restaurants in the second (high margin) category tend to depend less on convenience foods and to cater to customers who are looking for fresh foods, often prepared gourmet-style, and more service. This type of food preparation and service usually requires a greater number of personnel who are more highly skilled and often better paid. This tends to keep the cost of labor higher than in the first example, but the food cost percentage in such establishments will tend

FIGURE 1.4

Cost of food and beverages	40.0%
Labor cost, including payroll, payroll taxes, and employee benefits	20.0%
Other controllable and noncontrollable costs	30.0%
Profit before income taxes	10.0%
Total	100.0%

to be lower, partly because of higher menu prices. An analysis of the costs for such a restaurant might resemble those in figure 1.5.

FIGURE 1.5

Cost of food and beverages	25.0%
Labor cost, including payroll, payroll taxes, and employee benefits	35.0%
Other controllable and noncontrollable costs	30.0%
Profit before income taxes	10.0%
Total	100.0%

It is important to note that operations in the first category require greater numbers of customers to achieve a given dollar volume of sales. In the second example, partly because of higher menu prices, fewer customers are required to reach a given dollar volume. In general, it is possible to achieve a profit with fewer customers if menu prices are high.

In the two examples cited above, profit as a percentage of sales is shown at 10.0%. We must emphasize that these figures are not to be taken as industry standards, or even as necessarily desirable standards. Some experts feel that 5.0% profit is desirable, and others feel that a lower percentage of profit will help ensure customer return and lengthen the business life of a restaurant. The percentage of profit for any restaurant must be based on other factors, such as return on investment, the risk of being in business as opposed to other forms of investment, the return one might get in some other business, and a whole range of considerations involving the competition. In the last analysis, cost and profit determinations must be made on an individual establishment basis.

Now that we have taken a brief look at the types of costs involved in food and beverage operations and have found that some of them are controllable, it is time to take a closer look at what we mean by control and at what factors must be established before management can institute systems for keeping costs under control. However, before we do so, it will be useful to arrive at a working definition of a word that we have taken for granted thus far: **sales.**

SALES CONCEPTS

The term **sales** is used in a number of ways among professionals in the food service industry. In order for the term to be meaningful, one must be specific about the context in which it is used. It will therefore be useful to define the term and its various uses in the industry.

In general, a sale is the revenue resulting from a restaurateur's exchanging his or her products and services for value. We normally think of a sale in monetary terms, although there are other possibilities. The most commonly encountered uses of the term are the following.

Total Dollar Sales: Total dollar sales is a term used to refer to the total dollar volume of sales in any given time period, such as a week, a month, or a year. For example, total dollar sales for the Rush Hour Inn amounted to $658,000 for the year ending December 31, 19—.

Total Dollar Sales by Category: Examples of such uses are found in the terms Total Food Sales or Total Beverage Sales, referring to the total dollar volume of sales for all items in one category. By extension, we might see such terms as Total Steak Sales, or Total Seafood Sales, referring to the total dollar volume of sales for all items in those particular categories.

Sales Price: Sales price refers to the amount charged a customer for each unit sold. The unit may be one item—an appetizer or an entree—or an entire meal, depending on how a restaurant prices its products. The sum of all sales prices charged for all items sold in a given time period will be total dollar sales for that time period.

Average Dollar Sale: The average dollar sale is determined by dividing total dollar sales by the number of customers. For example, if total dollar sales for a given day in a restaurant were $1,258, and the restaurant had served 183 customers, the averge dollar sale would be $6.87. The concept is sometimes expressed as the average check, the average check price, or the average cover, all of which terms tend to be synonymous in our industry. The average dollar sale is used by food service operators for comparative purposes, to identify trends in sales, and to make judgments about the comparative effectiveness of various menus or menu listings, or even of sales promotions.

Sales per Serving Person: Sales per serving person is total dollar volume of sales for which a given server has been responsible in a given time period, such as a meal period, a day, or a week. There figures are sometimes used by management to make judgments about the comparative sales effectiveness of individual employees. It might be helpful to be able to identify those serving persons responsible for the greatest and for the least dollar sales in a given period.

Average Sale per Serving Person: Average Sale per Serving Person is total dollar sales for an individual server divided by the number of customers served by that individual. This too is a figure used for comparative purposes, and is usually considered a better indicator of the sales ability of a particular individual because, unlike that total sales per serving person, it eliminates differences caused by the mere fact of different numbers of persons served.

Average Sale per Seat: Average Sale per Seat is total dollar sales for a given time period divided by the number of seats in the restaurant. The normal time period used is one year. This figure is most frequently calculated by chain operations in order to compare sales results from one unit to another. In addition, the National Restaurant Association determines this average nationally so that individual operators may compare their results to other restaurants.

All of the above sales concepts are related to dollar sales and will be encountered by those entering the food and beverage industry. At the same time, there are a number of nonmonetary sales concepts and terms that should be understood. All of these have implications in both management and control, as will be increasingly apparent through the remaining chapters in the text.

Quantity of Items Sold: Quantity of items sold, often expressed as number sold, refers to the particular number of steaks, or shrimp cocktails, or any other menu item sold in a given time period. This figure is useful in a number of ways. For example, a restaurateur could use number sold to identify those menu items unpopular with customers, in order to eliminate such items from the menu. Additionally, historical records of number of particular items sold help in forecasting likely sales, and such forecasts are useful for controlling purchasing and production. The figure is also used in a variety of ways in controlling inventory and reconciling sales, as we will see in later chapters.

Average Number of Sales per Hour: Sometimes referred to as average number of covers per hour, this figure is determined by dividing the total number of customers served by one waiter or waitress by the number of hours he or she has worked. This figure may be of assistance to management for the purpose of scheduling appropriate numbers of servers for anticipated sales levels.

Seat Turnover: Seat turnover, most often called simply turnover or turns, refers to the number of seats occupied during a given period, or the number of customers served during that period, divided by the number of seats available. For example, if 150 persons were served luncheon in a dining room with 50 seats, seat turnover would be calculated as 3, obviously meaning that on average, each seat had been used three times during the period. This may be calculated for any given time period, but is most often determined per meal per day.

Sales Mix: This term is used to describe the relative quantities sold for any menu item compared to other items in the same category. The relative quantities are normally percentages of total unit sales and always total 100%. For example, assume a menu with five entree items represented by the letters A, B, C, D, and E. If total sales for all entree items in a given time period were 8,000—1,000 portions of A; 1,200 of B; 1,800 of C; 2,400 of D; and 1,600 of E—item A represents 12.5% of total unit sales, item B 15%, item C 22.5%, item D 30%, and item E 20%. That is the sales mix for this establishment, based on historical records.

MATCHING COSTS WITH SALES

For the restaurateur to stay profitably in business, total sales must be greater than total costs. If costs exceed sales for an extended period of time, the restaurateur will confront bankruptcy or at the very least will have to put additional funds into the business in order to keep it going. It is the job of the cost controller and manager to be constantly aware of the costs of operating the business and to keep them below sales. Cost information is gathered in many operations daily and compared with sales information for that day to determine the ratio of the various types of costs to sales. These ratios are compared to the same ratios from previous periods, and judgments are made as to whether the ratios are satisfactory. If not, remedial steps are taken to bring costs down to the point where the ratios are satisfactory. It is important that the comparative cost and sales information be from like periods. Customarily, comparisons are made for specific days of the week—Monday last week with Monday this week, for example. Comparisons sometimes are made of like weeks in two different months—for example, the first week in June compared with the first week in July. However, this information may not be valid if there is a normal seasonal fluctuation in business for those two months. Often, last week and this week are compared so that trends can be established.

In many establishments, cost and sales information is compared only periodically. However, it is obvious that remedial action will be more effective if the cost and sales information is current. Establishments that gather cost and sales information only monthly, quarterly, or annually are oftentimes unable to take effective remedial action because the information is too old to deal with current problems.

CHAPTER ESSENTIALS

In this chapter, we defined cost as used in the food service industry, and showed that all industry-related costs can be viewed from several perspectives, including fixed versus variable costs (with some variable costs being directly variable and others being semi-variable), controllable versus noncontrollable costs, total versus unit costs, and historical versus planned or budgeted costs. We explained the term prime cost and showed how the components of the prime cost relate to one another as well as to total sales. We defined the cost-to-sales ratio and provided the formulas by means of which various calculations are accomplished. We also showed how cost-to-sales ratios may vary from one establishment to another throughout the industry.

We defined sales and illustrated a number of special terms commonly used in the industry to discuss and compare sales, including total volume of dollar sales, total dollar sales by category, sales prices, average dollar sales per customer, per waiter, and per seat, as well as quantity of items sold, and turnover. Finally, we illustrated the matching principle of accounting as it relates to the food service industry.

An understanding of these concepts will be necessary to anyone seeking to comprehend the control process in the food service industry.

QUESTIONS AND PROBLEMS

1 Calculate the cost percentages. Express your answers to the nearest tenth of a percent.

- **a** Cost $200.00. Sales $500.00
- **b** Cost $150.00. Sales $500.00
- **c** Cost $178.50. Sales $700.00
- **d** Cost $216.80. Sales $800.00
- **e** Cost $127.80. Sales $450.00
- **f** Cost $610.00. Sales $2,000.00.

2 Calculate cost when the cost percentage and sales are given.

- **a** Cost % 28.0%. Sales $500.00.
- **b** Cost % 34.5%. Sales $2,400.00.
- **c** Cost % 24.8%. Sales $225.00.
- **d** Cost % 31.6%. Sales $1,065.00.
- **e** Cost % 29.7%. Sales $790.00.
- **f** Cost % 21.2%. Sales $4,100.00.

3 Calculate sales when cost percentage and cost are given.

- **a** Cost % 30.0%. Cost $90.00.
- **b** Cost % 25.0%. Cost $500.00.
- **c** Cost % 33.3%. Cost $1,000.00.
- **d** Cost % 27.3%. Cost $1,300.40.
- **e** Cost % 24.5%. Cost $88.20.
- **f** Cost % 34.8%. Cost $1,113.60.

4 List three examples of costs in a restaurant that are fixed, other than those illustrated in the text. Are they controllable? Explain your answers.

5 List three examples of costs in a restaurant, other than those illustrated in the text, that are variable. Are they controllable? Explain your answers.

6 Define:

- **a** Labor cost
- **b** Food cost
- **c** Profit
- **d** Beverage cost percentage
- **e** Controllable cost
- **f** Variable cost
- **g** Unit cost
- **h** Prime Cost

7 Write a short paragraph illustrating why a comparison of raw costs in two restaurants would not be meaningful, but a comparison of significant cost percentages might be.

8 Present cost for one a la carte steak is $3.20. This cost is 40.0% of the menu sales price.

- **a** What is the present sales price?
- **b** At an annual inflation rate of 11%, what will this steak cost one year from today?
- **c** Using the cost calculated in *(b)* above, what should the menu sales price be for this item if the cost percentage is to be 38%?
- **d** If you were a banquet manager planning a function six months from now, using this item, what unit cost would you plan for?
- **e** The banquet manager in *(d)* above has already calculated that the other items included in this banquet menu will have increased in cost in six months from $2.00 to $2.11. What should the sales price per person be for this banquet if the desired cost percentage is 40%?

9 In the ABC Restaurant, total fixed costs for overhead for October 19 were $28,422.80. In that month, 14,228 customers were served.

- **a** What was the unit cost for overhead per customer?
- **b** Assume that overhead will increase by 2% in November. Determine the planned unit cost for overhead if a decrease of 10% in the number of customers is anticipated.

10 A certain restaurant purchased domestic burgundy wine at $4.20 per bottle. Each bottle contains three liters, the equivalent of 101 ounces. The wine is served in five-ounce glasses, and management allows for one-ounce spillage per three-liter bottle.

- **a** What is the average unit cost per drink?
- **b** What is the total cost of sixty glasses of wine?
- **c** The banquet manager is planning a function for 120 persons for next Friday evening. Each guest will receive one glass of wine. How many bottles should be ordered for the party?
- **d** What will be the unit cost of the wine? The total cost?

11 In your own words, distinguish between cash sales and charge sales.

12 Calculate the average dollar sale per customer from the following:

- **a** Sales: $1,000.00; number of customers: 125.
- **b** Sales: $1,300.00; number of customers: 158.
- **c** Sales: $8,720.53; number of customers: 976.

13 A certain restaurant served covers and had gross sales for a three-hour period as illustrated in the following table. Determine (a) the average number of covers served per hour per waiter, and (b) the average sale in dollars per waiter for the three-hour period.

Waiter	*Covers served*	*Gross sales per waiter*
A	71	$237.40
B	66	$263.95
C	58	$188.25

14 In question thirteen above:

a Calculate the average cover.

b Calculate the turnover for the three-hour period if there are sixty-five seats in the restaurant.

15 In questions thirteen and fourteen above, if there were 85,629 customers per year and gross sales were $352,783.40:

a Calculate average dollar sale per customer.

b Calculate average sale per seat.

16 The financial records of the Colonial Restaurant reveal the following figures: for the year ending December 31, 19—

Depreciation	$25,000
Food sales	$375,000
Cost of beverages sold	$30,000
Other controllable expenses	$60,000
Payroll	$130,000
Beverage sales	$125,000
Payroll taxes and employee benefits	$20,000
Cost of food sold	$127,500
Occupancy costs	$55,000

a Following the form illustrated in the introductory chapter, prepare an income statement for the business.

b Determine the following percentages:

1. Food cost percent
2. Labor cost percent (payroll, plus payroll taxes and employee benefits)
3. Beverage cost percent
4. Combined food and beverage cost percent
5. Percentage of profit before income taxes

c Assume that the restaurant has seventy-five seats, and determine average sale per seat for the year.

chapter 2

Control

Learning Objectives

After reading and studying this chapter, the student should be able to:

1 Define and illustrate what is meant by control.

2 Pinpoint who is responsible for control in a food and beverage operation.

3 Give examples of various techniques used in control.

4 Define the following terms as used in food, beverage and labor control:

- **a** standards
- **b** procedures
- **c** standard procedures
- **d** budget
- **e** cost control
- **f** sales control
- **g** standard costs
- **h** quality standards
- **i** quantity standards

5 Prepare an Operating Budget.

6 List the steps in the control process.

7 Describe the significance of the cost benefit ratio in control decisions.

A considerable part of the previous chapter on costs and sales was devoted to developing basic understanding of the meaning of those terms as they relate to the food and beverage industry. This chapter will define control, discuss the relationship of control to costs and sales, and outline how a manager institutes control in an enterprise. While later chapters will go into specific procedures used in food, beverage, and labor control, this chapter will primarily discuss control and the control process in general terms.

Before beginning the discussion, it will be well to point out that control really means controlling people rather than things. Obviously cans of food do not disappear all by themselves, excess amounts of liquor are not used unless a bartender allows it, incorrect hours of work are generally not recorded except to the extent that a paymaster has incorrect information, food is not consumed by rodents unless human beings make that food accessible; revenues will be missing to the extent that patrons are allowed to leave without paying for what they have consumed. In all these cases, the difficulties that can arise are the result of human action, or lack of it, and if a business is to proceed profitably according to plan, people's actions must be controlled.

The people involved may not be simply the personnel of the food and beverage operation; "people" may include guests and patrons of the establishment, and, in some cases, intruders who may seek to avail themselves of the resources of the establishment without the knowledge and agreement of the management. Thus, locks on both the front and back doors would be two of the most basic control devices to prevent intruders from entering and probably stealing food, beverages, equipment, and even cash during periods when the operation is closed. Another simple control procedure is to locate the cashier near the front door in an effort to prevent customers from leaving without paying their bills. A time clock for employees serves many purposes, one of which is to develop an accurate set of records of the numbers of hours worked by each of the hourly wage employees, and this is another kind of control. Still another good example is the bartender's use of a measuring device to ensure that each drink mixed will contain the correct amount of a particular alcoholic ingredient. Interestingly enough, the concept of control refers to nonhumans too. For example, the institution of various sanitation procedures serves effectively to control infestation by various insects and rodents; loss of food to nonhuman invaders surely constitutes unwarranted additional cost to any restaurant.

DEFINITION OF CONTROL

Control is a process by means of which managers attempt to direct, regulate, and restrain the actions of people in order to achieve desired goals.

An obvious first step is to establish goals for the enterprise. Probably the most common goal for all private enterprises is financial success, although this is by no means the only long-range goal of business. Others might relate to preserving the environment, promoting better health among the population, or aiding in the integration of minority groups into national economic life.

To achieve these goals, management must set up any number of subgoals compatible with its long-range plans. These tend to be more specific and usually more immediate in nature. For example, to achieve the goal of preserving the environment, it would be necessary to make rather immediate plans to process or dispose of waste materials in appropriate ways. A full discussion of general business goals and the planning for their achievement is not within the scope of this text. Rather we will restrict ourselves to a discussion of the control processes employed by managers in the hospitality industry to achieve the goal of profitable operation. This will entail a discussion of how costs and sales are controlled in food and beverage operations—the means employed by foodservice managers to direct, regulate, and restrain the actions of people, both directly and indirectly, in order to keep costs within acceptable bounds, to account for revenues properly, and to make profits.

COST CONTROL

The process whereby managers attempt to regulate costs and guard against excessive costs is known as cost control. It is an ongoing process and involves every step in the chain of purchasing, receiving, storing, issuing, and preparing food and beverages for sale, as well as scheduling the personnel involved. Exact methods for cost control will vary from place to place, depending in part on the nature and scope of operation; but the principle behind varying methods will be constant. The obvious goal is to eliminate excessive costs for food and beverages and labor—to exercise governing power over costs in all areas in order to ensure that the business will operate at a profit.

Two of the principal causes of excessive costs are inefficiency and waste. For example, storing food in refrigerators that are not cold enough, or liquor in bottles that are not tightly closed, will lead to spoilage and hence to excessive cost. So will the preparation of an inedible beef stew or an undrinkable martini. When the stew is thrown into the garbage can or the martini poured down the drain, costs of operation are increased but sales are not. Since profit is essentially the difference between sales and costs, it is apparent that any increase in costs that does not lead to corresponding increases in sales can only have the effect of reducing profits. Clearly, management must take steps to guard against the occurrence of these excessive costs.

SALES CONTROL

While cost control is critically important to the profitable operation of any business, it alone will not ensure profitability. Additional steps must be taken to ensure that all sales result in appropriate income to the business. For example, profits will be adversely affected if a steak listed in the menu for $8.95 is sold to a customer for $7.95, or the cocktail that is supposed to sell for $1.35 is sold for $1.15. Therefore, it is important in most instances to insist that employees record each sales clearly on a check.

In addition, it is useful to check recorded sales against production records to ensure that all quantities produced are accounted for. Various methods for ensuring that all portions that have left the kitchen or bar have been recorded as sales on checks will be discussed in Chapter 13.

Although it is unfortunate that not all employees are completely honest, it is a fact of life that must be taken into account in food and beverage operations. Therefore, guest checks are usually numbered to ensure accountability. Sometimes duplicate copies of the checks, clearly identified as duplicates so they are not confused with the originals, are used to reconcile kitchen production with recorded sales. When the checks and duplicates are numbered sequentially, missing numbers can be noted and investigated at once.

RESPONSIBILITY FOR CONTROL

The total responsibility for the operation of any food and beverage enterprise rests ultimately with management. A number of factors, including nature and scope of operations, will determine the extent to which the manager exercises direct control as opposed to delegating responsibility to a subordinate. In general, the larger the operation, the more likely it is that one or more subordinates will supervise and direct control procedures.

For the purpose of this text, the authors will assume the existence of both a food controller and a beverage controller, each of whom will be responsible for the supervision of all control procedures in that single area. By the same token, we will assume that the manager will personally retain direct control over labor cost. While we recognize that this is not the case in all operations, such assumptions do facilitate discussion of the principles of control. Given the variety and number of different types of food and beverage operations in existence, it would be all but impossible to pinpoint just who is responsible for what controls in which type of restaurant, and in our view such a discussion would require considerably more space than it would be worth. The important point to remember is that ultimate responsibility rests with management.

NEED FOR CONTROL

The food and beverage business can be characterized as one that involves raw materials purchased, received, stored, and issued for the purpose of manufacturing products for sale. In these respects many similarities exist between the food and beverage business and other manufacturing businesses. As an example, let us look at the steps involved in the production of wood furniture.

The furniture manufacturer must determine what kinds of woods are best suited to the types of furniture he or she intends to manufacture and must purchase appropriate numbers of board feet of lumber at favorable prices. When the wood is delivered, the shipment must be checked to ensure that the material delivered is exactly what was ordered. Then it must be moved into appropriate storage facilities, partly to prevent theft and partly to ensure that the characteristics of the wood will not be adversely affected by climate. The wood must then be issued in appropriate amounts for the production of various kinds of tables and chairs. During the manufacturing process, some effort must be made to maintain a balance in the production, so that one table top is made for each four legs. When the manufacturing process is completed and the furniture is sold to customers, care must be taken to ensure that each sale is properly recorded, that the correct price is charged for each piece of furniture sold and delivered, and that the total dollar value of each sale is collected.

A great number of similarities exist between the manufacturing industries and the food and beverage business. The motel coffee shop, the school cafeteria, the hotel dining room, the resort cocktail lounge—all these have in common with other manufacturing businesses the responsibilities for purchasing, receiving, storing, and issuing raw materials for the production of finished products for sale. In the food and beverage business, we talk about fruits, vegetables, meat, poultry, and a large number of other foods—fresh, frozen, and canned—but these really serve the same purposes in our business that wood serves in the manufacture of furniture. Similarly, we deal with wines, spirits, and a number of other beverages, both alcoholic and nonalcoholic, which constitute the raw materials from which drinks are produced for sale.

These raw materials must be carefully selected, always with the desired final products in mind, and appropriate numbers of each must be ordered to meet expected production needs. In each case, the order for any raw materials should be placed with the vendor who will deliver it at the most favorable price. As food and beverage items are received, they must be checked to see that the restaurant or bar is getting what it pays for. Then the materials must be stored appropriately with respect to temperature and security until needed. When a chef or a head bartender requests materials from storage, the raw food or beverage item must be made available for the production of menu items for sale.

At each stage of operation it is necessary to institute control in order to prevent the kinds of problems mentioned earlier. Control may be accomplished in a variety of ways, and anyone who attempts to manage a food and beverage operation should be aware of the techniques and devices available for use.

The selection of particular techniques and devices depends on the nature of the difficulty to be controlled and on the situation in which the difficulty exists, as well as on the management style of the individual making the selection. Thus, selection of the means of control is not always simple, and the student should be aware of some of the options available.

CONTROL TECHNIQUES

The variety of control techniques available to a manager includes the following:

1 establishing standards
2 establishing procedures
3 training
4 setting examples
5 observing and correcting employee actions
6 requiring records and reports
7 censuring and disciplining employees
8 preparing and following budgets

Establishing Standards

Standards may be defined as *rules or measures established for making comparisons and judgments*. In business, these standards are set by management and are used for judging the extent to which results meet expectations. Several types of standards set by knowledgeable food and beverage managers are useful in establishing control over operations. It will be important to develop a working understanding of the several kinds of standards before proceeding.

Quality standards refer to the degree of excellence of raw materials, finished products, and by extension, work. In one sense, establishing quality standards is a grading process. Most food items are graded according to degree of excellence—many of them by the United States Department of Agriculture—and management must establish a standard of quality for each item for purposes of purchasing. Beef, for example, is generally available in a number of different grades for restaurant and institutional use, and it is important to determine which grade will be used for the preparation of a particular menu item.

Beverage items may also be differentiated by quality. For example, some spirits improve with age, and a twelve-year-old scotch whiskey is generally considered to be of a higher quality than another that is only eight years old. Management in beverage operations must determine which beverage items are of appropriate quality to ensure customer satisfaction.

Quality standards must also be determined for the work force. In some hotels and fine restaurants, higher degrees of skill are required for the production and service of elaborate menu items than would be necessary in the average roadside diner.

Quantity standards refer to measures of weight, count, or volume. Thus, management must establish such quantity standards as portion sizes for menu items and drinks and, in many instances, work output for employees.

The portion size for every food item served must be clearly established. Each shrimp cocktail should contain a predetermined number of shrimp of specified size, and a certain measure of sauce, as well as clearly identified measures of garnishes. An order of soup should be identified as to size of bowl or cup to be used, or the size ladle to be used in dishing it out, and the quantity of garnish to be included. Entree items must be established as being of a certain number of ounces or pieces. Surrounding items such as vegetables should be served with a certain size spoon, as with peas, or be measured by count, as with asparagus spears.

In bar operations, management must establish a standard quantity (in ounces) for each shot of liquor used. In many instances, bars operate with standard drink recipes indicating the quantities of ingredients to be used in preparing a particular drink.

Quantity standards are often important in the control of labor cost as well. It is useful to know when staffing, for example, how many tables or seats a waiter or waitress can cover during a given period, or how many sandwiches a pantryman can make per hour when planning a luncheon schedule for the staff.

In addition to quality and quantity standards, it is ultimately necessary to determine and set cost standards for operation. Cost standards are usually referred to as standard costs.

A **standard cost** is the agreed-upon cost of goods or service used to measure other costs. Paradoxically, it is simultaneously both realistic and ideal. For example, if one quart of liquor costs $6.40 to purchase, each and every ounce has a real cost of $.20, the standard cost of one ounce. If the entire bottle is used to prepare drinks, each of which contains one ounce, the standard cost of each should be $.20. However, this price is an ideal, since it does not allow for spillage or evaporation, both of which are likely to occur in bar operations. Standard costs are determined in several important ways, each of which will be discussed in detail in succeeding chapters. In the case of labor, these standard costs may be determined by obtaining averages over a period of time. In the case of foods and beverages, they may be determined by actual test, the simplest form of which has been previously illustrated in the discussion of the standard cost of one ounce of liquor.

Standard costs are useful in measuring an operation's effectiveness. As we shall see, comparing standard costs with actual costs can help determine how effectively food and beverage materials and labor resources are being deployed in a business operation. Cost standards are necessary in cost control because they provide a means of comparing what we are doing with what we should be doing.

Establishing Procedures

In addition to establishing standards for quality and quantity, food and beverage managers must establish standard procedures. Procedures are the *methods employed to prepare a product or perform a job, and standard procedures are those that have been established as the correct methods, routines, and techniques for day-to-day operations.* As we shall see in later chapters, for management to achieve effective control over food, beverage, and labor cost, the establishment of these standard procedures at every stage of the "manufacturing" process is necessary.

Ordering and purchasing procedures must be standardized to ensure that the raw food and beverage materials are purchased in needed quantities and qualities and at favorable prices at appropriate times. Receiving procedures must be standardized so that all goods received conform in quality, quantity, and cost to those ordered. Standard storing procedures must be put into effect to guard against both spoilage and theft, either of which will lead to excessive costs.

Issuing must be standardized so that food and beverage items will be used in the order they are received, thus preventing spoilage and the resulting excess costs. To further guard against spoilage and theft, issuance must accord with carefully determined production needs. Moreover, records of issues must be maintained in order to calculate a cost per item produced; such costs can then be compared to standard costs to determine the effectiveness of operation.

Production procedures must be standardized for a number of reasons. In order to satisfy customers, any given item must be produced by the same method and with the same ingredients every time it is served. It should also be served in the same quantities each time, partly so that customers will not feel cheated and partly to maintain cost standards.

When standards have been instituted in each of these categories—quality, quantity, and procedure—it then becomes possible to measure each aspect of the business. The day-to-day operating realities can be compared to the standards established, significant variations noted, and changes made to bring products and practices more nearly in line with the standards set. To the extent to which realities compare favorably with the standards set, effective controls exist.

Training

While establishing standards and standard procedures is highly important, it is really only a first step in the process of control. None of the standards are of any significance unless the employees are aware of them, and they will become aware of such standards only if management is willing to commit itself to training, a process by means of which managers teach employees how work is to be done, given the standards and standard procedures established. If, for example, management has established that a hamburger is to be prepared in four-ounce portions, then those employees who are to produce portions of hamburger must be made aware of the fact that four ounces is to be the correct portion size. Moreover, each person must be trained to produce portions of that size at his or her work station, using whatever equipment and supplies are to be provided. Obviously, failure to make all employees aware of the relevant standards and standard procedures established for their work renders the standards useless.

Any food service manager who trains employees would doubtless agree that training is difficult, frustrating, time-consuming, and in the short run, costly. Perhaps that is why a substantial number of poor managers ignore it and simply put new employees to work without devoting any time to demonstrating and explaining what is to be done. Sometimes the new employee is introduced to a co-worker who is expected to train the newly hired individual. Occasionally this works reasonably well; more often it does not, frequently because the co-worker is either unwilling or unable to do it. After all, the typical restaurant employee is not hired for his or her ability to train others.

If employees are not suitably trained in the use of the standards and standard procedures, the control aspects of the manager's job become difficult, at best; sometimes control becomes impossible. Further discussion of this topic will be deferred to the suitable section of the text, the chapters on labor control.

Setting Examples

Often, establishing standards and standard procedures is not quite as formal as the foregoing sections might suggest. In many instances, they are actually established informally when the employees in an operation follow the examples set by the manager's overt behavior, responses to questions, and even by the manager's failure to speak or take action in some situation. In general, the behavior of individuals in a group tends to be influenced by the actions, statements, and attitudes of their leaders. Thus by instructing personnel in the particulars of how their jobs are to be done, managers are in effect controlling; since their particular goals are presumably consistent with their long-range business objectives, their instructions reflect the standards and procedures which they expect will lead to those goals. At the same time, the manager's individual behavior in performing any task will influence the manner in which an employee will perform that same task. If the manager who has occasion to work with employees plating food for the dining room serves excessive portion sizes, employees will be inclined to do the same when the manager is not there. Similarly, if a manager is inclined to wrap up parcels of food to take home for personal use, employees will be so inclined as well. And if the manager observes them doing so and fails to end the practice, the amount of food leaving the premises will usually escalate.

It must be noted that any manager must be consistent in setting examples as well as in directing, regulating, and restraining employees and their actions. In far too many cases managers appear not to have long-range and short-range goals clearly in mind as they go about the business of managing, and their examples, actions, directions, and responses to employee questions do not offer a clear picture to subordinates. Such inconsistency confuses employees and has the effect of breaking down whatever control might otherwise exist.

Correcting and Observing Employee Actions

If management observes a bartender mixing drinks without measuring ingredients and fails to direct the individual to measure quantities carefully as drinks are mixed, then the bartender could reasonably assume that such work was acceptable and the manager would be missing an opportunity to control behavior. Should the manager observe the receiving clerk receiving meats without verifying that quantities received agree with the quantity on the invoice and fail to correct the practice, the employee could not possibly know that his or her performance was unacceptable.

One of the manager's important tasks is to observe the actions of all employees continually as they go about their daily jobs, to judge those actions in the light of what employees should be doing, and correct them to the extent necessary at appropriate times.

Requiring Records and Reports

Obviously the manager cannot be in all places at all times to observe employee actions. In smaller food and beverage operations, the owner/manager can observe employee actions to a far greater extent than can the manager of a larger operation consisting of one or more bars and dining rooms seating hundreds of people and employing hundreds of personnel. The larger the establishment the more likely it is that management observations cannot be direct but must be abstracted and inferred from a variety of records and reports. The variety and extent of these will be discussed in great detail in later chapters. One such report already discussed is the Income Statement which summarizes cost and sales information for a particular period, and from which can be determined such factors as cost-to-sales ratios of various kinds. If the ratios are acceptable to management, this implies in general terms that the performance of employees has been acceptable during the period covered by the statement. If these ratios are not acceptable, the implication is that the employees have not followed some or all of the standards and standard procedures formally or informally established. We may not be able to pinpoint specific problems from such a general report as the income statement; other more specific and more timely reports and records are often required. Some of these may be developed daily; others, weekly and monthly, as will be seen in succeeding chapters. Of significance is that the manager needs timely information to determine whether or not long-range and short-range goals and subgoals are being met. If not, the timeliness affords the opportunity of taking corrective action.

Censuring and Disciplining Employees

Censure and disciplinary action are two commonly employed control techniques. For example, the manager whose financial performance did not compare favorably with plans may have this fact pointed out to him by top management in any number of ways. The possibilities may range from quiet discussion to heated admonition, or from demotion or transfer to termination. On another level, an employee who has been informed about performance standards and who then does not meet these expectations is likely to learn about it from a supervisor or manager. At first, this might be simply called to his attention in an objective and unemotional way, and he could be given an opportunity to improve performance. If that improvement is not forthcoming in a reasonable period, then admonition on a second occasion is likely to be more severe. Most responsible managers would hope that a second such occasion would be the last and would bring about the necessary improvement. However, if it were not, then a manager would find it necessary to take progressively more forceful actions, the final one of which would be termination. This last should normally be used only if it is simply impossible to control and modify the employee's job performance. After all, if an employee was worth hiring, he or she should be worth keeping, and all suitable efforts should be made to bring his job performance into line. In addition, a high rate of employee turnover because of excessive firings can be very costly, leading perhaps to such additional costs as classified advertising for new help, increasing rates of unemployment insurance contributions in some states, lower rates of productivity, higher training costs, and others.

On the one hand, it must be understood that the object of censuring and disciplining employees is to change or modify their job performance—to control performance in such a way that the job activity of each employee is consistent with the standards and procedures that management has determined are likely to enhance the firm's goals and objectives. On the other hand, it should be apparent that censure and disciplinary action generally have negative connotations in the minds of employees, most of whom would normally prefer to avoid any such unpleasantness. If certain behavior patterns—those that follow the standards and procedures established by management—lead to positive and pleasant rewards, and others—those that ignore management's standards and procedures—bring the negative and unpleasant rewards of censure and disciplinary action, then most employees will generally prefer to strive toward the former and to avoid the latter. The very fact that employees know that transgressions lead to unpleasantness tends to have the desirable effect of making job activity conform with management's planned standards and procedures.

Preparing and Following Budgets

Perhaps the most common technique for controlling business operations is the use of budgets. A budget is a realistic expression of management's goals and objectives expressed in financial terms. Large businesses establish budgets for specific aspects of operation—such as sales budgets, cash flow budgets, capital equipment budgets, and advertising budgets, as well as others.

Restaurants need many of these budgets too. Capital equipment budgets, for example, are often prepared because of the ongoing need to replace equipment that wears out and purchase new types of equipment that come on the market. Capital equipment is typically very costly, and plans must be made to provide the necessary cash to purchase it. Advertising budgets are established so that expected sales can be generated without excess spending that will either cause the restaurant to lose money or cause a decline in profits.

The most important type of budget a restaurant can prepare is the **operating budget.** Stated in dollar terms, it is a forecast of sales activity and an estimate of costs that will be incurred in the process of generating those sales. By extension the budget suggests the profit that should result after the costs of producing those sales have been met, and also represents a financial plan for operations for the period it covers. In this text, we will restrict our discussion to the preparation of an operating budget because it is most closely aligned with the subject of food, beverage, and labor control. For established restaurants the operating budget is prepared with the help of historical information coupled with anticipated changes in the various categories in the budget, and in the business environment as well.

Thus, if federal or state legislation will affect wage rates paid to employees in the period covered by the budget in preparation, this information must be used in planning. If real estate tax rates have been increased or decreased in a particular community, this information, too, should be reflected in the budget. More difficult to deal with, but equally important, are the effects of poor weather conditions on future crops, anticipated shortages of beef due to cattlemen's reduction in herds, and general conditions in the economy that may affect the size of the restaurant's clientele.

In new establishments that do not have previous financial statements, information from a market analysis and from a manager's previous experience provides the best alternative sources of data for budget preparation. When no market analysis is available, when the manager is not widely experienced in the food and beverage business, or when both of these are true, budgets are often not prepared at all, and management misses an opportunity to employ one of the most useful of all control techniques.

PREPARING THE OPERATING BUDGET

As previously stated, the operating budget is normally prepared using historical information from previous budgets and other financial records. This information, together with anticipated changes in sales and costs, provides the data needed to prepare the operating budget for the coming period. Operating budgets can be prepared for any period of time—a day, a week, a month, a quarter of a year, six months, or a full year. Typically, the yearly budget is prepared first and then broken down into smaller time periods. Time periods will not reflect the same sales and costs because of the seasonality of the restaurant business. Thus, for example, if the budget for a restaurant forecasts $400,000 in sales for the year, each quarter would not necessarily forecast sales of $100,000. The first and fourth quarters may be the busy time for the restaurant and the second and third the slowest. So the restaurant may forecast $125,000 in sales for the first and fourth quarters and only $75,000 in sales for each of the second and third quarters. In addition, the restaurant might forecast sizable profits for the busy quarters and break even for the slow quarters.

The following illustration of budget preparation is a **static budget.** That is, it is a budget prepared assuming only one given level of business activity for the year (i.e., $400,000 in sales). One must recognize, however, that budget projections are often not correct. Sales levels can be higher or lower than projections because managers and people who prepare budgets often are not very good at seeing into the future, or they do not take all of the information at hand into account when preparing the budget. A new office building down the street may generate additional luncheon business not anticipated and planned advertising may bring in additional customers, or conversely, road construction out front may cause business to drop off for a period of time, or a factory down the road may close and cause a loss in business. To counteract such possibilities, managers often prepare budgets for different levels of business activity. These are called **flexible budgets** and are prepared for business volume above and below the expected sales level. When sales levels appear to have changed from expectations, management is prepared with a new set of budgeted cost figures for that sales level.

To illustrate the preparation of a budget, let us use as the example the Graduate Restaurant mentioned in the Introduction. The income statement and relevant percentages are reproduced in figure 2.1.

Previous discussion has also distinguished between controllable and non-controllable costs, and between fixed and variable costs. To prepare an operating budget, it is necessary to determine which categories of expenses are fixed and which are variable. Each restaurant must make its own determination. For purposes of this illustration the following assumptions will be made.

Fixed costs	
Depreciation	$ 16,250
Occupation costs	32,500
Other controllable costs	48,750
Fixed labor	39,000 (60% of 65,000 labor cost)*
Payroll taxes on fixed labor	9,750 (60% of 16,250)
Total fixed costs	$146,250
Variable costs	
Cost of food	35% of food sales
Cost of beverage	25% of beverage sales
Payroll costs	9.4% of food sales**
Payroll taxes	25% of variable payroll

*Payroll is a semi-variable cost, so it must be broken down into its fixed and variable components. The illustration has assumed that 60% of the total payroll cost is fixed and that the remainder is variable.

**Given total payroll cost of $65,000 and assuming that 60% of this is for fixed labor, the balance of 40% is for variable labor. As a dollar figure, this is $26,000 (40% of $65,000). As a percentage of food sales, this $26,000 is 9.4%. This is done on the assumption that in this particular restaurant, increases or decreases in labor cost are the result of increases or decreases in food sales volume, not beverage sales volume.

It is now possible to begin preparation of the budget for the Graduate Restaurant for the coming fiscal year. The initial step in this process is to examine sales figures from the recent past to note any trends that may be evident. In some establishments, such examination of sales records might reveal regular increases in sales from year to year; in others, decreases might be evident; in still others, changes from year to year, if any, might reveal no discernible pattern. In any case, it is the job of the owner or manager of a given establishment to analyze past sales performance and to identify reasons for that performance. Information proceeding from such analysis will be of great value in projecting sales levels for the period to be covered by the budget.

The next step in the budgeting process would be to look at the external climate surrounding the business and assess those factors that may affect sales

FIGURE 2.1
The Graduate Restaurant Income Statement for the Year Ending December 31, 19—

Sales			*Percentages of Sales*
Food sales	$276,250		85%
Beverage sales	48,750		15%
Total		$325,000	100%
Cost of sales			
Cost of food sold	$ 96,687		35% (of food sales)
Cost of beverage	12,188		25% (of bev. sales)
Total		$108,875	35.5% (of total sales)
Gross profit on sales		$216,125	66.5%
Controllable expenses			
Payroll	$ 65,000		20%
Payroll taxes, etc.	16,250		5% (25% of payroll)
Other controllable expenses	48,750		15%
Total		$130,000	40%
Profit before occupancy costs		$ 86,125	26.5%
Occupancy costs		$ 32,500	10%
Profit before depreciation		$ 53,625	16.5%
Depreciation		$ 16,250	5%
Profit before income tax		$ 37,375	11.5%

volume in the coming year. Such factors would probably include general economic conditions in the nation and in the immediate geographical area; population changes; changes that could affect transportation to the establishment, including new highways, bus routes, and so on; and any number of others.

Another important step is to review the operation's internal conditions, planned changes in which will affect sales volume. For example, any plans to increase or decrease menu prices will clearly affect sales volume, and the impact of such changes must be clearly assessed. So must such varied possibilities as anticipated changes in the number of seats in the restaurant, in the items listed in the menu, and in levels of advertising.

After investigating sales as discussed above, the next logical procedure is to determine the nature and extent of changes in cost levels, some of which will be dictated by anticipated changes in sales volume, and others of which will occur independent of volume changes. Variable costs are sure to be affected by changes in volume but may also be affected by other factors. Increased sales volume may necessitate hiring additional waiters or waitresses, but a union labor contract may include a new hourly wage figure for all employees. There are many other possibilities for cost increases, including a clause in a lease dictating a rent increase effective on a particular date, or higher utility rates, or anticipated increases in the costs of particular foods. Any anticipated changes in cost and sales levels must be considered and factored into the new budget.

Let us assume that the management of the Graduate Restaurant has carefully examined past cost and sales figures and has assessed the impact of various anticipated changes in both internal and external conditions on those figures. The following changes are anticipated:

1 Both food and beverage sales are expected to increase by 10%.
2 Fixed payroll costs will increase by 8%.
3 Variable payroll will continue to be the same percentage of sales.
4 Payroll taxes will increase proportionately with the increase in payroll costs.
5 Other controllable costs will increase by $65,000.
6 Occupation costs will increase by $2,000.
7 Food and beverage cost percentages will remain the same.

Based on these anticipated changes, the budget for the Graduate Restaurant for the coming fiscal year would be as illustrated in figure 2.2.

FIGURE 2.2
Operating Budget Graduate Restaurant For Fiscal Year Ending December 31, 19—

Sales	Previous Year	Change	Upcoming Year
Food sales	$276,250	+ $27,625	303,875
Beverage sales	48,750	+ 4,875	53,625
Total	325,000	+ 32,500	357,500
Cost of Sales			
Cost of food sold	$ 96,687	+ $ 9,669	$106,356
Cost of beverages sold	12,188	+ 1,218	13,406
Total	108,875	+ 10,887	119,762
Gross profit	216,125		237,738
Controllable expenses			
Fixed payroll	39,000	+ 3,120	42,120
Variable payroll	26,000	+ 2,564	28,564
Total payroll	65,000	+ 5,684	70,684
Payroll taxes	16,250	+ 1,421	17,671
Other controllable expenses	48,750	+ 6,500	55,250
Total	130,000	+ 13,605	143,605
Profit before occupation costs	86,125		94,133
Occupation costs	32,500	+ 2,000	34,500
Profit before depreciation	53,625		59,633
Depreciation	16,250		16,250
Profit before income taxes	$ 37,375		$ 43,383

Assuming that projections for sales, costs, and profits are considered acceptable to management, the budget would be adopted as the plan of action for the covered period. If the projections were considered unacceptable, management would reexamine both the assumptions on which the budget was based and the budget figures themselves. Such reexamination might suggest to management the desirability of additional changes affecting sales or costs that might lead to more acceptable results. Before the adoption of the budget, the effects of such potential changes could be tested by means of the techniques of Cost/Volume/Profit analysis, to be discussed in the following chapter.

Once an acceptable budget is adopted for an upcoming period, it becomes a standard against which operating performance is measured as the fiscal year progresses. To use it effectively for this purpose, management often apportions sales and cost figures into quarterly or monthly segments, which serve as standards or targets for the covered periods. If cost and sales figures do not meet expectations as identified in the budget for a given period, investigation into the causes of such differences will be made. Once the causes have been identified, it is possible and desirable to take remedial actions to ensure better performance in the next operating period. If, for example, sales do not increase to the extent predicted, it will be necessary to adjust costs so that desired profit levels may be maintained. If payroll or any other controllable cost is greater than the amount budgeted, then management will attempt to determine the reasons for the excessive amounts, and take appropriate measures to control future costs at more suitable levels.

THE CONTROL PROCESS

From the foregoing discussion of the techniques of control, it is possible to generalize four basic steps that lie at the heart of the control process:

1. Establish standards and standard procedures for operation.
2. Train all individuals to follow established standards and standard procedures.
3. Monitor performance and compare actual performance with established standards.
4. Take appropriate action to correct deviations from standards.*

To illustrate the manner in which the control process follows these steps, let us assume a restaurant, the owner of which wants to serve the finest food. To reach this goal the owner must establish those standards and standard procedures that will define the meaning of "the finest." In the case of one menu item—prime sirloin steak—the standard is *prime,* a term that specifies certain identifiable characteristics. The instructions to appropriate employees must reflect the fact that only prime beef is to be purchased for the production of this menu item. Whoever receives beef from the purveyor should check to see that it is the correct quality

*It should be noted that investigation will sometimes reveal that an established standard is unrealistic or inappropriate. In those instances, it will probably be desirable to change the standard.

by examining the meat and checking for the USDA Grade stamp on the outside fat. From time to time, the manager must make some observations to see that the meat purchased meets the standards set. This may require either examining raw meat hanging in the refrigerator or sitting down in the dining room and ordering a steak. If the manager is lax, customers will often note the divergence in quality from their past experiences there, and some will undoubtedly complain; others will merely not return. If the manager finds that the beef purchased is not in compliance with the standards set, then some remedial action is called for if the goal of offering the finest food is to be met.

It is possible to develop a set of analagous circumstances in virtually any other area of the operation where control must be instituted. Wherever control is needed in restaurant operations, it can best be accomplished by means of following the four aforementioned steps.

COST-BENEFIT RATIO

One additional important concept must be introduced before leaving the general subject of control and proceeding to the specific controls available to food and beverage operators—the relationship between costs incurred and benefits obtained.

The student can appreciate that all control measures bring some cost to a business, sometimes relatively insignificant, at other times great, and occasionally even prohibitive. A relatively insignificant cost is required to institute the simple control measure of locking the front and back doors at night to prevent burglary. Relocating a cashier's desk to a position judged more suitable for preventing customers from leaving without paying, costs somewhat more. Establishing a system of the time clocks presided over by timekeepers is of even greater and ongoing cost. Establishing a control department within the restaurant and hiring a food controller and a beverage controller, with appropriate secretarial and other assistance, together with all of the paper, supplies, and equipment these individuals would need, would surely entail large and possibly prohibitive sums of money.

One must remember that the purpose of cost and sales control measures is to guard against excessive costs and to ensure that all sales result in appropriate income. In other words, the business must benefit from the introduction of any control device, procedure, or personnel. For example, if recent telephone bills have reached unwarranted levels because of nonbusiness-related long-distance calls placed on the office telephone, a simple control expenditure for a telephone lock might result in considerable savings. In similar fashion, hiring a cashier to record sales and collect cash would probably go further toward ensuring that sales resulted in income than could a procedure that permitted waiters and waitresses to collect for the food and beverages they served. In each of these cases, as in all examples of incurring cost for purposes of control, the amount of such cost incurred should be exceeded by the benefits derived by the business.

Before instituting any new procedures for control, management must first determine that the anticipated savings will be greater than the cost of the new systems. Any manager must look critically at the various methods and procedures available for improving control to ascertain whether their imposition will save more than they cost. If the control procedures cost more than the price of instituting them, they will probably eventually worsen the restaurant's financial position. It is usually unwise in business to attempt controls whose cost exceeds their benefit. In its simplest form, it is safe to say that no one in business should spend a dollar if the anticipated saving is less than a dollar. In addition, one must also look at the nonquantifiable effects, beneficial and otherwise, before instituting any control procedure and incurring the consequent cost.

Control systems and procedures generally affect many aspects of the operation, sometimes in a negative way not anticipated by the manager. For example, a system that verifies that all food going from the kitchen to the dining room is appropriately recorded on sales checks may have the effect of slowing down service, reducing turnover, and even resulting in cold food being served to guests. By the same token, the installation of a time clock to develop accurate payroll records might cause resentment among certain long-time, loyal, and valued employees, some of whom might seek other employment rather than punch a time clock.

CHAPTER ESSENTIALS

In this chapter we established working definitions of the important terms control, cost control, and sales control. We fixed responsibility for control, and demonstrated the need for control through all operating phases in a successful enterprise. Eight commonly used control techniques were defined and illustrated. Managers frequently employ one or all of them in implementing the four-step process of control. Particular emphasis was given to the preparation and use of the operating budget as a control technique. Finally, we described the significance of the cost/benefit ratio in determining the extent to which control measures are to be implemented.

QUESTIONS AND PROBLEMS

1. Using one standard portion of chicken for an example, compare the quality standards one might find for that item in a school cafeteria with the standards one might expect to find in use in a fine restaurant.
2. How would the quality standards for labor in a fine restaurant compare with those of a school cafeteria? Why?
3. Are censure and discipline the only control techniques that have negative connotations? Why?
4. For purposes of establishing control, the management of a certain cocktail lounge has directed a bartender, who was formerly permitted to mix drinks without measuring, to use a device that automatically measures

quantities poured. What positive and negative effects can this new procedure have on bar operation?

5 From your own personal experience, cite an instance where a manager's inconsistency in setting examples or giving directions has led to confusion in day-to-day operations.

6 How can budgets be used as control devices in food and beverage operations?

7 What is the purpose of cost control?

8 Imagine that you are the manager of a fine restaurant and are confronted with the problem of a waiter who refuses to follow the service standards and techniques established by the owner. It is apparent to you that the waiter's approach results in faster but sloppy service. Two of the owner's goals are profitability and fine service. Discuss the possible actions that you might take under these conditions to control employee behavior and to work toward achieving the owner's goals.

9 A certain restaurant offers chopped steak as one of the items on the menu, and each cook who prepares one has his or her own ideas as to what constitutes chopped steak. Using the four steps in the control process as the basis for your response, show how a new manager might eliminate this problem.

10 The manager of a certain restaurant decides that all employees should be searched before they leave the premises each day because he believes this will reduce the problem of employee theft. Discuss the possible costs and potential benefits that the manager should consider before instituting this policy.

11 If the standard cost of a one-ounce drink (excluding mixer) is $.25 and the actual cost averages out to $.27 per drink, calculate the amount of excess cost in thirty-two drinks. How much liquor does that additional cost represent?

12 If the standard cost of a $1\frac{1}{2}$-ounce drink is $.40 and the real cost is $.43, calculate the amount of money wasted in thirty-two drinks. How much liquor does it represent?

13 If the standard cost of a $1\frac{1}{4}$-ounce drink is $.30, and the real cost is $.35, calculate the additional cost in thirty-two drinks and the amount of the liquor the additional cost represents.

14 Calculate the following standard costs, if the quart bottle costs $6.40:

- **a** for a 1-ounce drink
- **b** for $1\frac{1}{4}$-ounce drink
- **c** for a $1\frac{1}{2}$-ounce drink

15 Define standard procedures in your own words and give two examples from your own experience.

16 Given the following information reflecting the manager's expectations for the coming year's operation of The Market Restaurant, prepare the operating budget for the year, using the illustration provided in this chapter.

Food Sales: $420,000

Beverage sales: $90,000

Cost of food: 36.0% of food sales

Cost of beverages: 24.0% of beverage sales

Variable payroll: 20.0% of food sales

Fixed payroll: $42,000

Payroll taxes and employee benefits: 25.0% of total payroll

Other controllable expenses: $63,000

Depreciation: $25,500

Occupation costs: $36,000

17 The manager of the Downtown Restaurant has been following an operating budget for the current year; it is reproduced below:

Sales:		
Food sales	$630,000	
Beverage sales	140,000	
Total sales		$770,000
Cost of sales:		
Cost of food sold	$252,000	
Cost of beverages sold	35,000	
Total costs		287,000
Gross profit on sales		$483,000
Controllable expenses:		
Payroll	$173,250	
Payroll taxes and employee benefits	45,045	
Other controllable expenses	82,000	
Total controllable expenses	$300,295	$300,295
Profit before occupation costs		$182,705
Occupation costs		64,000
Profit before depreciation		118,705
Depreciation		38,500
Profit before income taxes		$ 80,205

For the upcoming year, the following changes are expected:

Food sales will increase by 10%.

Beverage sales will increase by 6%.
Food cost percentage and beverage cost percentage will remain the same.
Fixed payroll—$69,300 for this year—will increase by $8,000.
Variable payroll will be 16% of expected food sales.
Payroll taxes and employee benefits will remain the same percentage of payroll.
Controllable expenses will increase by $12,000.
Occupation costs will increase by $5,000.
Depreciation will remain the same.

Given these expected changes, prepare the operating budget for the coming year.

18 Referring to question 17, assume that the prepared operating budget has been adopted. After the first six months of operation, financial records reveal the following:

Sales of food have increased by 12% rather than by 10%.
Beverage sales have increased by 5% rather than by 6%.
Food cost percentage is 1% lower than budgeted, but beverage cost percentage is 2% higher.
Variable payroll is 14% of food sales, rather than the expected 16%.

Assuming that the trends evident in the first six months continue for the balance of the year, and that both sales and expenses are equally divided between the two halves of the year, prepare a revision of the budget for the second six-month period.

chapter 3

Cost, Volume, and Profit Relationships

Learning Objectives

After reading and studying this chapter, the student should be able to:

1 Explain the importance of the Cost/Volume/Profit relationship to cost control.

2 Solve problems to determine:

- **a** sales in dollars and units
- **b** variable costs
- **c** fixed cost
- **d** profit
- **e** contribution rate
- **f** contribution margin
- **g** variable rate
- **h** break-even

3 Graphically illustrate break-even computation.

4 List and illustrate ways in which the break-even point can be changed.

No discussion of costs, sales, and control would be complete without an understanding of the relationships of cost, sales volume, and profit. In the Introduction we pointed out the substantial profit made by the Graduate Restaurant, noting that the cost percents were in more favorable relation to sales than the Rush Hour Inn. We should not assume, however, that good cost-to-sales relationships automatically result in profit for a restaurant or that higher or lower cost percents are necessarily desirable for a given restaurant. Indeed, it is possible that a higher cost percent (which means lower menu prices or more food given each customer) might result in sufficient additional customers to provide a substantial profit even with high cost percents. Nevertheless, it is obvious that the sum of the cost percents cannot exceed 100% if the operation is to be profitable. It will be useful to examine illustrations from the examples in the Introduction (see figure 3.1).

FIGURE 3.1
The Graduate Restaurant

Sales	$325,000	100.0%
Cost of sales	108,875	33.5%
Cost of labor	81,250	25.0%
Cost of overhead	97,500	30.0%
Profit	37,375	11.5%

At the given level of sales and costs, satisfactory profit has been earned.

It is possible to earn acceptable profit at sales levels other than $325,000 even though prime cost, as percentage of sales, increases. Figure 3.2 illustrates how this may be possible.

FIGURE 3.2
The Graduate Restaurant

Sales	$500,000	100.0%
Cost of sales	200,000	40.0%
Cost of labor	150,000	30.0%
Cost of overhead	97,500	19.5%
Profit	52,500	10.5%

Although the cost-to-sales ratios for the prime costs have increased (cost of sales from 35.5% to 40%, and cost of labor from 25% to 30%), a satisfactory profit was still realized. The reason for this is that overhead has accounted for the same number of dollars in both cases. Consequently, as sales volume increases, this number of dollars has represented a smaller percentage of sales.

Now let us hypothesize a decrease in sales in the restaurant as illustrated in figure 3.3.

FIGURE 3.3
The Graduate Restaurant

Sales	$200,000	100.0%
Cost of sales	67,000	33.5%
Cost of labor	50,000	25.0%
Cost of overhead	97,500	48.75%
Profit (loss)	(14,500)	(7.25%)

In this instance, cost percents for the prime costs were the same as they had been at sales level $325,000. However, the operation shows a loss rather than a profit because the fixed element for overhead, still $97,500, now accounts for 48.75% of sales dollars, rather than the 30% it represented in figure 3.1.

The key to understanding the Cost/Volume/Profit relationship lies in understanding that fixed costs exist in an operation regardless of sales volume, and that it is necessary to generate sufficient total volume to cover both fixed and variable costs. This is not to say, however, that variable cost percents are to be ignored. In fact, if variable cost percent is high, it may not be possible to generate sufficient volume to cover fixed costs. After all, a dining room can be turned over only a limited number of times in any given meal period. On the other hand, if variable cost percents are too low, it may not be possible to generate sales volume simply because potential customers perceive prices as too high for value received, and thus dine elsewhere.

All this is by way of saying what by now should be obvious:

$$\text{Sales} = \text{Cost of Sales} + \text{Cost of Labor} + \text{Cost of Overhead} + \text{Profit (or minus Loss)}^{*}$$

Because cost of sales is considered variable, cost of labor includes both fixed and variable elements, and cost of overhead is largely fixed, one could shorten and simplify the above equation to:

$$\text{Sales} = \text{Variable Cost} + \text{Fixed Cost} + \text{Profit}$$

This is the basic equation of Cost/Volume/Profit analysis.

In proceeding with the chapter, the reader will do well to keep three points in mind.

1 Within the normal range of restaurant operations, a relationship exists between variable costs and sales that tends to remain relatively constant. That relationship is normally expressed as either a percentage or a decimal and tends to have a stable quality.

* The effect on loss will be implicit in all future statements of this formula and will not be restated each time.

2 Fixed costs, on the other hand, tend to account for stable numbers of dollars regardless of dollar sales volume. Consequently, expressed as either a percentage or a decimal, the relationship between fixed costs and sales changes as sales volume increases and decreases.

3 Once acceptable levels are determined for costs, they must be controlled at those levels if the operation is to be profitable.

Before attempting detailed discussion of Cost/Volume/Profit relationships, it will be necessary to introduce and define some important terms, concepts, and abbreviations. These will be illustrated using figures from the income statement for the Graduate Restaurant because they are now familiar to the student. The figures from the income statement are reproduced in figure 3.4.

FIGURE 3.4
The Graduate Restaurant Income Statement for the Year Ending December 31, 19—

Sales			*Percentages of Sales*
Food sales	$276,250		85%
Beverage sales	48,750		15%
Total		$325,000	100%
Cost of sales			
Cost of food sold	$ 96,687		35% (of food sales)
Cost of beverage	12,188		25% (of bev. sales)
Total		$108,875	35.5% (of total sales)
Gross profit on sales		$216,125	66.5%
Controllable expenses			
Payroll	$ 65,000		20%
Payroll taxes, etc.	16,250		5% (25% of payroll)
Other controllable expenses	48,750		15%
Total		$130,000	40%
Profit before occupancy costs		$ 86,125	26.5%
Occupancy costs		$ 32,500	10%
Profit before depreciation		$ 53,625	16.5%
Depreciation		$ 16,250	5%
Profit before income tax		$ 37,375	11.5%

By referring to figure 3.4, it should be clear that cost of sales ($108,875) is variable cost; the cost of labor is partly variable and partly fixed; and the breakdown of these figures was presented in Chapter 2 as 60% fixed and 40% variable. Therefore, 60% of $81,250 (or $48,750) is fixed and the balance ($32,500) is variable. The major portion of cost overhead is fixed; because the variable portion is comparatively small, as is the degree of variability, the cost of overhead ($97,500) will be treated as fixed in this analysis. (The figure above may be found in summary in figure 3.1.)

Given the above, the basic Cost/Volume/Profit equation for the Graduate Restaurant at this point would be:

Sales ($325,000) = Variable cost ($141,375, or $108,875 + $32,500)
+ Fixed cost ($146,250, or $97,500 + $48,750)
+ Profit ($37,375)

By letting the first letters of the terms stand for those terms, this could be written as a formula:

$$S = VC + FC + P$$

For the balance of this work, then

S = Sales
VC = Variable Cost
FC = Fixed Cost
P = Profit

In addition, the variable cost percent referred to earlier will henceforth be called by its more common name, Variable Rate, and will be abbreviated as VR. Thus,

VR = Variable Rate

The VR is determined by dividing VC by S.

$$VR = \frac{VC}{S}$$

For the Graduate Restaurant, variable cost of $141,375 is divided by sales of $325,000 to determine that variable rate is .435

$$\frac{\$141{,}375}{325{,}000} = .435 \text{ VR}$$

This is much the same as saying that 43.5% of the dollar sales is needed to cover the variable costs, or that $.435 of each dollar of sale is so needed.

If 43.5% of dollar sales is needed to cover the variable costs, then the remainder of 56.5% is available for other purposes. Those other purposes are meeting fixed costs and providing for profit. Thus $.565 of each dollar of sale is available to contribute to covering fixed costs and providing profit. This percentage (or ratio, or rate) is known as the Contribution Rate, and is abbreviated as CR.

Thus,

$$CR = \text{Contribution Rate}$$

The CR is determined by subtracting the VR from 1, as

$$CR = 1 - VR$$

In the case of the Graduate Restaurant, the CR is .565, found by subtracting VR .435 from 1.

$$1 - .435 = .565$$

Each dollar of sale, then, may be divided imaginatively into two portions: that which must be used to cover variable costs associated with the item sold and that which remains to cover fixed costs and to provide profit. The dollar amount remaining after variable costs have been subtracted from the sales dollar is defined as the Contribution Margin, and is abbreviated as CM. Thus,

$$CM = \text{Contribution Margin}$$

It should be noted that the ratio of Average Contribution Margin to Average Sales Price is the Contribution Rate.

$$\frac{CM}{SP} = CR$$

$$SP = \text{Sales Price}$$

The student will recognize at once that there can be no profit until all of the fixed costs have been met. If dollar sales volume is insufficient to cover both variable and fixed costs, the business will operate at a loss. If dollar sales are sufficient to cover both variable and fixed costs exactly, but insufficient to provide any profit (i.e., profit is zero), the business is said to be operating at the Break-even Point, usually abbreviated as BE. Thus,

$$BE = \text{Break-even Point}$$

When sales reach a level sufficient to cover all variable and fixed costs with an additional amount left over, that additional amount is obviously profit. Moreover, since CM is going to cover fixed costs until BE is reached, after BE is reached, CM becomes profit.

In the case of the Graduate Restaurant, fixed costs are $146,250. Each dollar of sale is divided into the VR (.435) to cover variable costs, and the CR (.565) to cover fixed costs, then to provide profit. Now, if each sales dollar is providing \$.565 CM, then it is possible by division to determine how many sales dollars, each providing \$.565 CM, will be required to reach BE. Therefore, we will divide the fixed costs (FC) of \$146,250 by the contribution rate (CR) of .565 to determine the sales requirement for break-even (BE), which is \$258,849.56, and which we will round off to \$258,850.

$$\frac{\text{FC } \$146{,}250}{\text{CR } .565} = \text{BE } \$258{,}850$$

At that level of sales, variable costs (VC) will be \$112,599.75, or 43.5% of sales. We round this off to \$112,600. This added to FC of \$146,250 totals \$258,850, leaving no profit.

$$\text{S } (\$258{,}850) = \text{VC } (\$112{,}600) + \text{FC } (\$146{,}250) + \text{P } (0)$$

However, the Graduate Restaurant did not operate at BE. The sales level achieved was \$325,000—\$66,150 beyond BE. While there were no fixed costs to cover beyond BE, each dollar of sale above it does have variable costs associated with it, here found to have been \$.435 for each dollar of sale, or .435 VR multiplied by S (sales). If we multiply the dollar sales of \$66,150 by VR (variable rate) .435, we find variable costs associated with those sales beyond BE to be \$28,775.25, rounded off to \$28,775.

$$\text{VC } (\$28{,}775) = \text{S } (\$66{,}150) \times \text{VR } (.435)$$

If the variable cost of \$28,775 is subtracted from sales of \$66,150, the result (\$37,375) is equal to the profit (P) for the period, and is made up of \$.565 out of each dollar sale beyond BE.

$$\text{P } (\$37{,}375) = \text{S } (\$66{,}160) \times \text{CR } (.565)$$

It should be stressed that this is true only for sales beyond BE; before reaching BE, there is no profit.

At this point it is important to point out that the foregoing analysis as well as those that follow are based on certain assumptions that an owner or manager must understand before attempting Cost/Volume/Profit analysis. The assumptions are that:

1 costs in a particular establishment can be classified as fixed or variable with reasonable accuracy;

2 variable costs are directly variable, as defined in Chapter 1;

3 fixed costs are relatively stable and will remain so within the relevant range;

4 sales prices will remain constant for the period covered by the analysis;

5 the sales mix in the restaurant will remain relatively constant.

To the extent that these assumptions are not accurate for a particular establishment, any analysis attempted will be less than accurate. However, even if somewhat less than wholly accurate, the analysis can be entirely useful. For most establishments, the inaccuracies within the normal business volume range do not seriously inhibit the use of such analyses.

COST CONTROL AND THE COST/VOLUME/PROFIT EQUATION

Earlier in this chapter, the point was made that for operations to achieve planned profits, cost must be kept under control by means described in Chapter 2. It will be useful now to illustrate what happens to planned profits when costs are not kept under control. For illustration, we will refer to the operating budget for the Graduate Restaurant for the coming year as developed in Chapter 2, and reproduced in figure 3.5.

FIGURE 3.5
Operating Budget
The Graduate Restaurant

Sales		
Food sales	$303,875	
Beverage sales	53,625	
Total sales		$357,500
Cost of sales		
Cost of food sold	106,356	
Cost of beverages sold	13,406	
Total cost		119,762
Gross profit		237,738
Controllable expenses		
Payroll	70,684	
Payroll taxes and employee benefits	17,671	
Other controllable expenses	55,250	
Total controllable expenses		143,605
Profit before occupation costs		96,133
Occupation costs		34,500
Profit before depreciation		53,633
Depreciation		16,250
Profit before income taxes		43,383

In order to determine the variable rate (VR) for the coming year, we must add the budgeted variable costs for food and beverages ($119,762) and the variable portion of both payroll and payroll taxes and employee benefits, given in Chapter 2 as 40%.

In the discussion of the budget for the Graduate Restaurant for the coming year in Chapter 2, it was stated that sales were to increase by 10% and that variable costs would therefore increase accordingly, although the cost percent would remain the same. Therefore, the ratio of variable costs to sales (the variable rate, or VR), calculated as .435 from figures in the income statement earlier in this chapter, is budgeted to remain the same for the coming year. Since this is true, the contribution rate (CR), defined as 1 − VR, will also be the same, or .565. Budgeted fixed costs for the coming year are:

Fixed payroll	$42,120
Fixed payroll taxes and employee benefits	10,530
Other controllable expenses	55,250
Occupation costs	34,500
Depreciation	16,250
Total fixed costs	$158,650

Assume that the new year has begun under the budget and that the manager fails to control variable costs adequately. Excessive variable costs develop because of this lack of control, largely through inefficiency and waste. Such problems as spoilage of raw materials and poor scheduling of staff are common causes of these excessive costs.

Now assume that these excessive variable costs have had the effect of increasing the variable rate from the .435 to .515, which is to say that the amount needed to cover variable costs has risen from a planned 43.5% of each sales dollar to 51.5%.

Let us now examine the effect of this on financial operations for the year. If this trend is allowed to continue and appropriate control measures are not instituted, figures by the end of the year will show a decrease in profit from the planned $43,383 to $14,737.50, as shown in figure 3.6.

FIGURE 3.6

Sales	$357,500.00
Variable costs (at .515 VR)	− 184,112.50
	173,387.50
Fixed costs	− 158,650.00
Profit	14,737.50

Thus, the profit as a percentage of sales will have decreased from a planned 12.1% to the projected 4.1%. This profit figure will not provide the owner with the profit projected in the budget and will present a low return on sales.

One could then ask what level of dollar sales would be required to earn the planned profit of $43,383 given this variable rate of .515 and fixed costs of

$158,650. It is possible to calculate the required dollar sales volume by means of the formula

$$\text{Sales level} = \frac{\text{Fixed costs} + \text{Profit (or planned profit)}}{1 - \text{Variable rate}}$$

Substituting in the formula, we see that

$$\text{Sales} = \frac{\$158{,}650 + 43{,}383}{.485\ (1 - .515)}$$

which equals $416,562.98 in dollar sales required, an additional $59,062.89 in sales. It should be obvious that these additional sales are required to make the planned profit simply because of the excessive variable costs that have had the effect of unnecessarily increasing the variable rate. The planned profit could have been earned at the sales level $357,500 if management had done a better job of controlling variable costs. This could have been done, conceivably, without any change in quality or quantity standards, and without raising prices.

DOLLAR CALCULATIONS

We have established a formula for determining the dollar sales level required to earn any planned or targeted profit, given a dollar amount of fixed cost and an expected variable rate, summarized as

$$S = \frac{FC + P}{1 - VR\ (\text{or } CR)} \qquad \textit{(Formula \#1)}$$

This formula may also be applied when seeking break-even point, merely by letting P = O.

Algebraically, this formula may be restated in several ways, such as those listed below, in order to solve for any unknown component.

$$CR = \frac{FC + P}{S} \qquad \textit{(Formula \#2)}$$

$$P = (S \times CR) - FC \qquad \textit{(Formula \#3)}$$

$$FC = (S \times CR) - P \qquad \textit{(Formula \#4)}$$

These formulas have useful applications for restaurateurs. For example, suppose that an owner knows the fixed costs and the anticipated sales level for a given restaurant, has a particular profit target in mind, and wants to determine what variable rate must be maintained to achieve the targeted profit. Assume the following figures:

Fixed costs	\$160,000
Sales potential	500,000
Profit target	40,000

Using Formula #2, we can determine a projected CR of .4.

$$\frac{\text{FC } \$160{,}000 + \text{P } \$40{,}000}{\text{S } \$500{,}000} = .4 \text{ CR}$$

Since CR = 1 − VR, then VR must be .6, which is to say that variable costs may not exceed 60% of the sales dollars at the expected sales level, or that \$.60 out of every dollar of sale is the maximum that can be used to cover variable costs.

Using figures selected from those above, we might then use Formula #3 to solve for potential profit in a restaurant with fixed costs of \$160,000, sales of \$500,000, and a projected variable rate of .6. Thus,

$$(\text{S } \$500{,}000. \times \text{CR } .4) - \$160{,}000. = \text{P } \$40{,}000.$$

Using Formula #4, solving for FC, we see that

$$(\text{S } \$500{,}000 \times \text{CR } .4) - \text{P } \$40{,}000. = \text{FC } \$160{,}000.$$

All of the foregoing problems and discussions of Cost/Volume/Profit relationships have addressed questions of dollars, either dollar costs, dollar sales, or dollar profits. However, there are occasions when owners and managers are interested in determining numbers of sales (covers) or customers required to achieve a given goal.

UNIT CALCULATIONS

In general, determining the numbers of sales needed to cover given fixed costs is possible if one also knows average sales price per unit sold and average variable cost per unit. Average sales price per unit may be determined by dividing total dollar sales by the number of customers served in the period. This is commonly known as the average cover. Average variable cost may be determined by dividing total variable costs by this same number of customers. For example, if a small restaurant recorded sales of \$24,000 and variable costs of \$15,000 in a period when 3,000 customers had been served, then:

$$\frac{\$24{,}000 \text{ sales}}{3{,}000 \text{ customers}} = \$8.00 \text{ average sale or Sales Price or cover}$$

Similarly,

$$\frac{\$15{,}000 \text{ variable cost}}{3{,}000 \text{ customers}} = \$5.00 \text{ average variable cost}$$

With this information, it is possible to determine average contribution margin (CM), defined previously as average sale minus average variable cost. Thus,

Average sale	$8.00
less Average VC	5.00
Average CM	$3.00

Before using this figure to complete calculations to determine required unit sales levels, one important limitation on its use must be noted. An establishment with a stable sales mix will gain more reliable data from the ensuing calculations than will one with wide fluctuations in the sales mix. Fluctuations in the sales mix typically cause fluctuations in the variable cost structure, and wide fluctuations may introduce serious distortions.

Mathematically, sales volume required to break even may be calculated by means of the following formula:

$$\text{Unit sales required} = \frac{\text{Fixed costs}}{\text{Contribution margin/unit}}$$

For example, suppose that the small restaurant referred to is selling one item only for $8 on the menu and that the variable cost for that item is $5. This particular establishment has total fixed costs to be covered of $9,000. Each time one order of this item is sold, the sale generates a contribution margin (sales price − variable cost) of $3.00. Therefore, in order to cover the $9,000 fixed cost, the restaurant must sell 3,000 units of the item, each producing its $3 contribution margin. This may be calculated as follows:

$$\text{Unit sales required} = \frac{\text{FC } \$9{,}000}{\text{CM } \$3}$$

$$\text{Unit sales required} = 3{,}000$$

This is further illustrated in figure 3.7. Note that the amount of the loss at each level of sales volume is represented by the space between the total cost and total sales lines to the left of the break-even point. The amount of profit is described by those same two lines, but to the right of the point.

If the sales price were $7 instead, the contribution margin would be reduced to $2, and sales of 4,500 units would be needed to cover the same $9,000 fixed cost. This point, where all costs are exactly covered by revenue with neither profit nor loss, has been defined as the **break-even point.** Many times restaurants

FIGURE 3.7
Break-even Analysis

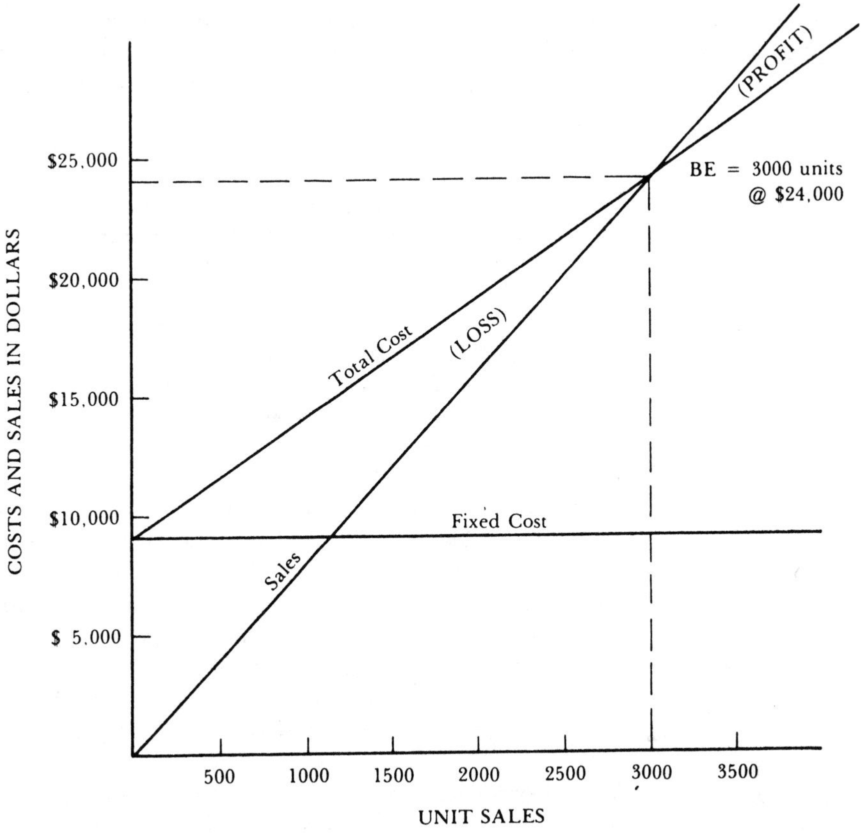

reduce selling prices in the hope of gaining additional unit sales to cover costs and earn greater profits. It should be obvious, however, that one cannot reduce selling price to the point where it is less than the variable unit cost of the item. This would result in a dollar loss on each unit sold, and the greater the number of units sold, the greater would be the dollar loss. On the other hand, trying to increase profit by increasing sales prices, or by reducing variable costs per unit, or by doing both of these at once, may result in greater profit per unit sold but may also reduce total number of sales and prove to be a costly attempt at increasing profit.

CALCULATING AVERAGE VR

It is apparent that food and beverage operations do not offer one product, as in the preceding analysis, but rather have a large number of items with different selling prices and various costs. Each item has a different contribution margin, and the calculation of break-even points for restaurants is rather more complex.

This problem is solved by establishing an average acceptable variable rate, recognizing that if that average rate is too high, an unrealistic or impossible number of customers or unit sales may be required for the operation to be profitable. For example, a restaurant may sell four items with the variable costs and selling prices given in figure 3.8.

FIGURE 3.8

	VC	*S*	*VR*
Steak	5.00	8.00	.625
Scallops	3.00	6.00	.5
Chicken	2.00	5.00	.4
Spaghetti	1.00	4.00	.25

To arrive at an average variable rate, it is first necessary to make some assumptions about the percentage of revenue likely for each of these items to represent a given period. If past records of sales are available, this information will be more accurate. If none are available, estimates must be made. For simplicity, we will assume that each of the items will be ordered by 25% of the customers. If that is true, then the relationship between dollar sales for any item and total sales for all items will hold constant, regardless of whether the restaurant has 40, 200, or 300 customers in a given period. To illustrate at the forty-customer level:

> Ten will order steak at total variable cost of $50 and total sales of $80. Another ten will order scallops at total VC of $30 and total S of $60. Still another ten will order chicken at VC of $20, bringing in total dollar S of $50, and the final ten will order spaghetti at VC $10, bringing sales up by another $40. Total VC for all items will be the sum of the above, or $110, while total S will be $230.
>
> Since VR equals VC/S in this instance, the calculation is:

$$\frac{\$110\text{ VC}}{\$230\text{ S}}, \text{ or a 47.8\% average variable rate.}$$

If the total anticipated number of customers were to increase from 40 to 200, and the proportional number of persons ordering each item were to remain unchanged, calculations would reveal a total anticipated variable cost of $550 and total anticipated sales of $1,150. These figures also reveal an average variable rate of .478 (see figure 3.9).

FIGURE 3.9

Estimated Unit Sales	*Item*	*Unit VC*	*Unit SP*	*Total $ VC*	*Total $ S*
10	Steak	5.00	8.00	50	80
10	Scallops	3.00	6.00	30	60
10	Chicken	2.00	5.00	20	50
10	Spaghetti	1.00	4.00	10	40
40				110	230

Another way of determining average VR, particularly when the specifics of past customer orders are absent, is to determine the percentage of total revenue represented by revenue for each of the items being sold. Thus, if steak has been responsible for $80 in sales out of a total of $230, as in the preceding charts, that revenue is equal to 34.78% of total sales. By following this method, it is possible to determine the proportional share of total sales (PSTS) attributable to each item as shown in figure 3.10.

FIGURE 3.10

	Total Revenue	*PSTS*
Steak	$ 80	.3478
Scallops	60	.2609
Chicken	50	.2174
Spaghetti	40	.1739
Variable	$230	

The individual variable rate of each item may then be multiplied by the proportional share of total sales (PSTS) represented by each item and added together in order to determine the total average VR (see figure 3.11).

FIGURE 3.11

	VR		*PSTS*		*Weighted VR*
Steak	.625	×	.3478	=	.2174
Scallops	.5	×	.2609	=	.1305
Chicken	.4	×	.2174	=	.0870
Spaghetti	.25	×	.1739	=	.0435
				VR Total Average	.4784

At this point, it becomes possible to determine the break-even point as previously illustrated. For example, if the above restaurant had fixed costs of

$64,328, then BE would be:

$$BE = \frac{\$64,328}{1 - .478}$$

Therefore, for this establishment BE = $123,233.72. Sales above that dollar level will be profitable; sales below that dollar level will result in a loss.

This analysis can be carried further. The $123,233.72 figure represents a certain number of customers. This number can be determined by finding out what the average check price is and dividing that figure into the break-even figure. To determine the average check price, take any number of customers and apply that figure to sales at that level. For example, in the case above, we used forty customers as an illustration. The average check price is $230 divided by forty, or $5.75. This same figure would be arrived at if different numbers of customers were assumed, provided the proportional numbers of sales for each menu item remain the same.

Therefore, dividing BE gross by $5.75 yields 21,432 customers necessary to break even. This can be further broken down into the number of customers per month and per week. Management can then make a determination if the potential market exists to reach the break-even point and various actions taken if the results are disappointing. The break-even point can be changed in one or more of the following ways:

1 Adjust menu prices upward.
2 Attempt to reduce variable costs.
3 Attempt to increase sales volume.

Figure 3.12 illustrates the effect of adjusting menu prices upward using the information from Figure 3.7. Let us assume that the price of the product was raised from $8 to $9. No change is made in fixed costs ($9,000) or in variable cost ($5.00). Break-even is determined as follows:

$$VR = \frac{\$5}{\$9} = .5556$$

$$BE = \frac{\$9,000}{1 - .5556}$$

$$BE = \frac{\$9,000}{.4444}$$

$$BE = \$20,252.03$$

This represents approximately 2,250 customers, a decrease of 750 customers necessary to break even ($20,252.03/$9.00).

Raising prices has the effect of changing the slope of the sales line and shifting the break-even point to the left and downward. If the business is able to

FIGURE 3.12
Breakeven Analysis at Increased Menu Price

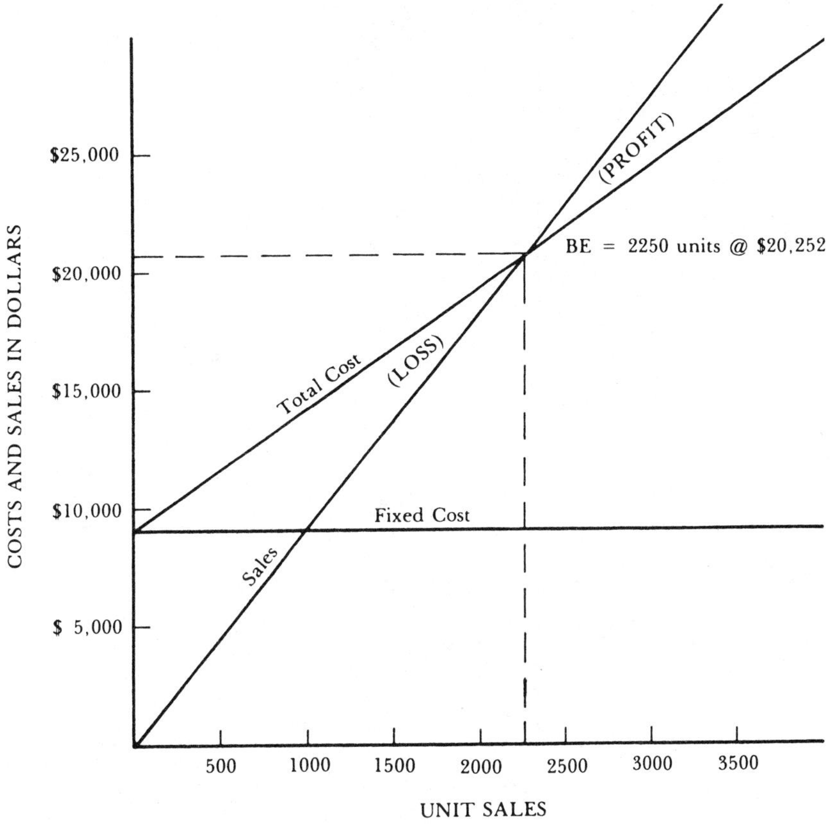

maintain its previous unit sales of 3,000 customers, a profit of $3,000 would now be obtained.

Figure 3.13 illustrates the effect of reducing variable costs. Going back to our original example, if we reduce portion sizes or take other measures to reduce the cost of the portion served by $.50, the new break-even point is calculated as follows:

$$VR = \frac{\$4.50}{\$8} = .5625$$

$$BE = \frac{\$9,000}{1 - .5625}$$

$$BE = \frac{\$9,000}{.4375}$$

$$BE = \$20,571$$

FIGURE 3.13
Break-even Analysis at Reduced Variable Cost

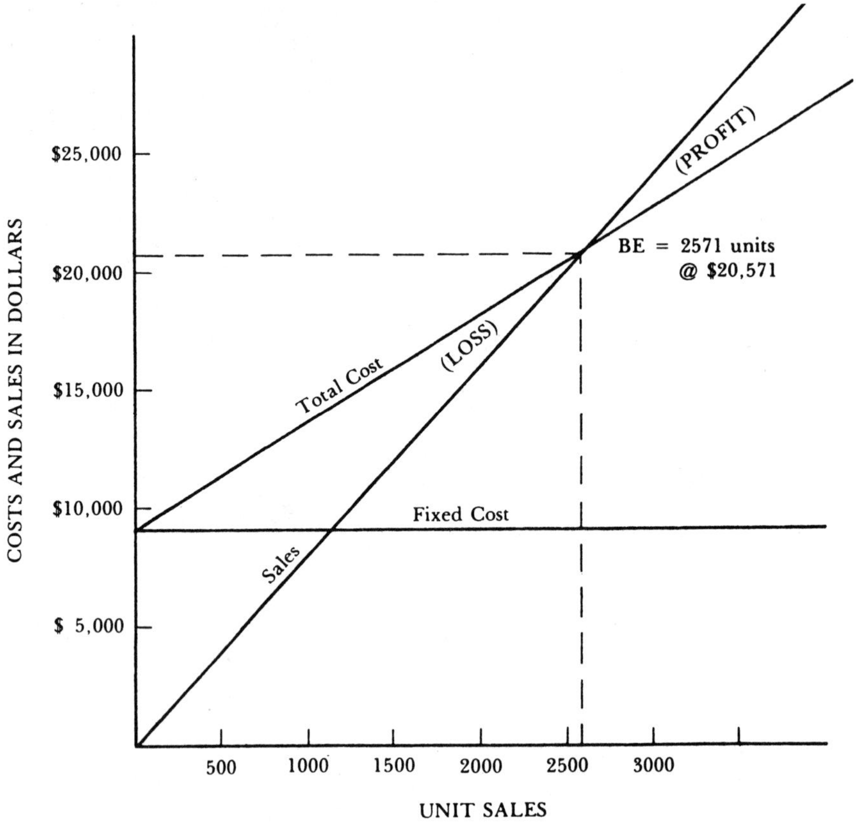

This represents 2,571 customers, a decrease of 429 customers necessary to break even ($20,571/$8.00). Lowering prices has the effect of changing the slope of the total cost line and again shifting the break-even point to the left and downward.

The third alternative, attempting to increase sales volume, is typically accomplished through advertising and other promotional efforts. However, one must note that costs increase as a result of advertising and will consequently increase the break-even point. If the additional volume and profit is not greater than the additional costs, then the restaurant will be in a worse position than it was before advertising.

Restaurant managers typically do not attempt just one of the three prior ways of changing the break-even point. They usually attempt all of them at the same time: raising prices a little, reducing costs somewhat, and undertaking limited advertising. It is hoped that current customers will not react adversely.

One Final Point

A primary objective in any business is to make a profit, not just to break even. Many food and beverage managers treat profit as a fixed cost and include it when determining the break-even point. The amount of profit to be added to fixed costs is a discussion outside the scope of this text and includes such considerations as rate of return on investment capital, desire to build sales volume, and alternative investment opportunities.

CHAPTER ESSENTIALS

In this chapter we showed how an understanding of Cost/Volume/Profit relationships is useful to those who attempt to institute cost control, by illustrating the effect of excessive or uncontrolled costs on profits. We provided the essential formulas required for Cost/Volume/Profit analysis, illustrated their use and listed their limitations. We defined the new terms break-even point, contribution margin, variable rate, and contribution rate. Graphic representation of the Cost/Volume/Profit equations was illustrated, and formulas and procedures for determining average variable rate for complex settings were explained. Finally, we offered possible alternate courses of action for managers who find unsatisfactory results from current Cost/Volume/Profit analyses.

QUESTIONS AND PROBLEMS

1 In your own words define the following terms:

- **a** break-even point
- **b** contribution margin
- **c** contribution rate
- **d** variable rate

2 Given the following information, find contribution margin:

- **a** Average sales price per unit \$8.22; average variable cost per unit \$3.78.
- **b** Average sales price per unit \$7.50; average variable rate .36.
- **c** Average sales price per unit \$6.20; average contribution rate .55.
- **d** Average variable cost per unit \$4.20; average variable rate .3.
- **e** Average variable cost per unit \$3.60; average contribution rate .6.

(From this point on, the use of the term "average" will be eliminated. This will have no effect on the problems or their solutions.)

3 Given the following information, find variable rate:

- **a** Sales price per unit \$9.25; variable cost per unit \$3.70.
- **b** Total sales \$164,328; total variable cost \$72,304.32.
- **c** Sales price per unit \$8.80; contribution margin \$5.72.

d Sales price per unit $6.37; total fixed costs $62,408; total unit sales 19,364; total profit $12,952.80.

4 Given the following information, find contribution rate:

a Sales price per unit $8.50; contribution margin $4.08.
b Sales price per unit $7.50; variable cost per unit $4.95.
c Total sales $64,726; total variable cost $40,130.12.
d Sales price per unit $6.50; profit $13,381.80; total unit sales 18,440; total fixed costs $56,137.

5 Given the following information, find break-even point in dollar sales:

a Fixed costs $48,337.80; contribution rate .6.
b Variable rate .45; fixed costs $155,410.31.
c Variable cost per unit $1.85; sales price per unit $7.40; fixed costs $64,065.60.

6 Given the following information, find break-even point in unit sales:

a Fixed costs $113,231.64; contribution margin $2.28.
b Sales price per unit $7.22; fixed costs $95,035.68; variable cost per unit $3.98.
c Contribution rate .6; sales price per unit $8.20; fixed costs $119,423.16.

7 Given the following information, find dollar sales needed:

a Fixed costs $60,000; profit $18,000; sales price per unit $8; variable cost per unit $5.
b Variable rate .45; profit $21,578.10; fixed costs $58,382.
c Sales price per unit $6.60; profit $21,220.00; contribution margin $4.29; fixed costs $56,000.

8 Given the following information, find unit sales needed:

a Fixed costs $58,922; profit $9,838; contribution margin $3.82.
b Profit $11,603; sales price per unit $7; fixed costs $47,197; contribution rate .6.
c Variable cost per unit $3.30; profit equal to 18% of $101,000; sales price per unit $6.30; fixed costs $36,609.
d Sales price per unit $6.20; fixed costs $59,425.36; variable rate .4; profit $14.000.

9 Given the following information, find fixed costs:

a Total sales $104,672; profit $18,000; variable rate .42.
b Profit $12,000; unit sales 18,392; variable cost per unit $2.63; sales price per unit $5.34.
c Sales price per unit $4.60; profit $24,00; unit sales 26,712; variable rate .35.
d Contribution rate .65; sales price per unit $8.40; unit sales 16,549; profit $13,000.

10 Given the following information, find profit:

- **a** Fixed costs $82,449.40; total sales $167,543.20; variable cost $55,629.60.
- **b** Variable rate .4; unit sales 26,412; fixed costs $93,764.40; sales price per unit $7.60.
- **c** Total sales $90,830.66; variable cost per unit $3.64; fixed costs $35,919.70; sales price per unit $6.22.

11 The following information is from the records of the Hassle Inn Restaurant:

Sales	$400,000
Cost of sales	140,000
Cost of labor	104,000
Cost of overhead	120,000

Assume that the given cost of labor is apportionable as 30.0% variable and 70.0% fixed.

- **a** Calculate profit.
- **b** Calculate break-even point in dollar terms.
- **c** Calculate required dollar sales level to earn a profit of $50,000.
- **d** If variable costs increase by $8,200, what level of dollar sales will be required to earn a profit of $36,000?
- **e** If cost of overhead increases by 10%, what level of dollar sales will be required to earn the $36,000 profit?

12 Given the following information, determine break-even point in unit sales volume:

- **a** Fixed cost $24,000; contribution margin per unit $3.20.
- **b** Fixed cost $37,192; contribution margin per unit $4.91.
- **c** Contribution margin per unit $2.27; fixed cost $8,722.48.

13 Given the information below, determine the break-even point in dollar sales volume:

- **a** Fixed costs $12,419; variable rate .39.
- **b** Average sale $6.25; average variable cost per unit $2.38; fixed cost $26,427.40.
- **c** Fixed cost $14,827.

Menu Items	*% of Revenue*	*VR*
A	40	.45
B	25	.60
C	35	.50

- **d** Fixed cost $21,617.43; contribution rate .443.

14 Determine dollar sales volume needed to achieve each of the following:

- **a** Annual profit before taxes of $20,000 in an operation with fixed costs of $35,422, and an average variable rate of .545.

b Annual profit before taxes equal to 12% return in invested capital of $200,000 in a restaurant with fixed costs of $47,387, and a contribution rate of .415.

c Annual profit before taxes equal to 11% return on invested capital of $250,000 in an operation with fixed costs of $56,725, offering a simple menu of the following items:

Menu Item	*% of Return*	*VR*
A	30	.60
B	20	.45
C	35	.35
D	15	.25

15 Determine the unit sales volume needed to achieve each of the following:

a Annual profit before taxes of $24,000 in a restaurant with fixed costs of $32,000, an average sale of $7.22, and an average contribution margin of $2.25.

b Annual profit before taxes equal to 14% return on invested capital of $300,000 in an establishment with fixed costs of $44,500, an average sale of $8.40, and an average variable rate of .625.

16 In a certain restaurant with fixed costs of $24,000, and a projected average sale of $8, the owner wants to earn profit before taxes equal to a 10% return on $120,000 of invested capital. The owner is projecting 15,000 unit sales for the coming year. What average variable rate should be planned for? At that level, what will be the average contribution margin per sale?

17 **a** Given the following information, determine the break-even point in dollar sales volume:

Fixed cost, $15,000
Variable cost per unit, $3
Sales price, $5

b Determine the break-even point for the above establishment if the variable cost per unit is reduced by $1.

c Determine the break-even point for the establishment in (**a**) above if the sales price is increased to $9 per unit.

18 Following the example provided by Figure 3.7, prepare break-even analysis graphs of the three problems in question #17 above.

19 The XYZ Restaurant has fixed costs of $36,400 annually. Management operates at an average variable rate of .65. The average check price is $5. For the upcoming year, management plans to decrease the variable rate to .6, and at the same time to adjust menu prices upward so that the average check price will be $5.50.

a What has the break-even point been in dollar and in unit sales for the year now ending?

b What will the break-even point be in the upcoming year in dollar and in unit sales if management makes the changes described above?

c Prepare break-even analysis graphs to illustrate both (**a**) and (**b**) above.

d If management's target profit for the upcoming year is $19,000, how many unit sales will be needed to achieve this goal?

20 A certain restaurant offers a simple menu to the public as follows:

Menu Item	*% of Revenue*	*Variable Rate*
A	15	.30
B	20	.35
C	28	.42
D	18	.55
E	19	.48

Fixed costs total $101,010.

a Determine the break-even point in dollar sales.

b At an average check price of $6.50, determine the break-even point in unit sales.

c Prepare a break-even analysis graph to illustrate the above.

d If the management in this operation achieves 17,500 unit sales, how much dollar profit should result?

e If only 13,000 unit sales are achieved, what will be the amount of the dollar loss?

chapter 4

Electronic Data Processing and Control

Learning Objectives

After reading and studying this chapter, the student should be able to:

1. Outline the development of data processing from its probable beginnings to the present.
2. Define the following terms as used in data processing:

a	Computer	**g**	Terminal
b	Output	**h**	Hardware
c	Storage	**i**	Software
d	Input	**j**	Programs
e	CPU	**k**	Hard copy
f	VDT	**l**	Soft copy
		m	Media

3. Describe the process by which a computer provides output to management.
4. List the reasons why computers are now just beginning to come into common use in the food service industry.
5. List various outputs food service managers require from computers.
6. List the two factors that enable managers to make intelligent selections among alternate systems.

Before proceeding to specific control procedures and techniques, one important topic must be introduced: the electronic data processing (EDP) for control purposes in food and beverage operations. Because various EDP systems—including computer systems, some of which are more sophisticated and complicated than others—are more and more commonly used in hotels and restaurants, it will be increasingly necessary to understand their present and future roles. The authors therefore recommend that any student planning a career in hotels and restaurants take at least some introductory course work in computer operations. This chapter will provide some elementary understanding of control applications of EDP, some historical perspectives, and basic terms, as well as describe computer operations in simple terms and suggest some control applications.

HISTORICAL PERSPECTIVES

Business has used systems and procedures for processing data for several thousand years. Quite possibly the predecessors of today's hoteliers and restaurateurs used early data processing (DP) devices to facilitate bill calculation and help ensure accuracy. Those devices would not have resembled the ones used today, nor could they have performed many of today's sophisticated operations, but technically they were DP equipment. Perhaps the earliest was the abacus of ancient China. The abacus consisted of beads strung on wires within a rectangular frame. A skilled operator could use it to add, subtract, multiply, and divide.

Other devices invented for processing data include the adding machine, invented by Pascal in 1642, and the calculating machine, which Leibnitz developed around 1700. Such devices were operated manually and would be considered quite slow by today's standards. The development of electric motors in the late nineteenth and early twentieth centuries made possible the processing of data with electromechanical devices that worked at considerable speed. Twentieth-century advances in electronics have eliminated the mechanical aspects of data processing. Mechanical equipment for these purposes is now disappearing, and such devices will probably be museum pieces by the end of the twentieth century. (Interestingly, the abacus—the earliest of the devices—was neither mechanized nor electrified, and is still commonly used in some parts of the world.)

Taking the place of mechanical and electromechanical equipment are electronic, nonmechanical devices of varying degrees of complexity. Such devices use electrical impulses transmitted through circuits to perform calculations and otherwise process information, rather than the gears and other moving parts that characterized the earlier equipment. Most people are familiar with the small, hand-held calculators commonly used for basic arithmetic, as well as for some rather more complex operations, and have seen the various electronic replacements for the mechanical cash registers used in earlier days.

After the Second World War, an entire electronic data processing industry began to develop in the United States. Many of the pioneering organizations in this field were outgrowths of companies that formerly produced electromechanical devices. Soon after the war, business and industry leaders recognized the useful applications of EDP, and company employees at many levels began to work with various EDP systems and devices, many of which were the forerunners of those used today.

COMPUTERS AND THEIR RELATION TO HUMAN WORK

Most people have some basic familiarity with that special class of EDP equipment known as computers. However, computers differ significantly from other classes of EDP equipment in some important technical ways. The development of EDP equipment has enabled information to be processed at speeds billions of times faster than was possible before. The words used to refer to these speeds are nanosecond (the billionth part of a second) and picosecond (the trillionth part of a second). Such speeds enable people to accomplish many complicated tasks that were impractical or even impossible before the advent of this new equipment.

As used today, the term **computer** refers to an EDP device with capabilities far beyond those of any earlier EDP equipment. Computers can store, manipulate, and otherwise process information at incredible speeds, without direct human intervention at each step during processing; they can also produce reports based on the stored and processed information. A computer, then, may be defined as a machine that processes data automatically, in a programmable way. For those who have not studied computers formally, some general information about what computers do and the terms used to discuss them will be useful.

Anyone who has been in a restaurant knows that considerable "data" must be processed, particularly by a cashier. A restaurant cashier is a very busy individual who must process guest checks, verify their accuracy, collect money and make change (or process credit card transactions for those who do not pay in cash), and prepare some elementary reports of sales activity. Because the job of cashier is common to most restaurants, an analysis of some aspects of the job can help identify the parts and functions of a computer system.

For purposes of the following discussion, imagine a cashier named Leslie, who is expected to process guest checks accurately and give the manager a daily report of both charge and cash sales. This report is Leslie's expected **output** (information retrieved), and is to be produced only with the aid of paper, pencil, adding machine, cash drawer, and credit card imprinter.

To ensure the output's accuracy, Leslie must be certain that the prices charged customers are accurate. Therefore, Leslie must have at the work station information that can be used to check correct menu prices against those recorded by waiters and waitresses. This information could be a small file drawer containing one 3 × 5 card for each menu item, or a copy of the menu posted on the wall. Either way, Leslie would have some **storage** capability, to retain information that must be available for ready reference.

To produce a report showing total cash and charge sales, Leslie must be provided with information about each individual sale. This is accomplished when each departing guest presents Leslie with a guest check. This information is the **input** with which Leslie is to work.

For the report to be accurate, each individual check must be accurate; Leslie must add each to ensure the totals are correct and to determine the proper tax to be charged. In other words, Leslie must possess some **arithmetic** ability. Also, Leslie must be able to differentiate between cash and charge sales so that output will be correct. Therefore, Leslie must be able to exercise some **logic** in discriminating the one from the other (see figure 4.1).

So far Leslie has been responsible for several capabilities—output, storage, input, arithmetic, and logic. All of these capabilities must be coordinated so that each is used at the appropriate time. For example, Leslie must know that a guest check must be totaled before the tax is computed, and that these tasks must be completed for all checks before a report can be provided. Somehow these capabilities must be made to work together. Because Leslie understands the job of cashier in this establishment and can efficiently coordinate all the required capabilities, **control** is present.

The manner in which Leslie performs the job of cashier provides some insights into the way a computer operates. Just as information must be provided to a cashier, so data must be provided (or input) to the computer. This is usually

FIGURE 4.1

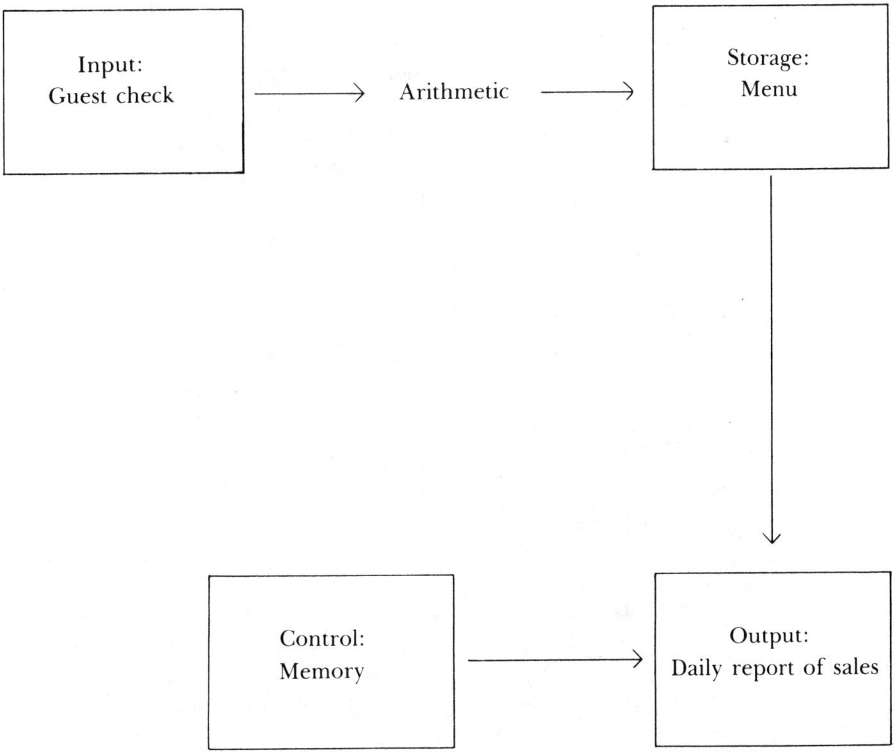

accomplished by special devices, the most common of which is known as a terminal. **Terminal** is a term used to describe a device for inputting or outputting data. It usually consists of a keyboard and either a printer or screen, or both. Input data can be stored, manipulated, and retrieved.

The storage, arithmetic, and logic process for which Leslie is responsible are carried out in a part of the computer commonly referred to as its "brain," but more accurately called a **Central Processing Unit,** or CPU. This highly sophisticated device is composed of several major components that process and otherwise manipulate data, provide storage capacity (or memory), and coordinate and control the computer's internal operation.

If the cashier's job were as simple as described, the development of sophisticated EDP equipment for food service operations would not be necessary. But some aspects of the cashier's work can be very complex. For control purposes many managers nowadays seek summaries and reports that cashiers can provide in reasonable time only with electronic assistance. Such summaries and reports enable management to monitor operations in a more timely manner than would be possible with manually prepared data, some of which could take hours or even days to calculate.

COMPUTER TERMINOLOGY

The computer field is really quite new and is advancing daily. Therefore, not surprisingly there is not always complete agreement on the exact meaning of some terms. This text will attempt to use terms and definitions that have reasonably broad acceptance. These should be sufficient to provide the student with some general understanding of computers.

Several terms have already been used—input, output, storage, logic, arithmetic, control, central processing unit, and terminal. But these alone are not sufficient; some additional terms and concepts must be introduced.

Data Input and Output

Because computers store and process data in the form of electronic signals, an intermediary device is required to translate input data into these signals and to convert output data to human language. Input/output (IO) devices stand between the human user and a computer and assist in performing these functions. A number of I/O terminals are available to the food and beverage industry, including the visual display terminal (VDT), which characteristically consists of a keyboard and some form of visual display screen. As an operator inputs data by means of a keyboard, the data is displayed on the screen so that it can be verified before it is stored. Stored data may subsequently be requested via the keyboard and displayed on this screen. Such output displayed on a screen is called **soft copy;** output produced on paper—more common for management reports—is known as **hard copy.** The output of hard copy requires a special terminal called a line printer. The simultaneous output of hard copy and soft copy is possible in a system that includes both a VDT and a line printer.

Hardware and Software, Programs and Media

Two terms that inevitably come up in any discussion of computers are **hardware** and **software.** Hardware refers to the visible, tangible components of a system, including CPUs, VDTs, printers, and so on. Hardware can be seen and touched, and physical space must be allotted to it. Software, on the other hand, is a term used broadly to refer to computer systems.

Programs are instructions to computers—series of step-by-step directions the system components follow in processing data. Devised by people known as programmers, they enable computers to operate and accomplish specific tasks. Computers have no intelligence beyond what is reflected in the programs, without which computers are incapable of anything. Programs tell the system what to do and how to do it. They are typically found on **media,** which includes such physical items as paper cards and tapes, magnetic cards and disks, and magnetic tapes and tape cassettes.

APPLICATIONS OF EDP FOR HOTELS AND RESTAURANTS

Our industry has used some EDP devices for a great number of years, but it is generally agreed that hotels and restaurants have not been quick to adopt computers. In fact, except for a handful of the larger firms and properties only during the 1970s did one begin to see any widespread use of computers in hotels and restaurants. These larger organizations initially used them primarily to speed certain specific bookkeeping and accounting functions; and hotels used them for reservations. At first, even in these organizations, control applications were secondary to speedy record-keeping. There were a number of reasons for this:

1. The high cost of computer systems, designed primarily for major corporations, could not be justified by most individual hotel and restaurant units.
2. Systems reliable enough for most industries were simply not reliable enough for hotels and restaurants, which could not tolerate the "down time" resulting from system failure.
3. Early programs for hotels and restaurants required a level of operator sophistication that was uncommon among typical industry employees.

In the last decade the computer industry has made progress in three major areas, and the effect has been to increase the use of computers by our industry.

Miniaturization of computer components has made possible the production of comparatively small devices. The cost of systems has been reduced, and simultaneously their storage capacity has increased. Improvements in programming have enabled even those without extensive computer knowledge and training to carry out highly sophisticated operations. Such developments make the use of computers entirely feasible for an ever growing number of food and beverage operations.

Figure 4.2 shows a comparatively small restaurant that uses a system consisting of the following components:

CPU in manager's office

Two VDTs with printers at servers' stations

One VDT at manager's desk

Remote printers at service bar and cooks' station

Servers arriving for work change into uniforms on a lower level (not shown on the diagram), then proceed to their sidestands in the dining room. On each sidestand is a small VDT that dining room personnel use to log in—i.e., they record their arrival for work much as they would with a time clock. Other personnel log in at the terminal in the manager's office.

Guests enter by the dining room supervisor's station, leave their coats in the coatroom, and are seated by the supervisor, who leaves menus at the table. Servers greet the guests and take their orders for drinks; these are written on ordinary white pads rather than on guest checks. Each server proceeds to a terminal and opens an account equivalent to a guest check in computer memory. This is done by entering server number, table number, and a special code assigned for creating a new account. With the account opened, the server, using a numerical code, enters customer orders for drinks. This data, together with the time of the order, is stored in the CPU, which has been programmed with correct prices for each drink. The system is programmed to send the recorded drink orders to the service bar, where they are output on a remote printer. The hard copy provided to the bartender is an order to prepare the drinks, and includes the server number, table number, and order time.

The bartender tears the hard copy of the order from the printer and places it on the tray with the prepared drinks, thus eliminating questions about which drinks are for which server and what time the orders were entered. At the appropriate time, the server follows similar procedures for placing food orders. Different codes are used for foods, and the orders are output on those remote printers at the cooks' station. All ordered items are stored in memory, but the only items output on the remote printer at any preparation station are those appropriate to that station. Thus, food orders are not output at the service bar, and orders for coffee, handled by the servers themselves, do not appear on any remote printers.

At the end of the customer's meal, the server obtains a guest check by requesting from the terminal and printer at the sidestand a hard copy of the data stored by table and server number. This hard copy is torn from the printer and

FIGURE 4.2

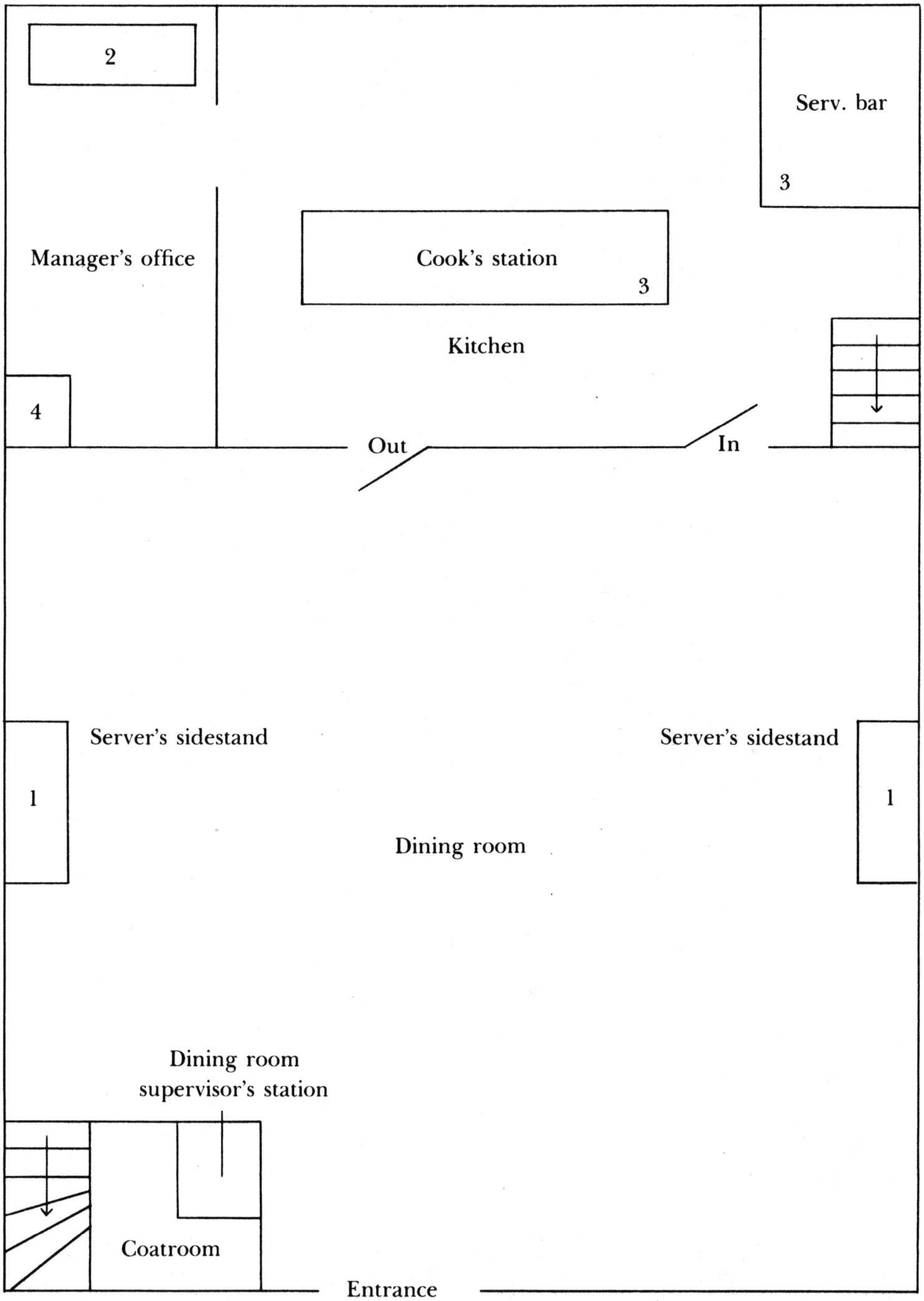

1. Server's terminals 2. Manager's terminal 3. Remote printers 4. CPU

given to the diner. In this particular establishment each server acts as a cashier for his or her own checks, and settlement is recorded for each check as the server receives cash or credit card.

At the end of a shift the server reports to the manager's office to settle the receipts. The manager uses his or her terminal to obtain summary data indicating charge and cash sales attributable to the particular server, and collects cash and charge vouchers accordingly. Before changing out of uniform and leaving the premises, the server logs out using the manager's terminal.

At the conclusion of business, a manager seeking a detailed breakdown of the day's business may request a wealth of data stored in the computer. A suitable program will provide such output as: total dollar sales categorized into cash sales and charge sales, with the charge sales divided by credit card; total dollar sales separated into food sales and beverage sales, with the food sales broken down into dollar sales by menu category or by individual menu items; average dollar sale per customer, per server, per seat, per table, or per hour, or any number of these; seat turnover; number of orders of each food and beverage item sold (a reflection of the sales mix); total dollar sales per hour; sales in any category for the period to date; total payroll cost for the day, for any part of the day, or for the period to date; and a vast amount of food and beverage cost data, including standard costs.

Management can monitor operations at will as the day progresses. Such data as gross sales volume, numbers of customers served, numbers of checks outstanding, sales mix, numbers of portions of particular items sold, and any number of other possibilities may be of special interest at given times through the day.

Conceivably, a clerical staff could produce all of the above information. However, it should be obvious that considerable time would be needed to produce such data, and the consequent cost would be great. In addition, the time required might render the data out-of-date before it is even produced. Finally, the very accuracy of the data might be questionable.

The foregoing illustration resembles a small, hypothetical system. However, larger and more sophisticated systems are already being used, particularly by some chain and other multiple-unit operations. Some require such output as hourly sales analysis, daily inventory data, unit financial reports, labor cost analysis, and customer counts on a unit, district, or system-wide basis. Computers with specialized hardware and individualized, more complex software, are essential in meeting such requirements.

Regardless of an operation's size or the size of a particular computer system, all have at least two important control applications in common:

1 Monitoring operations in a timely manner so that judgments can be made about such concerns as cost, sales, and employee performance; and

2 Increasing control over employee actions by requiring adherence to established standard procedures. For example, given the system previously described, a server would find it difficult to obtain food or a beverage without recording an item on a guest check.

Changes occur almost daily in EDP. New hardware and software packages continue to be introduced, and increasing numbers will be designed specifically for food service operations. Many chefs, stewards, managers, and other food service professionals will soon accomplish some of their normal work routines at computer terminals. Managers will soon face the problem of selecting an appropriate system from among an increasing number available from a growing list of vendors. The key to selection will lie in managers' ability to evaluate the capability, reliability, and compatibility of various hardware and software components; and their understanding desired outputs from the system. In the food service industry, desired outputs can be determined best through understanding food, beverage, and labor control processes, procedures, and goals.

CHAPTER ESSENTIALS

This chapter briefly traced the development of data processing equipment from early uses through recent advances that have brought electronic data processing equipment and computers within the reach of large numbers of businesses, including food service operations. By using the simple analogy of the restaurant cashier, we provided an explanation of the way that computers process data, and introduced a number of terms with which food service operators and managers should familiarize themselves as computers become more a part of the everyday life of the food service manager. We illustrated and explained the operation of a system resembling some currently used in food service, and suggested some applications for larger, centralized systems in organizations more complex than the individually-operated restaurant. Finally, we offered the two keys central to management selection of data processing systems for food service establishments.

QUESTIONS AND PROBLEMS

1. Explain why the abacus and mechanical adding machine can be considered data processing devices.
2. List three advantages of electronic data processing devices over mechanical devices used to process information.
3. List the five basic capabilities of a computer system.
4. Software is encoded on media. List five types of media used in EDP.
5. List the three primary reasons for the hospitality industry's delay in adopting computer systems.
6. What knowledge will a food and beverage manager need to make intelligent choices among alternate EDP systems?
7. How can EDP systems aid in establishing control in food service operations?

8 The third step in the control process discussed in Chapter 3 is to "monitor performance and compare actual performance to established standards." What outputs of the system illustrated in this chapter would help a manager do this?

9 Define each of the following terms:

Computer	Hardware
Output	Software
Storage	Programs
Input	Soft copy
CPU	Hard copy
VDT	Media
Terminal	

10 Using each of the terms in question 9 above, write a sentence relating to the food service industry.

part two

Food Control

With some understanding of the nature of costs, sales, controls, and EDP basics, it is now possible to begin an investigation of the subject rather loosely termed "food control." In the course of our investigation, we will look into various means of controlling food, as well as controlling, measuring, and judging food costs and food sales. Our approach will be to discuss the several accepted steps in the chain of daily events that make up the foodservice business—from initial purchase of raw materials to the sale of the products prepared from those materials. Following these discussions, we will look into several techniques for measuring food costs. Finally, we will investigate ways to judge food costs in relation to food sales and suggest approaches to improve performance from the figures determined.

We will begin with a discussion of the controls needed in purchasing foods.

chapter 5

Purchasing Control

Learning Objectives

After reading and studying this chapter, the student should be able to:

1. List and explain the four principal characteristics of effective purchasing control.
2. Distinguish between perishable and nonperishable foods.
3. Define purchase specifications.
4. Describe purchasing procedures for perishable foods.
5. Describe purchasing procedures for nonperishable foods.
6. Distinguish between the periodic order method and the perpetual inventory method.
7. Explain the significance of purchasing at competitive prices.
8. List and explain the advantages and disadvantages of centralized purchasing.
9. Explain and identify the advantages and disadvantages of standing orders.
10. Define par stock and briefly explain the considerations that may affect the quantity.
11. Explain one application of the computer for purposes of purchasing control.

The primary purpose for establishing control over purchasing is to ensure a continuing supply of sufficient quantities of foods, each of the quality appropriate to intended use, purchased at the most favorable price. Although it is not the job of the food controller to purchase foods, or even to assign responsibility for their purchase, he or she does become involved in the purchasing process to the extent of being responsible for setting up the control procedures. Under the direction of management, the food controller sees that appropriate standards for quality and quantity are set and that procedures are established for meeting these standards.

To a great extent cost will be governed by purchasing policies and techniques. Therefore, it will be useful to discuss purchasing in some detail from the point of view of a food controller, covering four principal characteristics of effective purchasing control:

1 Responsibility for purchasing is fixed.
2 Standards of quality are established.
3 Needed quantities are established.
4 Purchases of food are at the most favorable prices.

RESPONSIBILITY

Responsibility for purchasing can be delegated to any one of a number of persons in restaurant operations, depending on organizational structure and management policies. It is not uncommon to find the owners or managers taking the responsibility in some establishments, while in others, either the chef or the steward may be assigned the purchasing duties. In some hotel operations, foods may even be ordered by some individual in the office of the purchasing agent.

In order to facilitate discussions, we will arbitrarily fix responsibility for purchasing the necessary foods with the steward. This should not be taken to mean that the authors believe that this responsibility should always be given to the steward; on the contrary, the determination of who should be assigned this responsibility must be based on situations and conditions existing in each individual restaurant operation. The important point to be made here is that for control purposes, the authority to purchase foods, and the responsibility for doing so, should be assigned to one individual. One individual can then be held accountable for operating the system of control procedures established by the food controller.

KINDS OF FOODS TO BE PURCHASED

The types of foods to be purchased for any operation may be divided roughly into two categories: perishables and nonperishables. Because several significant differences will be presented in the techniques and procedures for the purchase of them, it will be useful at this point to differentiate between them.

Perishables are those items, typically fresh foods, that have a comparatively short useful life after they have been received. Various kinds of lettuce and fresh fish, for example, begin to lose their quality very quickly. Some meats and cheeses will retain their quality for somewhat longer periods, but they too will begin to lose their quality far sooner than, say, a can of tomato puree. Perishables, then, should be purchased for immediate use in order to take advantage of the quality required at the time of purchase. If a steward is always careful to purchase the best quality available for intended use, then it would be wasteful and costly not to make use of that carefully selected quality.

Nonperishables are those food items that have a longer "shelf life." Often referred to as groceries or staples, they may be stored in the containers in which they are received, often on shelves and at room temperature, for weeks or even months. They do not deteriorate quickly, at least as long as they are kept in sealed containers. They are typically purchased and stored in jars, bottles, cans, and boxes; the storage area in which they are kept, called a storeroom, would resemble the shelves of a supermarket to the layman.

Because these foods do not deteriorate quickly, it is possible to keep a reasonable supply of each on hand, for use as needed. For example, a restaurant that used an average of four No. 10 cans of whole, peeled tomatoes daily (more than four cases per week), could conceivably keep a supply of eight cases on hand without running any risk of spoilage. Foods that typically fall into this category of staples include salt, sugar, flour, canned fruits and vegetables, spices, and flavorings.

QUALITY PURCHASING

If a restaurant is to produce products of consistent quality, it must use raw materials of consistent quality. Therefore, it is important that the food controller, in cooperation with other members of the management team, draw up a list of all food items to be purchased, and list in appropriate detail those specific and distinctive characteristics that will best describe the desired quality of each. These carefully written descriptions are known as **standard purchase specifications.** These specifications are often based on grading standards established by the federal government, or in some instances, when federal grading standards are considered too broad, specifications are based on grading standards common to the appropriate commodities market. However, the restaurant is not restricted to these possibilities. Many knowledgeable individuals write specifications that are far more precise, and thus more useful for indicating to purveyors the exact quality desired. Once these standard purchase specifications have been written and agreed upon by the management team, they are often duplicated and distributed to potential purveyors to ensure that each will fully understand the exact requirements of the restaurant. Figure 5.1 gives five examples of standard purchase specifications.

Standard purchase specifications, if carefully prepared, are useful in several ways:

1 They force the management team to determine exact requirements in advance for any commodity.

FIGURE 5.1
Standard Purchase Specifications

Strip Loin	Bone-in 10″ cut. USDA Prime, upper half. Range #2, minimum 14 lbs., maximum 16 lbs. One-half to three-quarters of an inch fat except for seam fat. Moderate marbling, light red in color to slightly dark red. New York cut, chilled upon delivery. Free from objectionable odors, deterioration, and evidence of freezing or defrosting.
Flounder (grey sole)	Whole, dressed, fresh day of delivery. Minimum 2 lbs., maximum 4 lbs. Fish should be twice as long as is broad, with oval body. Flesh should be firm and elastic, meat should be white and slightly translucent, color should be bright and clear. Gills should be free from slime and reddish-pink in color, and scales should adhere tightly to the skin. No stale odors of ammonia. Yield of 40% to the fillet.
Grapefruit	Florida. Medium to large; 3-3/4″ to 4″ in diameter. Light yellow in color; approximately 12 to 14 sections; oval to round. Thin-skinned, tender, delicate flesh. No visible spotting or bruising on skins. Medium acidity and sweetness, faint bitterness. Packed 36 to a crate.
Canned Peaches	Yellow, cling halves—canned. US Grade A (Fancy), heavy syrup. 19–24 Brix, minimum drained weight. 66 ounces per #10 can. Count per #10 can: 30 to 35. Quote by dozen #10 can. Federal Inspector's certification of grade required.
Asparagus tips, frozen	Tips large, all green, frozen. US Grade A (Fancy). Packed in 2-1/2 lb. cartons, 12 cartons per case. Must be delivered 10°F or below. Quote by pound net. Federal Inspector's certification of grade required.

2 They are often useful in menu preparation, in that it is possible to use one cut of meat, purchased according to specifications to prepare several different items on the menu.

3 They eliminate misunderstandings between the steward and purveyors if they are circulated.

4 Circulation of specifications for one commodity to several purveyors makes competitive bidding possible.

5 They eliminate the need for detailed verbal descriptions each time a commodity is ordered.

6 They facilitate checking food as it is received, the importance of which will be discussed in Chapter 6.

Although specifications are written down at one particular time, they need not be considered fixed for all time. If conditions change, they can be rewritten and recirculated.

This critically important step, the determination of quality standards and the consequent writing of standard purchase specifications, helps to ensure that all commodities purchased will be of the desired quality for the intended use.

QUANTITY PURCHASING

Although purchase specifications can be established at one particular time and merely reviewed and updated on occasion, quantity standards for purchasing are subject to constant review and revision, often on a daily basis. All foods deteriorate in time, some more quickly than others, and it is the job of the food controller to provide a system that will ensure that only those quantities are purchased that will be needed immediately or in the relatively near future.* In cooperation with the steward, the food controller does this by instituting procedures for determining the appropriate quantities of each item that should be purchased. These procedures are based principally on the useful life of the commodity.

For purchasing purposes, foods are divided into the two categories previously discussed, perishables and nonperishables. The procedures for determining quantities to purchase vary somewhat and will be discussed separately.

Perishables

The very nature of perishable commodities suggests the importance of continually using up those already on hand before purchasing additional quantities. Therefore, the purchasing routine must provide for determining amounts already on hand. Decisions also must be made as to total quantities needed. Once these have been arrived at, the difference between them is the correct amount to order.

A basic requirement of the purchasing routine is that the steward take a daily inventory of perishables. This daily inventory may be an actual physical inventory in some cases. In others, it may be only an estimate based on physical observation. For example, the steward would probably count the actual number of ribs of beef but might only estimate the quantity of chopped beef. Or the steward might count the avocados individually but only count the cases of lettuce.

A very important and useful tool for the steward to use in taking this daily inventory is a standard form called the "Steward's Market Quotation List," illustrated in figure 5.2. This form, generally available from stationers who cater to the hotel and restaurant industry, is a listing of the most common perishables, arranged by types, with several blank lines provided for the special requirements of each restaurant. (Restaurants that offer menus so specialized that this particular form

* It must be noted that there are exceptions to the rule from time to time, as, for example, when the opportunity arises for purchasing a four-month supply of a nonperishable commodity at a substantial discount.

FIGURE 5.2
Steward's Market Quotation List

On Hand	Article	Wanted	Quotations	On Hand	Article	Wanted	Quotations	On Hand	Article	Wanted	Quotations	On Hand	Article	Wanted
	BEEF				**Provisions (*Cont'd*)**				**FISH (*Cont'd*)**				**Vegetables (*Cont'd*)**	
	Corned Beef				Pig's Knuckles Fresh				Carp				Estragon	
	Corned Beef Brisket				Pig's Knuckles Corned				Codfish, Live				Egg Plant	
	Corned Beef Rump				Pig, Suckling				Codfish, Salt Boneless				Garlic	
	Corned Beef Hash				Pork, Fresh Loin				Codfish, Salt Flake				Horseradish Roots	
	Beef Chipped				Pork, Larding				Eels				Kale	
	Beef Breads				Pork, Spare Ribs				Finnan Haddie				Kohlrabi	
	Butts				Pork, Salt Strip				Flounders				Lettuce	
	Chuck				Pork Tenderloin				Flounders				Lettuce, Ice Berg	
	Fillets				Sausages, Country				Flounders, Fillet				Lettuce, Place	
	Hip Short				Sausages, Frankfurter				Fluke				Leeks	
	Hip Full				Sausages, Meat				Haddock				Mint	
	Kidneys				Shoulders, Fresh				Haddock, Fillet				Mushrooms	
	Livers				Shoulders, Smoked				Haddock, Smoked				Mushrooms, Fresh	
	Loin, Short				Shoulders, Corned				Halibut				Okra	
	Strip				Tongues				Halibut, Chicken				Onions	
	Shell Strip				Tongues, Beef Smoked				Herring				Onions, Yellow	
	Ribs Beef				Tongues, Fresh				Herring, Smoked				Onions, Bermuda	
	Shins				Tongues, Lambs				Herring, Kippered				Onions, Spanish	
	Suet, Beef				Tripe				Kingfish				Onions, White	
	Tails, Ox								Mackerel, Fresh				Onions, Scallions	
					POULTRY				Mackerel, Salt				Oyster Plant	
	VEAL				Chickens				Mackerel, Spanish				Parsley	
	Breast				Chickens, Roast				Mackerel, Smoked				Parsnips	
	Brains				Chickens, Broilers				Perch				Peppermint	
	Feet				Chickens, Broilers				Pickerel				Peas, Green	
	Fore Quarters				Chickens, Supreme				Pike				Peas	
	Hind Quarters				Cocks				Porgies				Peas	
	Head				Capons				Pompano				Peppers, Green	
	Kidneys				Ducks				Redsnapper				Peppers, Red	
	Legs				Ducklings				Salmon, Fresh				Potatoes	
	Liver				Fowl				Salmon, Smoked				Potatoes, Bermuda	
	Loins				Geese				Salmon, Nova Scotia				Potatoes, Idaho	
	Racks				Goslings				Scrod				Potatoes, Idaho	
	Saddles				Guinea Hens				Shad				Potatoes, Sweet	
	Shoulder				Guinea Squabs				Shad Roes				Potatoes, New	
	Sweet Breads				Pigeons				Smelts				Potatoes, Yams	
					Poussins				Sole, English				Pumpkins	

MUTTON	Squabs	Sole, Boston	Romaine
Fore Quarters	Turkeys, Roasting	Sole, Lemon	Radishes
Kidneys	Turkeys, Boiling	Sturgeon	Rhubarb, Fresh
Legs	Turkeys, Spring	Trout, Brook	Rhubarb, Hot House
Racks		Trout, Lake	Sage
Saddles	**GAME**	Trout, Salmon	Shallots
Saddles, Hind	Birds	Weakfish	Sorrel
Shoulder	Partridge	Whitebait	Sauerkraut
Suet	Pheasant, English	Whitefish	Spinach
	Rabbits	Whitefish, Smoked	Squash Crooked Neck
LAMB	Quail		Squash Hubbard
Breast	Venison, Saddles	**VEGETABLES**	Tarragon
Fore Quarters		Artichokes	Thyme
Feet	**SHELL FISH**	Asparagus	Tomatoes, New
Fries	Clams, Chowder	Asparagus	Tomatoes, Hot House
Kidneys	Clams, Cherrystone	Asparagus, Tips	Turnips, White
Loins	Clams, Little Neck	Asparagus, Fancy	Turnips, Yellow
Legs	Clams, Soft	Beans	Turnips, New
Lamb, Spring	Crabs, Hard	Beans, Lima	Watercress
Racks, Double	Crabs, Meat	Beans, String	
Racks, Spring	Crabs, Oyster	Beans, Wax	**FRUIT**
Saddles	Crabs, Soft Shell	Beets	Apples, Cooking
Shoulder	Crabs, Soft Shell Prime	Beets, Tops	Apples, Baking
	Lobsters, Meat	Broccoli	Apples, Crab
PROVISIONS	Lobsters, Tails	Brussels Sprouts	Apples, Table
Bacon	Lobsters, Chicken	Cabbage	Apricots
Bologna	Lobsters, Medium	Cabbage, Red	Bananas
Bologna	Lobsters, Large	Cabbage, New	Blackberries
Crepinette	Oysters, Box	Carrots	Blueberries
Salami	Oysters, Blue Points	Carrots	Blueberries
Hams, Corned	Oysters	Cauliflower	Blueberries
Hams, Fresh	Scallops	Celery	Cantaloupes
Hams, Polish	Shrimps	Celery Knobs	Cantaloupes
Hams, Smoked	Turtle	Chicory	Honey Balls
Hams, Virginia		Chives	Melons, Casaba
Hams, Westphalia	**FISH**	Corn	Melons, Honeydew
Head Cheese	Bass, Black	Corn	Melons, Persian
Lard	Bass, Sea	Chervil	Melons, Spanish
Lyon Sausage	Bass, Striped	Cranberries	Cherries
Phil. Scrapple	Blackfish	Cucumbers	Cherries
Smoked Butts	Bluefish	Dandelion	Cherries
Pig's Feet	Bloaters	Escarole	Currants
Pig's Head, Corned	Butterfish	Endive	Chestnuts

is useless—such as Chinese or Near-Eastern restaurants—are well advised to devise their own and have them duplicated.)

In order to take the daily inventory of perishables, the steward will usually go through the refrigerators and freezers with the form in hand and, next to the appropriate items in each category, fill in the column on the left, marked "on hand." After completing this survey, the steward has a relatively accurate inventory of perishable commodities.

The next step in the routine involves determining anticipated total needs for each item, based on future menus, and often on experience as well. Depending on the restaurant, these figures for total anticipated needs are determined sometimes by the chef, sometimes by the steward, and often by the two working together. Two heads are usually better than one. As in the illustration in figure 5.2, it is helpful to write this figure for total anticipated needs in the "article" column, just after the name of the item in question.

Following this determination, the steward enters the difference between total anticipated needs and the amount on hand in the "wanted" column at the right. This difference is the amount that should be ordered to bring supply up to the total quantity required.

Nonperishables

While nonperishable commodities do not present the problem of rapid deterioration, they do represent considerable amounts of money invested in material in storage. Obviously cash tied up in nonperishable commodities is not available to meet other operating expenses of the business. Therefore, one goal of the purchasing routine for nonperishables should be to avoid excessive quantities on hand. Additional benefits to be derived from reducing quantities on hand include the elimination of some possibilities for theft, the reduction of storage space requirements, and possibly the reduction in the number of personnel required to maintain the storage area.

Fixing labels on shelves is one important step that should be taken in every storeroom to identify permanently the location of each item maintained in stock. In this way no item will ever be found in two or more different locations at one time. When items appear in several different locations, there is a tendency to order additional quantities in the unwarranted belief that the stock is running low. Moreover, when locations are identified, it becomes easier to find things when regular personnel are off duty or when personnel change.

For the convenience of stewards, a form available from stationers lists nonperishables, just as the Steward's Market Quotation List itemizes perishables. It is not widely used, however, since lists of groceries are not as universally applicable from restaurant to restaurant. A great number of stewards prefer to make up lists of their particular storerooms' contents and to have them inexpensively duplicated. These serve the same purpose: To list amounts to be ordered and competitive prices.

While there are a number of specific systems for maintaining grocery inventories at appropriate levels, most are variations on the following methods.

Periodic Order Method

Perhaps the most common method for maintaining stores' inventories at appropriate levels is the so-called periodic method, which, by contrast with methods for ordering perishables, permits comparatively infrequent ordering. Because nonperishable items have longer shelf life than perishables, it is both possible and desirable to order them less frequently, thus leaving the steward free to attend to perishables, which typically require considerable time. When this method is followed, a steward will normally establish with the advice of management periods for ordering purposes. On a regular basis—once every week, or every two weeks, or even once each month, depending on the policies of management as to the amounts of money to be tied up in inventory—the steward reviews the entire stock of nonperishable items and determines how much of each to order to ensure a supply sufficient to last until the next regularly scheduled order date. The calculation of the amount of each item to order is comparatively simple:

  Amount required for the upcoming period
− Amount presently on hand
+ Amount wanted on hand at the end of the period to last until the next delivery

= Amount to order

For example, in a certain restaurant ordering once a month, one of the items ordered might be #2½ cans of sliced pineapple, packed twelve cans to a case. The item is used at the rate of ten cans per week, and delivery normally takes five days from the date an order is placed. If the steward in this establishment found fifteen cans on the shelf, anticipated normal use of forty cans during the upcoming period of approximately four weeks, and wanted fifteen cans on hand at the end of the upcoming month, the calculation would be

  40 cans required
− 15 now on hand
+ 15 to be left at the end of the month

= 40 to be ordered on this date

However, since orders are normally placed for this item in cases rather than in cans, it is likely that the steward would round the order up to the next highest purchase unit and that the order placed would be for four cases consisting of forty-eight cans. While this rounding procedure may appear to lead to overpurchasing, in fact the steward is subtracting quantities on hand at the beginning of each period before placing the orders, and thus any such small overpurchases are likely to be used up at the beginning of the next period. Additionally, the order for the next period is, in effect, reduced by the amount of the small overpurchase in the current period.

The student might well ask how the steward knows the requirements for the upcoming period. Storerooms have hundreds of items, and it is impossible for a person to know without records how much is needed of most items. Fortunately, the steward is aided by the salespersons. In addition, many establishments keep appropriate records of amounts used. Smaller establishments typically rely on salespersons to keep track of previous orders. The steward can then look on the storage shelf and make an approximate calculation of the amount used by subtracting what is remaining from what was ordered. While this is probably a better method than having no knowledge of usage, it is unreliable because it fails to take into account the amount on hand at the beginning of any period. Nevertheless, this method is very common in the food and beverage industry. One additional note: If an establishment orders every time a salesperson calls, the order period will vary from item to item as salespersons do not all call with the same frequency.

A more systematic method of determining usage requires that certain additional steps be taken. A desirable first step is to enhance the utility of shelf labels by including additional information on them. For example, if the label were somewhat larger than standard size, it would be feasible in many establishments to record the quantities added to and taken from shelves right on the label. When used in this form, labels become known as bin cards, an example of which is shown in figure 5.3. As each delivery is received and placed on the shelf, both the date and number of units so placed is entered on the bin card. As quantities are issued for use, those dates and amounts are recorded as well. More spaces are provided for items issued than for items received for the obvious reason the purchases are comparatively infrequent, but issues may be daily. A balance column is provided so that a steward may determine and enter amounts on hand at any desired time, such as when a salesperson called or when the periodic ordering date arrived.

FIGURE 5.3
Bin Card

ITEM Pineapple Slices — DESIRED ENDING INVENTORY 15

DATE	IN	DATE	OUT	DATE	OUT	DATE	OUT	BALANCE
10/1								15
		10/2	2	10/3	2	10/4	2	9
10/6	48	10/5	2					55

At such times, it is quite simple to determine approximate usage by looking on the card for the balance on hand on the date the last order was placed, adding to that figure the number of units placed on shelves when the last order was received, and subtracting the balance currently on hand. The result will be approximate usage in the most recent period, regardless of the length of that period. The assumption is made that this quantity was used productively, although this may not always be the case, and should be considered in determining the amount to order for the next period. When such a system is followed, it is normally wise to compare the balance on the bin card with the number of units of the item actually on the shelves in order to be sure that all items issued have been suitably recorded. If a discrepancy exists, the balance shown on the bin card will not be entirely reliable in measuring actual usage during the period, and the missing items, presumably issued, must be added to the derived usage figure to achieve a more accurate figure.

If the amount used in the preceding period were the amount ordered for the coming period, the strong possibility exists that the establishment would end the coming period with no units of that item left on the shelf. Since this might make it impossible to produce certain items on the menu, or might make it necessary to secure some emergency supply in order to carry on to the next delivery date, most restaurants that follow this periodic method establish the amount that should be on hand at the end of any period and that should be sufficient to last until the next delivery is received. Once established, this is known as the desired ending inventory, and is entered on the bin card. Both delivery time and daily usage for that time must be used in determining the desired ending figure. Furthermore, it is advisable to add on to this figure some carefully considered amount as a safety factor, in case of delay in delivery. In many cases this safety factor may also include some amount to be kept on hand in the event that business volume in the coming period arises above normal levels.

It is important for anyone planning to enter this business to realize that none of the amounts mentioned in the preceding paragraphs should be determined and then never again reevaluated. After all, many changes occur in usage from period to period, and the steward or manager who fails to take changes into account is taking risks needlessly. For example, as the weather and menus change, some foods will be used in greater quantities. If demand for some items increases, usage is likely to increase as well; the converse would also be true. Thus, before ordering, it is normally advisable to compare usage in similar periods in preceding years. If menus and sales volume have changed as well, these too must be taken into account.

Perpetual Inventory Method

While better for control purposes than the periodic method, the perpetual inventory method is not as widely used. This is because its successful use requires that specialized personnel maintain rather complete and accurate records, and also because none but larger establishments can normally justify maintaining such personnel. However, because some larger operations, particularly those in chain organizations, do employ these methods, students should be aware of their underlying purposes, and the procedures necessary for their successful implementation.

The primary purposes of the perpetual inventory system are to ensure that quantities purchased are sufficient to meet anticipated need without being excessive and to provide effective control over those items that are being stored for future use.

This method requires the use of perpetual inventory cards, such as that illustrated in figure 5.4. These cards, while similar to the bin card illustrated in figure 5.3, include some additional information and are used rather differently. One very important difference is that the perpetual inventory card is not normally affixed to the shelf on which the covered item is maintained but is typically kept outside the storeroom and maintained by persons who do not work in the storeroom. The amounts of food purchased are recorded on the appropriate cards, and as items are issued for use, those amounts issued are similarly recorded. If the amounts recorded accurately reflect the movement of items into and out of storage, then it is possible at any given time merely to consult the perpetual inventory card to determine how much of an item is in stock at the moment. This system makes it possible to compare balances on the perpetual inventory cards with actual items on shelves to determine if any items are not accounted for.

FIGURE 5.4
Perpetual Inventory Card

ITEM	Pineapple Slices	COST	$9.84 per 12 can case
SIZE	#2½ can	PAR STOCK	32
SUPPLIER	ABC Co.	REORDER POINT	15
	18 120th St.	REORDER QUANTITY	24
	N.Y.C.		

DATE	ORDER #	IN	OUT	BALANCE
10/1	#222 - 24		2	15
10/2			2	13
10/3			2	11
10/4			2	9
10/5			2	7
10/6		24		31
10/7				
10/8				

The additional information, including the name and address of the supplier, as well as the most recent purchase price for the item, facilitates the ordering of additional quantities of the item. Three additional terms used on the card—par stock, reorder point, and reorder quantity—are also of considerable use in facilitating purchase, and require further discussion.

The reorder point is, quite simply, the number of units to which the supply on hand should decrease before additional orders are placed. Thus, if the reorder point for a given item is twenty-two cans, then no order for that item should be placed until the supply, as shown in the balance column, has reached that number. To establish a reorder point for any item, it is necessary to know both normal usage and the time needed to obtain delivery. Furthermore, it is advisable to include in the calculations a certain additional amount to allow for delivery delays and for possible increased usage during that period. In effect, the reorder point in the perpetual inventory method is the equivalent of the desired ending inventory in the periodic method and may be calculated in the following manner. If normal usage is two cans per day, and it takes five days from date of order to get delivery, then the basic number needed is ten cans. However, because delivery may be delayed, or because usage may increase for unforeseen reasons, or because both of those possibilities may occur at once, it is advisable to increase that amount somewhat, possibly by as much as 50%, thus establishing a reorder point of fifteen cans. Under the periodic method, the desired ending inventory would similarly be calculated as fifteen cans.

The perpetual inventory card also provides for a par stock figure for each item in stock. While it is generally acknowledged that par stock is a number of units related to usage and the time needed to get delivery, there is no general agreement on an exact definition of the term. Since the term is used in a variety of ways in the industry, the student should be aware of some of its more common uses. In some places, their term **par stock** is taken to mean a maximum quantity of a given item that should be on hand after the most recent order has been received. In others, it means a normal quantity that should be on hand at all times. Still another possibility is to treat par stock as a range defined by maximum and minimum quantities between which the actual quantities on hand should vary.

For purposes of this discussion, we will take par stock to be the maximum quantity of any item that should be on hand at any given time. That maximum quantity can be determined only after careful weighing of the following considerations:

1 storage space
2 limits of inventory valuation prescribed by management
3 desired frequency of ordering
4 usage
5 purveyors' minimum order requirements

Because storage space is limited for all but a few most fortunate operators, it is obviously necessary to calculate the maximum amount of space available for all nonperishable storage and then to allocate wisely the use of that space. For example, with those items normally purchased in comparatively large packages, such as bulk flour and sugar, it may be necessary to restrict space to that required for the storage of only a one-week supply.

To the extent that management chooses to restrict the amount of cash invested in inventory, it becomes necessary to restrict the amount of any item that one can maintain on hand. If the cash for meeting payroll and for paying outstanding bills is in comparatively short supply, then management will often choose to reduce the size of inventory and direct rather more frequent ordering of smaller quantities. In some cases, it is possible to accomplish this by restricting only the purchase of the more expensive items in the inventory, without effecting any change in purchase procedures for the less costly commodities.

Obviously, some schedule of desired frequency must be set up by management. In addition, while the foods involved are typically referred to as nonperishables, some are, in fact, rather more perishable than others, and this should be taken into account.

Determination of par stock should always take into account the relative quantities of an item used, which may change over time. If anticipated consumption of an item is expected to be high in a given period, then the par stock should be higher than at, say, another time or season when consumption is rather low.

Because a considerable number of purveyors prefer to supply items in standard wholesale purchase units, such as cases and fifty-lb. bags, the minimum order requirements of purveyors must be taken into account as well. Once all of the foregoing have been considered and a par stock figure has been established for each inventory item, each is entered on the appropriate perpetual inventory card.

The final consideration is the establishment of a reorder quantity—the amount that will be ordered each time the quantity of a particular item diminishes to the reorder point. The quantity ordered should be sufficient to bring the total inventory up to the par stock level. At first glance, that quantity would appear to be the difference between established par stock and reorder point. However, that figure would fail to take into account normal usage between order date and delivery—previously calculated as ten cans for the example in figure 5.4. This quantity must be added. Therefore, the calculation of reorder would be

	Par stock	32
−	Reorder point	15
	Subtotal	17
+	Normal usage until delivery	10
	Reorder quantity	27

However, food is normally purchased in case lots of six, twelve, or twenty-four, or some other quantity per case, depending on the item and size of container, and this must be taken into account. If the establishment needs twenty-seven units of something packed twelve to the case, the order placed must be in some multiple of twelve. In this case, the reorder quantity will be two cases, or twenty-four cans, rather than the twenty-seven determined above. Upon delivery, the stock is brought to thirty-one units, or approximately to par.

Many establishments choose not to use either of these systems in precisely the forms described above. There are a number of reasons for this. Some appreciate the value of perpetual inventory records removed from the control of those who receive and issue food, but are unwilling or unable to place orders on the daily basis presupposed by pure perpetual method. Others fear the comparative absence of control in the periodic method. For these and other reasons, some have developed what amount to hybrid systems that selectively employ the more desirable features of both systems.

One such system is essentially a perpetual method, but with reorder points and par stocks set sufficiently high so that orders need not necessarily be placed at precisely the moment that reorder points are reached. Such establishments might use the reaching of a reorder point merely as a signal that a particular item should be ordered on the next regularly scheduled day for placing orders, and would merely add the item to a list. If reorder point were high enough, there would be little danger of consuming the remaining quantity through normal usage prior to next delivery.

The final determination of routine—whether one of the illustrated procedures or some variation—must be based on the needs of the individual operation, and the policies established by management. The important point to be made is that the purchasing procedure must take into account the need for determining on an ongoing basis the quantities of each commodity that will be adequate for anticipated demand. It must guard against overpurchasing—the purchasing of unneeded quantities. In the case of perishables, overpurchasing increases the possibilities for both spoilage and theft. In addition, it increases the possibilities for overproduction and consequent waste. In the case of nonperishables, overpurchasing clearly increases the possibilities for theft; it may increase the need for personnel, and it certainly ties up unwarranted amounts of money in inventory. Because these are the very conditions that control systems are established to guard against, it is obviously important to set up procedures for determining appropriate quantities for ordering.

Once we have established purchase specifications so that we know what quality to buy, and inventory procedures so that we know what quantity to buy, it is time to discuss the question of price. Since it is normally desirable to buy commodities of the appropriate quality in adequate quantities at the lowest possible price, it is desirable to ensure that the steward will purchase foods on the basis of competitive prices from several possible suppliers.

SOURCES OF SUPPLY

The availability of sources of supply will vary considerably from location to location. Major cities, for example, tend to offer a greater number of possibilities, both in terms of different categories of suppliers and number of suppliers in each category. On the other hand, isolated areas offer few possibilities; sometimes establishments in remote areas must be content with what they can get. In general, depending on ownership policy, availability of suppliers, and general market conditions, foodservice operators look to suppliers who fall into the following general categories:

- wholesalers
- local producers

- manufacturers
- packers
- local farmers
- retailers
- cooperative associations

In most instances, the restaurant operator will deal with several of the sources of supply to obtain the necessary foods. For example, it is possible that a restaurant might turn to a local producer for dairy and bakery products, a packer for canned meats, a wholesaler for fresh meats, a different wholesaler for canned fruits and vegetables, and a local farmer for eggs. In recent years there has been a trend for wholesalers to diversify their product lines in an attempt to better meet the needs of their restaurant customers. In some instances, they are able to supply virtually all of the food-related needs of a restaurant. In general, one will deal with as many as may be necessary to ensure the supply of foods of appropriate quality at the lowest prices.

COMPETITIVE PRICES

To ensure that purchases are made at the lowest favorable price, the steward must secure prices from several competing suppliers for each commodity he or she intends to buy. The procedures differ for perishables and nonperishables.

Perishables

Because prices for perishables often fluctuate daily, it is necessary for the steward to telephone several different suppliers of the same commodity to ascertain current prices each time an order is to be placed. Assuming that copies of specifications have previously been sent to each, the steward can be assured that each supplier is quoting on commodities of comparable quality. It will be noted that the Steward's Market Quotation List, shown in figure 5.2, provides four columns for price quotations on each commodity with provision at the top of each column for the name of the supplier. Ideally, the steward will obtain prices from at least three suppliers for each item, and select the lowest price. In reality, other things also should be taken into account, such as different delivery times from supplier to supplier, the manager's possible preference for one dealer over another, the reliability of the dealers in sending foods that adhere to specifications, and so forth. Once prices have been obtained, the steward makes a selection of the supplier to be used and calls that dealer to place the order. Normally it is placed with the lowest bidder. As the order is placed the steward circles that particular price quotation next to the item to be supplied. Thus, when all perishables have been ordered, the steward has a complete record of commodities ordered, as well as a record of prices, quantities, and suppliers. As we shall see in the next chapter, this list will be valuable for checking purposes when the food is delivered.

Nonperishables

Procedures involved in securing competitive prices for nonperishables are somewhat different. Usually the steward will deal with fewer sources of supply in the case of nonperishables. It is often possible to obtain price lists from wholesale supply houses, each of which may be able to supply most of the groceries the steward intends to order. The steward can compare prices and make selections at greater leisure than he or she can in the case of perishables. Although the steward will normally select the lowest price consistent with quality desired, note that there are exceptions here as well. For example, if dealer A were offering all but one item at a lower price than dealer B, and dealer B's price for that one item were only two cents per can lower, the steward would be likely to place his order for twelve cans with dealer A in spite of the higher price, the difference being only a matter of $.24. The expenditure would be more than justified by the simplification of the ordering. In addition, it is possible that dealer B might not accept an order as small as twenty-four cans of a single item because the profit might be more than offset by the cost of making the delivery.

CENTRALIZED PURCHASING

No discussion of purchasing procedures would be complete without some mention of the existence of centralized purchasing systems, widely used by chain operations, and occasionally established by small groups of independent operators with similar needs. Under a centralized purchasing system, the requirements of individual units are relayed to a central office, which determines total requirements of all units and then purchases that total, either for delivery to the individual units by the dealer, or for centralized delivery. This last method obviously requires that a whole system for distribution be maintained and operated by the organization doing the centralized purchasing. There are both advantages and disadvantages to these centralized systems, and these should be understood by anyone involved in food management.

Advantages

1. Foods and beverages are purchased at a lower price because of volume purchasing.
2. It provides a better opportunity to obtain desired quality because purchaser has a greater choice of markets.
3. Goods can be purchased to the purchaser's exact specifications.
4. Larger inventories can be maintained assuring a more constant supply to individual units.
5. Greater control over dishonesty of individual unit food purchasers can be maintained.

Disadvantages

1. Unit must accept the standard item in stock and has little freedom to purchase for its own peculiar needs.
2. Units cannot take advantage of local "specials" at reduced prices.
3. Menus usually must be more standardized, thus limiting the individual unit manager's freedom to change a menu.

Finally, it should be noted that decisions about whether or not to become involved in centralized purchasing systems are normally made by top management, not by food controllers. However, there are times when food controllers may be called upon for advice and opinions, and they should understand what is involved in centralized purchasing.

STANDING ORDERS

Although it is desirable for needed quantities to be carefully determined each time orders are placed, stewards commonly make arrangements with certain purveyors for the delivery of goods without specific orders. These arrangements are known as standing orders, and typically take one of two forms.

One arrangement calls for the delivery of specific numbers of certain items each day; for example, twelve loaves of bread. The number would remain constant unless specifically changed by the steward.

The second arrangement usually calls for the replenishing of stock each day up to a certain predetermined number. For instance, the steward might arrange with a dairy supplier to leave sufficient quantities of bulk milk each morning to bring the total supply up to a predetermined figure, such as twenty gallons.

While these arrangements are convenient, they do present a number of possibilities for both waste and excessive cost to develop.

SUMMARY

Any system of food control must address itself to the question of purchasing. Controls must be established for purchasing if the food control system is to be effective. Poorly controlled purchasing procedures may lead either to reduced sales if the restaurant constantly runs out of food, or to excessive costs if the restaurant overpurchases perishables or purchases perishables of improper quality for intended use. The goals of the procedures discussed in this chapter are the establishment of control over costs and the elimination of excessive costs inherent in overpurchasing, which leads to spoilage, waste, and increased risk of pilferage. As we have seen, special procedures must be established to control the purchasing of perishables and nonperishables.

EDP APPLICATIONS

With computer systems currently available for restaurants, it is possible to input and store most or conceivably all of the previously discussed data. This will allow management easy access to the information required for informed purchase decisions.

For example, assume that management elects to maintain supplies of nonperishables by the perpetual inventory method, and all relevant data—including stock, reorder point, reorder quantity, previous purchases and issues, as well as such other information that would be important in making purchase decisions—is input through terminals. If the above is input for all nonperishable items, then management may quickly obtain current information reflecting current inventory status, including a list of those items at or below reorder point. In effect, the perpetual inventory card for each item would be in computer storage, rather than on paper in a file drawer. For chain organizations that use centralized purchasing techniques, this would offer obvious advantages.

This is but one example of the many possibilities offered by computer systems for more effective management of the purchasing function in food service.

CHAPTER ESSENTIALS

In this chapter, we described elements of a control system for food purchasing, including the fixing of responsibility for purchase, the establishment of appropriate quality and quantity standards, and determining of optimum purchase price. Specific procedures for the purchase of perishable and nonperishable foods were outlined, including the two most common methods for purchasing store: periodic order method and perpetual inventory method. The most common sources of supply used by food service operators were listed, and various considerations that affect selection of particular suppliers were suggested. We described centralized purchasing and discussed the advantages and disadvantages of centralized purchasing systems. We discussed the use of standing orders by some establishments and pointed out various risks associated with their use. Finally, we showed an application of the computer for better purchasing management and control.

QUESTIONS AND PROBLEMS

1 List ten food items you would consider perishable. Do the same for ten nonperishable food items.

2 Write a standard purchase specification for each of the following:

- **a** rack of lamb
- **b** lug of tomatoes
- **c** case of No. 10 cans of string beans

3 Write a one-paragraph explanation of why the standard purchase specifications would differ for eggs, depending on whether they were used for the breakfast menu or in the bake shop for bakery items.

4 Assume a certain restaurant uses the periodic order method. Determine amounts to order for canned peaches if orders are placed every two weeks and

- **a** normal usage is one case of twenty-four cans per week
- **b** ten cans are presently on hand
- **c** the amount desired as an ending inventory is sixteen cans

5 Assume a restaurant uses the periodic order method. Determine amounts to order for tomato juice if the steward orders once a month and

- **a** normal usage is one case of twelve cans per week
- **b** six cans are presently on hand
- **c** the amount desired as an ending inventory is eighteen cans
- **d** the coming month is expected to be very busy, requiring 50% more tomato juice than normal

6 Assume a restaurant uses the perpetual order method. Determine the reorder point, and at that point, the amount of canned pears to order given the following:

- **a** normal usage is twenty-one cans per week
- **b** it takes four days to get delivery of the item
- **c** par stock is set at forty-two cans
- **d** cans come packed twelve to a case

7 Assume a restaurant uses the perpetual order method. Determine the reorder point for canned green beans, and the amount of canned green beans to order given the following:

- **a** normal usage is two cans per day
- **b** it takes five days to get delivery of the item
- **c** par stock is set at twenty-nine cans
- **d** cans come packed six to a case.

8 Assume you have been hired as the purchasing steward of a new restaurant located in an area that is completely unfamiliar to you. How would you obtain information on sources of supply for perishable and nonperishable foods?

9 How can the computer help management establish control over the purchasing function?

chapter 6

Receiving Control

Learning Objectives

After reading and studying this chapter, the student should be able to:

1. List and explain the three principal characters of effective receiving procedure.
2. Describe the duties of a receiving clerk.
3. List the essential equipment and supplies needed for receiving control.
4. Identify an invoice and explain its use.
5. Explain the significance of the invoice stamp and list five reasons for its use in food and beverage operations.
6. Identify a meat tag, describe how the meat tag is used, and explain why it is used.
7. Identify the receiving clerk's daily report, list the information entered on the report, and explain how and why it is used.
8. Distinguish between Directs and Stores.
9. Explain one application of the computer for purposes of receiving control.

If great care is taken to establish effective controls for purchasing but no attention is given to receiving controls, all earlier efforts may be wasted. After all, ordering specific quantities and qualities at optimum prices constitutes no guarantee that the commodities ordered will actually be delivered. Either by accident or by design, purveyors may deliver foods in incorrect quantities, of higher or lower qualities, or not at the prices quoted, or all three. Receiving controls, therefore, have as a primary purpose verifying that quantities, qualities, and prices conform to orders placed.

THE RECEIVING CLERK

In our discussion, we will assume the existence of a receiving clerk to whom management will assign the full responsibility for receiving food deliveries and carrying out the control procedures set up by the food controller. In larger operations, particularly those with complete food control systems, this is often the case. In smaller operations, which deem the payroll expense of a receiving clerk unwarranted, food deliveries may be received by any one of several individuals, including the owner, the manager, the chef, or the steward. Although we use the title of receiving clerk here to facilitate discussion we are aware that others do receive deliveries. The point to be made here does not involve the title of the person doing the receiving; what is important is the development of a set of standard procedures for receiving food deliveries, and the verification that these deliveries conform to orders in every respect.

The person who is receiving has several duties, including checking quantities delivered and unit prices, which is comparatively easy, and at the same time checking for quality, which is rather more difficult because it requires more knowledge and experience.

In order for the receiving clerk to check deliveries thoroughly, certain supplies and equipment must be available, including:

1 a permanent copy of all standard purchase specifications
2 appropriate equipment, such as platform scale, hanging scale, and hanging racks
3 certain paper forms, tags, rubber stamps, and related office supplies, the importance of which will become apparent later in the chapter

The receiving clerk also must thoroughly understand the control procedures themselves in order to carry them out effectively. Effectiveness in complying with the receiving routine must be checked from time to time.

Because the receiving procedure does take a certain amount of time to follow, it is helpful for managers to arrange staggered delivery times with purveyors, beginning as early as possible in the day. The staggering of delivery times gives the receiving clerk a better opportunity to comply with routines. The early delivery times maximize preparation time available for those foods to be used on the day delivered.

THE INVOICE

All food deliveries should be accompanied by an invoice, which is another word for a bill. A typical invoice form is illustrated in figure 6.1. This is usually presented to the receiving clerk in duplicate by the person making the delivery, who will expect the receiving clerk to sign and return the second copy, thus acknowledging to the purveyor that the establishment has received the commodities listed. The original is, in effect, a bill that must be paid and routed to the bookkeeper or other individual responsible for paying bills. This routing procedure will be dealt with later in this chapter.

Invoices not listing prices should be discouraged. Prices should be checked on receipt of the goods. Otherwise, an opportunity exists for the purveyor to bill at the wrong prices by accident or by design.

FIGURE 6.1

Invoice
Market Price Meat Co.
300 Market St.
New York, N.Y.

Date June 11

To The Graduates Restaurant

Quantity	Unit	Description	Unit Price	Amount
30	lbs.	Strip Steak	4.95	148.50
10	lbs.	Breast of Veal	3.65	36.50
				185.00

THE INVOICE STAMP

It is generally good practice to provide the receiving clerk with a rubber stamp to be used on all invoices. This invoice stamp, a suggested form for which is illustrated in figure 6.2, is used for a number of reasons.

1. It verifies the date on which food has been received.
2. It provides for the signature of the clerk who has received the food and vouches for the accuracy of quantities, qualities, and prices.
3. It provides for the steward's signature, thus acknowledging that he/she is aware that the food has been delivered.
4. It provides for the food controllers verification of the arithmetical accuracy of the bill.
5. It provides for signatory approval of the bill for payment by an authorized individual before a check is drawn.

FIGURE 6.2
Invoice Stamp

Invoice Stamp

Date __________

Received __________

Steward __________

Prices and
Extensions
Verified __________

OK for
Payment __________

RECEIVING PROCEDURE

Although exact procedures and techniques for verifying deliveries will vary from establishment to establishment, procedures for receiving control should have the following characteristics:

1. Quantities delivered should be the same as those listed on both the invoice and the Steward's Market Quotation List or Steward's Staple List.
2. Quality of the food delivered should conform to the standard purchase specifications for each item delivered.
3. Prices on the invoice should be the same as those circled on the Steward's Market Quotation List and the Steward's Staple List.

Any exceptions to these three rules should be noted at once and appropriate steps taken. Sometimes this will involve returning inferior foods with the delivery truck. At other times it may involve changing the quantities listed on both copies of the invoice and having the deliverer initial both copies. For purposes of this discussion, it is important only to note that each variation should be attended to at the time and place of delivery.

Once deliveries have been checked in the light of the foregoing, it is recommended that foods be moved to appropriate storage areas as quickly as possible, with those that will most quickly deteriorate at room temperature being put away first. The spoilage and theft that may readily occur between receiving and storing foods can be a major cause of excessive cost. Therefore, the food controller should check from time to time to be sure that foods are being moved to storage areas at optimum times.

THE MEAT TAG

In the majority of restaurants, meats, poultry, fish, and shellfish constitute the most costly group of foods on the menu. Because of this comparatively high cost, establishments with complete food control systems set up special controls for these items. Each package or piece received is tagged by the receiving clerk before it is placed in storage. In general, the rule followed is that items typically purchased to be sent to the kitchen for immediate use are not tagged; those that are typically held in inventory for one or more days before use are tagged.

A meat tag (figure 6.3) is usually printed on heavy card stock for durability and is perforated for convenient division into two parts. The tags are purchased from any number of stationers catering to the industry, and are numbered sequentially, with the number appearing on both parts. They are used in numerical order. The receiving clerk fills in all information except the date of issue, which cannot be filled in until the meat is issued to the kitchen for preparation. After filling out the tag, the receiving clerk detaches the smaller part and sends it to the food controller. The receiving clerk will dispose of the larger part by either (a) attaching it securely to the piece or package of meat, or (b) sending it to the steward. Because both approaches have advantages and disadvantages, there is no general agreement

FIGURE 6.3

No. 20624
Date Rec'd. 6/11
Item Strip Steak Grade U.S. Prime
Weight 15 Lbs. @ $4.95
Dealer M P M Extension $74.25
Date Issued ________
William Allen & Co., N.Y. Stock Form 9247

No. 20624
Date Rec'd. 6/11
Item Strip Steak
Wt. 15 Lbs. @ $4.95
Ext. $74.25
Dealer M P M
Date Issued ________

as to which is preferable, and decisions as to which procedure to follow are often made by the food controller on the basis of practicability in a particular establishment.

The further use of meat tags and their importance to the operation with a complete control system will be discussed in detail in Chapter 8.

RECEIVING CLERK'S DAILY REPORT

Larger operations with complete food control systems will require that foods typically purchased for immediate use be charged to cost as received. The balance will be included in inventory and charged to cost as issued. In food control, all foods that are charged to cost as issued are called Stores, and all foods that are charged to cost as received are called Directs. An understanding of the differences between the two, as well as working definitions for both, will be increasingly important in future chapters.

Directs are those foods that, because of their extremely perishable nature, are purchased on a more or less daily basis for immediate use. The quality of these foods tends to diminish quickly, and if they are not used very soon after the time of purchase, they will become unusable for their intended purposes. Foods that typically fall into this category are fresh fruits and vegetables, fresh baked goods, and most dairy products. Ideally, the quantities of each purchased on any given day should be sufficient for that day alone. Therefore, since they should be purchased for immediate use, they will be issued as received and included in food cost figures on the day of delivery. The **working definition** will be that Directs are those items that will be issued and charged to food cost as received.

Stores, on the other hand, are those foods that, while ultimately perishable, will not significantly diminish in quality if they are not used immediately. They can be held in storage and carried in inventory for a day or so, or in some instances for considerable periods of time. Meats, for example, if stored under proper conditions, can be maintained for reasonable periods of time. So too can those grocery items that are purchased in cans, bottles, and boxes. All these items are purchased on the basis of anticipated needs, not necessarily immediate, and will be kept in inventory until they are needed. When the need arises, they are released from inventory, and **issued** to the kitchen. Since we have seen that cost occurs when food is used, these items will be included in the food cost figures when they are issued for use. The **working definition** will be that Stores are those items that will be charged to food cost as issued.

It is possible to go into long, elaborate discussions—even arguments—about the category into which any given item should be placed. Unquestionably, there are differences from restaurant to restaurant. In some establishments, for example, fresh fish is included with Directs, because it is purchased for use on the day of delivery. Other places may buy whole fish, which are cleaned and otherwise prepared for use the following day, and thus include fresh fish with Stores. Such discussion serves no useful purpose within this context. It is sufficient to say that the food controller in each establishment must make those decisions individually

FIGURE 6.4

Receiving Clerk's Daily Report — No. 1 — Date June 11, 19XX

Quant	Unit	Description	✓	Unit Price	Amount	Total Amount	Purchase Journal Distribution: Food Direct	Food Stores	Sundries
		Market Price Meats							
30	lbs.	Strip Steak	✓	4.95	148.50				
10	lbs.	Breast of Veal	✓	3.65	36.50				
						185.00		185.00	
		Ottman Meats							
15	lbs.	Pork Tenderloin	✓	2.50	37.50	37.50		37.50	
		Jones Produce & Fruit							
1	Crate	Lettuce	✓	12.50	12.50				
1	Bag	Onions		6.75	6.75				
1	Box	Grapefruit	✓	9.50	9.50				
1	Crate	Peaches	✓	12.00	12.00				
						40.75	40.75		
					263.25	263.25	40.75	222.50	

on the basis of use and then must consistently include each item in the preselected category.

When food is received, most larger establishments require the receiving clerk to complete a form listing all items received on a given day, usually divided by purveyor, and listed in the order received. One form is called the Receiving Clerk's Daily Report and is illustrated in figure 6.4. In addition to listing the dollar values of each item received, the form provides for the division of costs into three categories: Directs, Stores, and Sundries, which are nonfood items such as paper supplies and cleaning supplies, the cost of which is not a part of the cost of food.

By the time all deliveries for the day are in, preferably as early in the day as possible, the receiving clerk will have stamped and signed all invoices and entered each on the receiving sheet. The sheet with the invoices attached should then be sent to the steward, who signs the invoices, and then be routed to the food controller who will check the arithmetical accuracy of each invoice.* When

* In some establishments the food controller will not be concerned with arithmetical accuracy, because the accounting department will verify all bills prior to payment.

the checking has been completed, the controller sends the receiving sheet and the invoices on to the accounting department, where the figures will be entered in the purchase journal.

However, while the food controller still has the receiving sheet, one very important total figure is recorded: the total cost of Directs. Because Directs are charged to the food cost as received, the food controller will need this figure in order to compute the daily cost of food sold. When we reach the chapter concerned with computing daily food cost, it will be important to keep in mind that the daily cost of Directs comes from the receiving sheet.

In smaller establishments that do not have complete food control systems, many or all of the foregoing steps will be skipped, and the invoices are merely given to a bookkeeper by the person receiving the deliveries. However, this precludes a number of important possibilities for effective control. For example, such simplification makes it virtually impossible to compute a daily food cost. We will see that operating without knowledge of the daily food cost may be somewhat risky, and possibly a great disadvantage.

We have seen then that the purpose of establishing control procedures for receiving is to ensure that the establishment receives food in the quantities ordered, in the qualities specified, and at the prices quoted. These steps are basic and should be common to all foodservice operations, regardless of size. More complete systems of control, operated as they are with greater number of personnel and more equipment and procedures for checking, obviously offer greater measures of protection, but do so at greater cost. However, even the small owner-operated restaurant should take the basic steps to guard against excessive costs that may develop from the receiving of improper quantities or qualities, or the charging of improper prices.

EDP APPLICATIONS

If a restaurant or chain of restaurants is to make purchase decisions on the basis of data stored in computer memory, then it will be important to input data reflecting all items purchased as received. All this data is listed on the invoices checked by the receiving clerk. Management might designate some individual to input data for all foods received, and thus keep stored data current, both for quantity and price. In effect, this replaces the work presently done manually in those operations that keep data on perpetual inventory cards. Moreover, depending on the individuals involved and on the decisions of particular managers, it is possible to eliminate the receiving clerk's daily report because the essential information about purchase journal distribution and accounts payable may be input as the invoices are input to update quantities.

Another possibility might be to require that the steward placing orders record in a terminal the items and quantities ordered, and to provide the receiving clerk with a terminal for outputting this data as deliveries are received. This would provide a means for comparing items and quantities ordered with items and quantities received. Depending on management policy, prices could also be compared by this means.

CHAPTER ESSENTIALS

In this chapter, we described the principal characteristics of effective receiving procedure—that foods received should conform to orders placed in respect to quality, quantity, and price. We listed and described various forms, procedures, and pieces of equipment necessary to establish control over receiving, including invoices, invoice stamp, receiving clerk's daily report, scales, and meat tags. We then established a useful, working distinction between Directs and Stores, and pointed out the importance of effective receiving controls in preventing the development of excessive cost. Finally, we showed how the computer may aid in establishing control over the receiving function.

QUESTIONS AND PROBLEMS

1 In your own words explain several significant effects of improper receiving controls.

2 Why are the following pieces of equipment necessary for effective receiving control?

- **a** platform scale
- **b** hanging scale

3 Assume fifty pounds of strip steak were ordered and received, but the invoice showed an incorrect quantity and price. How would you rectify the errors?

4 Why is it desirable, even necessary, for the receiving clerk to have a complete set of the establishment's standard purchase specifications?

5 What possible cost effects might there be if food deliveries all arrived at the same time?

6 Distinguish between Directs and Stores.

7 Is it possible for proper receiving to take place in the absence of standard purchase specifications? Explain your answer.

8 The authors have indicated that some establishments do not use a receiving clerk's daily report form but check each item against the invoice. What are the possible advantages and disadvantages of this alternative procedure?

9 A certain restaurant does not use meat tags but treats meats as Directs. What are the immediate effects of this procedure on food cost? What are the possible ultimate effects?

10 The receiving clerk in a certain restaurant is also the dishwasher and has had no previous education or training in foods or in the food and beverage business. Discuss the possible effects on restaurant operations of having such an employee in this position.

11 In many restaurant operations, the steward who purchases food also functions as the receiving clerk. What are some of the possible positive and negative effects of this procedure?

12 How can the computer aid management in establishing control over the receiving function?

chapter 7

Control of Storing, Issuing, and Transfers

Learning Objectives

After reading and studying this chapter, the student should be able to:

1. List and explain the principal causes for the development of excessive costs while food is in storage.
2. List optimum temperatures for the storage of the various classifications of perishable foods.
3. Explain the significance and effect of temperature, storage containers, shelving, and cleanliness and facility location in food cost control.
4. Explain the principle of stock rotation as applied to the foodservice industry.
5. Distinguish between issuing procedures for Directs and Stores.
6. Price and extend an issue requisition.
7. List and define various types of transfers.
8. Explain the significance of transfers in determining accurate food costs.
9. Explain how the computer can aid management in establishing control over the storing, issuing, and transfer of foods.

Efforts to control costs by instituting the standards and procedures discussed in previous chapters can be largely wasted if excessive costs develop between the time goods are received and the time they are used in production. Although not responsible for the actual storing and issuing of foods or for the transfer of any items to any other part of the unit or to another unit (in the case of chain operations), the food controller does have the responsibility to establish standards and procedures that will minimize the possibilities for such unwarranted costs.

Before discussing specific causes and remedies for the excessive costs that develop while foods are in storage, it is important to emphasize that the receiving area should never be considered a storage area. Foods, especially perishable foods, should be moved to appropriate storage areas speedily and in appropriate order. The shelf life of most perishable items is considerably reduced if they remain on a warm receiving platform for any length of time, and of course the possibilities for theft are increased.

STORING CONTROL

The principal causes of excessive costs while food is in storage are spoilage, pilferage (the industry term for theft), and wasted labor. The food controller should understand the problems that lead to these causes and should use them as guides in establishing appropriate standards and procedures. In general these problems may be divided into four categories:

1 condition of facilities and equipment

2 arrangement of foods

3 location of facilities

4 security

Conditions of Facilities and Equipment

The factors involved in maintaining proper internal conditions include temperature, storage containers, shelving, and cleanliness. Any or all of these may lead to spoilage and waste.

Temperature

One of the key factors in the storing of foods, particularly perishables, is temperature. Food life can be maximized when food is stored at the correct temperature and humidity. The food controller should occasionally check the temperature gauges on the refrigerated storage facilities to see that the appropriate temperatures are being maintained. The temperatures that follow are generally accepted as optimum for storing the foods indicated.*

* While these temperatures are acceptable in very general terms, there are numerous exceptions. Bananas and potatoes, for example, should be stored at higher temperatures. For

- Fresh Meats: 34 to 36 degrees F.
- Fresh Produce: 34 to 36 degrees F.
- Fresh Dairy Products: 34 to 36 degrees F.
- Fresh Fish: 30 to 34 degrees F.
- Frozen Foods: −10 to 0 degrees F.

If temperatures are permitted to rise above these levels, shelf life is shortened, and the risk of food spoilage is increased for perishables.

Temperature also can be important in keeping nonperishables. Storage facilities for staple commodities should usually be room temperature, approximately 70 to 72 degrees F. On a number of occasions, particularly in older establishments, staples are kept in facilities that are either too warm because of their proximity to hot stoves or steam pipes running through the ceiling, or too cold because of location in an unheated part of the building. While the degree of risk is not quite so great with staples, it should be remembered that all foods are ultimately perishable, and that food life is increased by storage at proper temperatures.

Storage Containers

In addition to maintaining foods at proper temperatures, care must be given to storing them in appropriate containers. In the case of staples most, but not all, are purchased in airtight containers. Some, however, are purchased in unsealed containers, often paper bags, boxes, and sacks, which are susceptible to attack by insects and vermin. Whenever practicable, such commodities should be transferred to tight, insect-proof containers. In the case of perishables, both raw and cooked, care should be given to storing them in whatever manner will best maintain their original quality. Many raw foods such as apples or potatoes may be stored as purchased for reasonable periods; others, such as fresh fish, should be packed in shaved ice. In general, cooked foods and opened canned foods should be stored in stainless steel containers, and either wrapped or appropriately covered.

Shelving

For perishable foods, shelving should be slatted to permit maximum circulation of air in refrigerated facilities. For nonperishables, solid steel shelving is usually preferred. At no time should anything be stored on the floor. Appropriate shelving raised a few inches above the floor level should be provided for those large and heavy containers that must occasionally be used in storerooms or refrigerators.

Cleanliness

Conditions of cleanliness should be enforced in all storage facilities at all times. In refrigerated facilities, this will prevent the accumulation of small amounts of

---

specific temperature for storage of any particular commodity, consult such authorities as Kotschevar, *Quantity Foods Purchasing*, second edition (New York: John Wiley and Sons, Inc., 1975), or various publications of the United States Department of Agriculture.

spoiling food, which will give off odors and may affect other foods. In storeroom facilities, it will discourage infestation by insects and vermin. Storerooms should be swept and cleaned daily, and no clutter should be allowed to accumulate. Extermination should be accomplished on a regular basis to prevent rodents and vermin from reaching population levels large enough to cause damage and disease.

Arrangement of Foods

The factors involved in maintaining appropriate internal arrangement include rotating stock, fixing definite locations for each item, and keeping the most-used items readily available.

Fixing Definite Location

Each particular item should always be found in the same location, and attention should be given to ensuring that new deliveries of the item are stored in the same location. All too often, one commodity can be found in several locations at once—for example, six cans on a shelf, and two partially used cans in two other unrelated areas. This increases the chances for overpurchasing, spoilage, and theft. In addition, it makes difficult the monthly process of taking a physical inventory, which will be discussed in the next chapter. Incidentally, separate facilities for storage of different classes of foods should be maintained whenever practicable and possible. Eggs, for example, should not be stored with fish, cheese, or other foods that give off odors, because their shells are quite porous and will absorb flavors from other foods. Fish should always be stored in separate facilities.

Rotation of Stocks

It is very important that the food controller ensure that older quantities of any item are used before any new deliveries. This is known as the **First-In, First-Out** method of stock rotation, commonly called FIFO in the industry. The steward and his or her staff must be held responsible for storing new deliveries of an item behind the quantities already on hand, thus ensuring that older items will be used first. This reduces the possibilities for spoilage. If this procedure is not followed, if those who store foods are permitted to put new food in front of old food on shelves, the chances are increased that the older items will spoil before they are used. This is particularly important with perishables, but it should not be neglected with nonperishables.

Availability According to Use

It is usually helpful to arrange storage facilities so that most-frequently used items are maintained closest to the entrance. Although it has no effect on spoilage and theft, it does tend to reduce the time required to move needed foods from storage to production, and thus tends to reduce excessive labor costs.

Location of Storage Facilities

Whenever possible, the storage facilities for both perishable and nonperishable commodities should be located between receiving areas and preparation areas, and preferably close to both. Such locations facilitate the moving of foods from the receiving areas to storage and from storage to the preparation areas. A good storage facility will have the effect of

1 speeding the process of storage and issue
2 maximizing security
3 reducing labor requirements

All too often, storage facilities are located in areas that are unusable for other purposes. Often that policy is penny wise and pound foolish, because temperature, security, and sanitary conditions are not adequate.

Dry storage should be sealed to reduce the risk of infestation, Obviously, it is impossible to seal an area if its location is susceptible to rodents.

Security

Food should never be stored in a manner that permits pilferage. This is another reason for moving foods from the receiving area to storage as quickly as possible. Once in storage, attention must be given to maintaining appropriate security at all times. In the case of a storeroom for staple commodities, the room should never be left unattended. Employees should not be permitted to remove items at will. It is typical for a storeroom to be open at specified times for specified periods well-known to the staff, and otherwise closed to enable the attendant to perform other duties. When the storeroom is closed, it is locked, with the one key in the storeroom clerk's possession. In such cases, one additional "emergency" key is usually kept by the manager or in the office safe.

Security is also an important consideration in storing perishables, particularly in the case of high-cost items such as meat and fish. The importance of security obviously increases with the value of the items stored. It is sometimes advisable to establish separate control procedures for steaks, liquor, and other high-cost items.

DATING AND PRICING

It is desirable to date items as they are put away on shelves, so that the storeroom clerk can be certain of the age of each item and make provisions for use before spoilage sets in. Of particular concern are those items that are infrequently used. The storeroom clerk should visually check the stock frequently to ascertain which items are beginning to get old and then inform the chef so that items can be put on the menu before they spoil.

In addition, all items should be priced as goods are put away, with the cost of each container clearly marked. Following that procedure will greatly facilitate issuing, because the storeroom clerk will be able to price requisitions with little difficulty. If items are not priced as goods are put away, the storeroom clerk will waste considerable time looking up prices when goods are sent to the kitchen.

ISSUING CONTROL

In Chapter 6, a distinction was made between Directs and Stores. Directs were defined as those foods charged to cost as received and Stores as those carried in inventory and charged to cost as issued. From the food controller's point of view, that distinction becomes particularly important in a discussion of issuing procedures. Its importance will become increasingly apparent as we approach the discussion of the calculation of food cost.

Directs

Directs are charged to the food cost as received on the assumption that the quantities of these perishable items are for immediate use. In effect, these foods move directly from the receiving area to the kitchen, where they are used immediately to meet daily production needs. Although this is not strictly true in every instance, it does simplify the maintenance of cost records. In order to determine the cost of Directs for any given day, the food controller merely looks at the receiving sheet for the day and takes the total figure in the Direct column. If these perishables are being purchased in reasonable quantities, the cost of Directs may be artificially high on one particular day, when leftover quantities are used up, but are not reflected in cost for that day.

Because Directs are "issued" to the kitchen the moment they are received, no further record is kept of particular quantities of particular items. If there is waste or spoilage, or even pilferage, it will be reflected in an excessively high food cost figure, which will bear investigation. That entire question will be discussed in detail in Chapters 8 and 9.

The alternative to considering Directs issued as received would be to follow an issuing procedure such as that described below for Stores. It will be readily apparent that such a procedure for Directs would probably involve greater amounts of record keeping than would seem warranted to most establishments.

Stores

The food category known as Stores was previously described as one consisting of (a) staples and (b) tagged items, primarily meats. When purchased, these foods are considered part of inventory until issued for use and are not included in cost figures until they are issued. Therefore, it follows that records must be kept of issues in order to determine the cost of Stores. For control purposes, some system must be established to ensure that no Stores are issued unless the kitchen personnel submit lists of the items and quantities needed.

The Requisition

A requisition, illustrated in figure 7.1, is a form prepared by a member of the kitchen staff, listing the items and quantities needed from Stores. Each requisition should be reviewed by the chef, who should check to see that each item appearing is genuinely required in the amount listed. The requisition is then approved and signed by the chef. It is next given to the storekeeper, who fills the order.

Whenever practical, it is advisable to require that these requisitions be submitted in advance to enable the storekeeper to prepare the order without haste. In some places, it has been found quite practical to insist on requisitions being submitted the day before food is needed. This has the desirable effect of forcing kitchen personnel to anticipate needs and plan for the following day's production.

It is also desirable, in many instances, to set definite times for the issuing of food by the storekeeper, who, after all, has a number of other duties to perform, including keeping the storerooms and refrigerators clean, maintaining stocks of staples on shelves, rotating stock, and doing considerable paper work. Some operations have achieved good results by restricting the times for issuing food to

FIGURE 7.1
Requisition

Date 9/8, 19—

Supply Main Kitchen Dept.

Quantity	*Description*	*Unit Cost*	*Total Cost*
6	#10 Cans Green Peas		
50	Lbs. Sugar		
40	Lbs. Ground Beef		
6	Loins Pork		

Charge to Food Dept.

J. J. Lemon
Chef

two hours in the morning and two in the afternoon. Naturally, such decisions must be left to management in any particular operation.

Pricing the Requisition

After Stores have been issued from the appropriate stockroom, refrigerator, or freezer, it is the storekeeper's responsibility to list on each requisition the cost of listed items, and to determine the total dollar value of the foods issued. As will be discussed in Chapter 9, this information is necessary for a daily determination of food costs.

Meats and Tagged Items

As meats are issued, the tag is detached from each piece and the dollar value recorded on the requisition. If one listing requires the issuing of several pieces of meat, the tag values are totaled before entering. When meat tag values are entered, the tags are attached to the requisitions.

Staples

The unit cost of each listed item must be entered and multiplied by the number of units issued in each case. This is called extending the requisitions. The unit cost will come from one of the following, depending on the system in use.

1. The unit cost of each item is marked on each container as it is stored, making it readily available to the storekeeper.
2. A book or card file is maintained for all staple items, one page or card per item. The most recent purchase price is always entered as prices change.
3. The most recent purchase price is indicated on a perpetual inventory card for each item.
4. The storekeeper keeps a mental index card for each item and usually has the purchase price of each in mind from constant use.

While the first method is generally preferred, it unquestionably involves considerable labor and consequently is costly to maintain. Therefore, though preferred, it is not the method in general use. More often than not, prices come from the storekeeper's head. Although this "system" leaves much to be desired in terms of accuracy, it is the method requiring the least time and labor. Many operations have found the resulting inaccuracies have no significant effect over the long run.

Once the values of tagged items have been entered, and the unit costs of staples entered and extended, each requisition is totaled. At the end of the day, with meat tags attached, all requisitions are sent to the food controller.

It should be pointed out that on the following morning the food controller will have figures available for the principal components of a daily food cost:

1 Cost of Directs from the receiving sheet
2 Cost of Stores from the requisitions, with meat tags attached

FOOD AND BEVERAGE TRANSFERS

So far in our discussions we have assumed that a restaurant purchases, receives, stores, and issues food for use in one kitchen in which all production is accomplished. By doing so, we have quite purposely ignored the existence of a number of possible complications, which it will be useful to consider at this point. For example, even in smaller restaurants, food production in the kitchen may require the use of certain beverage items, such as wines and liquors, not purchased specifically for kitchen use. Conversely, many establishments purchase some food items knowing that they will be used at the bar for drink production. Whole oranges and lemons, as well as heavy cream, are good examples of this possibility. In addition, in some of the larger hotel and motel operations, more than one kitchen may be in operation and it may be necessary or desirable from time to time or even regularly to transfer food from one to another. Transfers may occur in chain operations, where one unit may produce such items as baked goods for other units, or where one unit in the organization, running short of needed items, may be encouraged to secure them from another unit.

Since the goals in food control include determining food cost as accurately as possible and matching food cost with food sales, it is often necessary to maintain records of the cost of the food transferred. When the amounts involved are relatively insignificant and have little appreciable effect on cost and on the cost-to-sales ratio, they may be, and usually are, disregarded. But when the amounts become somewhat larger and have rather more significant effects, records of some type must be developed.

Intraunit Transfers

Between Bar and Kitchen

Food and beverge transfers between the bar and the kitchen frequently occur in operations of all sizes. Many kitchens use such beverage items as wine, cordials, brandy, and even ale for the production of sauces, parfaits, certain baked items, and rarebits. Occasionally, these items are purchased by the food department for use in the kitchen, kept in a storeroom until needed, and then issued on requisitions directly to the kitchen. In such cases additional records are not required; the quantities and values listed on the requisition are sufficient to permit accurate calculations of cost. However, in most instances when these beverage items are needed in the kitchen, appropriate amounts are secured from the bar. After all, if sufficient supplies are already being maintained at the bar, it makes little sense to keep additional quantities for specific use in food production.

The same may be said of certain food items in the Directs category used by bartenders in drink production: if supplies of oranges, lemons, limes, heavy cream, and eggs are already available in the kitchen, it makes little sense in most operations to purchase specific supplies of these items for exclusive use at the bar. It is far simpler merely to secure the needed items from the kitchen. When it becomes necessary or desirable to achieve a high degree of accuracy in determining costs to match with sales, records of these transfers between the food and beverage departments must be maintained. The form used to maintain these records is the Food/Beverage Transfer Memo, illustrated in figure 7.2. As transfers are made, items and amounts are recorded on such memos by authorized individuals. When these memos have been completed, they may be sent to the food controller, who may use them to adjust food cost figures to achieve greater accuracy, and then routed to an accounting office, where the appropriate entries may be made in the financial records.

Between Kitchen and Kitchen

In some hotel and motel operations with more than one kitchen and dining room, it is common practice to determine food costs for each separately and to match the costs for each operating unit with the sales generated by that unit. Where some food items are transferred from one kitchen to another, higher degrees of

FIGURE 7.2
Food/Beverage Transfer Memo

Food/Beverage Transfer Memo

Date 9/8, 19—

From Bar

To Main Kitchen

Quantity	Description	Unit Price	Amount
1	750 ml Sneed's Sherry	3.95	3.95
1	750 ml Red Wine	2.65	2.65
		Total	6.60

Sent by Joe - bartender

Received by Paul - Chef

accuracy in determining food costs may be achieved by keeping records of items and amounts so transferred. In cases where, for example, one unit closes earlier than another, and cooked foods may be conveniently transferred from a closing unit to one remaining open until a later hour, it would be possible to achieve a higher degree of accuracy in determining costs for each unit by crediting cost for the early closing unit for the value of the items transferred and by adding the same amount to the cost for the later closing unit.

Even in cases where items are not so transferred but are merely returned to a central kitchen or commissary for reissue to the same or to other units on succeeding days, recording the value of the items returned on transfer memos or on other similar forms makes possible more accurate determination of food costs, and consequently of cost-to-sales ratios for operating periods.

Interunit Transfers

The two examples that follow illustrate the problem of interunit transfers, and the effect of such transfers on food costs.

In a number of instances small chains produce some items—baked goods, for example, in only one unit—and then distribute those items to other units in the chain. If the ingredients for the baked goods come from that particular unit's regular supplies, then some record must be made of the cost of the ingredients used. Failure to do so would result in overstating the food cost of the producing unit by the value of the ingredients used, and in understating the food costs of the receiving units by the value of the foods they receive. In addition, if the matching principle is to be followed, and if food sales are reported separately for each unit, then food cost figures that do not include the cost of all those foods sold, including the baked goods from another unit, cannot be said to be truly matched with sales. Under such conditions, if one of management's goals is to match costs and sales with a reasonably high degree of accuracy, it is necessary to use the transfer memo or some similar form to record the value of ingredients used in the production of finished products for transfer to other units.

With such records available, it is possible to credit cost of the producing unit. Appropriately increasing the food cost figures of the receiving units may pose more of a problem. If each unit receives an equal share of the goods produced, then one could simply divide the cost of the goods produced and credited to the producing unit by the number of units to which items had been transferred, and increase the food cost of each by one equal share. However, if the total produced for distribution to the various units is not divided among them equally, then some more equitable means for apportioning cost must be found. One possible means of dealing with this problem is by recording the values of transferred items at standard costs. The question of calculating standard costs of production for this and for other purposes will be deferred to Chapter 10.

Another problem involving the value of foods transferred from one unit to another may be found in those chain organizations that permit or encourage unit managers to use foods from other units when their own supplies run low and when additional purchases are precluded by time. When units are comparatively close to one another and offer identical menus, occasions may arise when one of the units nearly exhausts the supply of some important item and does not discover this shortage until it is clearly too late to purchase an additional amount. In some organizations, items are borrowed and returned within a day or so as a matter of course, and no complications arise as long as all borrowed items are appropriately returned. However, not all cases are quite so simple, as, for example, when a perishable item borrowed by one unit does not appear on the menu again for some considerable period of time. Rather than maintain records over long periods in order to ensure the return of borrowed items, it is often simpler to record such transfers of foods on transfer memos, and to use the information so recorded to increase the cost of the unit that has borrowed, and correspondingly to decrease the cost of the supplying unit.

An interesting problem that may arise in connection with this procedure is the extent to which it influences some managers purposely to maintain short supplies of some high-cost and perishable items. If the organization permits one to secure needed supplies from other units at the same prices one would pay in the market, some managers will be encouraged to reduce the possibilities for excessive costs due to spoilage and pilferage in their units simply by maintaining adequate supplies. Under such conditions, discouraging managers from taking advantage might entail establishing a price for transfer purposes somewhat higher than the current market price.

It is quite probable that there are in this industry a reasonably large number of transfers of the various types discussed above, but it is equally probable that a large number of these involve comparatively small amounts of food of relatively insignificant value. Consequently, because the amounts involved are usually negligible in most places, records are often not used. However, if and when the amounts become significant, provision must be made for maintaining adequate records to ensure that good cost figures include the cost of beverages used in food preparation and exclude the cost of food items sent to the bar for beverage preparation, and that food cost figures for one unit of a larger organization include the cost of food items sold in that unit. In every case, to the extent feasible, the cost of items sold in a department, division, or unit should include the cost of all items reflected in sales figures.

EDP APPLICATIONS

From the previous chapter, the student will recall that computer memories can record quantities purchased and received, as well as purchase prices. It would also be possible, if desired, to establish a computer code for all storage locations, such that each particular item in storage be assigned a particular location. Before any food purchases were stored, it would be useful to determine from computer memory the correct storage location for each item, in order to help ensure that all available quantities of a given food item were consolidated in one particular location.

Issuing control offers many possibilities for computer assistance. For example, rather than require the chef to write out a requisition and present it to the steward, management might ask that the chef enter the needed items in a terminal. By so entering these needs, the chef would be helping to update stored data reflecting inventory levels, for the items would be treated as issued when entered by the chef. If a printer were installed in the storeroom, the chef's clearly legible order would be available to those who would fill it. The requisition as entered by the chef could be printed instantly or at a later time if that were considered more feasible. Thus, the handwritten requisition so commonly used now could be eliminated. Another desirable feature of this procedure would be that the chef could output data as needed reflecting quantities of particular items presently in storage. This would have obvious benefits for purposes of menu planning.

Transfers may be processed in much the same way as requisitions. If a bartender were to need fruit or other Directs for making drinks, these needs would be entered in a terminal at the bar and printed out in the storeroom so that delivery to the bar might be made. Beverages required for food production would be entered by the chef and printed out at the bar. Any transferred items would be stored in memory until needed for accurate food cost determination.

CHAPTER ESSENTIALS

In this chapter, we listed and explained the principal causes of excessive costs that develop while food is in storage: spoilage, pilferage, and wasted labor. We showed how food service operators manage these problems through controlling the food storage conditions, including temperature, storage containers, shelving, cleanliness, location of foods, and rotation of stock. We suggested the need for proper location of storage facilities and discussed various security measures designed to prevent pilferage. A distinction was made between issuing procedures for Directs and Stores, and we indicated the importance of the requisition and the meat tag in issuing Stores and in determining the cost of issues. We discussed the possible effects on food costs caused by food and beverage transfers, both interunit and intraunit, and described the means for maintaining records of such transfers. Finally, we showed how computers may be used to assist management in establishing control over the storing, issuing, and transfer of items in inventory.

QUESTIONS AND PROBLEMS

1 What are some of the possible problems implicit in allowing the chef, receiving clerk, or dining room manager to have keys to the storeroom?

2 Even with restricted access to storeroom keys, it is sometimes desirable to change locks. Under what specific conditions would you as a food controller advise the manager to change locks?

3 In your own words, explain how excessive food costs may be reduced through proper rotation of stock.

4 List and explain the disadvantages in locating a storage area at some distance from the receiving and preparation areas. Are there any advantages?

5 If a new storeroom clerk discovered an item on his shelves still in good condition, but six months old, what, if anything, should he or she do about it? Why?

6 Referring to the price list below, calculate the total value of the following requisitions.

Storeroom Price List and Requisitions.

A Most recent storeroom prices obtained from the steward

Item	*Purchase Unit*	*Unit Price*
Applesauce	#10 can	$2.10
Beets, sliced	#10 can	1.62
Carrots, diced	#10 can	2.63
Clams, minced	#10 can	4.29
Cocktail sauce	gallon	5.75
Coffee	pound	1.15
Corn, whole kernel	#10 can	2.13
Cranberry sauce	#10 can	1.89
Flour, all purpose	pound	.23
Fruit cocktail	#10 can	2.05
Garlic powder	pound	3.48
Ketchup	12 oz.	.48
Linguine, #18	pound	.32
Mushrooms, whole	#10 can	3.21
Mustard	8 oz.	.25
Olive Oil	gallon	3.72
Peaches, halves	#10 can	2.45
Pepper, black	pound	2.54
Pepper, white	pound	2.98
Pineapple, crushed	#10 can	1.89
Rice	pound	.18
Salt	pound	.10
Sauerkraut	#10 can	2.23
Sugar, granulated	pound	.39
Tomato puree	#10 can	1.98
Tomatoes, whole peeled	#10 can	1.49
Vinegar	gallon	2.58

B Storeroom requisitions:

1. July 6th

Quantity	Item	Unit Price	Extension
24–8 oz.	Mustard		
24–12 oz.	Ketchup		
20 lb.	Salt		
2 lb.	Black pepper		
5 gal.	Olive Oil		
5 gal.	Vinegar		
10 lb.	Sugar		

Total: ______

Authorized by: H. Sneed, Maitre D'

2. July 6th

Quantity	Item	Unit Price	Extension
12—#10	Tomatoes, whole		
12—#10	Tomatoe puree		
10 lb.	Coffee		
2 lb.	White pepper		
50 lb.	Salt		
50 lb.	Flour, all purpose		
2—#10	Sauerkraut		
3—#10	Carrots, diced		
1—#10	Fruit cocktail		

Authorized by: P. Noir, Sous Chef

Total: ______

3. July 7th

Quantity	Item	Unit Price	Extension
3—#10	Corn, whole kernel		
6—#10	Beets, sliced		
3—#10	Peaches, halves		
2—#10	Applesauce		
25 lb.	Rice		
3—#10	Cranberry sauce		
1 gal.	Cocktail sauce		
2—#10	Mushrooms, whole		
Authorized by: G. Chambertin, Chef		Total:	

3. July 8th

Quantity	Item	Unit Price	Extension
2—#10	Clams, minced		
5 lb.	Linguine #18		
1 lb.	Garlic powder		
6–10	Pineaple, crushed		
Authorized by: P. Chardonnay, Relief Chef		Total:	

7 The Somerset Restaurant Company owns and operates three small units in one community. Gross food sales and food costs as recorded on the books of each unit are as follows:

	Unit A	*Unit B*	*Unit C*
Sales	$155,400	$98,300	$228,000
Food Cost	80,808	30,473	77,520

The above figures do not include the values of food transferred from Unit A to the other two units, including all baked goods used in the chain, which are produced in one bake shop located in Unit A. During the period, transfers from Unit A to the other two units totaled $20,000, of which $8,000 was sent to Unit B, and the remainder to Unit C.

a Calculate food cost percent before transfers are taken into account.
b Adjust food cost figures by the amounts of the transfers to determine more accurate food costs.
c Calculate food cost percents based on the costs determined in (**b**).

8 Food cost percent is often one of the elements used to judge a manager's ability to control food costs. Explain how failure to take the value of transferred foods into account before calculating food cost percents can affect the performance ratings of managers who send food items to other units, and of managers who receive food from other units.

9 A certain small chain operates four units in one small city. Each unit purchases for its own needs and produces for its own sales on premises. Each produces its own rolls, cakes, and pies. However, when one unit underproduces, the manager is encouraged to secure needed quantities from another unit in the chain before purchasing from outside. One item, apple pie, costs $1.35 to produce in-house, and is available outside for $2.75 from nearby bakeries. What would be an appropriate transfer price for apple pies sent from one unit to another? What effect would the transfer price you decide on have on the volume of transfers between units?

10 Why should food not be stored on the floor at any time? What may happen to food so stored?

11 Explain how computers may be of assistance to management in each of the following areas:

a storing control
b issuing control
c control of transfers

chapter 8

Monthly Inventory and Food Cost Determinations

Learning Objectives

After reading and studying this chapter, the student should be able to:

1. Describe the procedure for taking physical inventory at the end of the month.
2. List and explain five ways to assign costs to units of food in inventory.
3. State the formula for calculating cost of food consumed.
4. Explain the difference between cost of food consumed and cost of food sold.
5. Describe the effect on food cost of each of five acceptable methods of assigning cost to the closing inventory.
6. List and explain the adjustments needed to translate cost of food consumed into cost of food sold.
7. Define the terms *opening* (or *beginning*) *inventory* and *closing* (or *ending*) *inventory*.
8. Explain the relationship between monthly calculation of cost of food sold, and the monthly income statement.
9. Devise a simple monthly food cost report to management, given the necessary figures.
10. Calculate cost of food consumed, cost of food sold, food cost percent, and cost per dollar sale, given appropriate figures.
11. Explain the possible shortcomings in a system that calculates cost of food sold only once a month.
12. Explain how computers may assist management in determining both inventory values and employee adherence to standard procedures for food issue.

MONTHLY INVENTORY

In most business establishments, including food and beverage operations, one universally accepted practice is the taking of a physical inventory. This is done at the close of an accounting period, typically after the close of business on the last day of a calendar month. In our discussion here we will be concerned only with those dealing in food and beverage items purchased primarily for making and selling food and beverage products.

The process of taking a physical inventory requires that one physically count the actual number of units on hand of each item in stock, and record that number in the appropriate place in an inventory book, such as that illustrated in figure 8.1, or in some other similar place. It is normally considered good practice to list the items in stock in a book specifically for that purpose, in the same order in which they are maintained in stock, rather than in any other order. This facilitates a procedure that can be long and tedious, depending on the number of commodities in the inventory.

Taking a physical inventory in a storeroom, for example, commonly requires two people, one to count the units on shelves and the other to record the amounts in the inventory book. If the storeroom is arranged as suggested above, it is possible for the two to begin in one logical spot and to work their way around

FIGURE 8.1
Storeroom Inventory

Month of	September, 19—							
Articles	Quantity	Price	Amount	Quantity	Price	Amount	Quantity	Price
Brought forward								
Tomato Paste #2½ cans	16	24	3.84					
Tomato Paste #10 cans	6	1.49	8.94					
Tomatoe Puree #10 cans	8	1.29	10.32					

in order, finding items on shelves in the same order as that listed in the inventory book.

Once quantities are determined for each item, total values can be calculated for each. To do this, one must record the unit cost for each commodity and then multiply it by the number of units of each in the physical inventory. Once the total value of each commodity has been determined, these totals can be added to determine the total dollar value of the inventory. This dollar figure is known as the closing inventory valuation for the period and automatically becomes the opening inventory valuation for the next period.

One of the principal difficulties with the above procedure is determining unit costs or values for each item, since all purchases are not made at the same price. It is not uncommon for the price of any one item in the inventory to change several times during the course of the month. Determining what value to assign to units remaining in inventory at the end of the month raises the question of which, if any, of the various prices should be assigned to the unit item for purposes of inventory valuation.

There are at least five possible ways of assigning values to units of commodities in inventory, each of which will be explained. Because each provides a different answer to the question of inventory value at the end of any given period, the student is advised to become familiar with these approaches, any one of which management might select as appropriate for use in a particular establishment given a particular set of circumstances.

Because it would be unwieldy and possibly confusing to illustrate each of the five by attempting to treat a complete set of inventory figures, we will restrict ourselves to only one item in the stores inventory of a particular restaurant, #10 cans of fruit cocktail. Records from the restaurant for a certain month reveal the following:

Opening Inventory on the 1st of the month:	10 cans	@	$2.35	=	$23.50
Purchased on the 7th of the month:	24 "	@	2.50	=	60.00
Purchased on the 15th of the month:	24 "	@	2.60	=	62.40
Purchased on the 26th of the month:	12 "	@	2.30	=	27.60

A physical inventory on the 31st of the month showed that twenty cans remained in stock. From this we may deduce that fifty cans were consumed in the course of the month in this manner:

Opening Inventory	10 cans
+ Purchases during the month	60 "
= Total Available for use	70 "
− Closing Inventory (number of units still available)	20 "
= Amount consumed (number of units no longer available)	50 cans

Because both the value of the opening inventory ($23.50) and the purchases of this item ($150.00) are known, it is also possible to add both values together to determine the value of the total number of units available, or $173.50. It should be obvious that it is possible to determine the value of the amount consumed only if one can somehow determine the value of the number of units in the closing inventory and then subtract it from the value of the total available. The following are five accepted methods of assigning these unit values.

Actual Purchase Price Method

Perhaps the most reasonable approach would be to value the remaining items—those in the closing inventory—at actual purchase price. However this can be done only if those prices are marked on the units. If the cans are marked with actual purchase prices, totaling their value is obviously a simple clerical job requiring no more complex procedure than addition. Hence, it is possible to determine the value of the 20 cans as:

4	@	$2.35	=	$ 9.40
12	@	2.30	=	10.40
4	@	2.60	=	10.40
20			=	47.40

If cans were not marked, an alternative procedure would be necessary.

First-In, First-Out Method

If actual purchase prices are not marked on the cans, an alternative procedure is to assume that stock has been rotated during the period and that the units consumed were the first to be placed on the shelf, so that those remaining on the shelf are in fact those most recently purchased. In many cases, these are not valid assumptions, but we will make them for purposes of discussion.

In order to establish a value for the closing inventory under this method, it would be necessary to know that the latest purchase on the twenty-sixth of the month was for twelve cans and that the next previous purchase on the fifteenth was for twenty-four cans. With that information available it is possible to determine the value of the twenty cans as:

12	@	$2.30	=	$27.60
8	@	2.60	=	20.80
20			=	48.40

However, if there were no particular assurances that the stock on the shelves had been properly rotated during the month, this would not be the safest possible course, since it rests largely on the assumption of rotation.

Weighted Average Purchase Price Method

Where no certainty exists that stock had been rotated, and where large quantities of goods are involved, it would be possible to determine a weighted average purchase price by multiplying the number of units in the opening inventory and in each purchase by their individual purchase prices, adding these values to determine a total value for all units together, and then dividing by the number of units involved. By following this procedure, the weighted average value of one unit could be determined by dividing seventy units into their $173.50 total value, which yields $2.48. Therefore, the value of the closing inventory would be:

20 @ $2.48 = $49.60

It should be apparent that, while this procedure makes logical sense on paper, it requires access to extensive documentaton. In fact, it is rather cumbersome and far too time-consuming to be used in most food and beverage operations.

Latest Purchase Price Method

A simpler, faster and more widely employed approach is to use the latest price in valuing the closing inventory. One justification for this approach is that if it were necessary to replace the remaining cans, the cost of replacement at the present moment would likely be the latest price at which the items were purchased. If this method were followed, as it frequently is in the food and beverage business, the value of the closing inventory of this item would be:

20 @ $2.30 = $46.00

Last-In, First-Out Method

In certain specialized circumstances, particularly in periods of high inflation, and when management chooses to minimize profits on financial statements in order to decrease income taxes, it is possible to maximize cost by minimizing the value of closing inventory. If management directs that costs are to be kept at a relatively higher level in order to minimize profits, this can be achieved in times of rising prices by valuing the units remaining in inventory at the close of a period at the earliest purchase price. By following this procedure with the current example, the value of the twenty cans would be:

10	@	$2.35	=	$23.50
10	@	2.50	=	25.00
20			=	48.50

It should be carefully borne in mind that a food controller does not normally determine the method to be used in valuing inventories. Although he or she may contribute to discussion of the question, the decision would probably lie with the firm's accountant. Additionally, once the decision is made, it cannot be changed capriciously; various accounting conventions and Internal Revenue Service regulations preclude simple change.

Comparison of Methods

If the prices of goods purchased were fixed, the selection of method for valuing a closing inventory would be of no importance; all methods would yield the same figure. However, in a period of fluctuating prices—which, after all, describes most periods in our business—the selection of one method over another may bring a significantly different result. A comparison of the values of the twenty cans in closing inventory described above illustrate this point:

1	Value based on actual purchase price method:	$47.40
2	Value based on first-in, first-out method:	48.40
3	Value based on weighted average method:	49.60
4	Value based on latest purchase price method:	46.00
5	Value based on last-in, first-out method:	48.50

Using the lowest established value, $46.00, as a base, a difference of 7.8% exists between the highest value and the lowest value in this particular case. And while the dollar differences for this one example do not appear particularly great, the difference in dollars would be significant if one were dealing with an entire inventory.

With the information available from our discussions in this and previous chapters, it is now possible to calculate the cost, cost-to-sales ratio, or actual cost percentage of operation for any establishment, regardless of the size and the nature and complexity of the control procedures in effect.

MONTHLY FOOD COST DETERMINATION

Cost of food sold for the month is determined by means of the following formula:

Opening Inventory	(food on hand the first day of the month)
+ Purchases	(both Directs and Stores)
Total Available	(total value of all food available for sale)
− Closing Inventory	(food on hand the last day of the month)
= Cost of Food	(includes waste and pilferage)

Opening inventory for any accounting period is by definition identical to the closing inventory for the previous period and is available from accounting records.

Purchases include all Directs and Stores purchased during the period as listed on invoices and summarized on the receiving clerk's daily reports throughout the period. Total available thus reflects the total dollar value of all foods, both Directs and Stores, available for the production of menu items for sale during the period. From this total, one subtracts the value of closing inventory as established by means previously described. The resulting figure represents cost of food for the period, and includes the cost of all food whether used productively or not.

It should be noted that the closing inventory figure does not include the value of any Directs that may have been purchased but not consumed. This results in a food cost figure somewhat higher than it should be. In practice, this is often ignored on the theory that any error in this procedure in one month will be offset the following month. This is to say that some Directs that will be used at the beginning of each month will have been included in cost for the previous month, and since Directs are purchased in small quantities for nearly immediate use, the value of these should be fairly constant from month to month. In some large organizations, these Directs are in a category termed Foods in Process, which is subtracted from total available along with the closing inventory of Stores.

At this point it will be useful to illustrate the effect of the various methods of establishing value of closing inventory on the cost of food for a period, using the figures determined earlier in this chapter for #10 cans of fruit cocktail.

FIGURE 8.2

	Actual Purchase Price Method	*First-In, First-Out Method*	*Weighted Average Method*	*Latest Purchase Price Method*	*Last-In, First-Out Method*
Opening Inventory	$ 23.50	$ 23.50	$ 23.50	$ 23.50	$ 23.50
Purchases	150.00	150.00	150.00	150.00	150.00
Total Available	173.50	173.50	173.50	173.50	173.50
Closing Inventory	47.40	48.40	49.60	46.00	48.50
Cost of Food	126.10	125.10	123.90	127.50	125.00

While the above differences are illustrated with only one item out of an inventory, it should be apparent that these effects would be cumulative over an entire inventory. Thus, though owners and accountants should jointly decide which method to use, a knowledgeable food controller should be aware of the effects of the various inventory valuation methods on food cost.

Once food cost for a given period has been determined, food cost percent may be calculated. For purposes of the following illustrations, let us hypothesize a small restaurant. Assume that the records reveal the following figures for the month of March:

Opening Inventory	$ 2,000
Food Purchases	6,000
Closing Inventory	3,000
Food Sales	15,000

Given these figures, we may now determine the cost of food for March by means of the previously stated formula:

Opening Inventory	$2,000
+ Purchases	6,000
Total Available	8,000
− Closing Inventory	3,000
= Cost of Food	$5,000

Once the cost of food is known, the cost percentage can be calculated by using the formula discussed in a previous chapter

$$\frac{\text{cost}}{\text{sales}} = \text{cost\%}$$

$$\frac{5{,}000}{15{,}000} = 33.3\%$$

This is the same as saying that the cost of food has been $.333 per dollar of sales.

However, it must be emphasized that while the $5,000 figure represents the cost of food, it is really cost of food issued, and not necessarily the same as cost of food consumed. Determining cost of food consumed may require that the cost of food issued be adjusted to account for a number of possible alternate uses of the food issued.

ADJUSTMENTS TO COST OF FOOD ISSUED

If there have been transfers between the kitchen and the bar, adjustments must be made to take the value of the transfers into account. Similarly, if there have been transfers from units in a chain to other units in that same chain, these two must be totaled and used to adjust the cost figures of all concerned. In some hotel operations, where separate cost records are kept for the several food outlets in one hotel, certain similar adjustments must be made for food items transferred from one operation to another. And transfers, including the intraunit transfers of cooking liquor and food to bar (Directs), and the interunit transfers of such items as baked goods, are not the only possible adjustments to food cost figures. In order to achieve more accurate food costs, many operations make one or more of the following adjustments.

Grease Sales

In many establishments, particularly those that butcher meats on premises, raw fat is one of the byproducts of kitchen operation. Many of these places save the raw fat and sell it to rendering companies, which convert it to industrial fats and oils. The sale of this fat at so much per pound results in income to the establishment, which is generally treated as a credit to cost.

Steward Sales

In some hotels, and occasionally in restaurants, employees are permitted to purchase food at cost for their own use. Employees will sometimes take advantage of this possibility for special family occasions when, for example, a particular cut and grade of meat was not available in local supermarkets. When steward sales are permitted, the resulting income is considered a credit to cost, reducing periodic cost by the value of the raw foods sold to employees. Were this procedure not followed, the cost of these foods would be included wrongfully in cost figures.

Gratis to Bars

In many establishments the kitchen is expected to produce various hot and cold hors d'oeuvres that are given away at the bar. Since the purpose of this is to promote beverage sales, it seems logical to reflect the cost of the hors d'oeuvres in the cost of operating the beverage department, and to credit food cost for their value.

Promotion Expense

In cases where the owner or manager of the operation has occasion to entertain persons who may bring in business, food is consumed but sales revenue is not increased because no one pays the check. If management seeks food cost figures that are as accurate as possible, it becomes necessary to credit food cost for the value of foods so consumed and to charge their cost to another account, such as promotion expense.

DETERMINING COST OF FOOD CONSUMED

When the above are taken into account, the monthly determination of cost of food consumed takes the following form:

		Opening Inventory
	+	Purchases
	=	Total Available for Sale
	−	Closing Inventory
	=	Cost of Food Issued
Add:		Cooking Liquor
		Transfers from other units
Subtract:		Food to Bar (Directs)
		Transfers to other units
		Grease Sales
		Steward Sales
		Gratis to Bars
		Promotion Expense
		Cost of Food Consumed

While use of the above expanded formula will yield the cost of food consumed, it must be noted that not all of the food consumed results in increases in sales revenue. In most establishments, employees eat on premises as a matter of course and are not charged for the food they consume. Therefore, to determine the cost of food sold, it is necessary to subtract the cost of employee meals from the cost of food consumed.

Cost of Employee Meals

While there are numerous ways of dealing with the cost of employee meals, the four techniques that follow serve to illustrate those that foodservice operators most commonly employ.

One approach involves separate issue requisitions; this requires that employees be given food other than that which is prepared for customers. All food used in the preparation of employee meals must be issued separately and listed on requisitions, which are kept separately from all other requisitions used by the establishment. When the food issued is so listed, the requisitions may be costed in the normal way, thus determining the cost of food for employee meals. This approach is perhaps best suited to those establishments large enough to maintain a separate preparation area and separate dining room for employees. Thus it may be used in some of the largest hotels, but in few restaurants.

A somewhat more common approach is for the manager to direct the chef to prepare specific meals that will cost no more than a certain amount per employee. This amount will be credited to food cost for each employee, and it is then necessary only to keep some reasonable record of the number of employees who are fed each day. This number, multiplied by the preestablished cost per meal, will give the cost of employee meals for the day.

Because it is very difficult in some establishments to keep a record of the number of employees who are fed each day, management will sometimes take the simple course of telling the chef that food cost will be credited for a specific number of dollars per day to cover the cost of all employee meals, regardless of the number who actually eat. It is then up to the chef to estimate the number who may eat, and either prepare food that will not exceed the cost guideline or offer employees food prepared for customers that does not exceed the permissible cost.

Another technique requires that all employees who eat record their selections on checks that resemble guest checks used in the dining room. The menu price is recorded next to each selection. Employees are not asked to pay these checks, which are totaled for the month. The total is then multiplied by the average food cost percent in recent periods to arrive at a reasonable cost figure for employee meals for that period.

By means of one of these techniques, or some other alternative, it is possible to determine the cost of employee meals. When this has been determined, it may be deducted from the cost of food consumed to determine cost of food sold, the figure that should be used for establishing the cost-to-sales ratio, or cost percent. To the extent that some operators fail to take employee meals into account when calculating food cost, they are overstating cost and distorting the food cost percent.

DETERMINING COST OF FOOD SOLD

Using all of the above adjustments, the calculation of cost of food sold in the month of March for the restaurant previously described is as follows:

	Opening Inventory		$2,000
	+ Purchases		6,000
	Total Available for Sale		8,000
	– Closing Inventory		3,000
	Cost of Food Issued		5,000
Add:	Cooking Liquor	$200	
	Transfers from other units	$250	450
		subtotal	5,450
Subtract:	Food to Bar (Directs)	$ 68	
	Transfers to other units	$349	
	Grease Sales	27	
	Steward Sales	12	
	Gratis to Bar	72	
	Promotion Expense	22	550
	Cost of Food Consumed		4,900
Less:	Cost of Employee Meals		300
	Net Cost of Food Sold		4,600, or $.307 per dollar of sale.

Using the sales figure of $15,000 previously given, food cost percent is 30.7%, 2.6 percentage points lower than it appeared to be before the adjustments were made.

Although this information is interesting, it is not as relevant as when it is compared with figures for similar periods. Such comparisons are facilitated when current and past figures are recorded side by side on reports to management.

REPORTS TO MANAGEMENT

Once food costs and cost percentages have been determined, they can be reported to management. The nature of the report must be determined separately for each individual establishment or chain, based on management's information needs as well as the food controller's ability to supply it. When the food control system is somewhat complex, more detailed information can be furnished. In such instances, management is better informed, and thus better equipped to make decisions.

Although management reports differ from place to place, a reasonable number have some points in common. For this reason, it will be worthwhile to generalize these points of commonality and to illustrate several types of reports that some establishments might find useful—from the comparatively simple to the more complex.

In some smaller establishments, where there are few formal control procedures and no specific control personnel, it is often impossible to prepare formal reports more frequently than once a month. These monthly reports are based on information furnished by an accountant, who often prepares them between the first and tenth days of a month for the preceding month. The figures are taken solely from the accounting records of the business and indicate the food cost and food cost percentage based on purchases and inventory, as illustrated previously. Simple report forms are available from stationers. However, reports to management should always be based on management's need for information, not on the availability of a particular form. If no appropriate form exists, it is not difficult to devise one that will meet a particular operation's needs.

The form illustrated in figure 8.3 is possibly one of the simplest that might be devised for reporting to management.

FIGURE 8.3

	July 19X2	*July 19X1*
Food Sales	$15,000	$14,000
Net Cost of Food Sold	$ 4,600	$ 4,340
Food Cost Percent	30.7%	31.0%

Current figures are in the first column, and the figures for the previous year are in the second. When both are available, side by side, it is possible to compare them and to make a judgment about the relative effectiveness of current operations. Thus, if the 31.0% cost-to-sales ratio for the same period last year had been acceptable to management, it is likely that the 30.7% figure this year would also be acceptable, provided there had been no significant changes in menu or operating procedure and no significant drop in sales.

In some instances, particularly when figures for previous periods have been unacceptable, it is possible to judge the effectiveness of changes made with the goal of improving performance. If, for example, comparisons were made between two consecutive months, as in figure 8.4, it would be possible to tell whether changes instituted because of unacceptable results for one month had the desired effect in the following month.

FIGURE 8.4

	July 19X2	*June 19X2*
Food Sales	$15,000	$12,000
Net Cost of Food Sold	$ 4,600	$ 4,560
Food Cost Percent	30.7%	38.0%

If management had considered the cost-to-sales ratio of 38.0% in June unacceptable and instituted changes to bring about a reduction in the figure for July, it would be possible to make some judgments about the effectiveness of the changes. In the instance cited, it is possible that the reduction in the cost percentage from 38.0% to 30.7% would be considered acceptable and the procedural change judged effective, so that it would become a permanent part of the procedures used daily in the future.

The cost percentage may be a measure of the effectiveness of the business. It will be useful to compare it to similar measures of effectiveness for other months. If the cost percentage for this month is approximately what it was in other months, and if the cost percentage had been considered satisfactory in other months, then it might well be considered satisfactory now, providing there has been no significant change in menu or purchase prices. However, if there has been some major change, if the cost percentage is considerably higher or lower this month, we would probably want to discover the reasons for the change. Once the reasons are known, steps may be taken to ensure that it will or will not happen again.

Operating figures and comparisons between them are a little like sightings taken by mariners. No one sailing a ship across several thousand miles of ocean would dream of setting a course on leaving port and not taking various kinds of readings during the voyage. Anyone who did that would probably find himself some considerable distance from his destination at the end of the voyage. During the voyage, readings are frequently taken to determine the ship's location. Then comparisons are made with a chart of the course to determine how far the ship is off course, and corrections are made to bring the ship back to the course set for it. The more frequently this is done, the closer the ship will stay on its original course. If readings are taken infrequently, the ship will have strayed considerably off course, and considerable time and money may be lost in coming back on course. In the food business, monthly readings on the course of the business are usually too infrequent. The business can stray quite far off course during the month and can be brought back into line only at considerable difficulty and expense.

The difficulty with relying on the cost percentage calculation is that it is often impossible to determine why changes occur from month to month. One cannot always look back over a period of three or four weeks with any degree of accuracy, unless significant records are available. It is hard to recollect what happened two or three days ago, let alone what happened weeks ago. When causes cannot be determined, it is almost impossible to effect changes.

In addition, it is too late for any changes in methods and procedures to have any beneficial effects on what happened during the period that has passed. If the cost percentage for March was a disaster, we must still live with the results of March forever. The best we can hope for is that changes we make will effect significant improvements in April.

In recognition of this, many establishments operate with daily or weekly reports, with varying degrees of complexity. In general, the more frequent the reports and the more detailed the information rendered, the better will be the oportunities for management to control events and to ensure that the events conform to objectives.

For those reasons, many larger restaurants prefer to have cost percentages and other operating figures calcuated more frequently, often on a daily basis. The manager who can find out what happened yesterday has a better opportunity to get at the causes and direct necessary changes immediately, because the causes of problems can be better located when no great time span exists between the problem and the considerations of its causes.

Daily costing procedures and daily reports to management will be discussed in Chapter 9.

INVENTORY TURNOVER

Sound food management demands that sufficient supplies of food be available for use when needed. However, excessive amounts on hand leads to (1) spoilage, because food must be held too long before being used; (2) excessive capital tied up in inventory; (3) higher than necessary labor cost to handle the greater amount of food; (4) greater than necessary space allocated to storage; and (5) unwarranted opportunities for theft.

Large establishments need greater storage space and more food in storage than smaller ones. All foodservice establishments have slow periods during the year when less food than normal is needed on the premises. Thus, it is impossible to establish a set number of food items that should be in the storeroom or a set dollar valuation for food in inventory. However, management must in some way determine that appropriate—but not excess—levels of food are kept in inventory.

One commonly accepted method is to calculate how often the inventory of food on hand has been ordered and used during a period of time. For example, if one were to order sufficient food to last one full year, most reasonable people would agree that the amount was excessive and would lead to waste, inefficiency, and greater than necessary costs. On the other hand, if one were to order enough food to last only one day, reasonable people would agree that greater amounts should be ordered and that savings could result by purchasing in larger quantities. Somewhere between the two extremes is an idealized amount of food to have on hand for a specific period. This amount will vary from place to place and will be determined by many factors including the amount of cash available for such purposes, the space available for storage, and the time necessary to receive food once it is ordered. For most restaurants an amount to last one or two weeks is considered normal, and we will use that range as our guide.

To measure how often food has been ordered and used, food operators have historically calculated the frequency of turnover of the food in the inventory. For example, if a restaurant orders and uses an inventory two times each month, an inventory turnover of twenty-four times each year would result and is in approximate agreement with our guide. One should note that all food is not turned over during the prescribed period of time. Perishables will turn over daily, and some canned items will turn over much less frequently.

Calculations are typically made when physical inventories are taken—once each month. The formula for this calculation is as follows:

$$\text{Average Inventory for the Month} = \frac{\text{Opening Inventory} + \text{Closing Inventory}}{2}$$

$$\text{Inventory Turnover for the Month} = \frac{\text{Food Cost for the Month}}{\text{Average Food Inventory}}$$

Putting actual figures to the equation, the inventory turnover for Restaurant A might look like this:

$$\text{Opening inventory} = \$5{,}650$$

$$\text{Closing inventory} = \$5{,}350$$

$$\text{Food Cost} = \$9{,}900$$

$$\frac{\$5{,}650 + \$5{,}350}{2} = \$5{,}500 \text{ (average inventory)}$$

$$\frac{\$9{,}900}{\$5{,}500} = 1.8 \text{ (inventory turnover for month)}$$

If each month's results were the same, the total for the year would be 21.6 times each year, or once every 2.4 weeks, slightly greater than our guide of once every one or two weeks.

The astute student will question the accuracy of the average inventory figure calculated above, for there is an assumption, perhaps an invalid one, that the opening and closing inventory figures used truly represent levels of inventory during the month, and that is not always and perhaps might not typically be the case. It is possible for inventories to be at a much higher figure during the month, no ordering taking place the last week of the month, and the ending figure a result of a planned usage of food to bring inventory to a desired level. This does happen frequently. But the only alternative would be to take a physical inventory more frequently, a procedure that in itself is costly.

EDP APPLICATIONS

If all quantities received and issued have been entered into computer memory, then it would be possible for the computer to provide a report of the quantity of each item in inventory at any given time. The most appropriate time for this report would be at the end of a month, the time when physical inventory is taken. The computer would not eliminate the need for physical inventory, for it would not have data concerning actual quantities in inventory, but only data concerning the quantities that should be found in inventory. This is an important distinction. If, for example, food has been used or stolen without beng recorded in a terminal, then such usage or pilferage will not be reflected in computer output. However, if physical inventory is taken and compared item by item with computer output, management can determine the extent of unauthorized use of food. This would be considered some measure of the extent to which employees were following the standard procedures established for operation.

The physical inventory will provide information that can be used to update the data in computer memory. With this data updated and current at the end of the accounting period, it will be possible to obtain a report showing the value of inventory by one of the methods previously discussed. It will be readily apparent that the calculation of the closing inventory value can be completed much faster by computer than by manual means.

With the above data available in computer memory, it would be very simple to determine cost of food issued. It would also be possible to determine cost of food consumed and cost of food sold, but only if additional data were input.

The computer would be extremely useful for generating reports to management for the current period and for such previous periods as required, provided, of course, that the data for periods were retained in memory for future use. These reports could be either of the relatively simple variety illustrated in this chapter, or of the more extensive and detailed types to be seen in the following chapter.

CHAPTER ESSENTIALS

In this chapter we described the procedure for taking monthly physical inventory of food and discussed five methods for assigning values to the foods in this inventory. After illustrating each of these methods, we showed the calculations necessary to determine food costs. We defined and differentiated among cost of food issued, cost of food consumed, and cost of food sold, and described the way in which each of these is calculated, taking into consideration transfers, grease sales, steward sales, promotion expense, and employees' meals. We illustrated the calculation of food cost percent and cost per dollar sale and showed how these figures are commonly reported to management for the purposes of making comparisons with other operating periods and judging operational performance. We described and illustrated the calculation of inventory turnover rate and discussed its significance to foodservice managers. Finally, we described how computers can be used to determine employee adherence to standard procedures for issuing food, as well as inventory valuations and for preparing management reports.

QUESTIONS AND PROBLEMS

1 In each of several restaurants, the following totals values were recorded during the month of November. Calculate issues for each

a	Opening inventory	$1,500.00
	Purchases	4,600.00
	Closing inventory	1,722.00
b	Closing inventory	$12,083.00
	Opening inventory	10,371.00
	Purchases	28,468.00
c	Purchases	$65,851.08
	Closing inventory	18,335.10
	Opening inventory	19,874.77

2 Given the following information for each of several restaurants, calculate both cost of food issued and cost of food consumed for each.

a	Purchases	$8,300.00
	Opening inventory	2,688.00
	Closing inventory	2,540.00
	Grease sales	76.00
	Cooking liquor	94.00
	Gratis to bar	119.00
b	Food to bar (Directs)	$189.00
	Closing inventory	6,647.00
	Transfers to other units	339.00
	Purchases	19,472.00
	Steward sales	53.00
	Transfers from other units	223.00
	Opening inventory	6,531.00

c

Opening inventory	6,622.40
Transfers from other units	47.35
Cooking liquor	253.65
Purchases	24,182.55
Closing inventory	6,719.30
Transfers to other units	347.60
Food to bar (Directs)	337.40
Grease sales	91.85
Gratis to bar	177.35

3 In each of the following cases, determine the cost of employee meals for the month.

- **a** In March 337 employees were given lunch, and 381 were given dinner. Managment credits food cost figures $.70 per employee for lunch and $1.10 for dinner.
- **b** In September, in a certain restaurant the employees were required to record their food selections on checks and to enter next to each selection its menu selling price. The sales value of the food employees consumed was found to total $7,826.95. In recent months the food cost percent has been approximately 35%.
- **c** In the ABC Restaurant in February 19X1, the chef has been directed to prepare food for the employees at a cost not to exceed $25 per day, regardless of the number of employees fed. This particular establishment is closed on Mondays and open the other six days of the week.

4 Given the following information for each of several restaurants, calculate the cost of food sold for the month.

a

Cooking liquor	$210.50
Steward sales	27.58
Purchases	12,339.42
Food to bar (Directs)	201.38
Gratis to bar	267.50
Grease sales	95.60
Closing inventory	4,278.37
Opening inventory	4,031.19
Employee meals:	
328 lunch @ $.65	
449 dinner @ $.95	

b

Closing inventory	$3,427.30
Grease sales	92.60
Purchases	11,230.45
Opening inventory	3,012.80

Transfers from other units	128.65
Cooking liquor	298.40
Gratis to bar	427.80
Food to bar (Directs)	312.45
Transfers to other units	155.75
Employee meals: $2,576.45 sales value; recent average food cost percent: 34.0%	

c

Purchases	68,543.36
Promotion expense	81.17
Grease sales	167.42
Closing inventory	20,963.71
Gratis to bar	58.73
Transfers from other units	637.38
Food to bar (Directs)	296.35
Opening inventory	22,687.40
Transfers to other units	784.29
Cooking iquor	543.18

Employee meals:

Executives: $1,833.75 sales value; recent average food cost percent: 31.0%

Other staff: 1,422 Breakfasts @ $.55
1,208 Lunches @ $.80
1,012 Dinners @ $1.05

5 Use the food cost figures determined in question 4 to determine food cost percent and cost per dollar sale figures for each of the restaurants, given the sales figures below:

a $26,173.55
b $25,819.45
c $191,405.95

6 The inventory records of the Yellow Dog Restaurant reveal the following information about one of the items carried in the food inventory for the month of January:

1/1	Opening inventory	12 units valued at $1.05 per unit
1/5	Purchased	18 units @ $1.15 per unit
1/12	Purchased	18 units @ $1.20 per unit
1/19	Purchased	12 units @ $1.30 per unit
1/26	Purchased	6 units @ $1.40 per unit

On January 31, the physical inventory shows nine units left in stock.

Determine the value of the closing inventory of the item, as well as the cost of the units issued, using each of the five possible methods illustrated and discussed in this chapter.

7 Given the following information, taken from the records of several restaurants for the month of May 19X4, determine the rate of inventory turnover for each.

a	Opening inventory	$3,287.40
	Closing inventory	3,322.60
	Food cost	13,220.00
b	Food cost	$18,448.30
	Opening inventory	6,327.65
	Closing inventory	6,581.75
c	Closing inventory	$21,971.38
	Food cost	67,346.93
	Opening inventory	23,168.49

8 Define each of the following terms: Opening inventory, Closing inventory, Average inventory, and Rate of inventory turnover.

9 Explain and compare the following: Cost of food issued, cost of food consumed, and cost of food sold.

10 List as many possible causes as you can for each of the following:

a Food cost percent increase from one month to the next.
b Food cost percent decrease from one month to the next.
c Increase in inventory turnover rate from one period to the next.
d Decrease in inventory turnover rate from one period to the next.

11 Explain how the computer may be useful in determining the extent to which employees have been following standard operating procedures in withdrawing items from inventory.

12 Why would a computer printout of closing inventory quantities and values be less than accurate unless updated by data from a physical inventory?

chapter 9

Daily Food Cost Determination

Learning Objectives

After reading and studying this chapter, the student should be able to:

1. Compute the daily cost of food sold.
2. Compute the daily food cost percentage and cumulative cost percent.
3. Prepare and interpret a daily report of food sold and food cost.
4. Establish the value of the book inventory.
5. Explain the relationship between book and actual inventory.
6. Outline various causes for differences in book and actual inventory.
7. Discuss the use of computers for generating daily reports of food costs and food sales for management.

The difficulty with the monthly review of operating figures is the length of time between reports. When the figures for one month reveal the development of problems, and steps are taken to eliminate the problems, it is necessary to wait a full month to determine the effectiveness of the steps. If erroneous judgments are made about causes of excessive cost, and the measures taken are based on those erroneous judgments, it is a full month before the next report reveals that the steps have not had the desired effect. This delay can be very costly. To avoid this delay and to avail management of more timely figures for making day-to-day operating decisions, a number of the larger and better organized restaurant operations employ daily food cost calculations. It is possible to determine the daily cost for any operation if certain procedures and forms discussed in previous chapters are used. Since all foods are categorized as either Directs or Stores in food control, the total costs for these two will be the two basic components of the daily food cost.

All Directs are charged to the food cost as received. Therefore it is necessary to determine the total of Directs received on any given day. This figure is readily available if the receiving clerk's daily report is completed each day. The total figure in the Directs column on the report for any day is the figure a food controller will use in the daily calculations.

On the other hand, Stores are charged to the food cost as issued, so the food controller must determine the value of the Stores issued each day. Since all issues must be listed on requisitions, the determination is not difficult. To determine the value of the issues, the food controller merely totals the values of all requisitions for any day.

In some operations, where transfers are made between the food and beverage departments or between units in a chain organization, or where other types of transactions—such as grease sales, steward sales, and promotion expense—are common, other figures must be taken into account. For example, any Directs charged to food cost as received but subsequently transferred to the beverage department would be subtracted from food cost figures. These items—typically oranges, lemons, and the like—would be listed on a transfer memo. In this case it would be necessary to determine their value and subtract it from cost figures. By the same token, the value of any alcoholic beverages transferred from the beverage department to the food department for use in food preparation would be added to food cost. In addition, a reasonable number of establishments even take the cost of employee meals into account on a daily basis.

Thus, the daily cost of food can be determined in the following way:

  Cost of Directs (from the receiving clerk's daily report)
\+ Cost of Stores (from requisitions, or from requisitions and meat tags, depending on the procedure followed)
\+ Adjustments for transfers from the beverage department to the food department, or for transfers in from other units
− Adjustments for transfers from the kitchen to the bar

(including food to bar—Directs, and Gratis to Bar, steward sales, grease sales, and promotion expense)

= Cost of Food Consumed
– Cost of Employee Meals

= Daily Cost of Food Sold

Once the daily food cost has been determined, the daily sales figure must be obtained, usually from accounting records. When both food cost and food sales figures are known, the daily cost-to-sales ratio can be determined.

However, by itself this daily food cost percentage may not be a very meaningful figure. Direct purchases may be made every other day, for any one of a number of reasons, and this will affect the daily food cost, making it artificially higher on the days when they are purchased, and correspondingly lower on the other days. In addition, some foods may be issued on days prior to the days when they will be used. Salt, for example, might be issued to the kitchen once a week to avoid the necessity for daily requisitioning of that item. In other cases, wholesale cuts of meat might be issued a day in advance for butchering. Both cases will have the effect of raising the food cost percentage on the day of issue, because the food is not reflected in sales until one or more days later.

To partially overcome the problem of an artificially high food cost percentage one day and a low food cost percentage another, many establishments also calculate the food cost percentage to date, which is the cumulative food cost percentage for a period. The food cost percentage to date takes into account the costs for all the days so far in the period, as well as all of the sales so far. In order to arrive at a cumulative cost percentage to date, the cost to date is divided by the sales to date.

A simple form (see figure 9.1) can be devised and inexpensively reproduced to give the procedure order and continuity. In order to maintain simplicity for purposes of discussion, we have limited the number of adjustment columns to two—one for additions to cost and the other for subtractions from cost. However, in practice there is no barrier to increasing the number of columns to whatever number would be necessary for achieving the desired degree of accuracy in any particular operation. The procedure may be followed on a daily cumulative basis for any number of days, depending on the information needs of management. In many cases, the figures are maintained on a weekly basis, and in others they are maintained over the period of a month.

An alternative form (see Figure 9.2) is useful for those establishments that use meat tags and wish to have separate figures for meats and staples. Inasmuch

FIGURE 9.1

Date	Directs	Stores	Beverage to Food	Food to Beverage	Cost today	Cost to date	Sales today	Sales to date	Cost % today	Cost % to date
3/1	50	100	—	—	150		500		30%	
3/2	25	75			100	250	250	750	40%	33.3%

FIGURE 9.2

Date	Directs	Meat	Stores	Cook Liq.	Food To Bar	Total Cost		Total Sales		Food Cost%		Food Inventory		
						Today	To Date	Today	To Date	Today	To Date	Purchases	Issue	Balance
10/15	500	275	100	20	10	885	885	2,000	2,000	44.3%	44.3%			
10/16	325	275	100	20	20	700	1,585	2,100	4,100	33.3%	38.7%			
10/17	400	300	125	25	20	830	2,415	2,200	6,300	37.7%	38.3%			
10/18	375	290	115	30	25	785	3,200	2,450	8,750	32.0%	36.6%			
10/19	490	450	105	30	30	1,045	4,245	3,400	12,150	30.7%	34.9%			
10/20	80	525	140	40	40	745	4,990	3,600	15,750	20.7%	31.7%			

as meats represent the largest element in the food cost, the form gives a clearer picture of where the money is being spent. Since meat tags are attached to requisitions, the food controller can simply total the values of the meat tags attached to requisitions and subtract that total value from the requisition total in order to arrive at figures for both categories.

The form illustrated in figure 9.2 includes three additional columns on the right for purchases, issues, and inventory. These columns are used to maintain a daily balance of Stores inventory, and are discussed in detail later in this chapter (see figure 9.8).

In some very large establishments, where the need for detailed information is greater, and personnel exist to compile the figures, costs are sometimes divided into even greater numbers of categories. Directs might be broken down into the costs of vegetables, fruits, dairy products, and so on. Meats might be divided into figures for beef, veal, lamb, etc. Figure 9.3 illustrates a form on which such a breakdown is accomplished.

DAILY REPORTS

Given the tools developed in the preceding chapter, it is possible to construct a report that reflects the position of the operation for that day, and for all the days to date for the period, and that at the same time compares these figures to those for a similar period. A simple report that accomplishes this is illustrated in figure 9.4.

FIGURE 9.4
Report to Management 10/20/—

	Today	*To Date*	
		This Week	*Last Week*
Food Cost	$ 745	$ 4,990	$ 4,200
Food Sales	$3,600	$15,750	$12,600
Cost Percentage	20.7%	31.7%	33.3%

When the position is set forth daily in this manner and compared to one or more recent periods, and determinations are made about the current operations' effectiveness, the causes of undesirable results then can be investigated while the events are relatively fresh in the minds of those concerned. Thus, in effect, the course of operations can be reset daily. If, for example, investigation reveals that a high cost percentage is the result of overpurchasing of Directs, plans can be made to use up the quantities on hand before more purchases are made. This will keep the cost of Directs down for a day or so and will have immediate impact on the cost-to-sales ratio. Another instance, the requisitioning of too many items from Stores, might cause a high food cost. In such a case, plans might be made for using up the quantities issued to the kitchen before additional quantities are

FIGURE 9.3
Food Cost Analysis—October 19—

1 Date	2 Day	3 Vegetables	4 Fruits	5 Dairy	6 Bakery	7 Total Directs	8 Beef	9 Poultry	10 Provisions	11 Other
10/1	Mon.	150.00	100.00	75.00	75.00	400.00	200.00	100.00	50.00	25.00
2	Tues.	100.00	50.00	25.00	25.00	200.00	100.00	50.00	40.00	10.00
3	Wed.	175.00	125.00	25.00	25.00	350.00	225.00	125.00	20.00	20.00
4	Thurs.	100.00	50.00	50.00	25.00	225.00	100.00	75.00	15.00	30.00
5	Fri.	175.00	100.00	75.00	75.00	425.00	250.00	125.00	25.00	50.00
6	Sat.	—	—	50.00	25.00	75.00	70.00	10.00	—	10.00
		700.00	425.00	300.00	250.00	1,675.00	945.00	485.00	150.00	145.00
10/8	Mon.	175.00	125.00	100.00	50.00	450.00	225.00	100.00	75.00	20.00
9	Tues.	100.00	75.00	25.00	25.00	225.00	100.00	75.00	—	10.00
10	Wed.	125.00	100.00	25.00	50.00	300.00	200.00	100.00	50.00	15.00
11	Thurs.	75.00	50.00	25.00	25.00		75.00	25.00	40.00	20.00
12	Fri.	200.00	100.00	100.00	25.00	425.00	250.00	150.00	40.00	—
13	Sat.	—	—	50.00	40.00	90.00	75.00	15.00	—	15.00
		675.00	450.00	325.00	215.00	1,665.00	925.00	465.00	245.00	80.00
10/15	Mon.	225.00	125.00	100.00	50.00	500.00	200.00	50.00	25.00	—
16	Tues.	100.00	100.00	75.00	50.00	325.00	100.00	125.00	25.00	25.00
17	Wed.	150.00	100.00	100.00	50.00	400.00	150.00	100.00	30.00	20.00
18	Thurs.	175.00	100.00	75.00	25.00	375.00	125.00	115.00	25.00	25.00
19	Fri.	200.00	150.00	115.00	25.00	490.00	225.00	150.00	75.00	—
20	Sat.	—	—	40.00	40.00	80.00	300.00	150.00	50.00	25.00
		850.00	575.00	505.00	240.00	2,170.00	1,100.00	690.00	230.00	95.00

FIGURE 9.3
(continued)

12 Total Meat	13 Total Store-room	14 Bar → Food Cooking Liquor	15 Food → Bar Directs	16 Total Today	17 Costs to Date	18 Total Today	19 Sales to Date	20 Food Cost % Today	21 Food Cost % to Date
375.00	135.00	—	10.00	900.00	900.00	2,000.00	2,000.00	45.0%	45.0%
200.00	150.00	—	—	550.00	1,450.00	1,500.00	3,500.00	36.7%	41.4%
395.00	145.00	20.00	10.00	900.00	2,350.00	2,700.00	6,200.00	33.3%	37.9%
220.00	120.00	5.00	20.00	550.00	2,900.00	1,800.00	8,000.00	30.6%	36.3%
450.00	240.00	20.00	10.00	1,125.00	4,025.00	3,600.00	11,600.00	31.3%	34.7%
90.00	135.00	25.00	25.00	300.00	4,325.00	1,300.00	12,900.00	23.1%	33.5%
1,730.00	925.00								
420.00	160.00	30.00	10.00	1,050.00	1,050.00	2,000.00	2,000.00	54.5%	52.5%
185.00	135.00	10.00	5.00	550.00	1,600.00	1,600.00	3,600.00	34.4%	44.4%
365.00	115.00	—	5.00	775.00	2,375.00	2,200.00	5,800.00	35.2%	40.9%
160.00	90.00	—	—	425.00	2,800.00	1,400.00	7,200.00	30.4%	38.9%
440.00	215.00	30.00	10.00	1,100.00	3,900.00	3,400.00	10,600.00	32.4%	36.8%
105.00	105.00	25.00	25.00	300.00	4,200.00	2,000.00	12,600.00	15.0%	33.3%
1,675.00	820.00								
275.00	100.00	20.00	10.00	885.00	885.00	2,000.00	2,000.00	44.3%	44.3%
275.00	100.00	20.00	20.00	700.00	1,585.00	2,100.00	4,100.00	33.3%	38.7%
300.00	125.00	25.00	20.00	830.00	2,415.00	2,200.00	6,300.00	37.7%	38.3%
290.00	115.00	30.00	25.00	785.00	3,200.00	2,450.00	8,750.00	32.0%	36.6%
450.00	105.00	30.00	30.00	1,045.00	4,245.00	3,400.00	12,150.00	30.7%	34.9%
525.00	140.00	40.00	40.00	745.00	4,990.00	3,600.00	15,750.00	20.7%	31.7%
2,115.00	685.00								

requisitioned, thus keeping down the cost of issues. When daily food costs are determined, the effect of these kinds of measures can be assessed daily, with the expected effect that by the end of the operating period, costs will be in line with management's goals. This is not always the case, but it is always more in the realm of possibility when food costs are determined daily.

Making intelligent plans to eliminate undesirable effects is never possible until causes are known. Occasionally, the determination of causes is simple. More frequently, the causes are several and are not readily determined from the figures on the reports previously illustrated. In some smaller operations, it is possible to go into the kitchen and make a complete first-hand investigation of all possible causes until the correct ones are found. In larger operations, this is not usually the case. To reduce the amount of time and effort involved in finding the causes of higher-than-necessary costs and then simplify the task, some food controllers develop more complex figures and reports. Figure 9.5 gives an example of one possible set of figures to help accomplish this end.

FIGURE 9.5
Report to Management, 10/20/—

			To Date	
	Today	*Same Day Last Week*	*This Week*	*Last Week*
Food Sales	$3,600	$2,000	$15,750	$12,600
Food Cost	$ 745	$ 300	$ 4,990	$ 4,200
Food Cost Percentage	20.7%	15.0%	31.7%	33.3%
Cost Breakdown:				
Directs	$ 80	$ 90	$ 2,170	$ 1,665f
Stores	$ 665	$ 210	$ 2,800	$ 2,495
Meats	$ 525	$ 105	$ 2,115	$ 1,675
Groceries	$ 140	$ 105	$ 685	$ 820

A variation on this technique involves using the same form of report, but shows the cost breakdown in terms of ratios rather than raw-dollar figures. This is particularly useful in operations offering a relatively fixed menu. Ratios are established between direct costs and sales, both today and to date, and the same is done for other costs as well. In the example given in figure 9.6, it will be seen that while sales figures have varied somewhat, the ratio of cost components to sales have not, suggesting that no significant changes have taken place in operating procedures. If one or more of the ratios changes considerably over what it should be, based on past events, causes can be investigated and changes made. If, for example, the cost-to-sales ratio had gone up, and the ratio of meat cost to total sales jumped drastically while other ratios remained approximately the same, the cause of the increase would be effectively localized. The food controller could disregard Directs and groceries when searching for a cause for the increase, and instead look into possible problems in the category of meats.

FIGURE 9.6
Daily Food Cost Report

Day Saturday Date 10/20/— W/E 10/20

Description	*Today*	*To Date* *This Week*	*To Date* *Last Week*	*To Date* *Same Wk, Last Mo.*
Food Sales	3,600	15,750	12,600	
Food Cost	745	4,990	4,200	
Food Cost %	20.7%	31.7%	33.3%	

Item	*Vegetables*	*Fruits*	*Dairy*	*Bakery*	*Total Directs*	
This Week	850	575	505	240	2,170	13.8%
Last Week	675	450	325	215	1,665	13.2%

Item	*Beef*	*Poultry*	*Provisions*	*Other*	*Total Meat*		*Total Stores*	
This Week	1,100	690	230	95	2,115	13.4%	685	4.3%
Last Week	925	465	245	80	1,675	13.3%	820	6.5%

Item	*Cooking Liquor*	*Food to Bar (Directs)*
This Week	165	145
Last Week	95	45

Where time and personnel exist to do the job, it is possible to extend this approach and develop ratios of costs to sales for individual categories of foods, as illustrated in figure 9.7. This technique is even more effective in localizing problems and in permitting more intensive investigation than might otherwise be possible.

In many instances, changes in these ratios may be caused by changes in customer ordering habits. However, in cases where demand has remained constant and market prices relatively so, increases in these ratios will be due to problems existing in kitchen operation. When thus localized, they may be more easily uncovered.

BOOK VERSUS ACTUAL INVENTORY COMPARISON

In Chapter 8 we discussed the reasons and procedures for determining the value of closing inventory at the end of each monthly period. Once completed, the closing inventory valuation is considered a real or actual inventory valuation and is so recorded in the business's financial records and statements. This figure includes the value of all items counted in the inventory—those that were physically present and could be found, counted, and valued.

FIGURE 9.7
Daily Food Cost Report

Day Saturday   Date 10/20/—   W/E 10/20

		To Date		
Description	*Today*	*This Week*	*Last Week*	*Same Wk, Last Mo.*
Food Sales	3,600	15,750	12,600	
Food Cost	745	4,990	4,200	
Food Cost %	20.7%	31.7%	33.3%	

Item	*Vegetables*	*Fruits*	*Dairy*	*Bakery*	*Total Directs*
This Week	5.4%	3.7%	3.2%	1.5%	13.8%
Last Week	5.4%	3.6%	2.6%	1.7%	13.2%

Item	*Beef*	*Poultry*	*Provisions*	*Other*	*Total Meat*	*Total Stores*
This Week	7.0%	4.4%	1.5%	.6%	13.4%	4.3%
Last Week	7.3%	3.7%	1.9%	.6%	13.3%	6.5%

	Cooking Liquor	*Food to Bar (Directs)*
This Week	1.0%	.9%
Last Week	.8%	.6%

Some foodservice operators next determine what the value of the closing inventory should be, and compare that figure, known as book inventory, to the actual inventory figure established through taking a physical inventory at the close of the period. One method for establishing the value of the book inventory is readily available to those who maintain daily food cost figures in the manner illustrated in figure 9.2. Such a form provides the means for maintaining cumulative book inventory figures for any period, as shown in figure 9.8.

FIGURE 9.8

	Purchases	*Issues*	*Inventory (Balance)*
9/30			$6,305
10/1	273	510	6,068
10/2	946	350	6,664
10/3	498	540	6,622
10/4	734	340	7,016

The closing inventory for September becomes the opening inventory for October. To this figure of $6,305 must be added any Stores purchases received on October

1 as found recorded on the receiving clerk's daily report, described and discussed in Chapter 6. From those two must be subtracted the value of any Stores issued on that same day as found recorded on requisitions, or on a combination of requisitions and meat tags. Since the cost of meats and other issues from Stores has normally been recorded in appropriate columns on figure 9.2, one must really only transfer the total of those two to the Issues column. So to find the closing book inventory valuation for any day, one merely starts from the closing inventory valuation for the preceding day, adds any Stores purchases, and subtracts any Stores issues. This procedure may be followed daily throughout any period. If it is followed daily for a calendar month, the final figure represents the closing book value of the Stores inventory for that period.

It is possible to determine the closing book value of the Stores inventory in establishments that do not determine daily food cost figures, but only if some form of receiving report and daily issue requisitions is used. If such is the case, the calculation is as follows:

Opening Inventory (Closing Inventory for the preceding month)
\+ Purchases (total value of the Stores purchased for the period as listed on the receiving clerk's daily reports for the period)

= Total Available (total value of the Stores available for sale during the period)
− Issues (total value of foods listed on issue requisitions for the period)

= Closing Book Value of the Stores Inventory

Under ideal conditions, the values of the book inventory and the physical inventory should be the same. However, for a number of reasons, some usually acceptable and others never acceptable, this is seldom true. Some of the acceptable reasons include an occasional human error in costing out requisitions, the use of the most recent purchase price rather than actual purchase price in valuing the physical inventory, and the mismarking of actual purchase prices on items when that method is used. Reasons that are never acceptable include the issuing of Stores without requisitions, the disposing of meats that have been allowed to spoil, and the actual theft of food.

Depending on the volume involved, discrepancies of some small percentage between book inventory and physical inventory can often be attributed to acceptable causes and are of no further concern, except that discrepancies should be pointed out to the employees whose errors have caused them. However, when discrepancies reach an unacceptable level, the food controller has a responsibility to investigate the causes and take appropriate steps to ensure that the variance will be significantly reduced in future periods. This may involve reviewing control procedures for purchasing, receiving, storing, and issuing food and revising those procedures where necessary. It also may involve reviewing the practices of employees responsible for carrying out the control procedures and taking appropriate steps to ensure that established procedures will be followed more closely in the future. In extreme cases, the food controller may have to review all procedures and all employee practices in order to find causes. Once discovered, the causes can be reported to management for necessary action.

Taking an ending inventory is a vital part of the control procedure. As well as being necessary for accurately determining inventory values at the end of each month so that proper financial statements can be prepared, the determination of a closing inventory value permits the food controller to measure the effectiveness of receiving, storing, and issuing procedures. Significant differences between actual and book inventory figures serve as signals to the food controller that control procedures need investigating.

EDP APPLICATIONS

In previous chapters we discussed the possibility of entering into computer terminals data that reflect all purchases and issues of food. The entry of such data would be facilitated by assigning numerical codes to all food items. We might use four-digit codes. The first digit might differentiate between Directs and Stores; the second digit could be used to distinguish other food groups within either category (such as fruits, vegetables, baked goods, and dairy products within the general category of Directs); the third and fourth digits might identify the particular item (such as apples, bananas, grapefruit, and oranges). With a suitable applications program that records all Direct purchases as issues and thus charges to food cost, and all Stores issues as charges to cost, obtaining a report of daily food cost would be possible. This could be further refined by recording in the computer terminals any adjustments to cost, for transfers and other items, as the transactions occurred, thus making possible a daily food cost report of whatever degree of refinement were considered appropriate.

With the simple addition of one or more sales terminals of the type described in Chapter 4, management could ensure that all sales data were recorded in computer memory as well. This data, summarized by the computer into a daily sales figure and used together with a daily cost figure determined by the computer as described above, would enable management to obtain a daily food cost report of the type described earlier in the chapter.

By encoding in memory greater detail about food categories, possibly by the use of five- rather than four-digit codes, generating a more detailed report along the lines of that pictured in figure 9.3 would be entirely feasible. The form of such a report could also be structured similar to those in figures 9.6 and 9.7. Many managers would consider the summarized data included in such reports to be of greater value for day-to-day management decision making.

CHAPTER ESSENTIALS

In this chapter we showed how some establishments compute cost of food sold and food cost percent on both a daily and a cumulative basis, an elementary management information system designed to provide management with more timely data on operations than is available from monthly calculations described in the previous chapter. We illustrated and discussed various types of reports used to detail and compare information from the current operating period to that from previous periods. We demonstrated how book inventory may be calculated and how book and actual inventory figures may be compared for judging the effectiveness of various control and reporting procedures.

Finally, we described how using computers to obtain timely reports might enable management to make decisions much more quickly and easily than would have been possible if reports had to be presented manually.

QUESTIONS AND PROBLEMS

1 Compute the daily food costs, the cumulative food cost to date, and the corresponding cost percentages from the following data.

			Transfers		
Date	*Directs*	*Stores*	*Beverage to Food*	*Food to Beverage*	*Daily Sales*
5/1	$350	$350	-0-	-0-	$1,400
5/2	$250	$175	$25	-0-	$1,000
5/3	$135	$125	-0-	$10	$1,000
5/4	$ 75	$135	$10	$20	$ 500

2 Following the alternative form illustrated in Figure 9.2, compute the daily cost and cost percentage figures—as well as the cumulative cost, sales, and cost percentage figures—for the period indicated below from the figures given.

Date	*Directs*	*Meats*	*Stores*	*Beverage to Food*	*Food to Beverage*	*Daily Sales*
9/4	$400	$350	$150	-0-	$50	$2,550
9/5	$150	$200	$150	-0-	-0-	$1,500
9/6	$350	$450	$100	$50	-0-	$2,850
9/7	$200	$250	$150	-0-	-0-	$1,800
9/8	$450	$300	$150	-0-	$50	$3,325
9/9	$ 63	$ 47	$ 97	-0-	$ 7	$ 665

3 Use the information given below to prepare a daily and cumulative analysis of food costs, food sales, food cost percents, and inventory balances on a form such as that illustrated in Figure 9.2. The opening inventory figure for November 1 is $9,330.

November 1: From the Receiving Sheet: Directs, $403, and Stores, $736.
Meat Tags: $320. Requisitions: $271. Sales: $2,241.

November 2:	From the Receiving Sheet: Directs, $261, and Stores, $108. Meat Tags: $282. Requisitions: $183. Sales: $2,121.
November 3:	From the Receiving Sheet: Directs, $273, and Stores, $1,463. Meat Tags: $491. Requisitions: $330. Cooking Liquor: $33. Food to Bar (Directs): $24. Sales: $2,740.
November 4:	From the Receiving Sheet: Directs, $521, and Stores, $281. Meat Tags: $392. Requisitions: $552. Sales: $4,063.
November 5:	From the Receiving Sheet: Directs, $334, and Stores, $372. Meat Tags: $751. Requisitions: $470. Cooking Liquor: $19. Food to Bar (Directs): $29. Sales: $4,682.

4 Use the information given below to determine the book value of the Stores inventory on the morning of May 6.

Closing Inventory for April $11,353.40

5/1—Stores purchases:	$742.38	Stores issues:	$621.80
5/2—Stores purchases:	397.49	Stores issues:	516.76
5/3—Stores purchases:	619.66	Stores issues:	472.51
5/4—Stores purchases:	273.16	Stores issues:	845.26
5/5—Stores purchases:	824.93	Stores issues:	725.77

5 In each of the following cases, determine the book value of the closing inventory for the month of October.

a	Opening inventory:	$ 3,748.00
	Purchases:	22,162.00
	Issues:	21,477.00
b	Issues:	$44,227.60
	Purchases:	42,191.40
	Opening inventory:	15,308.70
c	Purchases:	$10,601.58
	Opening inventory:	4,219.66
	Issues:	9,862.43

6 Given the information below, find book value of the closing inventory as well as the dollar difference between book and actual inventory for the month of January.

a	Opening inventory:	$ 400
	Purchases:	1,200
	Issues:	900
	Actual value of closing inventory:	$600

b	Purchases:	$ 6,327
	Issues:	6,498
	Opening inventory:	2,184
	Actual value of closing inventory:	$1,912
c	Issues:	$12,395.62
	Opening inventory:	4,129.88
	Purchases:	11,623.71
	Actual value of the closing inventory:	$2,673.47

7 In each of the instances in question 6, calculate the difference between book and actual closing inventory figures as a percentage of issues.

8 Based on the dollar differences determined in question 6 and on the percentages calculated in question 7, which, if any, of the three cases in question 6 bears closer examination by a food controller? Justify your answer.

9 Assuming that one or more of the above cases need close examination, how would a food controller go about such an examination? What steps might you, as a food controller, recommend be taken?

10 What are some of the potential advantages of computing daily and cumulative food cost and food cost percents, rather than relying exclusively on end-of-month calculations?

11 Discuss the possible advantages and disadvantages of having reports for management of the complexity made possible by today's computers.

chapter 10

Production Standards and Portion Costs

Learning Objectives

After reading and studying this chapter, the student should be able to:

1 Define and illustrate by example:

  a standard cost of a food item
  b standard portion size of a food item
  c standard recipe for a food item

2 List reasons why standard cost, standard portion sizes, and standard recipes are important to the success of a restaurant.

3 Describe the need for the butcher test; outline the procedure used in performing the test; and perform various calculations leading to value per pound, value per portion, cost factor per pound, and cost factor per portion.

4 Apply the cost factors obtained in the butcher test and cooking loss test to determine the price per pound and price per portion of subsequent purchases of the same item.

5 Describe the need for the cooking loss test; outline the procedure used in performing the test; and perform various calculations leading to value per pound, value per portion, cost factor per pound, and cost factor per portion.

6 Calculate and use yield percentages to determine amounts to buy when planning a purchase.

7 Explain the use of computers in determining and updating standard portion costs, and in calculating purchase quantities.

We have discussed the computation of cost percentages and ratios of various kinds, and have concluded that it may be possible to uncover waste, inefficiency, and poor procedures once we have determined that percentages are unsatisfactory. However, it is difficult to determine specifically what that ratio should be. And as costs change, menu prices change, or portion sizes change, the ratios developed must also change. While ratios will give an indication that something may be wrong, they do not tell us the extent to which money is being lost because of waste or inefficiency.

In this and following chapters we will discuss ways of determining the extent of waste or inefficiency. Specifically, we shall point out that it is not safe to assume that a current food cost percentage to date of 32.5% is satisfactory just because it has been that figure for the past few weeks, or even the past few months. Such comparisons merely indicate that what probably has been happening in the past is still happening. Thus if overpurchasing leading to waste and spoilage has been the rule for some time, and that condition still exists, the food cost percentage would still be the same. Similarly, ongoing pilferage of consistent quantities will result in a consistent cost percentage, as will overproduction or constant overportioning.

Rather than simply comparing the cost percentage to what it has been, our discussion will concern itself with what costs and cost percentages ought to be. We shall begin with the development of standard production costs and then, having developed a concept of what costs ought to be for a particular item, we shall develop procedures for determining what the costs ought to be for an entire meal, day, or operating period.

It is not enough simply to say that a restaurant's food cost is 32.5, 34, or 35% and that it has produced a profit for the owner over the past several years. It is entirely possible that considerable waste and inefficiency exist and that the owner is able to charge enough for his meals to cover the loss and still make a profit. In areas where competition from other restaurants is not significant, it is often possible to get away with higher than justified prices to cover waste and inefficiency. However, many experts feel that lower prices, even in those areas where competition does not exist, will increase the number of customers. If lower prices can be offset with lower costs, profit will be increased, a desirable goal for every restaurateur.

STANDARD COSTS

It is important that management know not only what food costs actually are, but also what they ought to be. Determining what the food cost should be for any operation is not a simple procedure. In the first place, it presupposes the establishing of standards and standard procedures in all those areas discussed in previous chapters. Next it involves considerable precalculating of standard portion costs and the ongoing development of records of numbers of portions sold in the past. These records, known as a sales history, are used to predict likely future sales, based on experience. This method of prediction is called forecasting. If a restaurant can forecast portion sales with accuracy, then it can predict costs with accuracy once standard portion costs are known. In effect, this amounts to setting performance goals under perfect conditions. The goals become standards, and it then becomes possible to review performance to determine whether or not the goals have been met. It is possible to measure actual performance against standard performance, determine both the extent to which standards have not been met as well as the causes for failing to meet the standards, and make appropriate changes in operating procedures in the hope that the actual future performance will be more nearly in line with the standards set.

This is a reasonably sophisticated approach to the control of costs, particularly in the food industry, and represents an attempt to control costs in a manner like that used in other manufacturing industries. It is neither simple nor inexpensive, and in its entirety should not be undertaken unless the cost can be justified in terms of savings. However, this approach to cost control, generally known as the precost, precontrol method, contains many elements that by themselves can serve various useful and important functions in less complex systems. One of these elements is the determination of standard portion costs.

What costs ought to be are **standard costs**. These are determined on the basis of the size of the portion served to a customer (the standard portion size) and the ingredients that go into preparing a particular item (the standard recipe). Both the standard portion size and the standard recipe must be determined before a standard cost can be computed.

STANDARD PORTION SIZES

One of the most important standards that a restaurant must set is the portion size, the quantity of any item that is to be served each time that item is ordered. In effect, the standard portion size for any item is the fixed quantity that management intends to give each and every customer in return for a fixed selling price.

Standard portion sizes help reduce customer discontent, which leads to lost sales. No customer can compare his or her portion unfavorably with that of another customer and feel dissatisfied or cheated. In addition, repeat customers will be more inclined to feel they receive fair measure for their money on each visit.

Standard portion sizes help eliminate animosity between kitchen help and dining room personnel, which can lead to delays in serving and make personnel antagonistic to patrons. When portion sizes are left to the whims of the kitchen help, arguments can develop concerning whether or not some waiter is receiving larger portions to serve his customers, thus ensuring larger tips.

Standard sizes help eliminate excessive costs. Cost for any given item varies with the quanity served. The cost for any item will be proportional to the quantity served to the customer. It stands to reason that an eight-ounce portion of anything costs twice as much as a four-ounce portion of the same item—if four ounces cost $.40, eight ounces will cost $.80.

Except in rare instances, selling prices do not vary with portion sizes. Prices are typically printed in a menu and usually are not changed until the menu is reprinted. Even when not printed, prices cannot be changed from customer to customer. If an item is listed at $2 on a certain day, then each and every portion of that item will be sold for $2. If one customer receives a four-ounce portion costing $.80, and a second customer receives an eight-ounce portion of the same item costing $.80, it is apparent that costs are not under control, and probable that customers and serving personnel are dissatisfied.

Such situations often have a number of unpleasant consequences. Customers complain, never return, or both. Serving personnel argue and sometimes quit. From a food controller's point of view, perhaps the most important undesirable consequence is that costs are not under control and excessive costs develop. In addition, under such conditions, gross profits vary on sales of the same item. The gross profit is $1.60 on the sale to the first customer, and $1.20 on the sale to the second customer. As we shall see in a later chapter, such conditions make it impossible to determine the relative profitability of one menu item over another.

Once standard portion sizes have been set, it is obviously important to ensure that each person who produces an item knows what size portion to prepare. Methods of accomplishing this vary. One effective way is to post charts conspicuously on kitchen walls for ready reference. This approach is particularly effective in large establishments that experience a high rate of employee turnover.

STANDARD RECIPES

Another important production control is the standard recipe. A standard recipe lists ingredients and quantities to be used and a procedure to be followed each and every time a particular item is produced. The use of standard recipes helps ensure that the quality of any item will be the same each time the item is produced. Consequently, the standard recipe (see figure 10.1) also helps guarantee consistency of taste, appearance, and customer acceptance; if the same ingredients are used in the correct proportions, and the same procedure is followed using those ingredients, identical products should be produced each time the standard recipe is used, even in the face of rapid employee turnover. Moreover, each repeat customer will likely be served an item of identical quality each time he or she orders.

The term **standard recipe** does not necessarily imply a recipe developed by some outside agency for use in numerous restaurants. Standard recipe means that recipe which will produce an item of acceptable quality for a particular operation. These recipes can be, and often are, developed in individual kitchens. Recipes are tested and modified until an acceptable recipe that produces the intended product is agreed on. That recipe then becomes the standard—the recipe that will be used each time a certain item is made.

In many operations, these standard recipes are recorded on cards that are made readily available to those responsible for production. They are clearly and legibly written so that the standard recipes can be easily followed. At times, they

FIGURE 10.1

Seafood Newburg (10 4-oz. portions)

1 lb. lobster meat
1/2 lb. shrimps, raw, out of shell
1/2 lb. scallops
1/2 lb. filet of sole
1 cup heavy cream
3 cups cream sauce
1 cup butter
salt and pepper to taste
1 T. paprika
1 cup sherry wine
6 egg yolks
extra sherry wine

a. Sauté all seafood in the melted butter well.
b. Add a little sherry and simmer until wine is absorbed.
c. Add paprika and cream sauce; combine well and simmer for a while.
d. Beat egg yolks and cream and add slowly to pan; combine well.
e. Check for seasoning; pour into serving dishes and add sherry over it.

are printed on special cards that are then plastic-coated for durability. In some establishments, these cards include either drawings or photographs of the finished products to illustrate for the production staff exactly how the final product should look when served to the customer. In addition to providing uniform appearance, these cards are particularly important in those restaurants that choose to illustrate menus with photographs.

Standard recipes are very important to the food controller. If they are not in use, costs cannot be controlled effectively. If any item is produced by different methods, with different ingredients, in different proportions each time it is made, costs will be different each time any given quantity is produced.

Once standard recipes and standard portion sizes are established, and steps are taken to ensure that personnel follow necessary preparation and portioning procedures, standard costs for portions of items sold, and thus for entire meals, can be developed.

STANDARD PORTION COSTS

One of the first steps in predetermining operating costs is to calculate the cost of a standard portion of each item offered on the menu. This is not only a critical step in setting up a precost, precontrol system, but also a useful technique for anyone who wants to determine what a portion costs. With appropriate standards in effect, it is possible to determine the cost of one standard portion of any item by employing one or more of the four following procedures, depending on the nature of the item.

Determining Standard Portion Costs

By Formula

For many, perhaps even for a majority of the items served in restaurants, determining standard portion cost is very simple. For a large number of foods, one may determine portion cost by means of the formula:

$$\text{Standard Portion Cost} = \frac{\text{Purchase price per unit}}{\text{Number of portions per unit}}$$

For example, in an establishment serving eggs on a breakfast menu, where two eggs are the standard portion, one could determine the standard cost of the portion by dividing the cost of a 30 dozen case of eggs—say, $27—by the number of two-egg portions it contained—180—to find standard portion cost to be $.15.

$$\frac{\$27 \text{ purchase price per case}}{180 \text{ standard portions per case}} = \$.15$$

This simple formula could also be used to find the standard cost of each of the additional items served in a typical standard breakfast, including the juice, bacon, toast, butter, and coffee. The sum of the standard costs of the individual items would thus be the standard cost of the whole breakfast, possibly offered in some particular restaurant as Breakfast Special #3, at $4.95 menu price. In many restaurants today, large amounts of food are purchased already portioned by the vendor. Determining the cost of one portion of any of these items is comparatively simple—divide the purchase price by the number of portions bought. Frankfurters purchased twelve to the pound for $1.44 cost $0.12 each. Frozen heat-and-serve entrees are often purchased in individual units, in which case the purchase price is the portion cost. Most preportioned foods come in containers showing the exact number of portions in the container.

So, determining the portion cost of many menu items may be done rather simply, merely by applying the formula given above. However, not all foods may be so simply portioned after purchase, and other techniques must be developed to determine the standard portion costs of more complex items, such as those prepared from standard recipes.

By Recipe Detail and Cost Card

When standard recipes are used, it is possible to determine the standard cost of each item prepared with those recipes.

A standard recipe yields a predetermined number of standard portions. Thus it is possible to determine the cost of preparing one portion by dividing the number of portions produced into the total cost of preparing the recipe. To find the total cost, it is necessary only to list each item and quantity from the recipe on a form, such as that in figure 10.2, and multiply each by its unit cost. In the example given, the second ingredient is one-half pound of shrimp. If one pound of shrimp costs $3.75, then one-half pound of shrimp costs $1.88; that figure is entered on the right in the column headed "Ext.," the abbreviation for extension.

Determining the cost of an ingredient can sometimes be rather complex. If, for example, a recipe called for three diced onions, it would be necessary to

FIGURE 10.2
Recipe Detail & Cost Card

Recipe Detail & Cost Card

Item: Seafood Newburg | Menu: Dinner | S.P. $8.50 | Cost $2.44 | F.C.% $28.7

Yield: 10 portions Portion Size: 4 oz of Seafood, + sauce Date 6/22/8-

Ingredients	Quantity	Unit	Cost	Ext.	Procedure
lobster meat	1 lb.	lb.	11.25	11.25	Sauté all seafood well in melted
shrimps	1/2 lb.	lb.	7.50	3.75	butter. Add sherry & simmer
scallops	1/2 lb.		6.00	3.00	until wine is absorbed. Add
filet of sole	1/2 lb.	lb.	4.50	2.25	paprika and cream sauce, then
heavy cream	1 cup	qt.	2.40	.60	combine and simmer. Beat egg
cream sauce	3 cups	–		.75	yolks and cream, add slowly to
butter	1 cup	lb.	2.00	1.00	pan, and combine well. Check for
salt & pepper				.05	seasoning, pour into serving
paprika	1 T			.10	dishes, and add sherry. Serve
sherry wine	8 oz.	750 ml	3.20	1.01	over toast points.
egg yolks	6 ea.			.42	
sherry wine	1 oz.			.13	
toast	1 slice			.05	
Total				24.36	

determine the number of average size onions in the sack of onions, and then determine the price of one onion by dividing the total number into the price of the sack of onions. Multiplying the price of one onion times three gives the price for the onions in the standard recipe. If chicken stock were an ingredient, it would be necessary to refer to a recipe detail and cost card to determine the cost of one measure of stock prepared according to standard recipe.

In the case of an ingredient such as "a pinch of salt," it is not worthwhile to calculate the value. In such cases the figure entered in some token amount, usually more than enough to cover the cost.

When fresh meat, poultry, or fish are used, it is necessary first to follow certain procedures involving butcher tests or cooking loss tests, or both. These will be discussed later in this chapter.

Once the cost of each ingredient has been established, the total cost of preparing the recipe is determined by adding the costs of the individual ingredients. This total, divided by the number of portions produced, is called the yield, which gives the cost of one standard portion. As long as ingredients of standard quality are purchased at stable prices, this should be the cost of producing one standard portion, provided there is no waste. Measuring waste and other inefficiency in terms of the dollars involved will be covered in later chapters.

It must be recognized that standard costs of standard portions must be recalculated occasionally because the market prices of the ingredients vary. The frequency of the recalculations will depend largely on conditions in the market, as well as the availability of personnel to do the arithmetic. If market conditions and prices remain fairly constant, it should not be necessary to recalculate more frequently than every three or four months.

By Butcher Test

When meat, fish, and poultry are purchased as wholesale cuts, it is important to recognize that the purchaser pays the same price for each and every pound, even though, after butchering, the resulting parts may have entirely different values. For example, a beef tenderloin purchased from a wholesaler for preparing filet mignon is trimmed of most fat by a butcher in a restaurant before it is cut into portions. Because of the nature of the piece of meat, it is likely that the trimming may yield approximately 50% fat and 50% usable meat. These parts clearly have different uses and different values, although the purchase price per pound has been the same. A nine-pound beef tenderloin purchased at $3 per pound has a total purchase price of $27. The price yields 4 ½ pounds of fat and 4 ½ pounds of usable meat. Saying that the quantities of fat and usable meat each had a value of $13.50 would be unrealistic. It would be more realistic to say that the value of the fat was the amount that it would cost to buy it, or what one could get by selling it to a renderer. This might be only $.10 per pound, which would give the fat a total value of only $.45. However, since the cost of the entire piece was $27, and it is obviously important to account for that entire amount, it would then be necessary to set the value of the usable meat as the difference between the purchase price and the value of the fat, in this case $26.55 ($27.00 − $0.45). Once it has been determined that 4 ½ pounds of usable meat has a value of $26.55, it is possible to determine the value of one usable pound by dividing the weight into the value:

$$\frac{\$26.55}{4.5 \text{ lbs.}} = \$5.90 \text{ per lb.}$$

Meats are usually portioned in ounces, so it is then necessary to determine the value of each ounce in that pound by dividing 16 oz. into $5.90.

$$\frac{\$5.90}{16 \text{ oz.}} = \$.036875 \text{ per oz. or } \$0.37 \text{ per oz.}$$

If this meat is cut into eight-ounce portions, the cost of each portion can be calculated as eight ounces times $0.37 per ounce, or $2.96. This is a much more accurate way of determining portion cost than any method that relies solely on the dealer price and does not account for the relative differences in values after butchering. This butcher test permits the reordering of values of parts of wholesale cuts in a realistic manner.

A butcher test is usually performed under the supervision of a food controller, who presents a particular cut of meat to the butcher. The butcher then breaks it down into its respective parts, keeping the parts separate so that they can be weighed. As the work begins, the food controller detaches the meat tag from the piece and records information from the meat tag on the top of the butcher test card (Figure 10.3).

The butcher keeps the parts separated to determine their individual weights after the butchering. The names of the parts are recorded in the column at the left, marked "breakdown," and the weights of the parts go into the next column to the right. Ideally, the total weight of the individual parts equals the total original weight. However, some small measure of weight is usually lost during the butchering, and it is common to find an entry in the breakdown and weight columns for "loss in cutting."

The next column, labeled "Ratio to Total Weight," represents the percentage of each part in relation to the whole. The ratio of each weight to the whole is calculated by following the formula:

$$\frac{\text{weight of part}}{\text{weight of whole}} = \text{ratio to total weight}$$

This ratio is of particular interest to a food controller when comparing similar cuts of meat supplied by two or more dealers. Comparisons of ratios of usable parts may assist in determining which dealer is offering better value. In addition, food controllers often compare meats of different qualities to determine which is more economical to serve. This ratio is also known as a yield percentage. Specific calculations that use this yield percentage will be discussed later in this chapter.

The Value per Lb. column appears mysterious but is possibly the simplest to complete. The values per pound for all parts except the principal part—the desire for which occasioned the original purchase—are merely the current prices at which each of the parts would cost if purchased separately in the open market. In most instances, these figures are obtained from one of the regular suppliers of meat to the restaurant. The values per pound are determined in this manner on the theory that one would pay this price to buy each of the parts separately, and thus each price entered is its reasonable value. No value per pound for the principal part is entered. It will be determined after the total values for all the other parts have been calculated in the next column, marked Total Value.

The total value for each of the secondary parts is obtained by multiplying the value per pound by the weight. The total value of the primary part is determined by

1 adding the total values of the secondary parts, and

2 subtracting that figure from the Total Cost indicated at the top of the form.

Thus, the sum of all total values will equal the total original cost.

FIGURE 10.3

Butcher Test Card

Item Beef Tenderloin — Grade U.S. Choice — Date 3/21/—

Pieces One — Weighing 9 Lbs. 0 Oz. — Average Weight —

Total Cost $ 25.65 — At $ 2.85 Per Lb. — Supplier XYZ Meat Co.

Breakdown	No	Weight		Ratio to Total Weight	Value Per Lb.	Total Value	Cost of Each Usable		Portion		Cost Factor Per	
		Lb.	Oz.				Lb.	Oz.	Size	Cost	Lb.	Portion
Fat		4	8	50.0%	.10	.45						
Loss in Cutting			4	2.8%	-0-	-0-						
Usable Meat		4	4	47.2%		25.20	5.93	.37	8 oz.	2.96	2.0807	1.0386
Total		9	0	100.0%		25.65						

With both the weight and total value of the principal part known, the cost of each usable pound and ounce—the next two columns to the right—can be determined by division.

Management determines standard portion sizes. This figure, typically in ounces, is entered in the next column, Portion Size. The portion cost is calculated by multiplying the portion size in ounces by the cost of each usable ounce.

The remaining two columns are used for recording the cost factors per pound and per portion, both of which will require explanation.

Cost Factors

The price of meat is seldom if ever stable. Typically, meat prices change monthly, weekly, and sometimes even daily. As market prices change, the usable pound costs and portion costs change as well. Therefore it is desirable to find some means to calculate both the new usable pound costs and portion costs without having to complete a new butcher test with each change in market price. The cost factors serve this purpose and are calculated in the following manner:

$$\text{cost factor per pound} = \frac{\text{cost per usable pound}}{\begin{bmatrix}\text{dealer price per pound of}\\ \text{original wholesale piece}\end{bmatrix}}$$

$$\text{cost factor per portion} = \frac{\text{portion cost}}{\begin{bmatrix}\text{dealer price per pound of}\\ \text{original wholesale piece}\end{bmatrix}}$$

The cost of a usable pound at a new dealer price is:

$$\begin{bmatrix}\text{cost of usable pound at}\\ \text{new dealer price}\end{bmatrix} = \begin{bmatrix}\text{cost factor}\\ \text{per pound}\end{bmatrix} \times \begin{bmatrix}\text{new dealer price}\\ \text{per pound}\end{bmatrix}$$

The cost of a portion at a new dealer price is:

$$\begin{bmatrix}\text{portion cost at}\\ \text{new dealer price}\end{bmatrix} = \begin{bmatrix}\text{cost factor}\\ \text{per portion}\end{bmatrix} \times \begin{bmatrix}\text{new dealer price}\\ \text{per pound}\end{bmatrix}$$

These formulas provide the food controller with a technique for determining new food costs as market prices change, and enable him or her to suggest changes in selling prices when necessary to maintain a relatively stable cost-to-sales ratio.

In order to increase the accuracy in the figures derived by this method, it is necessary to perform these tests periodically on a reasonable number of pieces. The test on one piece alone is not reliable because it may not be a typical piece, even though it was purchased according to specifications. It is better to have test results on a number of different pieces in order to arrive at averages.

Establishments that do butcher tests find several other important uses for the results.

1. Butcher tests on pieces purchased according to specifications from two or more dealers give results that are useful in determining from which dealer to buy.
2. Butcher tests conducted on a periodic basis afford the appraisal of the extent to which any one dealer is adhering to specifications.
3. Menu prices can be more intelligently planned because exact costs are known.

The student should note that the butcher test is conducted far less frequently today than it was formerly. A primary reason for this is the availability of preportioned meats—steaks, chops, and other items portioned before cooking—from meat vendors. However, the butcher test can be extremely valuable to the manager who wants to compare the portion cost of a preportioned item purchased from a vendor with the cost of an identical item portioned in the restaurant. Typically, one would expect to find standard portion cost lower for the item portioned in the restaurant, but this figure would take into account only food cost for the item, not labor cost. On the other hand, the portion cost for the preportioned item purchased from a vendor would include the vendor's labor cost. Therefore, to make a valid comparison, management would have to make a judgment about labor cost per portion for items portioned in the restaurant.

Although the butcher test enables the food controller to determine portion costs for entree items portioned before cooking—steaks, chops, and filets—many other items cannot be portioned until after cooking. Consequently, portion costs for these items—typically roasts of beef, pork, lamb, and other meats—cannot be determined until after the cooking process is complete. A different procedure, known as the cooking loss test, is required.

By Cooking Loss Test

The cooking loss test is used to determine standard cost of the standard portion of any item that must be cooked before portions can be produced. It is similar to the butcher test in that the objective of determining portion cost is the same. But while the butcher test is used to determine portion cost for items portioned before cooking, the cooking loss test is employed for items that cannot be portioned until after they have been cooked, principally because the amount of loss that occurs during cooking—varying with cooking time and temperature—must be taken in account before portions can be cut. Although the butcher test is no longer used very often, the cooking loss test continues to be as necessary as ever.

The cooking loss test is perhaps best explained by illustration. Referring to figure 10.4, the leg of lamb weighing eight lbs. eight oz. was originally purchased at $1.60 per pound, at a total cost of $13.60 as shown on the first line, titled

FIGURE 10.4

Cooking Loss

Cooked One ______ Hours Ten ______ Minutes at 385 ______ Degrees

______ Hours ______ Minutes at ______ Degrees

Breakdown	No	Weight Lb.	Weight Oz.	Ratio to Total Weight	Value Per Lb.	Total Value	Cost of Each Usable Lb.	Cost of Each Usable Oz.	Portion Size	Portion Cost	Cost Factor Per Lb.	Cost Factor Per Portion
Original Weight		8	8	100.0%	1.60	13.60						
Trimmed Weight		6	8	76.5%		13.60						
Loss in Trimming		2	0	23.5%		-0-						
Cooked Weight		5	8	64.7%		13.60						
Loss in Cooking		1	0	11.8%		-0-						
Bones and Trim		1	8	17.6%		-0-						
Salable Weight		4	0	47.1%		13.60	3.40	.21	4 oz.	.84	2.1250	.5250

Remarks:

Original Weight. After trimming excess fat and shank, the trimmed weight, shown on the second line, was six lbs. eight oz. and represented 76.5% of the original weight purchased. The third line, labeled Loss in Trimming, is determined by subtracting line 2 from line 1, and represents the weight of the excess fat and shank previously trimmed.

After being cooked, the leg of lamb was weighed again, and its weight was recorded on line 4. It is apparent that the cooking process caused a loss in weight because of the evaporation of moisture and the melting of fat. This loss of weight is recorded on the fifth line and is calculated by subtracting the cooked weight from the trimmed weight. After carving, the salable meat is weighed, and the weight entered on line 7. The weight of the unsalable part—bones and fat—is recorded on line 6.

Once the weights are recorded in the manner previously described, the food controller calculates the percentages to be entered in the Ratio to Total Weight column. This is a most important step. These ratios may be used by the food controller to compare similar pieces of meat. Comparisons may be made, for example, to determine which of several available grades of meat would yield the maximum quantity of salable meat of a desired quality. In addition, important comparisons may be made between pieces cooked at different temperatures or for different lengths of time, or both of these, to determine the optimum cooking times and temperatures.

It is important to note in this illustration that the total value of the salable weight is identical to the total value of the original weight. The fat and shank, loss in cooking, and bones and trim are all of no value in this instance. Therefore, the salable weight must account for all the entire original value.

It is apparent that, while the weight has decreased because of cooking and trimming, the total value has remained constant. This stable value in the face of decreasing weight has caused a considerable increase in the real cost of each cooked, usable pound and ounce. This last point clearly underscores the need for the cooking loss test. It would be impossible to determine portion costs until cooking loss had been calculated and accounted for.

Once the weight and value of the salable meat are recorded and the portion size entered from the restaurant's chart of standard portion sizes, the remaining calculations are performed in the same manner as in the butcher test.

The foregoing discussion has been based on a piece of meat not requiring extensive butchering before cooking. However, in many instances meats require considerable butchering—for example, in cases where the parts trimmed away have usefulness and value to the establishment. In these instances, the original and trimmed weights on the cooking loss test will appear as very different figures. This is because a butcher's test has first been performed and values have been assigned to the secondary usable parts. The weight and value of the primary usable part becomes the weight and value entered on the cooking loss test as trimmed weight. The original weight and value remain that of the piece of meat as purchased.

USING YIELD PERCENTAGES FOR PURCHASE CALCULATIONS

Once determined, yield percentages can be used to calculate the appropriate amount to purchase for any given anticipated number of servings. The general formula for this is:

$$\text{Amount to purchase} = \frac{\text{Number of portions desired} \times \text{Portion size}}{\text{Yield percentage}}$$

Let us refer to the leg of lamb in the cooking loss test. Intuitively one can see that each leg of lamb would produce sixteen portions, because each portion weighs one-quarter of a pound and there are four pounds of usable meat. Thus one can also see that if thirty-two portions were desired, one would purchase two legs of lamb each yielding sixteen portions or seventeen pounds of raw lamb. However, for calculations not that easy one would have to use the mathematical formula above. It would be calculated as follows:

$$\text{Amount to purchase} = \frac{32 \times .25}{.471}$$

$$\text{Amount to purchase} = 16.985 \text{ pounds}$$

The minor discrepancy between the intuitive calculation and the mathematical calculation is due to the rounding of the yield percentage figure.

It is important to note that the above formula assumes that future purchases of lamb will yield the same proportional amount as the tested leg. This means that the meat would contain the same relative amount of bone, fat, and lean, and that it was cooked at the same temperature for the same period of time so that shrinkage was relatively the same as the tested lamb.

Depending on the nature of the menu item, using one or more of the foregoing techniques can help one determine with reasonable accuracy the standard cost of one portion of any item on a menu. Once the standard cost of one portion is known, it is possible to set or adjust the selling price.

If standard costs and selling prices for each menu item were known, one might predict what it should cost to prepare food and what sales should result, providing it were possible to determine in advance how many portions might be sold. For example, if a standard portion of item X has a standard cost of $1.25 per portion, and each portion sells for $5.00, we can predict that 100 portions will cost $125 to produce and will bring in sales of $500. The next step, then, is to find some way to predict for each future date the number of portions that can reasonably be expected to sell. This will be the subject of Chapter 11.

EDP APPLICATIONS

Once standard portion sizes have been established and standard recipes have been agreed upon, this information may be stored in computer memory. If, as discussed in previous chapters, we have also stored in memory all food purchases and current purchase prices, it is then possible, given the appropriate applications program, to obtain from the computer standard portion costs based on updated market prices. As one might imagine, manually updating standard portion costs can be so time-consuming that it is done very infrequently, but this problem may be entirely overcome with the aid of the computer.

It would also be possible to create a computer program in which data obtained from both butcher and cooking loss tests could be stored in computer memory; requisite calculations could be performed and updated in seconds. With a suitable program in place, the computer could determine cost factors, store them, and employ them to update standard portion costs with each new purchase of items previously tested. This could provide management with remarkably timely and accurate standard portion costs.

If yield percentages (yield factors) were stored in computer memory along with standard portion sizes, a very simple program could be written to determine appropriate quantities necessary to prepare any given number of portions of an item for any given time period. For example, it would be possible to determine the correct quantity of beef to be purchased to serve roast prime ribs to seventy-five people at a banquet, or to serve the number of sales forecast for a given week.

CHAPTER ESSENTIALS

In this chapter, we pointed out the importance of knowing what food costs should be as well as what they are. We showed what preliminary steps must be taken in order to do this: establishing standard portion sizes and standard ingredients and production methods, usually referred to as standard recipes. With these standards established, one can determine the standard cost of one standard portion of any item on a menu by means of one or more of the following: simple formula, recipe detail and cost card, butcher test, and cooking loss test. We also showed how cost factors derived from butcher test and cooking loss test can be used to calculate portion costs as dealer prices change, and how yield percentages derived from these tests can be useful in determining proper purchase quantities. Finally, we demonstrated how computers may be used to maintain and update standard portion costs, as well as to determine proper quantities to purchase for specific purposes.

QUESTIONS AND PROBLEMS

1 In each of the following cases, determine selling price for a recipe yielding thirty portions, when the standard recipe cost and desired cost-to-sales ratio are as indicated below.

Recipe Cost	*Desired Cost Percentage for One Portion*
$ 55.25	30.0%
22.58	18.0%
124.50	45.0%
105.00	21.0%
12.60	40.0%

2 Define each of the following:

a standard portion size
b standard portion cost
c standard recipe

3 Using the form illustrated in Figure 10.3, complete the Butcher Test calculations on a beef tenderloin, U.S. prime, from the information given below:

Weight as purchased: 8 lbs. 8 oz.
Dealer price: $4.19 per pound
Portion size for filet mignon: 8 oz.

Breakdown:

Fat	4 lbs. 12 oz.	Value per pound: $ .10
Tidbits	12 oz.	Value per pound 2.49
Filet Mignon	3 lbs. 0 oz.	

4 Using the forms for Butcher Test and Cooking Loss Test illustrated in Figures 10.3 and 10.4, complete the calculations for the Butcher Test and Cooking Loss Test on a rib of beef, U.S. choice, weighing 38 lbs. 12 oz., purchased from a dealer at $3.19 per pound.

Breakdown:

Fat	6 lbs. 8 oz.	Value per lb. $ .10
Bones	4 lbs. 4 oz.	Value per lb. .32
Short Ribs	3 lbs. 4 oz.	Value per lb. 1.49
Chopped Beef	2 lbs. 8 oz.	Value per lb. 1.59
Loss in Cutting	0 lbs. 4 oz.	Value per lb. -0-
Oven Ready Rib	22 lbs. 0 oz.	
Cooked Weight:	20 lbs. 4 oz.	
Bones & Trim	1 lb. 4 oz.	

Portion Size for Roast Beef: 10 oz.

5 Using the cost factors developed in question 3 above, determine:

- **a** cost of the eight-oz. portion if the dealer increases his price for beef tenderloin to $4.49 per pound.
- **b** cost of each usable pound at the increased dealer price in 5(a) above.
- **c** cost of a six-oz. portion at the increased dealer price of $4.49.
- **d** the maximum number of ounces that can be served for a $5.55 portion cost after the dealer has raised his price to $4.49 per pound.

6 A cooking loss test on a leg of lamb shows a yield percentage of 42.5%.

- **a** Determine how many pounds of uncooked oven-ready legs of lamb to purchase if forty-eight portions are needed and each portion weighs four ounces.
- **b** Determine how many pounds of uncooked oven-ready leg of lamb to purchase if fifty-five portions are needed and each portion weighs five ounces.

7 How much would each portion cost in 6(a) and 6(b) above if the price per pound of the uncooked leg of lamb were $3.19?

8 Illustrate three possible customer reactions to nonstandard portion sizes.

9 If standard recipes are not followed, how can that affect the price and quality of a particular item?

10 If one roast beef is cooked rare, another well-done, and the portion size remains the same, discuss how the cost of each portion might differ.

11 Select one standard recipe that could be used in a foodservice establishment, then use current market prices for the required ingredients to determine standard cost of one standard portion. Assuming a desired food cost percent of 35%, what would be an appropriate menu sales price for the item?

chapter 11

Forecasting Sales and Controlling Production

Learning Objectives

After reading and studying this chapter, the student should be able to:

1. Define sales history and list several ways information for a sales history is gathered.
2. List several ways sales history information is presented.
3. Compute the popularity index and interpret the results.
4. Explain how forecasts of portions sold are made.
5. Describe the production sheet and calculate needed production.
6. Describe the procedures used in controlling high-cost, precut entrees.
7. Describe several uses made of the void sheet.
8. Calculate portions consumed on the portion inventory and reconciliation form, and outline several reasons for differences in portions consumed and portions sold.
9. Explain the use of computers for maintaining sales histories and for forecasting.

It is essential that all restaurants know with some degree of accuracy what they can reasonably expect to sell so that intelligent purchasing, production, and labor scheduling can be made. Obviously, no one can know for certain what will happen in the future. But with knowledge of past events, estimates of future events can be forecasted, assuming circumstances will be reasonably similar to the past. In the restaurant business forecasts based on past experiences often can be made rather accurately (except for such events as holidays, unusual weather, and so on). The primary tool used to record information so that sales can be forecasted accurately is called a sales history.

SALES HISTORY

A sales history is a written record of the number of portions of each item sold every time that item appeared on the menu. In effect, it is a daily summary of portion sales. In some establishments, sales histories are maintained for every item on the menu, from appetizers to desserts. In others, information is developed only for entree items. In many instances, the extent and complexity of the sales history is related to the length and scope of the menu itself. In all instances, the best decisions on the nature of the sales history are based on the need for information that can be put to use in improving operations. Unless the information maintained is useful in leading to better control over costs, it cannot be justified.

Because the sales history records what customers have ordered, the basic source of information is developed by the sales personnel—the waiters and waitresses. In the majority of operations, orders are recorded on guest checks, all of which are typically assembled in one place at the end of the day. For this information to be read and recorded, each check must be clear and legible, a point that must be emphasized to the staff time and time again. If no one can read the checks, the information they reflect cannot be abstracted.

Abstracting of the information on the guest checks may be accomplished in any one of a number of ways. The simplest, and perhaps most widely used, method involves maintaining a running count of portion sales as they occur. This is most often done by a cashier, who records information from the checks as they are presented by customers. The information is recorded either on a copy of the menu, on a special score sheet (figure 11.1), or on one of several types of mechanical counting devices widely available to the industry. At the conclusion of a meal or at some other appropriate time, such as the end of the day, the information is sent to the food controller so that it can be added to the records developed from previous days. This method has the advantage of adding little or no cost to operations.

In some operations, where the cashier is too busy for this extra work, the food controller takes the guest checks after the meal, or at the close of business, and breaks down the sales, usually on a score sheet such as that in figure 11.1. While this method is time-consuming, it does present some advantages, which will be discussed in the chapter on sales control. A variation involves the cashier

FIGURE 11.1

Day Tuesday	Date 2/2/8-	Meal Dinner
Item	Number of Portions	Total
A	卌 卌 卌 卌 111	23
B	卌 卌 卌 卌 卌 卌 卌 卌 卌 卌 卌 卌	60
C	卌 卌 卌 卌 卌 卌 1111	34
D	卌 卌 卌 卌 卌 卌 卌 卌 卌	45
Total		162

giving the checks to someone in the accounting department, who records the necessary information and forwards it to the food controller.

Some rather large fast-food operations have been quite successful in using modern electronic data processing equipment to develop sales histories. In some instances, waiters and waitresses sense-mark guest selections on guest checks that are really computer cards that can be processed after the close of business. In other cases, guest selections are recorded on special punch cards and are tabulated as they are recorded.

When the food controller has the information on the number of portions of each item sold, he or she adds it to the master records, often kept either on file cards or in an analysis book. The records may be arranged in any one of a number of ways, depending on which is deemed most useful to a particular establishment. Some typical arrangements include the following.

1 By operating period, such as one week, so that sales for each day of one week are all recorded on the same page or card. (See figure 11.2.)
2 By day of week, so that sales for Tuesdays, for example, may be compared for a period of several weeks.
3 By entree item, in order that the popularity of an item may be determined on a particular series of days.

Many operators have found it desirable to combine two of these systems in order to provide an overall picture of sales for the entire week at one glance, in addition to providing some clues as to the relative popularity of items when they appear on the menu with other varying items. An illustration of the technique appears in figure 11.3. It should be noted that these forms often include provision for recording other information that may have a bearing on sales. In many establishments, bad weather leads to a decrease in sales. On the other hand, in many large metropolitan hotels, bad weather often leads to increased sales, particularly during the dinner hour.

FIGURE 11.2

Sales History—Portions Sold—Month of February 19—

Weather	Fair	Snow																
Day	M	T	W	H	F	S	S	M	T	W	H	F	S	S	M	T	W	H
Date	1	2	3	4	5	6	7	8	9	10	11	12	13	14	15	16	17	18
Item																		
A	75	23	60	63	70	82	73	72										
B	60	60	55	65	62	58	61	65										
C	6	34	22	18	15	12	16	20										
D	159	45	140	149	150	161	154	155										
Total	300	162	277	295	297	313	304	312										

FIGURE 11.3

Sales History—Month of February 19—

Item	Monday			Tuesday			Wednesday			Thursday			*Friday*			*Saturday*			*Sunday*	
	1	8	15	2	9	16	3	10	17	4	11	18	5	12	19	6	13	20	7	14
A	75	72		23			60			63			70			82			73	
B	60	65		60			55			65			62			58			61	
C	6	20		34			22			18			15			12			16	
D	159	155		45			140			149			150			161			154	
Total	300	312		162			277			295			297			313			304	

Special events can considerably influence sales and are often included in sales histories. The occurrence of a national holiday on a particular day, or the presence of a particular convention group in a hotel, can affect sales considerably. So can such varied conditions as faulty kitchen equipment, or a torn-up street in front of the restaurant, or a major sale at a neighboring department store. In general, an effort should be made to include in the sales history any information about events that may have affected sales and that should be considered in forecasting volume of sales at some particular time in the future. In hotel restaurants, the house count, or the number of people registered in the hotel on a particular day, is often included so that a determination may be made of the percentage of registered guests who are using the dining room, and judgments made in the future as to numbers of portions to prepare for any given date or rate of occupancy.

Popularity Index

In addition to maintaining histories of portions sold, many food controllers use the figures to determine the percentage of total portion sales represented by each item, as in Figure 11.4, often referred to as Popularity Index.

FIGURE 11.4

Item	*Portions Sold*	*Percent of Total Sales (Popularity Index)*
A	23	14.2
B	60	37.0
C	34	21.0
D	45	27.8
Total	162	100.0%

Such ratios to total sales can be very useful in determining whether to continue offering a certain item on the menu. If item C consistently represented only 2% of total sales whenever it appeared, serious consideration should be given to removing it from the menu or substituting a more popular item.

These ratios are of far greater use in determining an item's popularity than are raw figures that simply indicate number of portions sold. For example, the sales history might show portion sales of item B from a low of twelve portions to a high of seventy-eight. This knowledge would not be as useful as information indicating that the twelve portions had represented 20% of total sales that day, and the seventy-eight portions had represented 19%. Given this information, as well as the information that item B represented 18.5% of total sales on another recent day, we might conclude that this particular item accounted for 18.5% to 20.0% of sales each time it appeared on the menu. If this has been the trend for some time, the information should be useful in some way for predicting the future.

In some operations, particularly those with relatively stable menus, these sales ratios can be developed for particular time periods and used effectively in forecasting.

FORECASTING

Forecasting is a technique that uses appropriate and available data to predict what is likely to occur in the future. It amounts to intelligent, educated guesswork about future events. If the future can be predicted with reasonable accuracy, appropriate plans can be made in advance to prepare for likely happenings. In the food industry, which deals with highly perishable products, this advance planning can be a large factor in operating profitably.

Forecasting is a principal element in control. If sales volume can be predicted accurately, then plans can be made for purchasing appropriate quantities of food to prepare for anticipated sales. Purchasing unneeded quantities can be avoided, thus reducing some of the possibilities for waste, spoilage, and pilferage. In addition, plans can be made for producing particular numbers of portions for sale on particular dates, thus reducing possibilities for excessive costs to develop. Moreover, such planned control over purchasing automatically can lead to control over production; it is impossible to prepare a greater number of portions than necessary if the raw materials of overproduction do not exist.

A usual first step in forecasting is to predict total anticipated volume in terms of anticipated numbers of customers for particular days or particular meals. To arrive at a figure, reference is made to the sales history to find the total number of sales that occurred on each of a number of comparable dates in the recent past. When wide differences are apparent, every effort must be made to determine the reasons for the differences. The causes are often revealed by the information in the history relating to weather and other conditions that existed at the time of the sales. The effect of each of these conditions must be judged—some increase sales, others decrease them.

When the effects of surrounding conditions have been evaluated, it is important next to judge the extent to which they will exist on a particular date in the future. This usually involves checking the local calendar of coming events, weather forecasts, and any other pertinent sources of information.

After these steps have been taken, it is possible to guess the total business volume that may be anticipated for a particular date. If, for example, recent history reflected 275 to 300 sales for dinner on Tuesdays in pleasant weather, one could reasonably anticipate that the next Tuesday would bring approximately the same volume of business if good weather were expected. In this case, it would probably be safe to predict 300 sales. The next step is to forecast the anticipated number of sales of each item on the menu. This is simpler to do if the menu is identical to those that have appeared on Tuesdays in the past. However, it can also be done for changing menus if the sales history is set up to reflect relative popularity of certain items when they have appeared with other items in the past. This type of forecasting is more difficult, but by no means impossible.

When the sales history shows the sales ratio for an item over a period of time, this may be taken as the popularity index and used for predicting. For example, if item B usually represents 20% of total sales on Tuesday evenings, it would be fairly safe to predict that next Tuesday, item B would also represent 20% of the anticipated 300 sales, or 60 portions.

This procedure is followed for every item that will appear on the menu, and thus a forecast is made of anticipated sales for a particular date. However, it should be recognized that this forecast must be somewhat flexible, subject to change as conditions may change. A change in the weather forecast, for example, might necessitate changing the sales forecast sometime before the date in question.

Once the forecast is completed, usually by a food controller, it should be reviewed by someone else, often the manager. Forecasting is educated guesswork, and two heads are usually better than one.

The completed forecast represents management's best judgment of the sales volume anticipated, and the information should be shared with appropriate personnel in the operation. One member of the staff who can make valuable use of this information is the person in charge of staffing the dining room. He or she can better make plans to hire sufficient personnel, yet keep the total to the minimum necessary, thus maintaining control over labor costs.

Perhaps the most important person with whom to share the information is the chef, who must be aware of anticipated volume, partly in order to anticipate labor requirements. In addition, with information about anticipated portion sales for each menu item, the chef is better equipped to advise the steward on the appropriate quantities of food to have on hand. If sales of sixty portions of item B are forecasted for next Tuesday, the steward need not purchase a greater quantity of the perishable ingredients than is necessary for the item. The consequent control of purchasing can be one of the most important factors in limiting excessive costs. When needed quantities are known, only those quantities should be purchased.

THE PRODUCTION SHEET

Production sheets such as that illustrated in figure 11.5 are often prepared to reflect the forecast determined by the food controller. A production sheet lists each menu item and, by listing the number of portions of each that are expected to be sold, sets production goals for the chef and his staff. These sheets should be viewed as an effort by management to control production and eliminate waste.

Production sheets vary in form and complexity from kitchen to kitchen. One very simple form appears in figure 11.5. It should be completed by a manager or food controller as many days in advance as possible, and forwarded to the chef immediately. Upon receiving it, the chef would know both total anticipated volume for a particular meal and the anticipated number of portion sales of each

FIGURE 11.5
Production Sheet

Production Sheet

Day Tues. Date 2/9/— Meal Dinner

Volume Forecast 305

Menu Item	Forecast	Adjusted Forecast
A	75	80
B	60	65
C	20	20
D	150	165
	305	330

item on the menu. With this information in hand, he or she would be better equipped to determine needs for perishable foods, for which the steward would place orders, and for nonperishable foods, which would be requisitioned from the storeroom. Provision is made for adjusting the forecasted figures upward or downward on the basis of weather or other changes.

Ideally, the changes will be minor. In any case, adjustments can be made immediately before the forecasted date, often the night before, sometimes in the morning of the date in question. The final figures in the adjusted forecast column are production goals for the chef, who should be responsible for seeing to it that leftover foods are used in meeting those goals whenever possible, provided that their use does not violate the establishment's quality standards.

In some operations, this very simple version of the production sheet is not sufficient. Where additional control over production is desirable, a more elaborate form, such as that pictured in figure 11.6, might be used. This form establishes

FIGURE 11.6
Production Sheet

Production Sheet

Day Tues. Date 2/9/— Meal Dinner

Volume Forecast 305

Menu Item	Forecast	Adjusted Forecast	Portion Size	Production Method	Portions on Hand	Needed Production	Total Available	Left Over
A	75	80	6 oz.	Recipe #62	—	80	80	0
B	60	65	8 oz.	Recipe #4	5	60	65	5
C	20	20	4 oz.	Recipe #19	—	20	20	0
D	150	165	12 oz.	Broil	20	145	165	6
	305	330						

greater control in several ways. It restates the portion size for each item, thus continually reemphasizing management's concern that the size of each portion served be carefully controlled. This may be particularly important in those places that offer portions of different sizes for luncheon, for dinner, and for banquets. It also directs the kitchen staff in the production method to be employed, which might be of considerable importance when several recipes exist for the same item and management has particular preferences or wants to try a different one. The purpose of the portions on hand column is to force the chef, before beginning production, to take an inventory of leftovers from the previous day or meal. While this is not desirable in some places because of the quality standards established, it is perfectly permissible in others.

In such instances, the figure in the total available column equals that in the adjusted forecast column, and at the same time is the sum of the leftover portions and additional portions produced. As a further control, there is a column for portions left over. Whenever possible this figure should be carried over to the production sheet for the next day or meal, in order to ensure that these leftovers will be sold. If portions of uncooked meats have been left over, and the number recorded cannot be located for a following day or meal, immediate steps can be taken to eliminate the future possibilities for pilferage.

Regardless of the degree of complexity involved, the purpose of any production sheet is to establish control by setting goals for production in order to eliminate a major cause of excessive cost. Unsold portions appear in cost figures but are not reflected in sales figures for the day. Therefore, to keep costs in line, controlling food production is necessary and desirable. Under ideal conditions, no unsold portions would ever be left over after a meal. Everyone recognizes that this is impossible, but it is a desirable goal nevertheless. To the extent to which unsold portions can be eliminated, food costs can be better controlled and excessive costs eliminated. With this goal in mind production sheets are established and used.

In most operations, the cost of entree items represents the greatest part of food cost. Meats and fish, after all, usually constitute the largest portion of food cost per customer served, and thus it is not strange that additional control procedures to isolate instances of waste and inefficiency are often concerned with entree items.

PAR STOCK CONTROL OF PREPORTIONED ENTREES

Expensive cuts of meat, such as steaks and chops, either are purchased already portioned, or are portioned in the restaurant before cooking. These items are usually cooked to order and are typically held in a refrigerator close to the broiler or range. Under such circumstances, the cook will be usually responsible for putting the items on the fire when they are ordered.

FIGURE 11.7

Item	Portions Issued	Additional Issues	Total Issues	Returned to Steward	Portions Consumed
D	165	—	165	6	159

Day Tues.

Date 2/9/—

Issues received J. Jones

Additional Issues —

Returned portions received Paul Smith
steward

Therefore, many managers and food controllers find it useful to make that particular cook fully responsible for these expensive items, by asking that he or she sign a sheet such as that illustrated in figure 11.7. By signing, the individual acknowledges receipt of the number of portions of each item indicated.

The number of portions that the steward issues should be equal to the number of sales forecasted for that item. In case the forecasted number is incorrect, provision is made for additional issues, for which the cook also will sign. At the conclusion of serving hours, the number issued can be totaled in the next column. The number of portions returned, if any, will be entered in the Returned column, and the steward will sign for the returns. Total Issues minus Returns equals the number of portions consumed, and the steward fills in this figure before sending the form on to the food controller.

One advantage of this procedure is that it makes the cook accountable for a particular number of portions. Knowing the certainty of being questioned about missing portions, the cook will be less likely to give any away to staff members.

THE VOID SHEET

Every restaurant offering steaks, chops, and other similar a la carte entrees has probably had some experience with items being returned from the dining room for one reason or another. Often portions are returned because a customer is difficult, or impossible, to please. However, on many occasions, the portions are returned because some member of the staff was not listening carefully to the customer who consequently did not receive what was ordered. Sometimes this is because of a careless waiter or waitress; sometimes because of a careless or overworked cook. In any instance, these returned portions represent cost, and should be accounted for. Therefore, many restaurants use a void sheet similar to that illustrated in figure 11.8. Whenever a portion is returned, an authorized individual, such as a kitchen supervisor or chef, must make note of it, indicating the name of the item, the number of the check on which it appeared, and the reason for its return.

The entries on such sheets can be most revealing to an alert food controller. For example, if one particular waiter or waitress appears on the list with greater

FIGURE 11.8
Void Sheet

Void sheet

Day Tues. Date 2/9/—

Check #	*Waiter #*	*Item*	*Reason for Return*	*Authorization*	*Sales Value*
11031	6	D	Too Well Done	SJC.	7.95
11034	6	B	Dropped on Floor	SJC.	6.95
11206	4	D	Too Well Done	SJC.	7.95
11227	3	D	Too Well Done	SJC.	7.95

than usual regularity, the individual in question is possibly not paying careful attention to customer orders. Such negligence can be very costly and should be attended to quickly. On the other hand, it might be noted that the number of broiler items returned is far greater when one particular employee is working. This might suggest the need to observe this employee's job performance and perhaps suggest that the chef attempt to get him to improve. If the number of returns is consistently great, investigation might suggest the need for additional personnel in order to better satisfy customer demand.

There are other important uses of the void sheet, particularly when efforts are being made to control portions by some method such as that previously described as the par stock control of portions. If portions are not accounted for, kitchen personnel can easily claim that they were returned by a difficult customer and thrown away. If all such portions are required to be recorded on the void sheet and attested to by some member of the management team, it is more difficult for kitchen personnel to be careless with the food.

In addition, the recording of returned portions, taken with other techniques previously described, makes possible the reconciliation of kitchen records of portions produced and cashiers' records of portions sold.

PORTION INVENTORY AND RECONCILIATION

Another useful approach to controlling entrees involves the use of a form similar to that illustrated in figure 11.9. This procedure, typically used in conjunction with a production sheet, incorporates some of the features of the par stock control but

FIGURE 11.9
Portion Inventory and Reconciliation

Portion Inventory and Reconciliation

Day Wed. Date 10/8/—

Portion Production:

Item	*Opening Inventory*	*Portions Prepared*	*Additional Preparation*	*Total Available*	*Closing Inventory*	*Portions Consumed*
AB	—	180		180	15	165
BH	5	60		65	5	60
CJ	—	110	10	120	14	106
DZ	20	145		165	8	157

Sales Reconciliation:

Item	*Portions Sold*	*Portions Void*	*Total*	*Consumed (From Above)*	*Difference*	*Comment*
AB	165	—	165	165		
BH	58	2	60	60		
CJ	103	1	104	106	2	2 missing checks
DZ	156	1	157	157		

Prepared by: Bob Smith
Food Controller

Reviewed by: Jane Jones
Manager

goes several steps beyond. Each entree item is listed before preparation begins. Then an inventory is made of any portions left over from previous servings. If leftovers are to be used, the number of portions on hand is deducted from the quantity scheduled for production, and only the difference is prepared. That number is written in the Portions Prepared column. Additional quantities prepared, if any, are indicated in the next column. At the conclusion of the serving hours, an inventory of the portions on hand (Closing Inventory) is made. When these columns are completed, the form is sent to the food controller.

On receiving the form, the food controller determines the total available by adding and then subtracting the closing inventory to find the number of portions consumed. Following this determination of the number of portions consumed according to kitchen records, the food controller obtains from the cashier (or other source) the records of portions sold that have been prepared for entry into the sales history. Because this figure may not include records of small parties or banquets served in private rooms, provision is made for entering the number of portions of banquet items sold. The number of portions voided, or returned to the kitchen, is subtracted from the total of these two, and the result is entered in the Total column. The next step is to determine the difference, if any, existing between the kitchen records and the portion sales records. That difference is written in the appropriate column. In the example given, kitchen records show the production of 106 cooked portions of CJ, while sales records indicate only 104 portions sold. The difference (2 portions) is entered and should be investigated immediately, while events are still fresh in the minds of the personnel involved. Once the causes of the discrepancy are known, steps can be taken to eliminate the problem in the future. After all, two portions unaccounted for represent 1.9% of portions produced. These portions will appear in the cost figures and, by not being reflected in sales figures, will raise the cost-to-sales ratio excessively.

While this technique is most useful in restaurants serving foods cooked to order, it can be helpful in other establishments as well. Its use requires that someone be able to estimate with some degree of accuracy the number of portions contained in, say, a steam table pan of beef goulash. The records resulting from the use of this reconciliation procedure will not be quite as precise in this type of foodservice establishment, but they can be helpful in attempting to isolate problems.

The number of missing portions can be a very useful figure in determining the extent of excessive cost in establishments that do not use the menu Pre-Cost and Abstract for computing standard costs. If portion sizes are carefully controlled and standard portion costs known, the number of portions unaccounted for can be translated into dollars quite simply. If in the previous example the missing portions of CJ have a standard cost of $3.35 each, then simple multiplication determines that the loss of these portions has increased costs by $6.70 on that particular day. Such a figure might not seem so great, but if equal losses occur seven days a week throughout the year, it indicates a weekly loss of $46.90 and an annual loss of $2,438.80, a substantial amount. The cost is excessive in every sense and should be eliminated. If the loss can be eliminated without increasing other costs, profits will be increased by the amount saved.

While the foregoing procedure for reconciling portion production and sales is useful, it does, after all, address itself only to entree items, and in most instances extending it to cover other items on the menu as well would be unwieldy. Although it is true that entree items usually represent the greatest proportion of cost, this does not mean that the cost of other items can be neglected. Also, this reconciliation does not take into account the waste, if any, that may have occurred in the preparation of the number of portions that were finally listed on the form. It is possible, for example, that several steaks were improperly cut and were discarded, never having been listed on the reconciliation form.

For these and other reasons, some large establishments, with the personnel and time necessary to complete the work, prepare various daily reports to determine the dollar difference between standard costs and actual costs. Once calculated, this dollar figure may be viewed as dollars wasted and gives knowledgeable managers an idea of the number of dollars that can be saved if the waste is eliminated. In this way, the dollar value of waste may be considered as potential savings. These topics are discussed in the following chapter.

EDP APPLICATIONS

Given the many electronic sales terminals available today, developing sales history data has become somewhat simpler and faster than it was in the past. With stand-alone sales terminals, it would be necessary at the end of a day or a meal period to print out a report of portion sales during that period for inclusion in a manually maintained history. With sales terminals integrated into a system, portion sales data may merely be stored in computer memory for future reference. The problem would be to create a suitable program for rendering the data in a form useful for forecasting.

With historical records of portion sales stored in memory, forecasting might take the following form. The manager or food controller would enter in a terminal the projected menu for whatever forecasting was to be done. The items would display in a column on the left side of the CRT. In columns to the right of each item, the manager would see numbers of previous sales from specific dates, or the popularity index for each, depending on the program employed. The cursor would appear on the top line at the right of the screen opposite the first menu item and would flash in that position until an entry had been made reflecting forecasted portion sales. Before making such an entry, the manager or food controller would obviously consider carefully all displayed records and make the necessary judgment about future sales.

As the manager entered his or her forecast, the cursor would move from line to line until sales had been forecasted for each menu item. At that point, it would be possible to obtain a print-out of the complete forecast, either as a simple forecast or in the form of one of the production sheets described in the chapter. As many copies as necessary could be obtained, so that various key individuals in the establishment could be informed of anticipated future sales forecasts.

CHAPTER ESSENTIALS

In this chapter, we discussed the importance of the sales history as a primary tool for forecasting future sales. We described and illustrated several approaches to maintaining sales histories. We identified the popularity index as used in the food service industry and showed how the popularity index is computed and used in forecasting. From the forecast, production sheets may be prepared, and these may take any of several illustrated forms. A method for controlling preportioned entree items was illustrated and discussed. The importance of a Void Sheet to management was stressed. The Portion Inventory and Reconciliation was offered as another useful approach to controlling entrees. Finally, we discussed the manner in which computers may be used to obtain and maintain sales histories, and how they can assist in forecasting sales and in preparing production sheets.

QUESTIONS AND PROBLEMS

1 Compute the popularity index for the following sales. Round percentages to nearest .1%.

a

Item	*Portions Sold*	*% of Total Sales*
A	60	
B	20	
C	80	
D	40	

b

Item	*Portions Sold*	*% of Total Sales*
A	30	
B	42	
C	73	
D	115	

c

Item	*Portions Sold*	*% of Total Sales*
A	86	
B	113	
C	55	
D	44	
E	25	

2 In 1 (**a**) above predict the sales for each item if sales for all items are expected to be 300.

3 In 1(**b**) above predict the sales for each item if sales for all items are expected to be only 150.

4 In 1(**c**) above predict the sales of each item if sales for all items are expected to be 450.

5 In question 2 above, assume that the adjusted forecast is 20% less than the original forecast, then prepare a production sheet, using figure 11.5 as a guide.

6 In question 3 above, assume that the adjusted forecast is 10% greater than the original forecast, then prepare a production sheet using figure 11.5 as a guide.

7 List and discuss four possible causes of discrepancies between figures listed in the Portions Consumed and Portions Sold columns on the form illustrated in figure 11.9.

8 Define sales history and list three ways information for a sales history is gathered.

9 What advantages and disadvantages do you see in each of the three ways sales history information is presented?

10 Describe a procedure used in controlling high cost, precut entrees.

11 If a food controller were looking for ways to reduce excessive food costs, would he or she find void sheets of any use? Why?

12 Of what use is an electronic sales terminal in developing a sales history?

13 Might it be possible for a computer to generate the portion inventory and reconciliation form illustrated in figure 11.9? In general, what hardware and data would be required?

chapter 12

Standard Versus Actual Food Costs: Potential Savings

Learning Objectives

After reading and studying this chapter, the student should be able to:

1 Define and calculate standard cost.
2 Describe how a Menu Pre-Cost and Abstract form is used.
3 List several ways an undesirable forecasted food cost percentage can be changed.
4 Define and calculate potential savings.
5 Distinguish between daily and periodic calculation of standard cost and potential savings.
6 Explain the role of the computer in determining potential savings.

In the preceding chapters, considerable discussion has been given to the desirability of and the means for establishing control over purchasing, storing, issuing, and preparing food products for sale. Attention was focused on establishing standards: standard purchase specifications, standard receiving and issuing procedures, standard production methods, and standard portion sizes. With the establishment of an additional standard—the standard portion cost—it becomes possible to measure operating efficiency with a greater degree of accuracy than would otherwise be possible, and thus to determine the extent to which the staff is adhering to the operating standards and procedures set by management. Actual costs can be compared to standard costs, and the difference between them will be a very useful measure of the extent to which standards are not being observed. The difference will indicate the degree of inefficiency in day-to-day operations and will suggest the extent to which costs could be reduced without any sacrifice in standards.

Generally speaking, there are two methods for comparing standard and actual costs. The first involves daily calculation of standard costs and actual costs and the development of cumulative figures over an operating period such as one month. Daily reports of the results to date are common and lead typically to a final summary report at the end of a period. The second method does not involve daily calculation but relies on periodic determination of standard costs from actual portion sales records for the period. The choice of one method over the other is left to management in any given operation and should be based on the type of menu in effect, management's need for information, and the availability of personnel to prepare the needed information.

While the first method offers the advantage of immediate information and all the attendant benefits of such immediacy, it does require considerable staff time for calculation. The second, although requiring less in the way of daily staff time, does not offer the advantage of immediacy, nor is it able to account for the fluctuations in market prices and their effect on standard costs. Because there are considerable differences in procedures, both methods will be discussed here.

DAILY COMPARISON

Once standard costs and selling prices for standard portions are known and forecasts have been made, it is possible to determine in advance what the cost percentage of operation should be. Of course, this figure will be accurate and reliable only if the forecast is accurate and the personnel adhere to all established standards.

At the end of the day or after the meal, when the forecasted sales have been made, the figures developed for the sales history can be substituted for the portions forecasted, and the standard cost percentage can be calculated. This will show what the cost percentage should have been, based on actual sales.

Both of these procedures are accomplished on a form known as the Menu Pre-Cost and Abstract, illustrated in figure 12.1.

Figure 12.1
Menu Pre-Cost and Abstract

Date Mon. 11/1/—

Menu Item	*Number Forecast*	*Forecast*			*Total Cost*	*Total Sales*	*Number Sold*	*Actual*			*Total Cost*	*Total Sales*
		Cost	*S.P.*	*F.C.%*				*Cost*	*S.P.*	*F.C.%*		
A	80	2.05	5.95	34.5%	164.00	476.00	75	2.05	5.95	34.5%	153.75	446.25
B	65	2.45	6.95	35.3%	159.25	451.75	60	2.45	6.95	35.3%	147.00	417.00
C	10	4.30	12.95	33.2%	43.00	129.50	6	4.30	12.95	33.2%	25.80	77.70
D	165	2.60	7.95	32.7%	429.00	1,311.75	159	2.60	7.95	32.7%	413.40	1,264.05
				33.6%	795.25	2,369.00				33.6%	739.95	2,205.00

THE MENU PRE-COST AND ABSTRACT

This form is divided into two sections. The part on the left is used in conjunction with the forecast, sometime before a day or meal. The part on the right is completed later, after the sales have taken place.

The Forecast

After sales have been forecasted, as described earlier, the food controller can enter both the items forecasted and the number of portions of each in the first two columns on the form. The next entries are the standard portion costs for each item, taken from recipe detail and cost cards, butcher test cards, or cooking loss test cards, depending on the nature of the item. In the sales column, the figures entered are taken from the menu. These are the prices for which each item will sell. In the cost percentage column, the figure will be the cost-to-sales ratio for one portion of each item.

When all of these entries have been made, the total standard cost of producing the forecasted number of portions is determined by multipying the portion cost by the number of portions forecasted. Thus, in the example given, eighty portions forecasted multiplied by a single portion cost of $2.05 gives the total standard cost of $164 for producing the needed quantity of item A. This is a standard cost figure. It presupposes that each portion will be produced in the exact standard size specified and according to the exact production method established by the standard recipe. This procedure is followed for each item listed, and the standard cost for producing the required number of portions of each item is determined. The total cost column is then added to determine the total standard cost for producing all items on the menu.

The same procedure is employed for determining the total sales that ideally will result from the production of the numbers of portions forecasted. The selling price for one portion of each item is multiplied by the number of portions forecasted to find the total dollar volume of sales that will result from the production of the portions specified for each item. Once total sales for each have been calculated, the total sales column is added to determine the total dollar income that will be generated by the portion sales forecasted.

In this manner, total anticipated costs and sales can be determined, provided, of course, that the forecast reflects all items that will appear on the menu and that the costs and selling prices of each are included. If, for example, the $12.95 selling price for item C includes such side dishes as potato, vegetable, and salad, the cost of each of these items must be included in the portion cost figures.

Once total costs and sales have been forecasted, a cost percentage can be predicted by simply dividing sales into cost and multiplying the result by 100. In the example cited, the total cost of $795.25 divided by the total sales of $2,369.00 is .33569, which multiplied by 100 shows a predicted cost-to-sales ratio of 33.6%. Again, it must be emphasized that this standard cost percentage will correspond to the actual cost percentage only under ideal conditions. However, the differences between the standard cost percentage and the actual cost percentage will give some indication of opportunities for improving operations.

The foregoing has presupposed the existence of a menu scheduled for production for a particular day in the near future, and the desirability of predicting cost and sales figures in connection with that existing menu. However, these techniques for forecasting costs and sales are also useful to the operator who is considering rewriting the menu. If accurate assessment can be made of public demand for the items on a proposed menu, the total costs and sales that should result can be predicted in advance. A manager can often avoid costly mistakes by obtaining from the food controller a forecast such as that above. Public demand for each item must be assessed and translated into the number of portion sales forecasted for each item. This number is multiplied by carefully determined standard costs and selling prices for each item. Total costs and sales are predicted for the proposed menu by adding the totals for each of the items, and the gross profit and cost percentage are forecasted. If the forecast is satisfactory, the manager can send the menu to a printer. If it is not, various changes can be made and their anticipated results should be assessed before the printing. Cost and sales figures may be raised or lowered, depending on which is desirable, by one of the following means.

1 Selling prices may be changed.
2 Costs can be reduced by changing portion sizes, standard recipes, or both.
3 Items may be eliminated.
4 Substitutions may be made.

Conceivably, all of these means might be employed in some instances and the final version of the new menu might bear little or no resemblance to that originally proposed. However, while the original proposal might have led to undesirable results, the new menu should not, provided that good judgment and careful calculations have gone into its preparation.

The Abstract

The abstract, or right-hand portion of the form under discussion, is prepared after sales have taken place. The person preparing the abstract, usually the food controller, refers to the figures developed for inclusion in the sales history, enters them in the Number Sold column, and multiplies each by the standard portion cost and selling price, copied from the forecast section, in order to determine the total standard cost for preparing the portions sold. This is a precalculated cost, based on precalculated standard costs for each portion. The total precalculated cost and the total sales are determined by adding each column. The standard cost percentage for actual sales is determined by dividing total costs by total sales.

The next step is to compare the forecasted cost percentage developed from the abstract. Differences will invariably exist. The differences occur because the total volume forecasted usually differs in some measure from actual volume, and because some items did not sell as well as was anticipated. In addition, some of the items may have sold in greater quantities than were forecasted, which sometimes raises questions about the extent to which the kitchen staff is following production schedules. This is worth noting because although the additional sales may have brought in additional income, failure to follow production goals established by management indicates that one of the control procedures is not operating effectively. In addition, it is possible that an appropriate quantity of an item was produced but that all portions were undersized. This is undesirable and may lead to loss of business, because it really means that customers have been cheated. For these reasons, among others, sales in excess of the number forecasted should always be investigated. One important reason for comparing the forecasted cost percentage with the percentage developed from the abstract is that the difference between the two measures not only the extent to which forecasting techniques can be improved, but also the extent to which the forecast has been wrong in terms of incorrect total volume, incorrect forecasted sales of particular items, or both. Such a comparison suggests possibilities for improving forecasting performance in order to bring the cost percentage from the abstract more nearly in line with that from the forecast. After all, this forecasted cost percentage has received some measure of approval as an acceptable goal, and therefore should not be ignored.

The forecasted cost percentage should reflect the cost acceptable to management to achieve a certain dollar volume of sales. In addition, it should be thought of as reflecting plans for meeting those goals, with the plans translated to established standards and standard procedures. So, to the extent that forecasted cost percentages are not in line with those calculated after sales, overall performance, including forecasting, is not all that it might be.

After a cost percentage has been calculated on the basis of the figures on the abstract side of the form, it may be taken as indicating what the cost percentage *should have been* if everything had gone according to plan. If the exact number of portions needed have been prepared according to the standards and procedures set by the management, this is what the cost percentage should be, and as such it reflects the dollar cost that should have been incurred to produce a certain dollar volume of sales.

If developed one meal at a time, or even one day at a time, and then put aside, these figures are not being used as effectively as they might be. It is possible and desirable to develop abstracts of standard costs and sales over a period of some weeks or months. If this period is taken as a test period, the results offer a very good indication of what the cost percentage of operation should be over a longer period of time. Figure 12.2 illustrates the results of such figures developed over a seven-day test period. In this case, the restaurant under consideration should generally operate with a cost-to-sales ratio of 33.6%. Such figures can be very useful in judging effectiveness of operations from week to week or month to month.

When standards are in effect for every item served, standard costs are known, and the Menu Pre-Cost and Abstract prepared daily reflects the total menu, it is

FIGURE 12.2
Summary of Daily Abstracts

Week of ______

Date	Standard Cost	Sales	Standard Cost %
1	$739.95	$2,205.00	33.6%
2	601.50	1,800.95	33.4%
3	782.97	2.316.50	33.8%
4	771.15	2,288.25	33.7%
5	735.50	2,195.55	33.5%
6	825.66	2,435.60	33.9%
7	747.80	2,225.55	33.6%
Total Standard Cost	$ 5,204.53		
Total Sales	$15,467.40		
Standard Cost %	33.6%		

possible to reconcile standard and actual costs on a daily basis, and thus to date throughout the period. Actual costs are determined from direct purchases and storeroom issues, as discussed in Chapter 9. The standard or potential cost of preparing all the items sold is taken from the Menu Pre-Cost and Abstract. Sales are taken from accounting department records. All figures are recorded on a form similar to that in figure 12.3. Actual cost percentage and standard cost percentage are calculated from the figures entered. Typically, the actual cost will be greater than the standard cost. The difference can be regarded either as waste or as excessive cost that can be reduced or eliminated if staff performance is improved. The raw dollar figures indicating that excessive costs have developed are not particularly useful in isolating the roots of inefficiency or other operating difficulties. In many instances, it is helpful to devise techniques for detecting the areas in which the waste has occurred.

Potential savings are the difference between the actual and the standard and may be recorded as dollars, as percentages of sales, or as both. Potential savings reflect the differences between conditions that exist and those that management would like to see if all plans were carried out to perfection. No kitchen will ever achieve that perfection, of course, but it is usually possible to find ways to improve operations so that the future results will be somewhat closer to perfection.

The conditions that lead to differences in standard and actual costs include overpurchasing, overproduction, pilferage, spoilage, improper portioning, and failure to follow standard recipes, among others. To the extent to which improvements are made and problems existing in these areas are eliminated, actual costs will be more nearly equal to standard costs, and potential savings will be reduced. In general, potential savings and waste are synonymous. The reduction in potential savings means the reduction of waste and the reduction of excessive cost.

When these figures are available daily and cumulatively for a period, it is possible to make daily investigations of the causes of the variance between standard

FIGURE 12.3

Summary of Actual and Standard Food Costs, Food Sales, and Potential Savings

Date	Actual Cost		Standard Cost		Sales		Actual Cost %		Standard Cost %		Potential Savings			
	Today	To Date	Today	To Date	Today	To Date	Today	To Date	Today	To Date	Today		To Date	
											$	%	$	%
1	786.00	786.00	739.95	739.95	2,205.00	2,205.00	35.6%	35.6%	33.6%	33.6%	46.05	2.1%	46.05	2.1%
2	612.33	1,398.33	601.50	1,341.45	1,800.95	4,005.95	34.0%	34.9%	33.4%	33.5%	10.83	.6%	56.88	1.4%
3	806.45	2,204.78	782.97	2,124.42	2,316.50	6,322.45	34.8%	34.9%	33.8%	33.6%	23.48	1.0%	80.36	1.3%
4	795.05	2,999.83	771.15	2,895.57	2,288.25	8,610.70	34.7%	34.8%	33.7%	33.6%	23.90	1.0%	104.26	1.2%
5	761.25	3,761.08	735.50	3,631.07	2,195.55	10,806.25	34.7%	34.8%	33.5%	33.6%	25.75	1.2%	130.01	1.2%
6	842.17	4,603.25	825.66	4,456.73	2,435.60	13,241.85	34.6%	34.8%	33.9%	33.7%	16.51	.7%	146.52	1.1%
7	759.05	5,362.30	747.80	5,204.53	2,225.55	15,467.40	34.1%	34.7%	33.6%	33.6%	11.25	.5%	157.77	1.0%

and actual cost figures. It will probably never be completely possible to eliminate the discrepancy between standard and actual costs. Management in any given situation must determine the extent to which reduction is possible, and be content to live with a discrepancy of some small percentage between the actual and the standard. No industry-wide figure for guidance exists. However, once management has determined a reasonable figure for the acceptable variance, exceptions can be noted at once, and investigation can begin immediately. Such immediate investigation is more likely to uncover causes than will investigation some days or weeks later. When causes are immediately known, one can take remedial action in the hope of correcting problems before their effects become more pronounced. Immediate consultation with the chef, steward, and other interested personnel will usually reveal causes and make corrective measures possible.

PERIODIC CALCULATION

In establishments in which daily calculations are impractical or impossible, one can still apply the principles of standard costing techniques periodically to determine the extent of waste under existing conditions. Like the daily techniques, the periodic approach presupposes that standards exist in all the areas previously discussed, that sales histories are maintained, and that standard portion costs are known. Under such circumstances a food controller can calculate standard costs for a test period of one week and compare the findings to the actual costs for that same period to determine the extent of potential savings. This might be done once every three months, or more frequently if time and need exist.

Using a worksheet such as that illustrated in figure 12.4, the food controller would enter from sales history records the items and the number of portions of each sold during the test period. Standard portion costs for each item would be recorded from appropriate recipe detail and cost cards, butcher tests, or cooking loss tests. The total standard cost for producing the number of items sold would be found by extending the items individually and then adding.

Actual costs for the period are determined from direct purchases, storeroom issues, and sales figures obtained from the accounting office. When daily cost figures are being developed, as discussed in Chapter 9, the figures are already available. The variance between actual and standard costs for the test period can then be determined, both in terms of dollars and as percentages of total sales. To the extent to which the test period is truly representative of day-to-day operations, the operational efficiency can be measured, and where necessary, corrective action taken to improve results by the next test period. It is usually advisable to select test periods at random, after the fact. The figures developed would be more truly representative than those that might be found if the employees knew in advance that a certain week were being taken as a test period. In such cases, employees would be likely to pay stricter attention to the standards set by management.

FIGURE 12.4
Periodic Potential Savings Worksheet

For Test Period ________ to________, 19—

Item	# Sold	Portion Cost	Total Standard Cost
A	520	$2.25	$1,170.00
B	731	3.85	2,814.35
C	322	4.10	1,320.20
D	903	1.85	1,670.55
E	611	2.45	1,496.95
			$8,472.05

Sales for Test Period:	$25,416.15
Actual Cost	8,877.45
Standard Cost	8,472.05
Potential Savings	$ 405.40
Actual Cost%	34.9%
Standard Cost %	33.3%
Potential Savings as a % of Sales	1.6%

While the results of their efforts might be wholly desirable, the measure of actual against standard cost for the period would give a distorted view of day-to-day wastefulness and potential savings.

Once determined, this standard cost percentage may be compared with actual cost percentage during the period between test periods. Thus, one can effectively judge the efficiency of operations during the intervening period. Where cost percentages are developed on a weekly basis, it is usually more desirable to compare the figures with a recently calculated standard cost percentage than with a cost percentage from the previous week. Of course, the menu should not have changed drastically in terms of content or price, and the cost of items should be pretty much the same as during the test period. If both assumptions are invalid, the concept of comparing the actual cost percentage with the standard would also be invalid. The important point to remember is that a comparison of the cost percentage with a previous period in no way by itself tells the manager if waste is occurring. Only by comparison with a standard can that determination be made.

One final word about potential savings is in order. To the extent that these amounts can be saved without incurring other costs, they will increase profits. If, for example, part of the potential savings figure is the result of overproduction and consequent spoiling of food, then by eliminating the overproduction, profits should theoretically be increased by the amount of the total savings. This is illustrated by the following figures.

	Actual	*Standard*
Sales	$10,000	$10,000
Food Cost	$ 3,800	$ 3,400
Gross Profit	$ 6,200	$ 6,600

It is immediately apparent that reduction in excessive costs brings about an identical increase in gross profit. If this reduction can be brought about without increasing any other costs–for example, the cost of labor—then literally every dollar saved will be an additional dollar in profit. This fact, perhaps more than any other, points up the importance of judging actual cost in comparison to standard costs, and of making every practical effort to eliminate the difference.

EDP APPLICATIONS

Given the computer's ability, with appropriate applications programs, to provide standard portion costs and to assist in forecasting, the development of the Menu Pre-Cost and Abstract is a comparatively simple matter. Provided that standard sales prices were also stored in memory, which would be quite likely with the use of modern sales terminals that feature price look-up, the Pre-Cost portion could be displayed or printed before the forecasted date so that any necessary adjustments could be made. The Abstract portion, printed after sales had taken place, would provide total standard cost for those items sold. It should be noted that preparing the Menu Pre-Cost and Abstract manually has been extremely difficult and time-consuming for those operators who have done it. In the future, however, with the aid of suitably programmed computers, it can become a comparatively simple document to prepare, and one that could become much more widely used than it is presently.

Once known, the standard cost for an operating period can readily be compared with the actual cost for the same period, determined by the computer in the manner suggested in Chapter 9. With both actual and standard costs for a period stored in computer memory, a report could be generated comparing the two; subtracting standard from actual costs can show potential savings for a period of any length. If determined on a daily basis, the data could be stored in memory and reported both daily and cumulatively for a period. Alternatively, the data might be stored daily but reported only periodically, possibly once a month, timed to coincide with the accounting cycle.

CHAPTER ESSENTIALS

This chapter presented two methods for determining total standard cost for a given operating period. We showed how a comparison of standard and actual cost for a period reveals a variety of inefficiencies in day-to-day operation, including poor forecasting, overproduction, failure to follow standard recipes, and some instances of overpurchasing. Four means for changing undesirable cost and sales were listed. Potential savings were defined as the difference between actual and standard cost. We illustrated how reductions in excessive cost will result in increases in gross profits and may result in increases in net profits as well. Finally, we described possible means for determining potential savings with a computer's assistance.

QUESTIONS AND PROBLEMS

1 List and discuss five possible conditions that can lead to differences between actual and standard costs, pointing out how each increases potential saving.

2 It has been said that potential savings, taken as a percentage of sales, may be used as one possible measure of operating efficiency. Do you agree or disagree? Why?

3 Discuss the advantages and disadvantages of using the daily method for determining potential savings over periodic calculations.

4 Using the figures given in each of the cases below, determine actual cost percent, standard cost percent, and potential savings both as a dollar figure and as a percentage of sales.

	Sales	*Actual Cost*	*Standard Cost*
a	$ 400.00	$ 120.00	$ 100.00
b	$ 860.00	$ 318.20	$ 301.00
c	$ 3,486.00	$1,394.40	$1,324.68
d	$11,198.00	$3,919.30	$3,695.34

5 Using the form illustrated in Figure 12.3 complete the calculation for a four-day period given the figures below:

	Actual Cost Today	*Standard Cost Today*	*Sales Today*
Monday	$110	$100	$300
Tuesday	$160	$145	$450
Wednesday	$175	$160	$505
Thursday	$185	$175	$520

6 Given the following information, prepare a complete Menu Pre-Cost and Abstract form. After completing the calculations, determine the forecasted cost percentage and the standard cost percentage.

Item	*Portions Forecasted*	*Portion Cost*	*Selling Price*	*Number Sold*
A	60	$2.50	$6.00	55
B	20	3.25	8.50	18
C	80	2.25	5.00	80
D	40	2.70	6.50	38

7 Given the following information, prepare a complete Menu Pre-Cost and Abstract form. After completing the calculations, determine the forecasted cost percentage and the standard cost percentage.

Item	*Portions Forecasted*	*Portion Cost*	*Selling Price*	*Number Sold*
A	30	$3.70	$8.50	28
B	42	3.00	6.80	42
C	73	2.75	6.00	70
D	115	2.50	5.50	106

8 Write a 300-word essay contrasting the approach to controlling costs using the Menu Pre-Cost and Abstract and the Portion Inventory and Reconciliation (Chapter 11).

9 Explain the role of the computer in determining potential savings.

10 Why might the increased use of computers in food service establishments make the Menu Pre-Cost and Abstract a more widely used control document?

chapter 13

Sales Control

Learning Objectives

After reading and studying this chapter, the student should be able to:

1. List and discuss the eight factors for which customers patronize one food service establishment rather than another.
2. Define the scope of sales control.
3. List the general topics included in menu making and discuss their relation to sales control.
4. Determine suitable menu prices, using any of three suggested methods.
5. Illustrate and explain the selling techniques that management advocates sales personnel use in controlling the sale of menu items.
6. List and explain the several control procedures employed to ensure that sales are suitably recorded and result in revenue.
7. Calculate the average sale for a foodservice establishment.
8. Balance and explain the purpose of a restaurant sales control sheet.
9. Explain two ways in which computers may aid managers in controlling restaurant sales.

For purposes of this text, the authors chose to view sales control in very broad terms. For many, sales control is simply a synonym for revenue control; however, the authors feel this position is entirely too narrow and restrictive. From our point of view, sales control also encompasses all of those activities undertaken by management to maximize sales volume. We believe that to control sales effectively, the manager must work to:

1. increase the number of customers,
2. influence what those customers purchase, and
3. ensure that all customer purchases result in appropriate revenue.

To think of sales control in any narrower sense would be to neglect a number of important management activities in most restaurants.

INCREASING THE NUMBER OF CUSTOMERS

It is comparatively uncommon for restaurants to operate at peak volume at all times. Most experience both high and low volume periods. Sometimes both are evident on the same day; at other times entire weeks of high volume may be followed by weeks when volume is comparatively low. Sometimes the differences are seasonal, sometimes annual.

At one time or another, most owners and managers are faced with the problem of lower sales volume than would be desirable. Consequently, in the light of operating costs that seem to increase continually, most are engaged in the business of attempting to increase sales volume in order to maintain or increase the level of profit. Productive efforts to increase sales are best made by those who understand the factors that cause customers to patronize one foodservice establishment rather than another. These factors include:

Business Location
Product Differentiation
Price Acceptability
Decor
Portion Size
Product Quality
Service Standards
Scope of the Menu

Purposely, these factors are not listed in any particular order. Every customer has his own important reason for patronizing a restaurant, and these will change under varying circumstances. To some, food quality might be the single most important reason for patronizing a particular restaurant. However, when time is short a convenient location might be the determining factor. To succeed, however, a restaurant must meet a sufficient number of the above characteristics to appeal to a large enough market and hence to cover costs.

Business Location

If one were to take a given population center and draw concentric circles around it, then place a restaurant at every mile on each of the circles as shown in figure 13.1, one could judge the effect of location in relation to the population center. Other things being equal, customers will normally choose the most convenient restaurant, and there is a maximum time any customer will travel to go to any particular restaurant.

FIGURE 13.1

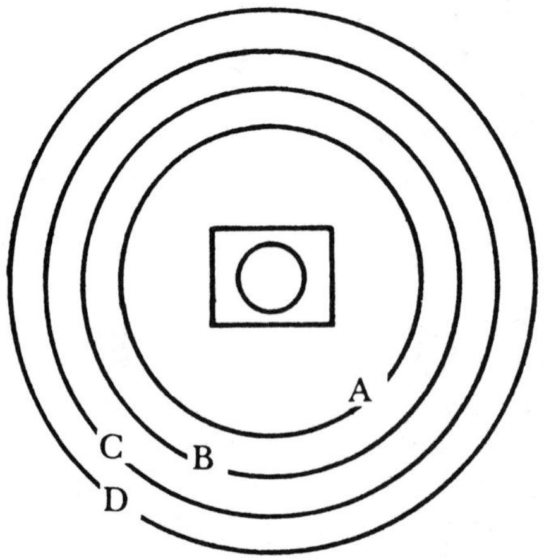

One would expect restaurant A to have more customers at any given time than restaurant B, and the numbers should decrease as one gets farther from the population center. At one extreme, it should be obvious that a restaurant located in the center of Death Valley in California would attract very few customers from Los Angeles because of the distance from that population center. Most people would be unwilling to travel that far for a restaurant, no matter how fine its reputation. On the other hand, the only Italian restaurant in a city of 100,000 can expect to do well, even if the quality of its product or its prices are not particularly attractive to potential clientele. In actuality the authors have noted that restaurants located in the financial district of New York City do an excellent luncheon business on weekdays, but many of them close for the evening meal and on weekends for lack of business. In midtown Manhattan, however, most restaurants do an excellent dinner business. A good location will not guarantee customers but is usually necessary for volume business. Fast-food operators recognize the importance of location. The national fast-food chains know very precisely how many customers they can expect in a given population center, and that is one reason why one seldom hears of a business failure for the "McDonald's" or "Burger King" type of establishment.

Product Differentiation

Economists characterize products and services as **homogeneous** or **differentiated.** This distinction is based on how similar or different products or services are from one another. A **homogeneous** product or service is one that is so similar to another that customers do not have a preference and will purchase whichever costs less. This means that a general "market price" exists for these products and services and the individual manager cannot raise prices without losing all or a number of customers. In the grain market, for example, a farmer can sell his entire grain supply for the "market price" but cannot sell any of it at a price one penny higher. This is because his grain is a homogeneous product and no buyer would pay higher than market.

A **differentiated** product or service, on the other hand, is sufficiently unique so that customers develop a preference for that product or service. The uniqueness can be real or imagined. As long as customers prefer one product or service over another, for whatever reason, that product or service is differentiated. Most businesses, including restaurants, fall into that category.

People have preferences, even among Italian restaurants. One may have a better decor or a better sauce; another has faster service. If food and beverage managers can differentiate their product and service sufficiently, they will get more customers than their competition and can charge higher prices, often resulting in greater profit. This is one of advertising's functions—to establish differentiation and customer loyalty, even though the product or service may be quite similar to another.

Price Acceptability

Figure 13.2 shows the relationship of prices to sales between two different products. Example A is a product that is only slightly differentiated. Note that as the price charged is increased, the number of unit sales drops considerably. This is because customers have no particular loyalty to that product and will purchase a similar one from a competitor who charges less; they may also either find a substitute for it or go without. Example B, on the other hand, is a more differentiated product and unit sales volume is less affected by price changes. Customers have a real loyalty to that product and are willing to pay higher prices for it because no other product or service similar to it is available and they desire it enough to pay the higher price. The product in Example A has what economists call an "elastic" demand curve, whereas the product in Example B has an "inelastic" demand curve. One is very price-sensitive, the other is not.

FIGURE 13.2

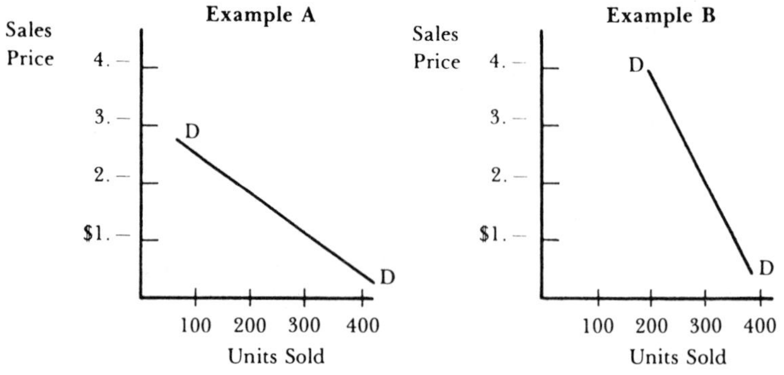

In the food and beverage business, generally the more homogeneous the product or service is, the more price-sensitive it is; the more differentiated the product or service, the less price-sensitive it is. That is why we find McDonald's and Burger King charging about the same for hamburgers. Hamburgers are reasonably homogeneous, and although both companies attempt to differentiate their products and service through advertising, different packaging, methods of operating, and other means, many customers feel that both are of about the same quality. The challenge for most food and beverage operators is to determine how differentiated their products or services are in order to set prices that will provide the maximum profit. If products and services are not sufficiently differentiated to enable operators to set high enough prices to make reasonable profits, the operators must either go out of business or find ways of changing the products or services.

Decor

There is an old saying that "beauty is in the eyes of the beholder." That is indeed true when it comes to restaurant decor. Every restaurant has a clientele that enjoys its particular decor. The decor differentiates one restaurant from another. However, what is pleasing to one person may not be pleasing to another. One key to restaurant success, then, is decor that will appeal to a sufficiently large clientele to ensure volume, and thus profit. Families usually prefer an informal, light atmosphere; persons who patronize gourmet restaurants usually prefer a more formal setting. Dark restaurants with limited visibility usually appeal to a select group of patrons. In effect, a restaurant's decor determines to a great extent the number and type of its patrons.

Portion Size

Portion sizes must be appropriate to the clientele that a food and beverage operator wishes to attract. Young, active persons are often more concerned with larger portions and sometimes patronize the restaurants that are the most generous with servings. Older persons, on the other hand, often eat much smaller amounts and sometimes stay away from restaurants with large portion sizes because they feel they will waste food or have to pay for food not consumed. Therefore, it is not true that large portions always attract great numbers of customers. Most customers want value for their money, and portion size is only one element in determining whether or not value is received. Of significance is the principle that portion sizes must satisfy the needs of the clientele the food operator wishes to attract. If they are smaller than desired, business will be lost. If they are larger than desired, greater cost than necessary will result, possibly causing reduced profit and certainly leading to wasted food.

Product Quality

Quality, like decor, means something different to each of us. Those with particularly refined tastes—sometimes referred to as gourmets—will often accept nothing but perfection in food, which for them means that all ingredients must be fresh rather than canned or frozen, that soups must be prepared from freshly made stocks, and that vegetables must be cooked only until just tender. Unless the products of a particular restaurant meet these exacting standards, such individuals will not patronize it. On the other hand, most of us do not have such demanding standards and are perfectly willing to consume and enjoy food products that might be rejected by the ultra-demanding connoisseur. At the same time, there are those who appear to be completely indifferent to what most of us would consider appropriate standards of quality for foodservice products. For them, food of almost any degree of quality, however poor to us, is acceptable. Their reasons for patronizing restaurants are not related to product quality as most of us would define it.

In a given population, various segments demand products of various levels of quality, and it is management's responsibility to assess the market and offer products of such quality as will appeal to a large enough segment of the market to ensure sufficient volume for profitability.

Service Standards

Anyone who has ever eaten out realizes the wide range of service available and the quality of service offered. Fast-food establishments and cafeterias tend to offer as little service as possible, while some of the older hotel dining rooms and many finer restaurants seem to have extraordinary numbers of attendants for each patron. And where greater service is offered the diner, it is occasionally of the very highest quality—swift, unobtrusive, and nearly approximating an art form—but more often it is somewhat indifferent, rather slow, sometimes sloppy and intrusive, and quite obviously untrained.

At the same time, each individual diner or party consciously or unconsciously considers what constitutes appropriate quantity and quality of service for each particular dining occasion. Often time is a factor, and the diner will select that establishment that he or she feels will afford the opportunity to consume the desired meal within the time frame available. On the other hand, there are those, often celebrants of some special occasion, for whom time is of no particular concern. For them, the pleasure of the dining occasion, consisting of the finest quality in both food and service, is of paramount importance. The former may select one of the nationally known fast-food chains or a popular local cafeteria, while the latter may prefer to travel some distance to seek out a well-known and widely respected restaurant that is renowned for offering service in the time-honored Old World tradition.

Additionally, there are those who are well aware that service means tipping serving personnel, which they prefer not to do. Many people on low or fixed incomes fall into this category. Of necessity they must be concerned with each penny spent and prefer to use their limited means for food purchase, rather than for tipping serving personnel.

Managers who seek to maximize restaurant sales should be aware of the extent and quality of service that their customers want. With that awareness in mind, certain aspects of the business can be adjusted to suit the patrons. For example, a full-service restaurant may reduce the amount of service by instituting a salad bar and instructing serving personnel to direct diners there between the appetizer and entree courses. This might facilitate a reduction in the number of serving personnel, and at the same time possibly speed up the dining process to suit the aims of both hurried diners and the restaurant manager, who wants to increase customer turnover during the peak dining hours.

Scope of the Menu

With the exception of those restaurants that offer homogeneous products—commonly accepted and even sought out by the public, consumed in vast amounts because of their comparatively low prices as well as their staple nature in the diet of the dining public—most establishments need a wider range of items on the menu. A menu that includes only two or three entree choices is obviously of more limited appeal than one that offers twelve or fifteen. Any given diner would be more likely to find an item of his choice on the latter menu. In establishments whose success depends heavily on repeat business, the more limited menu could substantially reduce the number of times in a given period when a particular customer would return.

However, the extent of the offerings on any menu must be governed by certain considerations, including the equipment available in the kitchen, the culinary abilities of the kitchen staff, and the cost considerations that arise when a large number of items are being offered and much leftover food results. As a general rule, the greater the scope consistent with these other considerations, the larger will be the segment of the market to which the menu appeals, and the more likely will be success.

It is probably not possible to find an ideal restaurant, in terms of all of the above considerations. After all, no location is perfect, and it is impossible to assess a market so perfectly that differentiated products can be provided at a price acceptable to all diners in a setting pleasing to all. However, for a restaurant to succeed, management must keep these considerations in mind and offer as great a portion of each as possible to the largest possible segment of the market. Failure to recognize these factors carries with it the risk of failing to attract a sufficient share of the foodservice market to cover costs and establish a successful and profitable enterprise.

INFLUENCING CUSTOMER PURCHASES

It is important for restaurateurs to exercise some form of control over the number and variety of menu items, because food is purchased in particular quantities in anticipation of reasonably specific numbers of sales. If sales do not materialize for each of the products, food might either be wasted, get spoiled, or be used to produce menu items other than those for which it was initially purchased. In the last case, this food might be used in place of some rather less costly ingredients, and consequently food cost per item produced is higher than necessary. Still another possibility is that the unsold food items may be used to feed employees, and thus generate no sales at all. For example, if fresh fish is purchased for use in a broiled fish dish, and if sales for that item fall short of anticipated numbers, then the fish must be put to another use before it spoils. It may go into a casserole or be fed to the staff. Whatever the use, the fish will usually generate a lower contribution margin per unit than was anticipated, and the item prepared will have a higher cost-to-sales ratio than the item for which it was intended. Overall cost and potential savings figures will be higher than desired, and profits will be reduced.

Still other problems may result. If customers do not order the anticipated items, a shift in demand may cause such difficulties as running out of another item for which high demand was not anticipated. This could lead to reduced sales volume and might strain the ability of the work force in the kitchen, with one kitchen station being overworked while another has little to do.

In addition, in many establishments, different menu items frequently have different contribution margins. Higher-priced items often provide more desirable contribution margins than lower-priced items. To guarantee maximum profit, the knowledgeable foodservice operator understands the advantages of selling those food items with the highest contribution margins. For this reason, the successful operator must distinguish carefully between actively selling food and passively taking orders for it. In this sense, establishing control over the variety and numbers of items sold may be accomplished by two means: by the preparation of the menu itself and by the sales techniques used by service personnel.

The Menu

The first means for influencing customer purchases begins with writing the menu—the primary selling tool in most restaurants. As such it is largely responsible for which items are sold in the greatest and in the smallest quantities. Those items that are presented most favorably—those featured on the menu—will typically outsell other items. Conversely, those items that are least favorably presented will not sell in as large numbers as they might. Since each menu item frequently has different costs, contributions margins, and cost percents, the foodservice operator has an opportunity to control the cost percent and gross margin through preparing menus that achieve maximum sales volume, especially for those items deemed the most desirable and most profitable to sell.

Menu preparation is a complete subject in itself, quite beyond the scope of a text in cost control. However, anyone interested in cost control in hotels and restaurants should have some acquaintance with the general topics involved.

Layout and Design

It should be apparent that the entire physical menu—the stock, the color, the printing, and so on—should suit the character and style of the restaurant. One would not, after all, expect an elaborate menu printed in raised type on parchment stock in a common roadside diner, nor should one expect to see the menu of a high-priced and exclusive Continental restaurant printed poorly on the cheapest paper available. Appropriate menu design and layout for each kind of restaurant is essential to satisfy the clientele and achieve maximum revenue.

Anyone unfamiliar with the principles of advertising layout and design would be well advised to consult one or more of the several excellent books on these topics*—as well as reviewing first efforts with a specialist in the field—before having a menu printed.

Variety

For a menu to have maximum public appeal, a suitable variety of foods, preparation methods, and prices is necessary. Variety will satisfy the needs of a broad market and will assist the restaurant operator in capturing the largest possible number of customers. Even in specialty and ethnic restaurants, variety is important. After all, even the chains of hamburger restaurants give the customers a choice of several types and styles of hamburgers.

Several authors and restaurant specialists have suggested that a good general menu should include among the entrees several different types of meat, fish, poultry, and egg dishes. One highly respected consultant has suggested that five is the minimum number of entrees acceptable for a restaurant menu and that the number should include at least one of each of the general types of dishes mentioned above.

In general, menus should also include various kinds of cooking methods. Some items should be sautéed, others roasted, some boiled, and so on. This not

*Lothar A. Kreck, *Menus: Analysis and Planning, 2nd Edition* (New York: Van Nostrand Reinhold Company, 1984); Jack E. Miller, *Menu Pricing and Strategy* (New York: Van Nostrand Reinhold Company, 1979); Albin G. Seaberg, *Menu Design, Merchandising and Marketing, 3rd Edition* (New York: Van Nostrand Reinhold Company, 1983).

only ensures acceptance by customers with various prefrences but also adds variety in the appearance of foods reaching the customers' tables.

Appearance of foods is of great importance. The number of combinations of foods that may appear together on plates is vast, and some are more interesting and attractive than others. The possibilities for providing pleasant and appropriate contrasts in color, contour, and texture are always in the mind of the able menu writer. Saying that people eat first with their eyes may sound trite, but it is true nevertheless and should be kept in mind by anyone writing a menu.

It is also desirable to include a reasonable variety of entree prices. Not all potential customers desire to purchase the most expensive items, and most restaurants risk losing a substantial number of customers if prices do not appeal to a broad market. This is particularly true when family trade forms a substantial segment of the market and when repeat business is necessary for profitable survival.

Item Arrangement

Perhaps the most significant menu-making principle to a food controller is the physical arrangement of items on the menu. Unless their attention is otherwise directed, American customers read a menu in the same way they would read a book—from beginning to end, from top to bottom, and from left to right. Items listed first and at the top of a list are seen first and make the greatest impression. It stands to reason that those items will sell in the greatest quantities, or at least will sell in greater quantities than if they were placed at the bottom of the list.

Another way of bringing customers' attention to a particular menu item is to feature it in larger type than the items surrounding it. Sometimes a different typeface can have the same effect. In some cases, not only is the type different, but the item is given its own featured spot on the menu. In addition, many restaurants use colored pictures or photographs of some menu items to capture customer attention and to build sales volume for the pictured items.

The significant point is that the items the food controller wishes to sell in the greatest quantities should be the featured items. These may be the item in greatest supply in the kitchen on a particular day, or those with the most favorable cost-to-sales ratios, or those that provide the greatest contribution margins. In some instances, the featured items might be those whose sale would most greatly enhance the restaurant's reputation and thus help build sales volume. Many operators place those with greatest contribution margins in the most prominent places on the menu and relegate those with lesser contribution margins to less conspicuous spots. On such menus, high-cost, high-price items will be more prominent, often appearing first on a list of entrees. Other operators may feature items that require extensive preparation and cannot be used up as leftovers. On such menus, less perishable a la carte items, such as steaks cut and cooked to order, will be far less prominent on the menu.

On a well-prepared menu, all foods will appear in just those physical locations and with just those degrees of prominence that will induce customers to order what management wants most to sell.

Descriptive Language

The dining experience begins well before customers taste the food they have ordered. It begins with the first impression of the food operation, when the restaurant is first described by a friend, when potential customers read a review or an advertisement, or when they first enter the premises. The physical appearance of the establishment and its staff, and the attitude of the staff toward the diners, will make or reinforce an initial impression, or change one.

The menu itself, and the language used in that menu to describe food offerings, may make a good impression and induce customer orders. The descriptions of foods may make the customer hungry and may help to build higher sales than might otherwise have been possible. On the other hand, a menu that poorly describes available items may actually decrease sales. A food and beverage operator can often greatly influence the average check revenue by using descriptions that make menu items sound interesting. Customers tend to react positively to these foods that are appealingly described, and negatively to those that are not.

Appropriate adjectives tend to increase customer satisfaction because they lead to higher levels of expectation. As long as food lives up to its billing, customers receive greater enjoyment from eating those foods that verbal description has suggested will be good. The successful operator knows that a menu item simply labeled "Broiled Steak" has considerably less appeal to the customer than one described as "U.S. Choice Sirloin Steak Prepared To Your Taste, Garnished With The Chef's Special . . ." And after all, "Deep Fried Maryland Chicken, Southern Style" does conjure up different feelings for the diner than does "Fried Chicken."

Kitchen Personnel and Equipment

There have been all too many horrible examples of zealous foodservice operators writing into their menus various items that are beyond the culinary skill of their kitchen staffs. In fact, the authors are aware of instances when foodservice consultants have set up menus that included items that could not properly be produced by the kitchen personnel commonly available in the labor market. Too, there have been cases where certain menu items were perfect delights to customers until one or more kitchen employees quit or were fired, and new employees simply were not able to prepare the items satisfactorily. Anyone writing a menu should have clearly in mind the performance abilities of present staff and should be realistic about the possibilities of replacing any staff member with another of equal skill.

At the same time, someone writing a menu should be aware both of the type and quantity of equipment needed to prepare the items being included, and of the condition of the available equipment. Before including some dish that requires precise oven temperature for successful preparation, one should be sure that oven thermostats are in proper working order. And before deciding to include french fried potatoes with every order, one should be sure that sufficient equipment and staff are available in the kitchen to meet projected demand.

In addition, many kitchens, particularly large ones, are organized into stations, and the menu writer must be sure that the menu produced will lead to a reasonable amount of work for each station, with none being either overloaded or underworked. If analysis of an existing menu suggests that the amount of work in the kitchen is not suitably balanced among the workers or the stations, it may be wise to consider rewriting the menu, adjusting the number of persons working at each station, or providing additional equipment, or all of these. If such situations are permitted to develop or continue, the possibilities for increasing the labor turnover rate in the kitchen are increased significantly.

Failure to take these potential problems into account before writing the menu raises the possibilities of increasing customer discontent over bad food, poorly prepared, served late, and served cold.

Pricing

Because virtually all menus include the standard prices, and because the sum of all such prices paid by customers represents total food revenues for restaurant establishments, it should be evident that the prices at which menu items are offered are critically important in determining the success or failure of a restaurant. The selling price or sales value of a product or service is normally set by the manager or someone in authority. It is generally printed on a menu, or in some instances, placed on signs appearing throughout the restaurant.

The sales price should be determined by cost. A higher-cost item will have a higher sales price than a lower-cost item. Steak usually sells for a higher price than spaghetti because the cost of the ingredients in the meal is usually higher. However, cost is not the only determinant of price.

Other considerations enter into price detemination. Of primary concern is the desire to maximize sales. Restaurants with highly differentiated products have more flexibility to raise or lower prices than those with homogneous products. If McDonald's raises its prices substantially and Burger King does not, McDonald's would most likely suffer a substantial loss of customers. In all probability, the increase in prices would result in less total revenue for McDonald's and lower profit. On the other hand, an exclusive French restaurant with a highly differentiated product might raise its prices with very little adverse reaction from its customers. Thus, it is important that each restaurateur have some understanding of price sensitivity as it relates to product and service, so that sales and profits might be maximized. This price sensitivity will vary among restaurants and locations. Typically, locations with low-income residents will have more price-sensitive customers than those with higher-income residents.

Sometimes restaurateurs set prices deliberately to exclude certain customers or to cater to a specific clientele; or sometimes changing conditions force concomitant change in pricing policies. For example, a certain restaurant in New England had an excellent location on a major highway and catered primarily to interstate traffic. Prices were quite low, and the restaurant did volume trade in excess of 1,000 customers per day. A new interstate highway was built a short distance from the restaurant, and interstate traffic no longer traveled by their front door. Customer count dropped off to about one-quarter of what it had been, and the restaurant could not profitably operate with low prices. They decided to cater to the local population and increased quality and prices. Profit margins were considerably higher, and once again they were profitable, although with fewer customers than before.

Many methods exist for establishing menu prices.* Most, however complex they may appear, are variations on one or more of the following:

1. competitors' prices
2. cost-to-sales ratios
3. contribution margins

Perhaps the most widely used approach to menu pricing might best be termed a "follow the leader" technique: pricing to meet the competition. It is commonly employed by those who have little or no idea of the costs of the items they sell, including those who feel that if a nearby competitor is managing to stay in business by selling hamburgers for $1.25, then they too will find hamburger sales profitable at that price. When such operators find themselves bankrupt, they can never quite understand why. But the use of this imitative approach is not restricted to the unknowledgeable; it is also employed by a substantial number of seasoned and successful operators.

Restaurateurs often feel that if their prices are higher than those of nearby competitors, they will lose business to the competition. Tacitly, they are defining their products as homogeneous rather than differentiated, and in many cases they are correct in doing so. Those restaurants featuring such common items as steak, roast beef, or hamburgers are often quite similar in product, service, and price. Decor is often the only feature that makes one essentially different from another. In such cases, the restaurant's accessibility to the market it serves is the primary determinant of the number of customers and sales. In many such instances, any increase in price over that charged by the competition may effectively eliminate the small advantage offered by location and lead to an unacceptable loss in sales.

While the policy of pricing to meet the competition can be successful for some operators in some markets, it may lead to disastrous results for others. If selling prices are low, substantially larger numbers of customers are necessary to cover fixed costs and show an operating profit. Typically all restaurants in a given area cannot maintain the necessary volume to survive when selling prices are low, and only the most able operators survive. Under such conditions, the failure rate for restaurants in a given area is normally very high.

The second means of dealing with menu pricing, via cost-to-sales ratios, may take either one of two possible approaches. In either case, portion costs

*For a detailed treatment of this topic see Jack E. Miller, *Menu Pricing and Strategy* (New York: Van Nostrand Reinhold Company, Inc. 1980).

must be carefully determined by means of the techniques discussed in Chapter 10.

Once portion costs are known, selling prices can be set for each item so that portion cost represents some fixed percentage of the selling price. If, for example, a restaurateur wanted food cost-to-sales ratio to be 40%, then he could set a selling price for each item merely by dividing .4 into the portion cost and adjusting the resulting answer to some suitable amount to print in a menu. Thus, $1.24 would be adjusted to $1.25, a more suitable menu price. If this approach were followed with literally every menu item, the cost percent for operation for any period would be 40%, provided that the staff followed all established procedures for purchasing, receiving, storing, issuing, and producing food. Also, if the 40% figure were a reasonable one, it would be determined by subtracting profit, fixed cost, and labor cost as percentages of sales from 1, or 100%.

Another approach based on cost-to-sales ratios requires not only that one have rather complete information about portion costs but also that one establish some tentative selling prices and then forecast sales volume for an upcoming period. The calculations of potential food cost percent based on the forecast, the portion costs, and portion selling prices may be accomplished on the Menu Pre-Cost and Abstract form illustrated and discussed in Chapter 12. If the resulting cost percent is unsatisfactory, then before printing a menu costs, selling prices, and the forecast can be adjusted until a realistic and satisfactory potential result is obtained. If the forecast for the period has been reasonably accurate, and if the staff has observed all standard procedures for all phases of operation, the resulting cost percent for operation should conform to management's expectations.

The third approach, dealing with specific contribution margins for each item on the menu, is becoming more accepted in the industry but is still not widely used. This approach requires that the foodservice operator, knowing the portion costs for each item sold, determine the average contribution margin for menu items needed to cover overhead and yield a desired profit at an expected level of sales volume. For example, a simplified Income Statement for food might appear as follows:

Gross Food Sales	$100,000
Less Cost of Food Sold	40,000
Gross Profit	
(total contribution margins)	$ 60,000
Overhead Costs	50,000
Profit	10,000
Number of customers served during the period:	30,000.

Each customer in this example spent an average of $3.33 and contributed an average of $2 to cover overhead and profit.

This method would suggest that each menu item should be priced at $2 above costs, regardless of the item. A steak with portion cost of $4 would be priced at $6, and a pasta item with cost of $.50 would be priced $2.50. If this approach were followed and if sales volume matched or exceeded forecasts, the minimum acceptable dollar profit would be assured, provided that costs were kept strictly under control in all areas.

In addition, many might consider this a more equitable method of setting prices. Assuming that no significant difference exists in the cost of producing menu items, each customer is bearing only his or her fair share of the overhead costs and profit, and no more.

Selling Techniques

The second means of influencing customer purchases is to develop a sales force of waiters and waitresses. They can greatly assist management in selling certain menu items, or for that matter, cause other menu items not to sell. Many successful foodservice operators use the following techniques to exercise some additional control over sales:

1 meeting daily with sales personnel
2 establishing standard selling techniques
3 periodically assessing the performance of sales personnel

Many establishments hold daily meetings with sales personnel (the waiters and waitresses) to review and discuss menu items that management wishes to emphasize and to provide the personnel with all necessary information about the preparation and contents of the dishes on the menu. This procedure offers a number of advantages to both management and the customers. For management, it ensures that the sales force will be thoroughly knowledgeable about product, a prime requirement in sales personnel in all businesses. Additionally, management has a fine opportunity to make sales personnel aware of the exceptional items that may appear on the menu for that particular day, including some that would not have been available had not prime ingredients been available in the markets. Obviously, these are the items that management has most interest in selling to the public, since prices have been structured to provide appropriate contribution margins and, because of the seasonality and freshness of such items, the necessity that all orders be sold.

The customer, on the other hand, has the distinct advantage of being able to learn from a knowledgeable salesperson whatever he or she needs or wants to know about the product before it is purchased. Customers then make realistic decisions about what to order or not to order. This helps to reduce the number of orders rejected by customers who make incorrect assumptions about certain food items.

The adoption of certain standard selling techniques can be of great assistance in maximizing sales. These techniques, if properly handled by the sales personnel, not only help to build volume sales but also provide each customer with some greater measure of personal attention than he or she might otherwise receive.

One of the useful selling techniques that many successful operators have their personnel employ is to suggest items to customers that they might not otherwise think of ordering. One common example is the cocktail before dinner, or the wine with the meal. In the case of the cocktail, the operator not only builds sales but also gives customers something with which to occupy their time until their meal is ready. This technique may be expanded to suggesting courses that the customer might not have considered otherwise—appetizers, salads, and desserts.

Another adaptation is to ask the sales personnel to make specific suggestions for particular courses. For example, if the restaurant particularly wishes to sell one item rather than another, the waiters and waitresses may be asked to suggest that specific item to all diners for a particular meal. If done properly, it can add a pleasant, personal touch to the meal for the customer, while at the same time building sales.

It is normally not difficult to secure employee cooperation in making suggestions to customers, particularly if the personnel are aware that customer tips are typically a percentage of the gross amount of the check and that higher dollar sales lead to higher tips.

When daily meetings with sales personnel are held, and standard selling techniques are adopted, management is well advised to review, at least periodically, the performance of the sales force. Performance can be assessed in a number of ways, including determining gross sales per employee or average sale per employee for a certain period, such as a week. Those whose performance is significantly below that of the majority may need reminding or coaching, or ultimately, replacing.

If the above sales techniques are established and implemented, and if the menu is prepared according to the principles discussed above, the food controller is better able to see that sales volume is maximized and that those items that are sold result in the highest profit for the establishment.

ENSURING THAT CUSTOMER PURCHASES RESULT IN REVENUE

Throughout the discussion of food control in the preceding chapters, references have been made to food sales. The assumption has been made tacitly that food sales have been accurately recorded in some way and that the total sales figure has been available to the food controller, who has accepted its accuracy without question. This is not usually the case. There exist any number of possibilities for errors in the recording of sales. Incorrect prices may be charged, and checks may be lost or stolen, before or after reaching the cashier. On some occasions, no checks are written, and food is prepared without charge, in effect. These are but a few of the many possibilities, but they point out the need for establishing some procedures for controlling sales.

The purpose of establishing procedures is to ensure that all food prepared by the kitchen and served in the dining room generates revenue for the operation, and that the revenue for each item is recorded in the correct amount by the sales personnel (the waiters and waitresses) and by the accounting personnel (the cashiers). Control over costs is important, but much of the effectiveness of cost control is dissipated if no control is exercised over sales. For example, imagine that the costs in a certain establishment are controlled to such an extent that the actual food cost of $350 approximates the standard cost. This food costing $350 should produce sales of $1,000, and result in a cost-to-sales ratio of 35%. If procedures are not established to control sales, it is conceivable that the sales might be recorded as $900, resulting in a cost-to-sales ratio of 38.9%. Gross profit on sales is reduced by $100, and the food cost is 3.9 points higher than it would have been if all sales had been recorded.

In such a case, additional controls over cost and additional efforts to improve kitchen performance will not be effective. Steps must be taken to control the recording of sales. While these steps are often under the jurisdiction of the accountant rather than the food controller, it is important that everyone in food control understand them and be able to put them into effect if called on to do so.

The Guest Check

One of the simplest steps to take in attempting to establish sales control procedures is to require that each item ordered and its selling price be recorded legibly on a guest check. This procedure, followed by the majority of commercial restaurants, with the possible exception of small owner-operated luncheonettes and some cafeterias, serves a number of useful functions; it

1. reminds the waiter what has been ordered;
2. shows the customer an itemized list of charges;
3. provides a written record of portion sales that can be abstracted and recorded in a sales history;
4. facilitates verification of the cashier's accuracy;
5. permits checking back to see that accurate prices have been charged for each item ordered; and
6. provides tax records, where applicable.

Although the use of guest checks provides a certain measure of control over sales, most establishments take the additional precaution of using numbered checks.

Numbered Checks

Most places that use guest checks purchase them in serially numbered quantities. In some instances, the checks are on pads in numerical order. In others, the checks are individual units but are numbered nevertheless. Not all establishments make use of the various possibilities offered by the numerically ordered checks, but those that do so find a number of benefits.

For example, when numbered checks are used, it is possible at the end of any serving period to reassemble them in order to determine if any are missing.

Checks may be missing because a waiter or a cashier is dishonest, or because a customer has taken the check with him and has not paid for the food consumed. Immediate investigation should be made when any check is missing, and steps taken to end the problem.

Numbered checks make possible the assigning of responsibility for particular numbers to particular employees who can be held accountable for incorrect entries and, to some extent, for missing numbers. In many cases, this responsibility is assigned by requiring that personnel sign for checks by the pad or book. Where this is the practice, it is typical to require that the personnel sign a book out before a serving period and turn it back in at the end, recording the numbers of used checks as they do so. Figure 13.3 illustrates a typical waiters' signature book set up for this purpose. In other instances, particularly in expensive restaurants serving haute cuisine from an a la carte menu, personnel sign for individual checks as needed. Figure 13.4 shows an example of a signature book used in this kind of operation.

While the numbering of checks is an important first step in establishing sales control procedures, the control established is not complete. A busy waiter or waitress can still make errors, either purposely or by accident. Incorrect prices can be charged for food recorded on the check; and it is also possible for the wrong items to be recorded. A charge of $5.95 might be made, for example, for a sirloin steak that should be sold for $8.95. Or the $8.95 steak might be recorded on the check as a chopped steak selling for $3.95.

The Food Checker

In an effort to eliminate some of these possibilities, many restaurants hired personnel who were known as food checkers. The job of food checker was to remain at a station in the kitchen, close by the exit door to the dining room, and to verify that each food item leaving the kitchen was recorded on a guest check. In many

FIGURE 13.3
Waiters' Signature Book

Date 10/1/8

			Checks			
Date	*Waiter No.*	*Book No.*	*From*	*To*	*Closing No.*	*Signature*
10/1	1	7	700	799		J.J. Jones
10/1	2	8	800	899		S.S. Smith

FIGURE 13.4
Cashier's Record of Checks Distributed to Waiters

H. Martin Cashier Sept. 3 198

Check No.	Waiter No.	No. Served	Table No.	Waiter's Signature
100	1	4	2	S. Smith
101	2	2	3	P. Jones
102				
103				
104				
105				
106				
107				
108				
109				
110	3	2	7	J. Crowley
111	4	3	8	B. Miller
112				
113				
114				
115				
116				
117				
118				
119				

instances, the job of recording selling prices was taken from the waiters and given to the food checker. Often these prices were recorded on the checks mechanically with a register similar to a cashier's register. This technique provided an extra measure of control, because at the end of a serving period the readings in the checker's register should equal the total of cash and charge sales recorded by the cashier, with allowance made for taxes and tips. When the food checker's figure exceeded the cashier's figure, investigation could be made into the causes of the discrepancy. When numbered checks were in use, the numbers of the missing checks could be determined and the waiter involved questioned. Another advantage of this system was that the independent pricing of checks by a food checker afforded some measure of protection against service personnel giving away food or underpricing items purposely in a misguided effort to get larger tips.

However, there are so many disadvantages to using food checkers that this system of sales control has all but disappeared today. One serious disadvantage is that lines tend to form at the food checker's station during busy periods. Service to customers slows down, turnover decreases, cold food is served, and customers are dissatisfied. In addition, particularly in inflationary wage periods, food checkers are considered to be too much of a burden on the payroll. In some instances, attempts have been made to combine the jobs of the food checker and the cashier, often with unsatisfactory results.

The Dupe System

One way of maintaining some of the desirable qualities of the food checker system while eliminating some of the attendant problems is to set up what is usually called a "dupe" system. **Dupe** is an abbreviation of the word "duplicate," and suggests that a duplicate copy is made of each order. There are several means of doing this. One is to use pads on which each check is followed by a carbon copy, usually on a paper of a different color and texture. There are variations on this procedure. The important point is that the dupe must be given to personnel in the kitchen before any food is issued, and management instructs kitchen personnel only to issue the food items recorded on the dupes in the quantities indicated. When food has been picked up by serving personnel, the dupes are left behind in the kitchen, and in many places deposited in a locked box through a slot in the top. At the end of a serving period, dupes bearing the same numbers as the original checks may be matched against the checks to locate any discrepancies.

Although it is conceivable that dupes could be used for all food orders in some kitchens, it is not usually the case. In most instances, dupes are used only for entree items and certain other high-cost items, such as shrimp cocktails, over which management wants to exercise control.

When dupes are used, many establishments match the duplicate to the original check to verify that nothing was given out from the kitchen without an original, and to verify that the cashier received all original checks. However, that is a time-consuming job, so some restaurants have taken additional measures to simplify the verification procedure. One such method requires that sales personnel write food orders and no prices on checks and dupes as the orders are taken. Then, on the way to ordering the food from the kitchen, each waiter must record prices on the checks with a register similar to that used by a food checker. The register dispenses a printed receipt, which must be attached to the dupe before kitchen personnel will issue any food. When this procedure is followed, it is possible at the end of a meal to compare the readings from the kitchen register with the cashier's register, and to locate missing amounts.

In addition to requiring that checks be verified against dupes each day, some establishments take the additional step of requiring that checks be analyzed periodically. Where this is required, the food controller periodically examines the checks for one day, noting the nature and extent of each error, as well as the name or number of the person responsible. Pricing errors and errors in addition and in calculation of taxes can be called to the attention of the person in charge of service personnel. In some instances, the list of errors is posted on an employee bulletin board, often with the desirable psychological effect. Few persons like seeing their errors posted for all to see, and often employees make considerable effort to improve.

The Cashier

In most establishments, one employee is usually hired as cashier and given the responsibility of recording cash sales and charge sales as customers leave the premises. The cashier is usually stationed somewhere near the exit. Whenever possible, it is desirable to require that sales be recorded in a register and that the registration of the sale be endorsed on each check, whether it is cash or charge. Some restaurants wisely require that all guest checks for cash be stamped "Paid" as the cash is received. Some even require the cashier to deposit all paid guest checks in a locked box as soon as the cash has been collected. The purpose of both these procedures is to prevent the reuse of paid guest checks, which sometimes occurs when serving personnel and cashiers form unhealthy alliances.

It is a frequent practice to require cashiers to record the number of persons served, as well as the breakdown of checks into food sales, taxes, and tips, and also to differentiate between cash and charge sales. While this is frequently done by cash register, it is best illustrated by the typical control sheet shown in figure 13.5.

FIGURE 13.5
Restaurant Sales Control Sheet

Check #	*Waiter #*	*# Covers*	*Food Sales*	*Tax*	*Tips*	*Cash*	*Charge*	*Detail*
101	6	2	4.00	.48		4.48		
102	3	5	20.00	1.60	5.00		26.60	Diners'
103	2	1	3.00	.24	1.00		4.24	Amex
104	2	2	7.00	.56		7.56		
105	6	4	12.50	1.00		13.50		
		14	46.50	3.88	6.00	25.54	30.84	

In this illustration, it should be noted that the total of sales, taxes, and tips equals the total of cash and charge sales. Thus, $46.50 + $3.88 + $6.00 = $56.38; also, $25.54 + $30.84 = $56.38. Where such a form is used, cashiers are typically required to list the checks in numerical order so that missing numbers will be readily apparent, and investigation can be made to determine if any sales are unrecorded. In establishments that require that printed receipts be attached to dupes before food is released, the total food sales recorded by the cashier should agree with the reading taken on the machine that dispenses the printed receipts. The same principle may be applied in those restaurants that employ food checkers to record selling prices on guest checks by machine. Moreover, the preceding systems are used in those establishments that rely on cash registers rather than the control form illustrated. These registers normally provide for the separate recording of food sales, taxes, and tips on the one hand, and cash and charge sales on the other.

As well as providing an accounting department with accurate sales information for inclusion in the financial records, these summary forms enable the food controller to determine the average sale per customer for each meal. This average is determined as follows:

$$\text{average sale} = \frac{\text{total dollar sales}}{\text{total number of covers}}$$

From the totals in figure 13.5, it is apparent that each customer has spent an average of \$3.32. This is of considerable interest to the food controller and the manager, both of whom are interested in following business trends. If the average sale decreases over a period of time, investigation can be made into the reasons for the changes in customer spending habits. Some possibilities might include a deterioration in service standards, customer dissatisfaction with food quality, inadequate sales promotion, and changes in portion sizes.

These are but a few of the methods and procedures knowledgeable food controllers and managers employ in their efforts to establish effective sales control procedures. The net effect of these efforts should be an accurate accounting of all sales so that undesirable food cost percentages will not be attributed to improperly recorded sales.

EDP APPLICATIONS

Computers and other EDP devices can be of great assistance to managers in their efforts to control sales. For example, the sales history developed with the aid of a sales terminal can provide management with a valuable body of information indicating customer preferences from among menu offerings. Properly used, this information can lead to the development of menus that include no items unpopular with the clientele of a particular restaurant. This, of course, is but a simple and obvious use.

Another possible use involves a sales terminal capable of generating sales reports quickly while sales are in progress—half-way through the dinner hour, for example. It would obviously benefit a manager to know during the dinner hour how portion sales of the various menu items compared to the forecast of sales, the basis for many purchasing and production decisions. If sales for some item were far less than had been forecast, the manager might want to make some judicious efforts to increase sales (as opposed to orders taken) for the item, possibly by offering some inducement for the waiters and waitresses to "sell" the item. If successful, this type of mini-campaign could have many beneficial outcomes, including a decrease in leftover food, lower costs, and possibly an increase in dollar sales.

Perhaps the most important use of the computer as a sales control device may be illustrated by its ability to eliminate the traditional need for the guest check and dupe. In at least one system currently available for restaurant use, the waiter records guests' selections on a simple pad of white paper. He signs into the terminal using his individually assigned code, and is then led through a program in the course of which data is recorded in computer memory indicating that a particular number of diners seated at a particular table have made particular selections from the menu. All this information is entered by means of pre-assigned codes, including the menu selections. At this time, a "check" with a particular serial number is opened in computer memory, where it will remain until a printed copy is requested, typically when the diners have completed their meals. As the menu selections are entered, they are transmitted to the various stations of the kitchen, where they display on printers. By this means, various stations are advised of orders placed, including correct number of portions, waiter placing the order, and time the order was placed. Orders are picked up by waiters at suitable times for delivery to diners. Additional menu selections for other courses are similarly recorded in the terminal, until finally the diners have finished their meals and requested their check. At that time, the waiter requests a copy of the check at the terminal, and it appears on the attached printer. The data on the check remains in memory, where it is stored as an open check until settled by payment or charge card. If not settled by the close of business, management will be so informed by printed report, which will show table number, number of guests, name or number of the waiter, and the outstanding amount. If required, a duplicate copy of the check can be printed.

This particular system offers a number of advantages to managers in their efforts to control sales. First, it helps to speed service in the dining room and to increase turnover by eliminating the need for each waiter to walk to the kitchen to place each order. Next, it completely eliminates the need to maintain traditional guest checks, to verify the accuracy of each, and to ascertain that none are missing at the end of a meal period. Finally, by means of the printers at various kitchen stations, it becomes possible to ensure that each food item ordered and picked up has actually been ordered by a guest in the dining room. The system offers many advantages for the control of both sales and costs.

CHAPTER ESSENTIALS

In this chapter we covered the scope of sales control and suggested it encompasses three areas of management concern: (1) increasing the number of customers, (2) influencing what those customers purchase, and (3) ensuring that all customer purchases result in appropriate revenue. We showed how business location, product differentiation, acceptable prices, pleasing decor, portion size, product quality, service standards, and scope of the menu influence the number of customers that patronize a restaurant. We discussed the general topics of menu making as well as techniques employed by service personnel and showed how these influence customer purchases. We illustrated specific techniques and procedures for ensuring that customer purchases result in revenue. Finally, we showed how computers may assist management in the ongoing effort to control sales in restaurants.

QUESTIONS AND PROBLEMS

1 Define the scope of sales control.

2 List and discuss five factors that could be important in setting selling prices for a neighborhood restaurant. Be specific in identifying the type of restaurant you choose.

3 In what ways can the portion size a restaurant offers have an effect on the number and type of customers who patronize the establishment?

4 How may location be important to the success of a new restaurant?

5 Distinguish between homogeneous and differentiated products (or services).

6 What is the normal effect of changing the price of a differentiated product? Of a homogeneous product?

7 What is meant by a "price-sensitive" product or service?

8 The owner of a certain small restaurant realizes that his establishment is offering homogeneous products, which are extremely price sensitive. Given his present cost and sales volume, the business is unprofitable, but he does not want to sell out. What suggestions could you make to help this owner make the business profitable?

9 The new manager of a certain restaurant learns that there is always a waiting line of customers on Friday and Saturday nights. Because of the apparent need to serve customers as quickly as possible to make seating available to those waiting in line, to what extent should this new manager suggest the use of selling techniques that tend to prolong service and result in customers spending additional time at tables?

10 Given the following information, determine an appropriate contribution margin to use in setting menu prices, and then determine suitable menu selling prices for each of the given items.

Gross sales:	$300,000
Cost of food sold:	$100,000
Number of customers served:	50,000

	Portion Costs
Item A	$1.85
Item B	2.60
Item C	3.50
Item D	6.28
Item E	4.12

11 What control procedures does the foodservice industry use to ensure that sales are recorded and result in revenue?

12 What sales techniques might management suggest that sales personnel use to:

a Improve gross revenue and average check?
b Increase tips?
c Sell a menu item prepared in excess quantity that must be thrown away if not sold?

13 In each of the following calculate the average sale.

	Number of Covers	*Total Sales*
a	20	$ 70.00
b	87	$ 372.40
c	142	$ 863.45
d	463	$2,309.00

14 Why would each of the following adversely affect the average sale in a restaurant?

a deterioration in service standards
b customer dissatisfaction over food quality
c inadequate sales promotion
d changes in portion sizes

15 Show by example how improper recording of sales affects the food cost percentage.

a A certain restaurant projects labor costs of 36%, fixed costs of 28%, and wants to plan for profit of 12%. What food cost percent should be projected?
b Using the food cost percent from (**a**) above, what menu selling prices would be suitable for each of the following:

	Portion Cost
Item A	$1.94
Item B	2.26
Item C	4.40
Item D	3.88
Item E	2.42

17 What six general topics make up the subject of menu making? Explain the meaning and significance of each. Rank the six in the order of their importance to a food controller, then explain and justify the reasons for the order you have established.

18 How can computers and other EDP devices aid managers in controlling restaurant sales?

part three

Beverage Control

In previous chapters we discussed the need for food, beverage, and labor control procedures and outlined in detail control principles and procedures for food. Beverage control is similar to food control in many ways. It is necessary to develop standards and procedures for purchasing, receiving, storage, issuing, production, and sales. Those standards and procedures will be closely akin to food control, only instead of dealing with highly perishable food items, we will be concerned with liquor items that in many cases can be kept indefinitely. The need for beverage control is as important as food control because of the nature of the product. The probability that employees will steal, or attempt to become silent partners with management, is greatest with beverages. Interestingly enough, although it is recognized that beverage control is most needed, it is an area where only limited controls can be successfully instituted.

chapter 14

Beverage Control: Purchasing, Receiving, Storing, and Issuing

Learning Objectives

After reading and studying this chapter, the student should be able to:

1. Identify the primary purposes of beverage purchasing control.
2. Explain the importance of fixing responsibility for beverage purchasing and identify the person(s) responsible for that job.
3. List the considerations that enter into the frequency and quantity of beverage purchases.
4. Distinguish between call brands and pouring brands.
5. Describe beverage purchasing routine in large operations, including the steps followed and the forms employed.
6. Describe and explain the importance of the beverage receiving report.
7. List and explain the important factors in beverage storing control.
8. Describe the procedure for controlling beverage inventories in large operations.
9. Distinguish between front bars, service bars, and special purpose bars, and explain the procedures for issuing beverages to each.
10. Define the following terms as they relate to beverage controls: *par stock, bin cards, full bottle sales, coding, perpetual inventory, mixers.*
11. Describe how managers can use computers to aid in the process of control over beverage purchasing, receiving, storing, and issuing.

BEVERAGE PURCHASING

The term **beverage** requires some definition. Technically, any liquid intended for drinking is a beverage, a word derived from the French verb **boire,** to drink. In a sense, all beverages can be divided into two groups—those that contain some measure of alcohol and those that contain no alcohol at all. Obviously, the former are normally called alcoholic, and the latter nonalcoholic.

Alcoholic beverages include some measure of alcohol, sometimes comparatively small. The production of all alcoholic beverages begins with a process known as fermentation, in which yeast acts on a mash, commonly of fruit or grain, to produce an alcoholic mixture. Sometimes corn, sugar cane, or other plant materials may form mash. Further processing of such alcoholic mixtures results in the production of three different types of alcoholic beverages: beers, wines, and spirits. Beers are produced from fermented grains; most wines come from fermented grapes. All spirits are produced by distilling fermented products—fruits, grains, or various others. Distilled products include whiskies, brandies, liqueurs, rums, gins, vodkas, and some few others.

Nonalcoholic beverages commonly include those normally found listed in restaurant menus under the "beverage" category—coffee, tea, and milk, as well as a host of others, some carbonated and some not. Carbonated nonalcoholic beverages include club soda, ginger ale, and a wide range of other flavored beverages. Nonalcoholic beverages that are not carbonated include fruit and vegetable juices, such as orange juice, tomato juice, and V-8. Many of the nonalcoholic beverages are used to dilute alcoholic beverages and to produce a vast number of drinks with a wide variety of flavors. When so used, these nonalcoholic beverages are called **mixers** and most commonly include club soda, ginger ale, lemon-lime soda, cola, tonic water, orange juice, tomato juice, and grapefruit juice.

For purposes of these chapters, we will use the term beverage alone to refer to alcoholic beverages, and the term mixers to refer to those nonalcoholic beverages that are typically used with alcoholic beverages to produce a variety of so-called mixed drinks. Some mixed drinks, usually produced according to recipe, require additional items, and they will be referred to simply as other ingredients. They typically include olives, pearl onions, sugar, cream, lime juice, lemon juice, and others.

The primary purposes of establishing beverage purchasing controls are to maintain an appropriate supply of ingredients for producing beverage products, and to ensure that the quality of each is appropriate to intended use, and that each is purchased at the optimum price. As with all control, the key is the establishment of standards and standard procedures.

The extent of the need for each of the three different types of alcoholic beverages must be determined before any purchase decisions can be made. Needs will differ from place to place, depending on clientele and inherent differences in the nature of operations. Some neighborhood bars will cater to customers whose tastes will run primarily to domestic beer, inexpensive wines, and comparatively few whiskies. On the other hand, cocktail lounges serving an upper-middle-income business clientele may offer imported beer, a great assortment of spirits, and possibly a few fine wines, while some relatively expensive restaurants may specialize in the finest of imported wines. And these are but a few of the infinite number of possibilities. Because all alcoholic beverages are comparatively expensive, carefully defining customer tastes is particularly important in an attempt to eliminate the purchase of beverages that will not sell. Purchasing beverages involves the outlay of cash for merchandise that must be carried as inventory until sold. It is usually undesirable to maintain an inventory of items that move very slowly. Once the operation is open and control procedures are in effect, a manager can identify slow-moving items and restrict or eliminate their purchase. However, this is a partial solution at best. It is of the utmost importance to restrict initial purchases to items that will meet customer tastes.

An ideal approach to the analysis of potential customer tastes is to do a market study. This may be as informal or formal as an owner might desire, ranging from simply surveying the types of customers in the immediate area and their preferences to engaging a reputable firm that specializes in market studies to do more sophisticated research.

Purchasing Responsibility

The nature and size of an operation will often dictate who is responsible for purchasing beverages. In smaller, owner-operated establishments, the responsibility will naturally fall to the owner. In others, it may be held by the manager. In some, particularly larger operations, the purchasing responsibility is delegated to a purchasing agent, a steward, or even a beverage manager. The job title of the individual responsible for purchasing is of little consequence. The important point is that one individual should be held responsible and accountable for all beverage purchasing. For control purposes, it is desirable to assign the responsibility to someone who is not involved in either the preparation or sale of drinks.

Quantity Purchasing

Purchasing is partly simplified by the nature of beverage packaging. All beverages are purchased in sealed containers and can be successfully stored for comparatively long periods if proper storage conditions are maintained. So long as bottles and kegs remain sealed, their contents will not rapidly deteriorate when stored at proper temperature. Storage life varies from a rather short time for kegs of beer, to many years for some wines, and indefinitely for whiskies. However, it is generally true that beverages need not be purchased for use on the day received, as is often the case with food. Once purchased, beverages are held in storage until needed. Therefore, purchasing may be done periodically. The freqency of beverage purchasing depends on a number of factors including management policy with respect to tying up money in inventory, as well as availability, delivery schedules, and the numerous and differing regulations imposed by various state and local governments. In many establishments, purchasing is done monthly, some time early in the month, and is based in part on the physical inventory taken at the close of the preceding accounting period.

In addition to establishing a periodic ordering schedule, it is important to determine the quantity of each item that will be needed between ordering dates. This should be based on experience. If a perpetual inventory system is used, as discussed later in this chapter, the figures that reflect experience are readily available. If perpetual inventory is not in effect, reference can be made to past invoices or bills. The purchases reflected on the invoices may be used with some degree of accuracy to infer quantities used. This, however, would be a laborious process at best and should be undertaken only as a last resort. Because it is usually desirable to issue bottles from inventory to a bar from requisitions, as discussed later in this chapter, it would be preferable, in the absence of perpetual inventory, to make references to bar requisitions for preceding months to determine levels of use for each item kept in stock.

It is desirable to maintain perpetual inventories of stocks, and the best method for determining quantities to order is tied to such a system. Perpetual inventory cards or books will often show a desired par stock for each item, which is a kind of idealized quantity that should be on hand. This will often equal approximately 150% of the quantity customarily used during a period. In addition, maximum and minimum figures may be given. The maximum will reflect management's determination of the limit to which the number of units on hand may be increased. The minimum will be, in effect, a reorder point. In many establishments, the rule is that no item is to be ordered unless and until the quantity on hand approximates or reaches the reorder point. In an effort to control purchasing, it is usually desirable for the beverage controller to work with the manager to establish realistic reorder points for all items in stock.

Quality Purchasing

Alcoholic beverages used by a bar may be divided into two classes according to use: **call** brands and **pouring** brands. A call brand is used only if specifically requested by the customer; a pouring brand is used whenever the customer does not request a call brand. If a customer simply orders a "Scotch and soda," he or she should be given the pouring brand. On the other hand, if the customer orders a specific brand of Scotch with soda, he or she is always given the call brand, the one specifically requested (if it is available). The usual practice is to designate one low- to medium-priced brand in each category of spirits as the pouring brand. The choice will vary with the clientele and the price structure. Once this is done, all other brands become call brands. The selection of pouring brands is an important first step in establishing both quality and cost standards. Although management usually does this, it is important that the beverage controller recognize its significance and check to see that the selection has been made and that the proper brands are being used at the bar.

The determination of quality for alcoholic beverages is a function of several factors including price, customer preferences, sometimes age, and often popularity based on advertising. Most people will agree on the extremes—that certain twenty-five-year-old Scotches are of high quality, and that various cheap gins are of very low quality—but there remains a vast area between the extremes for possible and legitimate differences of opinion. Thus, quality determination becomes a matter for decision by the individual operator.

Purchasing Procedure

Whenever practical, it is advisable to establish a purchasing routine that requires formal written purchase orders. In larger establishments formal purchase requests serve as the basis for ordering.

In a large hotel, the purchasing routine might be the following. The wine steward, the person in charge of maintaining the beverage inventory and stock room, would make up a purchase request such as that illustrated in figure 14.1, just after the first of the month. These are prepared in duplicate, and the original is forwarded to the purchasing agent in the acounting department. The purchasing agent in some places is required to secure management's written approval on the purchase request before placing any orders. The orders placed are recorded on purchase orders, shown in figure 14.2, made up in quadruplicate. The copies are distributed as follows: the original is sent to the firm from which the beverages have been ordered; a second copy is sent to the wine steward to confirm that the orders have been placed; a third copy is sent to the receiving clerk so that he or she will know what deliveries to expect and can determine the correctness of the quantities and brands delivered; the fourth copy is kept by the purchasing agent.

FIGURE 14.1
Purchase Request Form

Quantity	*Item*	*Unit Size*	*Supplier*	*Unit Price*	*Total Price*
12	Old Crow	750 ml	A.&C. Suppliers	$6.50	$78.00
6	Beefeater Gin	750 ml	A.&C. Suppliers	$8.50	$51.00

Requested by S.S. Smith　　　Approved by J.J. Jones

FIGURE 14.2
Purchase Order

Henry Hilson Hotel
New York City

Date 10/1/8×

M A.&C. Suppliers

Please Ship The Following Supplies
VIA Your Truck.

Quantity	*Unit*	*Item*	*Price*	*Amount*
12	750 ml	Old Crow	$6.50	$ 78.00
6	750 ml	Beefeater Gin	8.50	51.00
				$129.00

Ordered by B.H. Brown

Obviously not all establishments follow such detailed purchasing routines. Nevertheless, written records reduce misunderstandings and disputes that can rise in their absence; it is advisable in all instances to maintain some written record of purchases, preferably on a purchase order, to make comparisons with the goods delivered. Written purchase orders eliminate disputes over brands and quantities ordered, prices quoted, and delivery dates. Because the purchase of alcoholic beverages involves the outlay of considerable amounts of cash, it is wise to establish a system such as the purchase order method to reduce or eliminate the possibilities for error.

Establishing any particular system for purchasing will be effected in part by the varying laws of individual states with respect to the purchasing of alcoholic beverages. In approximately one-third of the fifty states, spirits must be purchased from state-operated monopolies and may not be purchased from wholesalers. In some of these states, sales of wines and beers are similarly controlled. In the remaining states, sales of wines, spirits, and beers may be purchased through wholesalers. In addition, various local restrictions may apply and typically vary considerably from one locale to another. Therefore, anyone responsible for purchasing alcoholic beverages must become familiar with the specific laws and restrictions that apply in a specific location.

In many establishments when state law permits, salespeople call on the wine steward, and it is common for purchase requests to be made up by the wine steward on the basis of these meetings. In some states, dealers may offer special discounts from time to time, and a wine steward can frequently save a considerable amount by taking advantage of them. In addition, in locations where prices are allowed to fluctuate, this kind of procedure enables the wine steward to list a quoted price on the purchase request. By listing a particular dealer's name, in states where this is possible, some of the purchasing agent's work is simplified.

RECEIVING

One useful technique in establishing control over beverage receiving is to require that deliveries be made at times when the receiving clerk can deal with them exclusively. It is undesirable, for example, for a clerk to receive beverage deliveries while receiving highly perishable food items. Pilferage is one of the most common causes of excessive beverage cost, and goods left unattended on a receiving platform create needless possibilities for such pilferage.

It is particularly important that a clerk receiving beverage items have information detailing what items are expected. This information can be furnished on a copy of the purchase order, and in fact, this is usually the simplest practical method in an establishment of any size. The receiving clerk can then check the invoice against the purchase order to see that they agree in quantity, brand label, and price. Any exceptions should be noted as directed by management and attended to in the manner prescribed. The receiving clerk should have a list of procedures to be followed in any possible eventuality. In major hotels, this list is likely to be quite detailed; in small restaurants there may be no written list, but a rule that the manager is to be called in case of any problem.

A principal function of a receiving clerk is to see that the items listed on the invoice are actually received in the quantities noted. The invoice is a bill, and the establishment will be held accountable for payment of the amount indicated on it. Therefore, it is important to guard against the possibilities of being billed for items that are not received, and the receiving clerk is responsible for checking to see that it does not happen. To accomplish this, the clerk must carefully count, sometimes weigh, all items received. In the case of wines and spirits delivered by the case, he should open each case and see that each contains the requisite number of properly labeled items. Each unit, or bottle, should be sealed. Any broken units should be returned for credit with the seal intact.

The Receiving Clerk's Daily Report in a Larger Establishment

Once deliveries have been received and checked, each invoice must be written up on a receiving report. This receiving report eventually makes its way to the accounting department and serves as the basis for making entries in the purchase journal. It also serves several other important purposes before it reaches the accounting department. These other purposes, which are important to the control system, include a clear listing of beverages received so that (a) the beverage controller can compare the received and ordered beverages, and (b) the information can be easily transferred to inventory records by the wine steward and controller.

For the control system to be accurate and effective, it is important that the receiving sheet be completed carefully by the clerk before the end of each day.

The most useful receiving report is one specifically designed for beverages. The beverage receiving report can take any of several forms, one of which is illustrated in figure 14.3.

FIGURE 14.3
Beverage Receiving Report

Date *10/5/—*

Distributor	*Item*	*# Units*	*# Cases*	*Unit Size*	*Unit Cost*	*Case Cost*	*Total Cost*
BCD, Inc.	Gin (Whitby)	24	2	750 ml	4.75	57.00	114.00
BCD, Inc.	Vodka (Holka)	12	1	750 ml	4.55	54.60	54.60
Fey, Inc.	Fey Chablis	24	2	750 ml	1.45	17.40	34.80

Distribution

Wine	*Spirits*	*Ale*	*Beer*	*Mixers*	
34.80	114.00 54.60				S. S. Smith Wine Steward B. B. Barton Receiving Clerk

Because the beverage receiving sheet is an accounting document, its specific makeup will vary considerably from place to place, depending on the nature and degree of complexity of the accounting practices in effect. However, it is generally desirable to establish a separate receiving report for beverages and then to design a report form tailored to an individual establishment's needs. In the case of beverages received, it is generally good practice to require not only that the receiving clerk sign a daily report, but that the wine steward sign it as well, thus acknowledging receipt of the beverage items listed on the receiving report.

STORING

All beverages received must be moved away from the receiving area as quickly as possible. Alcoholic beverages are always highly susceptible to pilferage, and often the receiving clerk cannot possibly keep watch over quantities of them for more than a very few minutes. Therefore, the wine steward should be notified of deliveries at once so that removal of all beverage items to secure storage can be arranged at once.

Security is one of the key elements in establishing control over the storage of beverages of all kinds. Whether alcoholic or nonalcoholic, all beverages should be stored in securely locked areas to eliminate the possibilities of pilferage. Each bottle represents a cash investment ranging from a few cents for mixers to several dollars for premium spirits and fine wines.

Keys to beverage storage areas must be carefully controlled to guard against unauthorized personnel gaining access to the various wines and spirits. An excellent practice is to have only two keys for each lock. One is kept by the wine steward; the second is kept locked in a safe accessible only to top management. Some establishments further tighten security by installing special locks that record, on a paper tape in the lock, the time at which it is opened and relocked. These time locks pinpoint the opening of storage areas at odd hours by unauthorized personnel. In any case, it is usually advisable to change locks on the beverage storage facilities from time to time to offset the possibility that duplicate keys have been made. It is particularly important that locks be changed when personnel changes occur among those who have had access to keys.

Storage Facilities

To reduce the amount of time required to distribute the supplies, beverage storage facilities should be located in an area reasonably close to bars. In addition, it is usually desirable to locate the storage facilities in an area where the entrance is readily accessible and under continual observation. This helps reduce the security problem as well as facilitate the issuing of supplies.

Internally, the storage area should be kept free of debris that can pile up as the result of emptying cases and stocking shelves. Once opened, cases should be completely emptied. All units in a case should be stored on the appropriate shelf and the empty carton removed at once. Control must be exercised to ensure that some personnel do not remove cartons that are not completely empty.

Appropriate temperature controls should also be established. These will vary considerably with the kinds of beverages stored. Alcoholic beverages other than wines should be stored at room temperature to minimize the chances of deterioration. Wines must be stored at very carefully controlled temperatures. Wines in corked bottles should be stored on their sides to prevent the corks from drying out and the wines consequently deteriorating during storage. As a general rule, red wines should be stored at about 55°F. White wines and sparkling wines should be stored at a slightly lower temperature, if possible. Depending on the nature and extent of the wine stores, both purposes sometimes can be accomplished in the same storage facility by means of professionally installed equipment for cooling and circulating air, and by storing items that must be kept cooler on shelves closer to the floor. Wherever and whenever possible, ales, beers, and mixers should be stored at lower temperatures—near 40°F. In the case of ales and beers purchased in kegs, this is often necessary to prevent spoilage. Where only bottled items are stored, it is still desirable to store at this lower temperature in order to reduce the time and the ice necessary to bring the items to proper serving temperature.

The physical arrangement of the storage area is important. Like items should be kept together. All gins, for example, should be kept in one area, rye whiskies in another, and Scotch whiskies in a third. This kind of arrangement simplifies finding an item when needed. It is helpful, too, for a floor plan of the storage area to be affixed to the door, so that authorized personnel can easily locate items.

One way of ensuring that items will always be found in the same location is to institute the use of bin cards like the one illustrated in figure 14.4. The bin card, a standard form available from appropriate stationery suppliers, is affixed to the shelf and serves as a label. It lists pertinent information concerning each item—type of beverage, brand name, and bottle size. It also may include provision for a certain number used to identify the particular item on the shelf. Some establishments assign each beverage item a code number from a master list (see figure 14.5), and that code number is recorded on the bin card. In many instances, the number is stamped by a mechanical stamping device on each bottle received.

This technique serves several purposes. In the case of wines, many of whose names are not easily pronounced or spelled, it simplifies the ordering by both customers and employees. In many instances, wine lists are printed with bin numbers. This is frequently a boon to wine sales, which can be highly profitable.

In the case of all alcoholic beverages, this technique provides a measure of control, as will become more apparent after Chapter 15. The number stamped on each bottle identifies the bottle as the property of the establishment. Thus, an employee cannot claim a bottle as personal property if one is found in his possession. In addition, empty bottles can be checked for numbers before they are replaced by full bottles, thus ensuring that no one is bringing empties in from outside and using them to get bottles from the establishment's stores.

The use of bin cards also permits the wine steward to maintain his own perpetual inventory record of quantities on hand. By using this card carefully to record the number of units received as they are placed on the shelves, as well

FIGURE 14.4
Bin Card

Item Old Crow Stock Number 153

Date	*In*	*Out*	*Balance*	*Date*	*In*	*Out*	*Balance*
10/1			4				
10/3		1	3				
10/7		1	2				
10/11		1	1				
10/12	4		5				

FIGURE 14.5
Illustration of Beverage Code Numbers

Sample Numbering Code for Wines, Spirits, and Beers

American Whiskies: 100 series
- Blended Rye: 100–139
- Straight Rye: 140–149
- Bourbon: 150–179
- Sour Mash: 180–189

Imported Whiskies: 200 series
- Scotch: 200–239
- Canadian: 240–249
- Irish: 250–259
- Other: 260–269

Gins & Vodkas: 300 series
- Gins: domestic 300–329
  imported 330–349
- Vodka: domestic 350–379
  imported 380–399

Rums and Brandies: 400 series
- Rum: 400–449
- Brandy: domestic 450–459
  imported: 460–479
- Cognac: 480–499

Cordials and Liqueurs: 500 series

Red Wines: 600 series

White wines (still): 700 series

Other Wines: 800 series
- Sparkling, Rosé, Dessert, Aperitif

Beers and Ales: 900 series

as the number of units issued as they are given out, the wine steward has a way of determining the balance on hand without resorting to counting bottles. In addition, the wine steward who carefully maintains such records has a way of determining that bottles are missing so that this important fact can be brought immediately to management's attention.

Inventory Control

For control purposes, it is important that records of beverage stocks be kept by someone other than the wine steward or bartender responsible for maintaining the stores. These records should be maintained on an ongoing basis and should reflect both additions to stores as a result of purchases and deductions from stores based on issues to operating bars. This ongoing record, kept by the beverage controller, is called a perpetual inventory. It is an indispensable feature of the beverage control system.

Perpetual inventories may be kept on cards or in books, both of which are available as standard forms from stationers. A sample of the perpetual inventory card is shown in figure 14.6.

FIGURE 14.6

Code # 153 Bottle Size 750 ml

Item Old Crow Unit Cost $6.50 Par Stock 4

Date	*Received*	*Issued*	*Issued*	*Balance*
10/1				4
10/3		1		
10/7		1		
10/11		1		
10/12	4			5

One card or one sheet should be maintained for each item in stock. Where code numbers are used, the perpetual inventory is typically maintained in code number order. The number of units received are entered from the receiving clerk's daily report or from the invoices attached to the report, depending on the form of report. Issues are recorded from requisitions. Since items are received in quantity and issued in units, more space is provided for issues than for purchases. This type of record would be used in an operation with one bar. In a hotel or restaurant with multiple bars, the perpetual inventory more likely would be found on a card like the one illustrated in figure 14.7.

FIGURE 14.7

Code # 153 Size 750 ml

Item Old Crow Unit Cost $6.50 Par Stock 8

		Issued To Bar				
Date	*Received*	# 1	# 2	# 3	# 4	*Balance*
10/1						6
10/4		1		1		4
10/10			1			3
10/11	4					7
10/12		1				6

In such establishments, each bar would be assigned a number, and requisitions would be prepared separately for each. By means of the card, separate records of issues to each bar could be maintained. It is particularly useful to have such records when the need arises to pinpoint such problems as missing bottles.

When the beverage controller maintains a perpetual inventory, it is possible to spot check the number of items on shelves from time to time, to guard against loss and to ensure that the wine steward is securely maintaining the supply.

The forms illustrated are used for maintaining records of number of bottles on hand. Some establishments maintain records that reflect inventory values as well. This is done on a separate form and is usually handled by the accounting department, although the beverage controller might do it in some places.

When a perpetual inventory is maintained, determining whether bottles are missing involves simply checking the stocks on the shelves from time to time during the month. A beverage controller commonly checks several items in this way every few days. When any discrepancy between inventory records and bottles on shelves occurs, immediate investigation into causes is begun, and appropriate remedial action is taken.

At the end of each month, standard accounting practice requires that a physical inventory be made of the stocks on hand. Typically, this physical inventory is the beverage controller's responsibility, often with the assistance of the wine steward. This monthly inventory is usually recorded in a bound inventory book. After the total number of units in each category is recorded, that number is multiplied by the unit cost to determine the dollar value of the units on hand. Comparing the results of the physical inventory with the records maintained in the perpetual inventory helps find any discrepancies. Where the physical inventory shows fewer or more bottles on hand than there should be according to the perpetual inventory, immediate investigation should be made to reconcile the difference. Sometimes these differences result from improper counting of items on shelves; sometimes from improper maintenance of perpetual inventory records from receiving sheets and bar requisitions. Either of these bookkeeping errors is easily remedied. However, when the difference cannot be traced to one of these causes, it is probable that items unaccounted for have been stolen. Management should be informed at once and take appropriate steps.

When bin cards and perpetual inventory cards are maintained separately, the first by the wine steward and the second by the beverage controller, comparing entries on the cards can help determine errors, and where a difference exists, one can check back to the appropriate receiving sheet or requisition.

ISSUING

Because beverage stores are all considered inventory, cost does not occur until beverage items are issued for use. Therefore, partly to maintain physical control over bottles and partly to determine costs, no bottles should ever be issued from stores without a written requisition signed by an authorized person, often the head bartender. A very simple form of requisition is illustrated in figure 14.8.

FIGURE 14.8
Requisition

Date 10/5

Quantity	*Description*	*Unit Cost*	*Total Cost*
1	Old Crow		
1	J & B		
1	C.C.		

Requisitioned by BSS

Issued by ______

Received by ______

The dated requisition is filled out by an authorized individual who determines quantities needed at the bar and signs the form. When the requisition is filled by the wine steward, he or she signs the appropriate line indicating that the items listed in the quantities shown have been issued. When the items are received at the bar, the bartender on duty (who may or may not be the person who ordered the items initially) checks them and signs the appropriate line acknowledging receipt of the listed items. After the items are delivered to the bar, the requisition is returned to the wine steward, who fills in the unit cost of each item and extends the requisition by multiplying the unit cost by the number of units issued to find the total cost of each. A grand total is then entered at the bottom for the cost of all items issued.

Many establishments further their control by requiring that each requisition be accompanied by empty bottles from the bar, so that in effect issuing the units listed replaces quantities that the bartender has already used. When this system is used, a par stock can be maintained at the bar. For example, five bottles of a particular brand of Scotch might constitute the par stock for that item. When one bottle is emptied, the bartender might put it aside until the end of the night when it would be listed on a requisition form. This form would be left for the morning bartender who would see to it that the empty bottles, together with the requisition on which they were listed, were delivered to the wine steward. The wine steward would check each bottle against the requisition and replenish the bar stock before the beginning of business. This would bring the stock at the bar back up to par. Such a system ensures a constant and well-controlled supply of beverage items at the bar. In addition, occasional spot checks of par stock against the par stock list would ensure that items are not missing from the bar. This affords an additional measure of control.

Establishments that operate more than one bar must prepare separate requisitions for each, so that bars may be controlled separately. Basically, there are three kinds of bars:

1 Front bars, where bartenders serve the public face to face.
2 Service bars, where customer orders are related to the bartender by waiters and waitresses who serve the drinks to the customer.
3 Special purpose bars, usually set up for one particular event, such as a banquet.

The par stock at a bar differs somewhat from par stock in a storeroom. Par stock at a bar should be listed in exact quantities for each type and size of items kept in stock. For example, the stock of gin should be listed according to brand names; it should include bottle sizes for each, as well as an exact number of bottles that should be at the bar at all times. One particular brand of gin, stocked in 750-ml sizes, might have a par stock of five bottles at a certain bar. This implies that someone could check the stock at any time and expect to find five bottles of that particular brand on hand. Not all would necessarily be full, but at least the number of bottles would be under control. In addition, replenishing the supply daily could be accomplished by exchanging a full bottle for each empty bottle turned in by the bartender, thus maintaining the par stock at all times.

Obviously par stocks for bars will vary greatly from bar to bar. In every case, however, the par stock figures should be related to quantities used and should be varied from time to time as customer demand varies. Drinks may go in and out of fashion for seasonal as well as for other reasons, and it is normally desirable that par stocks at the bar be adjusted to meet customer demand without being overstocked. In addition, since storage space at a bar is relatively limited, the quantity of any item should be limited to the amount necessary to meet no more than two days' demand.

In the case of front bars and service bars, par stocks should be established for each bar. However, this is not possible in the case of special purpose bars, which present unique problems. When these bars are set up, sufficient stocks must be issued to carry the bartender through the banquet. Typically, the quantities issued are greater than needed, and the remainder must be returned to the wine steward at the conclusion of the event. To avoid errors, great care must be exercised to insure against mishandling of bottles. Special banquet requisitions are often used, which make provision for all bottles issued, whether consumed or returned. An example is illustrated in figure 14.9.

Such requisitions are often made out by the banquet manager, particularly in hotels. They are given to the wine steward, who issues the items listed to the bartender or barboy in time for the bar to be set up for the event. Provision is made for recording additional issues that may be required. At the end of the event, it is desirable that some other individual, such as the beverage controller, check that all full, empty, and partially used bottles are acounted for. When this

FIGURE 14.9
Banquet Bar Requisition

Function Lions Club   Bartender Joe

Location Green Room   Date 10/15/—

Item	*Quantity*	*Original Issue*	*Additional Issue*	*Returns*	*Con-sumed*	*Unit Cost*	*Total Cost*
Scotch	2	2					
Gin	2	2					
Vodka	2	2					
Bourbon	1	1					
Canadian	1	1					
S. Vermouth	1	1					
Dry Vermouth	1	1					

Requisition by Joe
Issued by ______
Received by ______
Returns Checked by ______

is done, the correct amount for the quantities actually consumed can be charged to cost, and unused quantities can be returned to stock. Perpetual inventory and bin card entries are made from the consumed column on the banquet requisition.

Establishments in which most wines are sold by the bottle institute additional procedures for control purposes. In some, small stocks of the most popular wines are maintained at a front or service bar to eliminate the need for going to the wine cellar each time a bottle is ordered. Once the bottle of wine is taken from the bar and served to a customer at a table, it is effectively away from the bartender's control. The bartender may not have an empty bottle to turn in with his requisition on the following day to bring his stock up to par. Therefore, many establishments maintain additional control over full bottle sales by requiring that a form be filled out each time a bottle of wine is delivered to a table. One example is illustrated in figure 14.10.

Such a form is useful in hotels that serve full bottles of both wines and spirits to guests in their rooms, as well as in situations where par stocks of wines are not maintained at the bar and each bottle must come directly from the wine cellar. The full bottle sales slip serves as a requisition in such instances. When such forms are used, it is important to require that the server fill out each completely before the bottle is issued—to guard against potential problems. When completely

FIGURE 14.10
Full Bottle Sales Slip

Date 10/5/— Table # 8 Check # 1230

Code #	*Description*	*Quantity*	*Size*	*Cost*
602	Chateau Latour	1	Full	$75.00

Served by ____

Issued by ____

filled out, the form provides an excellent means for verifying each sale. It is possible to check each against the guest check number indicated and to hold the server accountable for errors.

EDP APPLICATIONS

Having established a system of beverage code numbers, as illustrated in figure 14.5, that code can be used for purposes of storing the entire beverage inventory in computer memory. Once perpetual inventory were so established, additions to the inventory and any such issues would be recorded as deliveries were received from vendors, or as bottles and cases were sent to the bar. Thus, a complete book inventory of beverages would be stored in computer memory. In addition, with reorder points and reorder quantities set and stored in memory, it would be possible to determine usage periodically, to make decisions about whether and when to place an order, and to charge reorder quantities, if necessary.

Later chapters will explain how data stored in computer memory can help determine the quantities of beverages that should have been consumed at the bar, given sales records and standard drink recipes. Such information, compared to a bartender's actual bar requisition, can reveal the extent to which the bartender is adhering to standards and standard procedures established for bar operation.

CHAPTER ESSENTIALS

In this chapter, we defined and classified beverages, identified the primary purposes of beverage purchasing control, and listed the considerations that determine the frequency and quantity of beverage purchases. We described and explained the use of the beverage receiving report and identified the duties of the beverage receiving clerk. The important factors in beverage storing control were listed and explained, and the important factors in beverage inventories in large operations were described. We distinguished between various types of bars and explained the procedures for issuing beverages to each, while at the same time defining a number of special terms used in beverage control. Finally, we showed how computers and other EDP devices may assist management in controlling beverage purchasing, receiving, storing, and issuing.

QUESTIONS AND PROBLEMS

1 What are the primary purposes of beverage purchasing controls?

2 Explain the importance of fixing responsibility for beverage purchasing, and identify the person(s) responsible for that job.

3 What considerations determine the frequency, timing, and quantity of beverage purchases?

4 Describe the beverage purchasing routines in large operations, including in your answer both the steps followed and the forms used.

5 What possible effects might an excessive inventory of beverages have on the overall beverage cost?

6 If the beverage purchasing responsibility is given to the same person who prepares and sells drinks, why might a measure of control be lost?

7 Of what significance are the terms **call brand** and **pouring brand** to beverage costs?

8 Why would a beverage receiving clerk's daily report form not necessarily be used in a small operation?

9 Distinguish between bin cards and perpetual inventory cards.

10 Distinguish between par stock at the front bar and par stock in the storeroom.

11 How can computers assist managers in maintaining perpetual inventory records of beverages?

chapter 15

Beverage Production Control

Learning Objectives

After reading and studying this chapter, the student should be able to:

1. Explain the need for beverage production control and identify measures taken to institute it.
2. Define each of the following terms: *shot glass, jigger, stemware, mixer, straight drink, mixed drink, cocktail, standard bar recipe.*
3. Calculate the standard cost of one standard drink, given a recipe and a list of current market prices.
4. Calculate the standard cost-to-sales ratio for one drink, given the standard cost and sales price.
5. Determine the number of standard drinks in bottles of various sizes, given the measure of the standard drink.
6. Explain the importance of standard selling prices to profitable bar operation.
7. Explain how computers can be used by managers to aid in beverage production controls.

A customer ordering a drink often has a preconceived idea of how the drink will taste. The customer orders a daiquiri, for example, because he or she has enjoyed the taste sensations experienced in the past from the subtle blending of lime juice, sugar, and rum by skillful bartenders. A customer who is served a cocktail that does not meet expectations may be dissatisfied and complain or simply not return. Therefore, any establishment offering drinks must recognize and accept certain standards of customer expectation and drink preparation, and establish procedures to ensure that these standards will be met. Control must be established over quantities of ingredients used in preparation, as well as over the proportions of each in a drink. In addition, drink sizes must be standardized. When standards of ingredients, portions, and drink sizes are set, the customer has reasonable assurance that the drink will meet expectations each time it is ordered. When these standards are set and enforced by management, they can be made to hold true even in the face of a high rate of employee turnover.

By establishing and maintaining these standards, management also provides a means for controlling costs. When drinks are prepared by formula and served in predetermined portion sizes, each daiquiri prepared by the bartender on duty should cost the same as every other daiquiri. Because the selling price is fixed, the cost-to-sales ratio for daiquiris should be the same for each daiquiri prepared. If all other drinks also are prepared according to standards appropriate for those drinks, the cost-to-sales ratio for other drinks should also be stable. When this is true, the cost-to-sales ratio for the overall operation should be stabilized, provided that the sales mix does not vary greatly. Simply stated, it becomes possible to develop a standard cost percentage for operation to which the actual cost percentage can be compared. This will be discussed in more detail in the next chapter.

QUANTITY CONTROL

One of the first steps in establishing control over production is to standardize the quantities of the most costly ingredients used: the alcoholic beverages. The amounts the bartender uses must be controlled. This involves predetermining the quantities to be used and providing a means of measuring those quantities.

In most beverage operations, the majority of drinks prepared involve combining one kind of liquor with a mixer. Scotch and soda, gin and tonic, rye and ginger ale, rum and Coke, are all examples of this type of drink. Management must determine the quantity of the expensive ingredient: the liquor. The amount varies from bar to bar, from three-quarters of an ounce in some places to as much as two ounces in others. This amount is set in advance by management and should be considered the amount management is willing to give in return for the selling price of the drink. Once the amount is settled, management must provide the bartender with the means for measuring this quantity each time a drink is prepared.* There are several methods for measuring quantities. The simplest and most widely used requires that the bartender physically measure the quantities poured. There

*Although wines and spirits are now purchased in metric units, most bars continue to measure and serve in ounces.

are four commonly used measuring devices: shot glasses, jiggers, pourers, and automated dispensers.

The Shot Glass

In some places, the bartender is provided with small glasses that are used for measuring. There are two kinds: plain and lined.

Plain shot glasses hold a predetermined quantity when filled to the brim. They are available in a number of sizes, from fractions of an ounce to several ounces. At any given bar, all should be the same size. In many places where these are used, the bartender is told to fill the shot glass and pour the exact measure into the drink. In others, the bartender is provided with shot glasses that hold slightly less than management is willing to give (three-quarters of an ounce, for example, if one ounce is the agreed on measure). The bartender is instructed to pour the three-quarters of an ounce into the drink and then in view of the customer, an additional small amount directly from the bottle to the glass. There is a psychological advantage to this method: customers think they are getting more than they are entitled to.

A lined shot glass is similar to a plain one, but a line is etched in it somewhere below the brim. In some places, the standard of fill is to the line, which is in full view of both the customer and the bartender. Other establishments use shot glasses that have deceptive lines so that when the bartender fills to the line on the inside of the glass, it appears to the customer to go above the line on the outside. This is an optical illusion, but it gives the customer a sense of getting something for nothing. Another variation on the lined glass approach involves using glasses that hold the standard measure when filled to the brim, but have lines etched somewhere below the brim. These are used for the same psychological reasons.

The Jigger

The jigger is a double-ended stainless steel measuring device, each end of which somewhat resembles a shot glass. They are of different sizes—one may hold 1.0 ounce and the other 1.5 ounces. Many believe the jigger is necessary for the accurate measuring that ensures perfect cocktails. It can be used for measuring straight shots as well, but is more useful for preparing cocktails calling for varying quantities of ingredients. For measuring these drinks, shot glasses are inappropriate. Some cocktails call for such varied measures as one ounce of one ingredient and one-and-one-half ounces of a second. To measure exact quantities of each ingredient, it is necessary to use the jigger.

The Pourer

Another way to control the quantity of liquor used in preparing drinks is by one of an assortment of devices that can be fitted on the top of a bottle and that permits the pouring of only a predetermined amount. These devices are known as pourers. A number of different types are available, but all operate on the principle of controlling the quantity poured each time the bottle is used. In an establishment where one ounce was the standard measure, the bottles could be fitted with devices that would dispense just one ounce. Each time the bartender tipped the bottle to pour, exactly one ounce would be dispensed. The psychological effect of these pouring devices is widely disputed. Some feel that the customer is given the illusion of the bartender pouring freely; others argue that the customer can feel resentful of management that neither trusts the bartender nor permits an extra drop to be dispensed to the customer. Still others feel that such attachments are useful at a service bar, which customers never see, but should never be used in a front bar, where the customer watches the bartender mix the drink.

The Automated Dispenser

In recent years, numerous companies have developed and successfully marketed various automated devices for dispensing predetermined measures of liquor. These range from comparatively simple systems for controlling only the pouring brands to highly elaborate control systems that not only control ounces but also mix drinks at the push of a button. These complex systems, costing thousands of dollars, are usually connected to a cash register in such a way that the sale is recorded on a guest check as the drink is prepared. In addition, meters record the quantities used and permit elaborate inventory control procedures. Many believe that these systems should be used in service bars but never at front bars except in cases where repeat customers are the exception rather than the rule, as in the case of an airport bar.

Free Pour

Another common system for controlling quantity is really a nonsystem. Where this is the practice, bartenders are permitted to "free pour." In effect, management relies on the experienced bartender to gauge by eye the quantities poured.

Although an experienced bartender can do this with great accuracy, the procedure clearly reduces the degree of management's control over the bar operation. In addition, in situations where rapid employee turnover is the rule, management is likely to find that it has no control at all over operations. In any bar operation, free pouring is likely to be abused by all but the most dedicated employees, leaving the door wide open for bartenders to operate more for their own advantage than for the general good of the business. However, many owners who permit free pouring seek to offset its disadvantages by adjusting selling prices upward to ensure the desired level of profit.

Glassware

In addition to controlling the quantity of liquor used in preparing each drink, it is desirable to control the overall size of the drinks. Standardizing the glassware used for service makes this comparatively simple. It is management's responsibility to predetermine the size of each drink and to provide the bartender with appropriate glassware for the service.

Beverage glassware is available in a wide variety of shapes and sizes. Therefore, management can furnish the bar with particular glassware for particular drinks. For example, stemmed cocktail glasses, holding 2½ ounces, may be used for all cocktails in a particular bar. Because the bartender cannot fill the glass beyond the brim, it is impossible to serve a portion size greater than 2½ ounces without changing glasses or giving the customer a "dividend." By furnishing the bar with 2½-ounce cocktail glassware, directing that all cocktails be served in these glasses, and declaring that no dividend will be given to customers, management can effectively control the portion size. Many fine hotels and restaurants consider the 2½-ounce cocktail glass too small. Management is willing to give a more generous portion for the posted selling price. In such cases, bartenders use so-called lined cocktail glasses—those holding 4½ ounces, with a line etched around the glass indicating a three-ounce measure.

In order to establish effective portion control, then, it is important to purchase glassware in appropriate sizes. Management must determine the kinds of glassware that will be needed (based on present or anticipated clientele and their preferences), then determine portion sizes. The purchasing of glassware must be based on these portion sizes determined by management, and bartenders must be instructed what glasses are to be used for serving particular drinks. While the neighborhood bar may be able to get by with just four or five types of glasses of as many sizes, the fine restaurant cannot. Neither can the hotel. Both may require as many as ten to fifteen different types and sizes of glassware for beverage service. Typically, a fine metropolitan hotel or restaurant would require a supply of glassware similar to that listed in figure 15.1. Samples of these are pictured in figure 15.2.

FIGURE 15.1

Standard Glassware ______________________ Restaurant

Item	*Size*	*Par Stock at Bar*
Shot Glass	1.25 oz.	24
Cordial	2 oz.	12
Cocktail	3.5 oz.	24
Cocktail	4.5 oz.	24
Champagne	4.5 oz.	24
Sour	5.25 oz.	24
Rocks	5.5 oz.	48
Brandy	5.5 oz.	12
Wine	8.5 oz.	24
Wine	6.5 oz.	24
Hi-Ball	8 oz.	48
Hi-Ball	10 oz.	48
Pilsner	10 oz.	24

FIGURE 15.2

Shot Glass
$1\frac{1}{4}$ oz.
Sour
$5\frac{1}{4}$ oz.
Footed Rocks
$5\frac{1}{2}$ oz.
Wine
$6\frac{1}{2}$ oz.
Cocktail
$4\frac{1}{2}$ oz.
Brandy
$5\frac{1}{2}$ oz.
Champagne
$4\frac{1}{2}$ oz.
Highball
8 oz.
Cordial
2 oz.

Thus, management standardizes portion sizes by purchasing particular glassware for particular purposes, and by carefully instructing bar personnel in its use. While the standardization of portion sizes helps control beverage costs, that alone is not enough. It is useful to stipulate that a gin and tonic will be served in an eight-ounce glass, yet this alone does not tell bar personnel what part of the standard portion should be gin and what part mixer. This consideration is important in cost control for, after all, the cost of gin is greater per ounce than the cost of mixer, and the relative amounts of each used in making the drink will affect the cost. The following two examples will show clearly the difference in the cost of ingredients effected by changing proportions.

Cost of Gin: $.15/oz.		Cost of Mixer: $.02/oz.	
Gin & Tonic "A"		Gin & Tonic "B"	
Gin—2 oz.	= .30	Gin—1 oz.	= .15
Mixer—6 oz.	= .12	Mixer—7 oz.	= .14
	.42		.29

In both cases, the result is eight ounces of gin and tonic. However, by varying the proportion, the costs differ considerably. If this particular drink is offered at a posted selling price of $2.00, there will be considerable difference between the cost-to-sales ratios as well.

$$\frac{\text{Cost } .42}{\text{Sales } 2.00} = \text{Cost \% } 21.0 \qquad \frac{\text{Cost } .29}{\text{Sales } 2.00} = \text{Cost \% } 14.5$$

STANDARD RECIPES

Clearly, if costs are to be controlled, the same control must be established over the proportions of ingredients that go into each drink. In other words, standard recipes must be established so that bar personnel will know how much of each ingredient to use to produce a certain drink.

Generally speaking, bartenders prepare and serve two kinds of drinks that require liquor: straight shots with mixers, such as the gin and tonic, and mixed drinks or cocktails, many of which involve a number of ingredients that must be combined in a certain way for the drink to be right.

In the case of the former, the standard drink is controlled by providing the bartender with appropriate glassware of predetermined size, as well as a jigger or other device for measuring the liquor content. The standard drink size is measured, poured over ice in the right glass, and then filled with the mixer. In effect, this constitutes the standard recipe. Each time a customer orders a Scotch and soda, the bartender will place a certain number of ice cubes in the right sized glass, measure in the standard quantity of the pouring brand of Scotch, and fill the glass nearly to the brim with soda. Every Scotch and soda prepared in this way will be the same. The customer's second drink will be the same as the first, and on returning to the bar in two weeks, he or she will be reasonably sure of receiving the same drink for the same price, barring changes in management policy. This is a major factor in establishing customer satisfaction and developing repetitive business.

Accomplishing the same end in the case of cocktails is somewhat more complicated. In most cases, there are two or more recipes for making any cocktail, the results of which are somewhat different. For example, two different mixing guides might list the following ingredients under recipes for the Manhattan cocktail:

A	*B*
2-½ oz. Blended Rye Whiskey	1-½ oz. Blended Rye Whiskey
¾ oz. Sweet Vermouth	¾ oz. Sweet Vermouth
Dash bitters	Dash bitters

While mixing the ingredients in the prescribed way will produce a Manhattan cocktail in each case, there are substantial differences between them. In the first case, the ratio of whiskey to vermouth is 3-to-1; in the second, it is 2-to-1. In addition, the first recipe makes a drink that is three-quarters of an ounce larger than the second. Finally, the first costs more to make because it contains an additional three-quarters of an ounce of blended rye whiskey.

It is apparent that management must decide which of several recipes will be the standard used to prepare the Manhattan. Similar decisions must be made for all cocktails. While the most frequent approach is simply to adopt one of the standard recipe guides for use at the bar, it is by no means uncommon, particularly in chain operations, to find that a special recipe book is prepared for use in the establishment. In every case, the standard recipe would include not only the measures of alcoholic beverages to be used in preparation but the quantities of all other ingredients including the garnish, if any, as well as mixing and serving instructions. In some cases, pictures of the drinks are provided to ensure uniformity, particularly in the face of high rates of employee turnover. Figure 15.3 gives examples of typical standard recipes for the Manhattan and the Brandy Alexander, two common cocktails. Both of these are among the standard recipes for the cocktails most frequently ordered in bars and lounges today, found listed in Appendix A at the end of the text.

Another important point to remember is that the book of standard recipes provides the bartender with instructions for preparing the unusual cocktails that are requested only on rare occasions. Although a number of bartenders are able to mix virtually any drink requested, many have few occasions to mix a Taxco Fizz, an Opal, or an Earthquake. The presence of a standard recipe guide at the bar has on many occasions helped to ensure the satisfaction of the customer requesting the unusual drink. Although standard bar recipes are a necessity from the point of view of someone interested in control, many bartenders and some managers view them with disdain. In some places, therefore, they are a controversial subject.

FIGURE 15.3

Manhattan	S. P. ______________
2-1/2 ounces blended rye whiskey 3/4 ounce sweet vermouth dash of bitters 4 ice cubes stem cherry	
Combine the whiskey, vermouth and ice cubes in a mixing glass and stir well. Strain into a 4-ounce stem cocktail glass. Garnish with the cherry.	
Brandy Alexander	S. P. ______________
3/4 ounce brandy 3/4 ounce Creme de Cacao 3/4 ounce heavy cream 3 ice cubes	
Combine all ingredients in a cocktail shaker and shake vigorously. Strain into a 4-ounce cocktail glass.	

It is theoretically possible to establish a standard recipe for each and every drink served by any bar, indicating the size of the drink and the quantities of each ingredient. As a practical matter, it is not possible to enforce standard recipes in all instances at all bars. One illustration of the problem should suffice.

Most people are familiar with the martini, a cocktail made of gin and dry vermouth, stirred with ice, strained into a cocktail glass, and served garnished with an olive. Many people order martinis every day. In some parts of the country it is surprising to find so little agreement of the proportions of gin and vermouth that should go into a "good" martini. For some, the best mixture for a three-ounce martini is two ounces of gin to one of vermouth; for others, it is three ounces of gin to one drop of vermouth. And there are an infinite number of variations. Because the bar business seeks to satisfy customer tastes, it is very difficult to set up an inflexible standard recipe for the martini for a particular bar. One single standard recipe might satisfy some customers, but make others very unhappy. In many instances, bartenders must be permitted a certain amount of freedom to alter standard recipes, not at their own whims, but at the request of customers. In such cases, the standard recipe should be a kind of average of all the martinis mixed in a certain bar over a period of time.

When standard recipes are established and standard portion sizes have been set, it becomes possible to calculate the standard cost of any drink.

DETERMINING STANDARD PORTION COSTS

Straight Drinks

The cost of straight drinks, served with or without mixers, can be determined by first dividing the standard portion size in ounces into the number of ounces in the bottle to find the number of standard drinks contained in each bottle. This number is then divided into the cost of the bottle to find the standard cost of the drink.

With the introduction of the metric system for beverage packaging, it has become necessary to convert the metric contents of bottles as purchased into their ounce equivalents. A simple table for conversion is shown in figure 15.4.

For example, the standard portion size for the pouring brand of Scotch in a certain bar is 1½ ounces. The bar uses 750-ml bottles of Scotch. The chart in figure 15.4 shows that a 750-ml bottle contains 25.4 ounces. Dividing the 1½ ounce standard drink into the 25.4 ounces contained in each bottle, one determines that each bottle contains 16.9 drinks, rounded off to the nearest tenth of a drink.

$$\frac{25.4 \text{ oz.}}{1.5 \text{ oz.}} = 16.9 \text{ drinks.}$$

FIGURE 15.4
Relationship of Approved Metric Sizes to U.S. Standards of Fill

DISTILLED SPIRITS

OLD SIZES *U.S. STANDARDS OF FILL*	*U.S. OUNCES*	*STANDARD METRIC SIZES*	
		LITERS	*MILLILITERS*
Gallon	128		
Half-Gallon	64		
	59.2	1.75	1750
	33.8	1.00	1000
Quart	32		
Fifth	25.6		
	25.4	3/4 liter	750
3/4 Quart (Cordials)	24		
	17	1/2 liter	500
Pint	16		
4/5 Pint	12.8		
3/4 Pint (Cordials)	12		
Half Pint	8		
	6.8	1/5 liter	200
1/4 Pint	4		
1/8 Pint	2		
	1.7	1/20 liter	50
1/10 Pint (Miniature)	1.6		

WINES

OLD SIZES U.S. STANDARDS OF FILL	U.S. OUNCES	STANDARD METRIC SIZES LITERS	MILLILITERS
4.9 Gallon	627.2		
3 Gallon	384		
1 Gallon	128		
Jeroboam (4/5 Gallon)	102.4		
	101	3	3000
Half-Gallon	64		
Magnum (2/5 Gallon)	51.2		
	50.7	1.5	1500
	33.8	1	1000
Quart	32		
Fifth	25.6		
	25.4	3/4 liter	750
Pint	16		
4/5 Pint	12.8		
	12.7	3/8 liter	375
1/2 Pint	8		
Split (2/5 Pint)	6.4		
	6.3	3/16 liter	187.5
4 Oz.	4		
	3.4	1/10 liter	100
3 Oz. Miniature	3		
2 Oz.	2		

Because there is a certain amount—hopefully minimal—of spillage and evaporation in all bar operations, this can be further rounded off to an average of 16.5 drinks per bottle. If the purchase price of the bottle is \$5.55, then each of the 16.5 drinks it contains has a standard cost of \$5.55 divided by 16.5, or \$.34, when rounded off to the nearest cent.

$$\frac{\$5.55}{16.5} = \$.33636$$

This same bar would normally offer a number of call brands of Scotch as well, and the same technique can be used to determine the standard cost of the standard drink of each. In the case of the premium Scotch costing $9.20 per 750-ml bottle yielding 16.5 drinks, the standard cost of each drink is obviously somewhat higher:

$$\frac{\$9.20}{16.5} = \$.5575 = \$.56 \text{ per drink.}$$

An alternative procedure for finding the standard cost per drink requires that one divide the cost of the bottle by the number of ounces it contains to find the cost per ounce, then multiplying the ounce cost by the standard drink size. For example, if the pouring brand of gin costs $6.20 per liter, the equivalent of 33.8 ounces according to the chart, each ounce would cost $.1834, or $.183.

$$\frac{\$6.20}{33.8 \text{ oz.}} = \$.183$$

This ounce cost, multiplied by the standard 1½-ounce drink size for gin in this particular bar, shows a standard cost for the standard measure of $.2745, or $.27.

$$1.5\text{-ounce standard size} \times \$.183 \text{ per ounce} = \$.27 \text{ per drink}$$

Some who employ this method might prefer to divide the bottle size in ounces, but by one ounce less. This has the effect of allowing for the usual evaporation and spillage.

The use of one method rather than another is purely a matter of the personal preferences of those who perform the calculations. Once these calculations have been performed, the usual practice is to record the results on a form similar to that illustrated in figure 15.5. These are updated whenever prices change. In this way, up-to-date cost figures are always available to management to use in several ways. One use for the figures is in calculating the cost of mixed drinks and cocktails.

FIGURE 15.5

Bottle Code	*Item*	*Bottle Size ml*	*oz.*	*Bottle Cost*	*Ounce Cost*	*Drink Size*	*Drink Cost*
201	Old Bagpipe	750	25.4	6.80	.268	1.5 oz.	.40
206	Highland Hiatus	750	25.4	8.45	.333	1.5 oz.	.50
302	Guttersnipe Gin	1000	33.8	5.84	.173	1.5 oz.	.26

Mixed Drinks and Cocktails

It is particularly important to determine the standard cost of a drink made by standard recipe in the case of cocktails and other mixed drinks. These drinks typically involve several ingredients and often require two or more alcoholic beverages. Consequently, mixed drinks are usually more expensive to make than straight drinks. Knowledge of the cost per drink is important in making intelligent pricing decisions.

To determine the standard cost of cocktails and other mixed drinks and to maintain records of the information, it is useful to obtain a supply of Recipe Detail and Cost forms similar to those illustrated in figures 15.6 and 15.7. Both are used farily commonly and can be made up either by a printer or by a secretary who has access to a duplicating machine.

The first step in determining the standard cost of the drink is to record on the form all the information from the standard recipe for each drink. It is essential that all ingredients used by the bartender in preparing the drink are taken into account in determining cost. The cost of any of these drinks should and does include the cost of all the various nonalcoholic ingredients that may be used. Various fruit juices, eggs, and heavy cream are but a few of the other ingredients that must be considered. In addition, various garnishes for the drinks must be included where appropriate. These might include such varied items as olives, stem cherries, cocktail onions, and slices of various fruits. To arrive at the true cost of the drink, the cost of all of these must be added to the cost of the basic alcoholic ingredients.

It should be noted that both the forms given contain space near the bottom for including the standard preparation procedure and the standard glassware. If this information is recorded from the bartenders' guide, management is provided

FIGURE 15.6
Standard Recipe—Detail and Cost

Item Martini — Bar Recipe # 53

Selling Price	$2.00
Cost	$ .42
Cost Percentage	21.0%

Ingredients	*Quantity*	*Cost*
Guttersnipe gin	2 oz.	.35
Dry vermouth	1/2 oz.	.05
Martini olive		.02
Totals:	2-1/2 oz.	$.42

Procedure: Pour gin and vermouth into glass mixer. Add cracked ice and stir gently. Pour into 3-oz. cocktail glass. Add olive and serve. Glassware: 3 oz. Cocktail

FIGURE 15.7
Standard Recipe: Detail and Cost

Item: Maurice Cocktail		Bar Recipe: 77	
	9/11		
	Date	*Date*	*Date*
Selling Price	$1.75		
Cost	.31		
Cost Percentage	17.7%		
	Bottle Data		
	9/11		
Ingredient Cost	*Date*	*Date*	*Date*
Guttersnipe gin	$5.84		
	Drink Data		
	9/11		
Ingredient Cost	*Date*	*Date*	*Date*
Juice of 1/4 orange	.03		
1/2 oz. sweet vermouth	.05		
1/2 oz dry vermouth	.05		
1 oz. gin	.17		
Dash bitters	.01		
Totals	$ .31		

Procedure: Combine all ingredients in glass shaker. Add cracked ice and stir. Strain into 4-oz. cocktail glass.

Standard Glassware 4-Oz. Cocktail

with a complete set of the standard recipes, in a loose-leaf book, or in a card file for ready reference.

Once the basic information has been recorded from the standard recipe, it is necessary to find the cost of each ingredient, both alcoholic and nonalcoholic. The location of this information will vary considerably from place to place. It is particularly helpful here to have the information in a form such as in figure 15.5. In some large establishments, the beverage controller will have the cost of beverages in perpetual inventory records or in an up-to-date price book.

Some smaller operations may find it necessary to refer to invoices, receiving sheets, or inventory books. In the case of nonbeverage items, such as the food items transferred from the kitchen, it may be necessary to refer to the relevant transfer memos. In other cases, the steward might be asked for the most recent purchase prices for each item. Here, too, the procedure will vary considerably from place to place. In general, the exact procedure followed is of no particular importance, so long as it results in ascertaining the correct cost figures for each item in the recipe.

The techniques for recording the data are different for the two forms illustrated. In the first instance, one must calculate the cost of the quantity used before recording any cost information on the form. In the example given, the cost of the two ounces of gin is recorded as $.35. This is determined by referring to the chart in figure 15.5, which indicates that one ounce of the pouring brand costs $.173. This multiplied by the two ounces in the recipe gives the cost figure to record, rounded off to the nearest cent.

If a form similar to the second example is used, the first step would be to record the size and cost of a bottle of the pouring brand. In the example shown, the 33.8-ounce bottle of gin is recorded as costing $5.84. The next step is to divide the number of ounces into the cost of the bottle, and to multiply the result by the number of ounces of gin in the recipe. This is exactly the same kind of calculating that one would have already performed in compiling the figures illustrated in figure 15.5.

The only real advantage of the form shown in the second example is that it provides space to recalculate drink costs as the costs of the ingredients change. When this form is adopted, it may thus be used for a relatively longer period of time before it beomes necessary to rewrite the cost records.

Once the costs of all ingredients have been determined, the figures are totalled and the result is the standard cost for preparing the drink according to the standard recipe.

This cost is recorded at the top on the line provided, and divided by the selling price to determine the cost-to-sales ratio for the drink. This is recorded as the cost percentage for that particular drink. If selling prices have not yet been determined, the cost per drink should certainly be one of the chief considerations in arriving at a reasonable figure. Even in those cases in which selling prices have been set before costs were calculated, all the selling prices should be reviewed in the light of the newly developed cost figures.

STANDARD SELLING PRICE

Once standard costs for standard drinks are known and listed, a similar list of selling prices should be estalished. One obvious reason for doing this is to enable management to post selling prices at the bar or to list them in a menu, depending on the type of establishment. It is generally good practice to maintain a complete list of these standard selling prices in the beverage controller's office. Many of the techniques for control to be discussed in chapter 16 depend heavily on selling prices.

The techniques for maintaining such lists of standard selling prices are many and varied. As in so many other cases, the simplest is often the best; and for that reason it is recommended that selling prices for cocktails and mixed drinks be maintained on the recipe detail and cost cards, and the prices for straight drinks be kept on an expanded version of the list first shown in figure 15.5, now shown in its expanded form in figure 15.8.

It is absolutely essential in any bar operation that the selling prices be standardized for each drink sold, for straight drinks as well as for cocktails and other mixed drinks. When selling prices are standardized, customers can be properly

FIGURE 15.8

Bottle Code	*Item*	*Bottle Size ml*	*oz.*	*Bottle Cost*	*Ounce Cost*	*Drink Size*	*Drink Cost*	*Drink S.P.*
200		750	25.4	5.35	.21	1.5 oz.	.32	1.50
202		750	25.4	8.10	.319	1.5 oz.	.48	2.00
203		750	25.4	8.14	.32	1.5 oz.	.48	2.00
206		750	25.4	8.45	.333	1.5 oz.	.50	2.00
207		750	25.4	9.20	.362	1.5 oz.	.54	2.00
210		750	25.4	8.90	.35	1.5 oz.	.53	2.00
212		750	25.4	12.10	.476	1.5 oz.	.71	2.50
213		750	25.4	14.20	.559	1.5 oz.	.84	2.75

charged for the drinks they order, and the prices will not vary from day to day. The possibilities for customer satisfaction are increased, for the customer who has been charged $1.25 for a particular drink on Tuesday has reasonable assurance that an identical charge will be made for the same amount for the same drink on Wednesday.

In some places, the list of standardized drink prices is posted on signs over the bar or printed in a menu. Such postings and listings have the additional effect of eliminating many possible arguments over drink prices.

Perhaps the most important purpose behind the standardization of selling prices is the maintenance of a planned cost-to-sales ratio for each drink sold. The drink that costs $.30 when prepared according to standard formula, and that sells for $1.50, has a cost-to-sales ratio of $.30 to $1.50, more commonly expressed as 20%. The sale of each such drink results in the addition of $1.50 to daily sales figures and $.30 to daily cost figures, the net effect being a gross profit on the sale of $1.20. In the case of this particular drink, this is the desired, preplanned effect of each sale. The net effect is not a matter of the bartender's whim; it is planned by management. Ingredients, and consequently costs, are planned. With this in mind, selling prices are set and have a predetermined relationship to the costs. In addition, each sale has a predetermined impact on the operation's overall gross profit. In effect, the profit on each sale is planned when management sets both cost and selling prices. Thus, planning and maintaining profit levels becomes possible.

EDP APPLICATIONS

Once management has stored in computer memory all data relative to the purchase of beverages, including standard bottle sizes and updated purchase prices, the computer may be used to determine the standard cost of each drink served, provided management programs contain certain additional data. This would include standard recipes for drinks and the conversion table shown in figure 15.4. The conversion table is needed simply because beverage purchases today are made in metric units, but most restaurants continue to measure in the more traditional ounces. Storing the conversion table in memory would provide the computer with means for changing the metric unit purchases into ounce measures as part of the determination of standard costs for drinks.

Another important use of EDP may be seen in those establishments that use the more sophisticated sales terminals, like bar registers. Many of these terminals inlude a feature known as automatic pricing, which is used in the following manner. The keyboard of the terminal has drink names rather than numbers on many of the keys. When a drink is ordered, the bartender inserts a check into the printer attached to the terminal, then depresses the key corresponding to the drink ordered. Drink prices have been preprogrammed into the terminal, and each time a given key is depressed, the name and correct price for the drink ordered are printed on the guest check. This procedure allows a bartender using the terminal correctly to charge only the standard price that management has preprogrammed into the terminal memory.

CHAPTER ESSENTIALS

In this chapter, we explained the need for beverage production control and identified a variety of means by which such controls may be instituted. We explained the importance of standard drink recipes and illustrated the calculation of standard costs from those recipes. We explained the problem of buying beverages in metric containers while measuring and selling drinks by ounces and provided a table for converting metrics to ounces. We discussed the importance of standard sales prices for drinks and explored several possibilities for employing computers as aids in controlling beverage production.

QUESTIONS AND PROBLEMS

1 The cost of the liquor in a certain drink is $.18 per ounce and the cost of the mixer is $.03 per ounce. Determine the cost of the drink in the following cases.

- **a** One ounce of liquor and six ounces of mixer are used.
- **b** 1½ ounce of liquor and seven ounces of mixer are used.
- **c** Two ounces of liquor and six ounces of mixer are used.

2 In each of the examples in question 1 above, determine selling price if:

- **a** A desired liquor cost of 20% is used.
- **b** A desired liquor cost of 25% is used.
- **c** A desired liquor cost of 18% is used.

3 In a certain drink, a one-ounce shot of liquor is used, which represents the entire cost of the drink. How much does the drink cost if a one-liter bottle of the liquor costs $5.76?

4 If the desired cost-to-sales ratio is 20% for a certain drink, determine the selling price if a 1½-ounce shot is used and the cost of the liter of liquor is $8.00.

5 If the desired cost-to-sales ratio is 20% for a certain drink, determine the selling price if a 1½-ounce shot is used and the cost of the liter of liquor is $6.40.

6 If the desired cost-to-sales ratio is 25% for a certain drink, determine the selling price if a 1½-ounce shot is used. The cost of the liter of liquor is $6.72 and the cost of the mixer is $.04.

7 How may portion control be instituted in bar operations?

8 Why is production control necessary in bar operations? What are some of the measures which can be taken to institute control?

9 Select recipes for any four common drinks from a book of drink recipes in Appendix A, then determine the standard cost of one standard drink of each using current prices in your calculations.

10 Identify each of the following:

Straight drink	Jigger
Mixed drink	Plain shot glass
Cocktail	Lined shot glass
Mixer	Stemware
Automatic pricing	

11 Assume that you are manager of a cocktail lounge that uses an Electronic Sales Terminal with automatic pricing as a bar register. There is no other register in the establishment. It is 5:00 P.M. on a busy Friday afternoon, and the terminal suddenly stops working. What instructions would you give the bartender to follow until the terminal was repaired?

chapter 16

Measuring the Effectiveness of Bar Controls

Learning Objectives

After reading and studying this chapter, the student should be able to:

1 Calculate the value of end-of-month beverage inventory, monthly beverage cost, and monthly beverage cost percent.

2 Calculate daily beverage cost and cost percent, taking transfers, wines, beers, ales, and mixers into account.

3 Determine the effectiveness of production controls using each of the following methods: ounce control, potential sales value.

4 Measure the effectiveness of production controls by the following:

- **a** Ounce control method.
- **b** Adjusted potential sales value methods.
- **c** Average potential sales value method.
- **d** Standard deviation method.

5 Explain the need for sales control in beverage operations and the steps that may be taken to institute such control in both large and small operations.

6 Define the following terms:

- **a** Inventory differential
- **b** Full bottle sales slip
- **c** Ounce control
- **d** Potential sales value
- **e** Mixed drink differential
- **f** Secondary ingredients
- **g** Automated bar
- **h** Ring in, ring out register

7 Describe how computers may be used to control bar operations effectively.

One important part of the control procedure is the regular measuring of the effects of operation to see if events are conforming to plans. There are many ways of measuring results. The differences in techniques arise chiefly from differences in the size and scope of operations, as well as from some differences in management philosophy. Regardless of differences, the techniques for measuring operations fall into three principal categories, one based on cost percentages, a second on ounce consumption, and a third on potential sales value versus actual sales. Each of the three categories will be discussed in this chapter.

MONTHLY CALCULATION OF COST PERCENTAGE

It is useful to compare cost and sales figures on a regular basis to see if the anticipated cost-to-sales ratio is being maintained. Methods for doing this vary considerably from operation to operation. So we shall look at several that might be found in operations of different sizes.

Smaller operations, often owner-managed with few employees, usually have no beverage controller. However, the owner must determine the cost-to-sales ratio. In many places, this is done monthly, with or without the help of an accountant. Cost is determined from inventory and purchase figures in the following manner.

A physical inventory of the storage area is taken, usually immediately after the close of business for the month. The number of bottles of each item in stock is counted and its value is determined by one of the five methods for inventory valuation discussed in Chapter 8. When the value of each item in stock is known, the values are added, and the result is the total dollar value of the closing inventory for the period. Because the closing inventory figure for any period is, by definition, the opening inventory for the following period, it is necessary to look back at the records to determine the closing inventory for the preceding period. To this opening inventory valuation, the owner adds the cost of all purchases for the month from bookkeeping records. The opening inventory plus the purchases shows the dollar value of all the stock available for sale during the period. To illustrate, consider the following example:

Closing inventory valuation—preceding period	$ 5,000
+ Purchases (from accounting records) this month	8,000
Total stock available for sale during month	$13,000

Of the stock available for sale, some has been issued to the bar, and some has not. To find the value of the stock issued to the bar, the ending inventory figure this month is subtracted from the total available figure previously determined.

Thus:

Total stock available for sale during month	$13,000
− Closing inventory valuation—this month	6,000
Value of stock issued this month	$ 7,000

While the $7,000 figure represents the value of liquor going to the bar, it does not necessarily represent the true cost of liquor sold at the bar. To determine that figure, the $7,000 must be adjusted by the change in inventory at the bar from the beginning to the end of the month. To illustrate:

Bar inventory valuation at the beginning of month	$1,500
Bar inventory valuation at the end of the month	800
Inventory differential	$ 700

That figure must be added to the $7,000 figure to compute the cost of liquor consumed for the month. Thus:

Issues to bar	$7,000
Inventory differential	700
Cost of liquor consumed	$7,700

If the differential at the bar were a negative figure, that amount would be subtracted, rather than added, to the value of issues to the bar.

Having determined the cost of liquor consumed at the bar, the cost percentage, or cost-to-sales ratio, is determined in the usual manner:

$$\text{Cost percentage} = \frac{\text{Cost}}{\text{Sales}}$$

Illustrating:

$$\text{Cost percentage} = \frac{\$7{,}700}{\$29{,}389.30}$$

$$\text{Cost percentage} = 26.2\%$$

The above procedure may be employed by even the smallest of bars and will require the barest minimum of paperwork on the manager's part. It merely requires that some basic bookkeeping records of purchases be maintained, and that a par stock be maintained at the bar by issuing full bottles in exchange for empties. From the point of view of control, it is not the best possible procedure, but it does enable one to determine the cost-to-sales ratio for a period in establishments where no staff is available for maintaining daily records of issues.

Many managers find that these simple procedures result in determinations of beverage costs and beverage cost percentages that are not suitably accurate for their particular operations, and thus they require some or all of the possible adjustments to cost of beverages issued, described below.

ADJUSTING MONTHLY FIGURES

Food and Beverage Transfers

Some operations do not consider the figures so derived accurate enough, because they do not reflect the cost of such food items as oranges, lemons, eggs, and heavy cream, which are often used for beverage preparation, but which are typically purchased by the food department and transferred to the bar. The cost of these items is significant and should properly be included in the beverage cost figures, not in the food cost figures. For this reason, such establishments maintain records of the transfer of these food items from the kitchen to the bar, and add the cost to the beverage cost, while subtracting them from the food cost. In the case of food items issued directly from food stores to the bar (such as cocktail cherries and olives), separate bar requisitions are prepared, often on a different color paper from food requisitions. When such is the case, provision must be made for adding the cost of these items to the beverage cost. The effect of their use is reflected in beverage sales, so their cost should properly be reflected in beverage cost.

Many operations use certain beverages in the preparation of food products for sale, and send them from the bar to the kitchen when needed. When the amount involved is deemed significant, separate records of these transfers are maintained as well. In the case of an establishment that featured a different parfait each day and used a certain amount of a different cordial from the bar to prepare them, records could be kept on transfer memos of the amounts of each cordial sent to the kitchen for food preparation; the value of the cordial would be subtracted from the beverages cost figures.

Other Adjustments

Possible additions to cost include:

1 Any food item used in beverage preparation, not included in transfer memos.

2 Cost of mixers, if not included as transfers.

Possible credits to cost include:

1 Cost of any officers' drinks that should more properly be charged to entertainment or to business promotion. In the event that sales revenue has

been recorded for any such drinks, this revenue should be subtracted from beverage sales figures and probably written off.

2 Cost of the beverages used in other promotional activities, such as free drinks to couples celebrating fiftieth wedding anniversaries, complimentary drinks offered to diners ordering before 5:30 P.M., and so on.

Using all such adjustments, the cost of beverages sold would be determined as illustrated in figure 16.1.

FIGURE 16.1

Cost of Liquor Consumed		$7,700
Add:		
Food to bar (Directs)		220
Storeroom issues		105
Mixers		525
	Subtotal	$8,550
Less:		
Cooking liquor		335
Officers' drinks		110
Special promotions		465
Cost of Beverages Sold		$7,640

Therefore, Beverage Cost Percent equals $7,640.00/$29,389.30, or 26.0%.

Once determined, the cost-to-sales ratio for a period may be compared to the ratio for other periods to see how results measure up to those of similar periods in the past. If, for example, the cost percentage for the current period is 26.0%, and the records reveal that the cost percentage for the last six months has fluctuated between 25.8% and 27.0%, a manager would likely conclude that the measured results were satisfactory, provided that the past results have been considered satisfactory. If, however, some dramatic change in the cost-to-sales ratio were revealed, and the change was both unexpected and undesirable, the manager would try to determine the reasons for the change and attempt to effect changes in the operation so that the undesirable results would not be repeated.

Monthly Calculation by Category

Some managers would consider the foregoing cost and cost percentage figures too general to be of maximum value for their operations. Many would prefer to see both cost and sales figures divided into spirits, wines, and beers, principally because the cost-to-sales ratios for these three may differ significantly from one another, and changes from one period to another would not be apparent in one cost percent figure that reflected all three.

Assuming that appropriate records are available, a form such as that illustrated in figure 16.2 may be devised both to distribute cost and sales figures for these

FIGURE 16.2

Beverage Sales:				
	Sales		*Adjustments*	*Net Sales*
Spirits	$20,572.50		$260.00	$20,312.50
Wine	5,877.80		50.00	5,827.80
Beer	2,939.00		50.00	2,879.00
Total sales	$29,389.30		$370.00	$29,019.30
Less:				
Cost of Beverages Sold:				
	Spirits	*Wines*	*Beer*	*Total*
Cost of issues	$3,496.30	$3,250.00	$953.70	$7,700.00
Adjustments:				
Additions				
Food to bar (Directs)	220.00	—	—	220.00
Storeroom issues	105.00	—	—	105.00
Mixers	525.00	—	—	525.00
Subtotal	850.00	- 0 -	- 0 -	850.00
Subtractions				
Bar to kitchen	45.00	220.00	70.00	335.00
Officers' drinks	65.00	25.00	20.00	110.00
Special promotions	105.00	360.00	—	465.00
Subtotal	215.00	605.00	90.00	910.00
Net adjustments	635.00	(605.00)	(90.00)	(60.00)
Net cost of sales	4,131.30	2,645.00	863.70	7,640.00
Cost percent	20.3%	45.4%	30.0%	26.3%
Cost per dollar sale	$.203	$.454	$.30	$.263

three major categories, and to reflect the various adjustments previously discussed as they affect the major cost and sales categories.

In Chapter 15, standard drink recipes were developed, partly to determine standard portion cost for pricing purposes. If, for example, sales prices for drinks made with spirits were established with a target cost percent of 20.0%, the overall cost-to-sales ratio of 26.0% determined in the earlier part of the chapter would not indicate to management whether or not the target was being achieved. However, when sales and cost figures, as well as adjustments for both wines and beers, are factored out, it becomes possible to determine, as in figure 16.2, the cost percent for spirits for the period has been 20.3%, and a judgment can be made about the effectiveness of the cost control measures instituted.

The analysis of the cost-to-sales ratio just once each month presents some obvious problems. A month is an accumulation of thirty yesterdays, and by the time the results of all those days are known, it is too late to do anything about them. If the figures indicate that October was a disaster, nothing can be done to change the results of October's operation. It may be possible to reduce the effects over the course of a year by improving results in other months, but nothing can be done to change the past. The best a manager can hope for is to show improvement in the operation for November and December, and thus offset the poor result of the October operation. It would be preferable to have some knowledge of the cost-to-sales ratio before the period has passed, so that efforts might be made to improve operations while there is still time for the improvements to affect the figures for the current period.

DAILY CALCULATION OF COST PERCENTAGE

If the manager could have figures for the first ten days of the month, changes could conceivably be effected in the operation in time for their positive effect to be reflected in the figures for the period. Some larger operations, in which staff exists to maintain the necessary records, do this. Where beverages are issued to the bar daily on the basis of requisitions that accompany the empty bottles, it is possible to determine costs daily. After beverages are issued, the requisitions are numbered and totaled to determine the cost of the issues for the day. This figure is taken as the cost of beverages sold on the preceding day and may be compared to sales for the day to determine a cost percentage. It is fairly obvious that this is less than completely accurate. The assumption is made that every ounce in every empty bottle was sold on the preceding day, and does not account for the possibility that the contents of a bottle might have been sold over a period of several days. The daily cost percentage is therefore unreliable. However, if the cost of daily issues is accumulated daily and compared to the accumulated sales over all the days so far in a period, a more accurate picture merges. The inaccuracies inherent in the figures for one day tend to be eliminated, and a reasonably reliable picture of overall operations is provided, as illustrated in figure 16.3.

FIGURE 16.3

	Cost		*Sales*		*Cost Percent*	
Date	*Today*	*To Date*	*Today*	*To Date*	*Today*	*To Date*
11/1	$300		$900		33.4%	
11/2	$240	$ 540	$970	$1,870	24.8%	28.4%
11/3	$220	$ 760	$920	$2,790	23.8%	27.3%
11/4	$225	$ 985	$995	$3,785	22.6%	26.0%
11/5	$170	$1,155	$930	$4,715	18.3%	24.5%
11/6	$190	$1,345	$920	$5,635	20.7%	23.9%

An even more reliable picture of daily operations might be obtained if management could take daily inventory of the stock at the bar and thus determine an inventory differential for each day similar to that discussed earlier in this chapter. If the manager were able to subtract each day's closing bar inventory from the opening bar inventory, the bar differential obtained could be subtracted (or added, in the case of a negative figure) to the daily issues figure to determine daily cost with greater accuracy.

If such daily differential figures were available, two more columns could be added to the form illustrated in figure 16.3, between the two columns headed Date and Cost Today. These two would be headed Beverage Issues and Bar Inventory Differential. With the addition of these two, Cost Today would become a net figure, incorporationg daily issues and bar differential, and the daily calculation of cost percent for the day and for the period to date would result in some greater degree of accuracy.

The cost percentage to date reflects the net effect of all costs and all sales for the number of days that have passed in the period, and may be fairly judged in the light of comparable figures from the recent past. When comparison reveals undesirable results, attempts may be made to reverse their effect during the current period in order that the total figures for the period will reflect more desirable results. An undesirable trend may be reversed well before the end of the period.

ADJUSTING DAILY FIGURES

Just as monthly figures can be adjusted in a variety of ways, so daily figures can be adjusted by the manager or beverage cost controller who seeks a more precise picture of operations. If records are available in the form of transfer memos, sales checks, and the like, the form illustrated in figure 16.3 could be expanded to resemble that in figure 16.4.

Figure 16.4 provides for increasing the daily issues figure by recording in the Additions column such items as transfers of Directs from the kitchen to the bar, mixers purchased directly for the bar, and food storeroom issues to the bar. If bar inventory were taken daily, positive differential could also be included in this column. In the Subtractions column, one could include transfers of beverages to the kitchen (cooking liquor), the cost of officers' drinks used for entertainment or promotion, and the cost of complimentary drinks used for special promotions. Negative bar differentials could be subtracted here, also. If one preferred, individual columns for each of the above could be included in place of the two columns illustrated.

Using one or another of these forms, a manager can monitor employee performance, note significant deviations from acceptable norms, and take the necessary corrective action while events are still fresh in the minds of participants and investigations are feasible.

In each method of maintaining cost figures discussed so far, the object has been to compare current figures with historical figures—the current cost-to-sales

FIGURE 16.4

Date	Beverages Issued	Additions	Subtractions	Total Cost		Sales		Cost Percent	
				Today	To Date	Today	To Date	Today	To Date
11/1	$300	$10	$35	$275		$900		30.6%	
11/2	$240	$20	$25	$235	$ 510	$970	$1,870	24.2%	27.3%
11/3	$220	$10	$20	$210	$ 720	$920	$2,790	22.8%	25.8%
11/4	$225	$ 5	$10	$220	$ 940	$995	$3,785	22.1%	24.8%
11/5	$170	$10	$15	$165	$1,105	$930	$4,715	17.7%	23.4%
11/6	$190	$ 5	$ 5	$190	$1,295	$920	$5,635	20.7%	23.0%

ratio with that ratio for a previous period. Judgments are made on the basis of the acceptability of previous figures and the degree to which current figures measure up. Various kinds of efforts are made to determine actual costs, and these actual costs are compared to actual sales. This is probably the most common approach to the problem of controlling beverage costs, but it is not necessarily the most desirable. After all, current figures may compare favorably to figures for a number of previous periods, but there is no adequate way of determining the extent to which the figures for previous periods were as they should have been. Very often this is not the case. The figures for previous periods may reflect any number of unknown problems, and the comparison of current to past figures may merely confirm that past problems continue to exist. Some method must be found for determining the extent to which problems exist. In short, some more accurate standard for judging the cost-to-sales ratio is needed.

OUNCE CONTROL

Another technique for beverage control is the quantity- or ounce-control method. Some years ago it involved taking daily physical inventory of bar stock in order to determine the number of ounces consumed, and the calculation from detailed sales records of the number of ounces sold. Ideally, of course, the number of ounces consumed should equal the number of ounces sold; in practice, they never do equal one another because of spillage, evaporation, and breakage. However, when a bar is operated carefully, paying strict attention to the standards set by management, the difference can be kept to a minimum.

In this form, the ounce-control method has virtually disappeared from the field. It is probable that the cost of maintaining the procedure daily would far outweigh the benefits to be derived from it. However, modern technology has made possible the reappearance of ounce-control procedures in a variety of forms. Some involve meters attached to bottles to measure quantities used daily, and others require the purchase and use of some rather expensive and sophisticated computerized devices that dispense ingredients, mix drinks, record sales, and maintain bar inventory records automatically. Because such sophisticated equipment generally becomes comparatively less expensive in the years following its introduction, it is probable that more of this equipment will be used in the future.

CALCULATING POTENTIAL SALES VALUE

In some beverage operations, efforts are made to determine what sales should result from the issuing of full bottles of various liquors from the storeroom. For example, if the standard drink of gin is one ounce, and gin is issued in one-liter bottles, then each bottle potentially contains 33.8 drinks. If the standard drink sells for a standard price of $1, then the potential sales value of the bottle issued is 33.8 drinks times $1 per drink, or $33.80. Hypothetically, then, each bottle of gin issued should produce $33.80 in sales. By extension, given standard drink sizes and standard selling prices, the total revenue that will be produced can be determined by issuing one bottle of any item kept at the bar. Therefore, when an empty bottle of any item is turned in with a requisition for replacement, it should be possible to find the potential sales value of the bottle reflected in actual sales. In a simple, hypothetical bar, for example, using only liter bottles and serving only straight drinks in one-ounce shots for $1 per drink, the consumption of one bottle each of gin, rye, and Scotch produces $96 in sales. With this in mind, one should find $101.40 recorded in the cash register at the end of the day.

From this information, it is possible to develop a chart of the standard sales values of bottles sold only by the straight drink (see figure 16.5). In practice, such a chart would necessarily include all brands so sold at the bar and would obviously be considerably longer than that in the figure.

FIGURE 16.5

Bottle Code #	*Item*	*Bottle Size*	*Drink Size*	*Drinks per Bottle*	*Drink Price*	*Sales Value Per Bottle*
301	Gin	1 liter	1 oz.	33.8	$1.00	$33.80
107	Rye	1 liter	1 oz.	33.8	1.00	33.80
217	Scotch	750 ml	1 oz.	25.4	1.00	25.40
352	Vodka	1 liter	1 oz.	33.8	.90	30.42
456	Brandy	750 ml	1 oz.	25.4	1.10	27.94

ADJUSTING SALES VALUES FOR MIXED DRINKS

However, beverage operations are seldom, if ever, quite this simple. Most bars do not sell spirits only in straight shots. Cocktails and other mixed drinks, involving varying quantities of spirits and other ingredients, account for some portion of sales in most establishments. Therefore, if control is to involve the use of potential sales values of bottles, some way must be found to account for the differences that arise from the production of various mixed drinks. The potential sales value of each bottle must be adjusted according to some formula that takes into consideration variations in both quantities of spirits used and selling prices.

In fact, control procedures involving potential sales values are generally quite complex and require considerable time and calculation. For these and other related reasons, they are not commonly used except in some very large operations. However, some basic understanding of these procedures is necessary for anyone who seeks to acquire a complete overview of beverage control. Several different approaches will be discussed here.

The problem in establishing control by the potential sales value of bottles lies in determining that sales value. This may be done in one of two methods. The first involves setting potential sales values based on sales of straight shots only and adjusting these figures daily or periodically by the so-called mixed drink differential. These adjustments to the values of bottles issued and consumed are made after sales have taken place. The second method involves analyzing sales during a test period and determining weighted average values per bottle in advance, based on historical sales records. These methods must be discussed separately.

MIXED DRINK DIFFERENTIALS BASED ON DETAILED SALES RECORDS

When detailed sales records are available and drinks are prepared according to standard recipes, one can calculate the sales value of the ingredients in each type of drink sold.

For example, the preparation of a martini in a certain bar may require two ounces of gin and one-half ounce of dry vermouth. Assuming that gin as a straight drink is sold in two-ounce measures for $2.00, and the martini sells for $2.25, $2.00 represents the sales value of the gin, and the remaining $.25 is called the mixed drink differential. Once the sales value of the primary ingredients has been calculated in this way, it is possible to determine the mixed drink differential for each drink sold. If the sales value of the primary ingredient in a drink is $.90, and the actual selling price is $1.50, each sale of that particular drink must be accounted for by the use of a differential of an additional $.60. On the other hand, if the drink with two ounces of primary ingredient with sales value of $1.80 were sold for $1.75, a differential of minus $.05 would be required. These differentials must be calculated for each drink sold, and appropriately recorded for frequent reference.

Each day, after sales have been analyzed from guest checks, the number of drinks of each type sold must be multiplied by the differential for that drink, and the total bottle sales value for spirits consumed is increased by the total of all plus differentials and decreased by the total of all minus differentials.

Figure 16.6 illustrates the calculation of potential sales values based on this method. Sales values per bottle are recorded from a chart similar to that shown in figure 16.5; multiplying the number of empty bottles of each primary ingredient by the recorded potential sales value per bottle determines total sales value of each primary ingredient. These are totaled to find sales values of the empty bottles from the bar. Next, this total must be adjusted for mixed drink sales, as shown in the lower half of the form. Mixed drink differential for each type of drink is multiplied by the number sold to determine total differential per item. These, in turn, are added to determine net differential for the day, which figure is typically added to sales values of empty bottles to determine an adjusted sales value. In rare instances the differential figure may be a negative, in which case it would be subtracted from bottle sales values. The resulting potential sales value should be very close to the actual sales figure recorded in the bar register.

Determining differentials by analysis of drink sales must be done daily, and the sales values of bottles issued to replace empties at the bar must be adjusted

FIGURE 16.6
Daily Analysis of Potential Sales Values

Date 11/11/8–

Bottle Code No.	*Item*	*Bottles Consumed*	*Sales Value per Bottle*	*Total Sales Value*
301	Gin	3	$33.80	$101.40
107	Rye	2	33.80	67.60
352	Vodka	2	30.42	60.84
			Total	$229.84

Adjustments for Mixed Drink Differentials:

Mixed Drink	*Primary Ingredient*	*Ounces of Primary Ingredient*	*Straight Drink Price*	*Mixed Drink Price*	*Mixed Drink Differential*	*Number Sold*	*Total Differential*
Martini	gin	2	$2.00	$2.25	+ $.25	22	+ $ 5.50
Screwdriver	vodka	1	.90	1.50	+ .60	18	+ 10.80
Martini	vodka	2	1.80	1.75	− .05	8	− .40
						Total	+ $15.90

Sales Values adjusted by differentials:

Sales Values of empty bottles from bar	$229.84
Adjustments for mixed drink differentials	+ 15.90
	$245.74

accordingly to determine the sales value of the spirits consumed. Many have found that although this method results in the development of useful and often highly accurate control data, it is somewhat cumbersome for day-to-day use in most establishments. To many, some simplification of the procedures seems necessary and desirable. Therefore, a method for determining average potential sales values of bottles has been developed.

AVERAGE POTENTIAL SALES VALUES

This method eliminates the need for determining mixed drink differentials daily. It requires establishing a test period during which careful records are kept of the number of each type of drink sold. These records serve as the basis for determining the average potential sales value of each bottle. Such records of actual sales are analyzed as shown in figure 16.7.

FIGURE 16.7

Primary Ingredient Gin

Drinks Prepared	*# Sold*	*Oz./Drink*	*Total Oz.*	*Drink Price*	*Total Sales*
Martini	90	2	180	$2.25	$202.50
Straight shots	150	1	150	1.00	150.00
		Totals	330		$352.50

Assuming that the test period truly represents the sales mix, a determination of the average sales value for one ounce of the primary ingredient can be made by dividing 330 ounces sold into $352.50 total sales. In this case the average sales value for one ounce of gin is $1.07. Because this primary ingredient is purchased and used by the liter, the average sales value of each liter is 33.8 ounces, multiplied by the average sales value of each ounce, or $36.17. In some places, the person performing these calculatons reduces the bottle size by one ounce in order to account for unavoidable spillage and evaporation, thus assigning a more realistic average sales value to each bottle. Once these calculations have been completed for all primary ingredients consumed during the test period, a chart is prepared of the average sales value of each item used in the bar, as illustrated in figure 16.8. It would thus replace the chart of standard sales value of bottles sold only by the straight drink, illustrated previously in figure 16.5.

With such a chart available, the potential sales value of the bottles consumed at the bar can be determined daily by multiplying the number of empty bottles of each brand by the potential sales value of the bottle taken from the chart. The procedure for doing this is illustrated in figure 16.9.

This total potential sales figure would then be compared to actual sales records for the day, as previously described, to uncover any remarkable instances of deviations from standards based on experience during a test period.

FIGURE 16.8
Chart of Average Potential Sales Values of Bottles

Bottle Code #	*Item*	*Bottle Size*	*Sales Value*
301	Gin	1 liter	$36.17
107	Rye	1 liter	37.73
217	Scotch	750 ml	29.60
352	Vodka	1 liter	30.90
456	Brandy	750 ml	28.35

FIGURE 16.9

Bottle Code #	*Item*	*Bottles Consumed*	*Sales Value per Bottle*		*Total Sales Value*
301	Gin	3	$36.17		$108.51
107	Rye	2	37.73		75.46
352	Vodka	2	30.90		61.80
				Total	$245.77

Although using average potential sales values per bottle is done more commonly than the method involving daily determination of differentials, it is by no means universal. The average method still requires considerable calculation and could be used only in establishments where one or more persons were available to perform the necessary calculations regularly. In many places this would not be practical. Moreover, the average method is useful only to the extent to which the sales mix at the bar remains relatively stable. Major changes in the sales mix because of changing times and changing customer preferences render the calculated averages far less reliable and dictate the calculation of new average potentials based on a new test period.

STANDARD DEVIATION BASED ON TEST PERIOD

In the interest of further simplifying and eliminating frequent and time-consuming sales analysis of the types discussed, some managements have attempted to adapt to beverage control some of the techniques of statistics. The technique that follows has a growing number of strong defenders but has so far not gained wide acceptance in the industry.

This approach requires establishing a test period during which management takes all appropriate steps to ensure strict employee adherence to all standards and standard procedures. In addition, all phases of the bar operation are kept under observation during the period in a further effort to ensure compliance. At the conclusion of the test period, bottle consumption is carefully determined on the basis of inventories and issues, and is translated into potential sales values by drink, as previously discussed. In effect, a potential sales value is determined that indicates what the total sales value might have been if all spirits consumed had been sold by the straight drink. Following this step, actual sales recorded are compared with the calculated potential sales. Typically, the potential sales figure is greater than the actual sales, and the difference between the two is taken to reflect the sale of cocktails and other mixed drinks as well as the normal spillage to be expected at the bar. Because the operation has been under careful observation throughout the test period, this difference is taken as a standard difference, which can be used for purposes of comparison in the future. The difference is divided by the potential sales figure to determine, as a percentage, the extent of the deviation from the potential. If, for example, potential sales value were $1,000, and actual sales were $950, the difference would be $50 divided by $1,000, or 5%. Expressed in another way, it could be said that during the test period actual sales were 5% less than potential sales. By reducing the potential sales figure by 5% to account for normal spillage and the sales of cocktails and other mixed drinks, it is possible to develop an adjusted potential sales figure, which can be useful in measuring bar operations in the future as long as the sales mix remains fairly constant.

With this in mind, one can calculate adjusted potential sales figures in the future and use these figures to determine the extent to which bar operations are measuring up to expectations. As long as the sales mix does not change greatly, this can be done without resort to the elaborate analytical techniques described earlier. However, if major discrepancies appear between actual sales and adjusted potential, sales analysis may be both necessary and desirable in the process of determining causes.

One important advantage of this approach is the ease with which differentials may be recalculated from time to time. As customer tastes change, and the sales mix is affected, it is comparatively simple to establish a new test period and calculate a new differential for use in measuring operations. Also, as costs or selling prices change, the percentage deviation should remain fairly constant.

Regardless of the techniques involved in their calculation, potential sales figures can be very useful in judging the bar operation. When compared to actual sales figures, they provide a means of measuring the extent to which actual operations are meeting management's expectations. For example, if actual sales of $1,400 are compared to potential sales of $1,500, it is apparent that the actual falls short of the potential by $100, or 6.7%. It is incumbent upon management in a particular operation to determine the extent to which deviation is to be tolerated. Assuming that the potential figure is reasonably accurate, the difference means that the staff is not using the raw materials of production in the manner prescribed by management. This difference reflects operational problems of all sorts, including failure to mix according to standard recipes, excessive spillage, errors in filling orders, overpouring, general waste, and even outright theft. All such problems are of concern to management and should be eliminated. However, in actual and potential sales figures, the amount to be tolerated will differ considerably from operation to operation. In some places, a discrepancy of 1% between actual and potential sales may cause extreme concern and lead to careful and detailed analysis of all phases of the operation. In others, a 3% deviation may be considered within the limits of tolerance. Such determinations are obviously within the province of management. In general, management is usually less tolerant of differences arising from failure to record sales than it is of any other cause. Poor pouring and mixing techniques may often be ascribed to, and tolerated as, the pressures of business at the bar. But failure to record sales often reflects the intention to steal. For this reason, effective management will never accept it as a tolerable reason for the discrepancy between actual and potential sales.

SALES CONTROL

In beverage operations, the opportunities for sales control are often somewhat limited. To a great extent, effective control procedures depend on division of work among several employees, a condition not found in a number of bars. In many instances, one employee—the bartender—is responsible for taking orders from customers, filling those orders, recording the sales, and collecting cash or securing signatures on charge vouchers. This dependence on one individual tends to reduce the opportunities for control, and often sets the stage for the development of a number of operational problems.

One indication that problems exist can often be found in certain work habits of some bartenders, as listed below. Most of the following are considered unacceptable in most well-managed bars, because the owners or managers are well aware of the problems likely to develop.

1. **Working with cash drawer open.** This enables dishonest individuals to make sales transactions without recording the sales in the register. This is a serious problem if the bartender is responsible at the end of the shift for only those sales recorded on the register tape.
2. **Under-ringing sales,** either as No Sale or as some amount less than the actual sale. Following from item 1 above, this could enable someone to pocket the difference between cash in the register drawer and sales recorded on the tape.
3. **Overcharging customers, but ringing correct amounts in register.** This too provides a source of pocketable cash amounting to the difference between amounts collected and amounts rung in the register.
4. **Undercharging customers.** This may be done to accommodate a bartender's personal friends or in an attempt to increase tips from others. It may be done in several ways, including giving call brands but charging for pouring brands, or by overpouring.
5. **Overpouring.** Giving the customer more than he or she pays for, often through willful failure to measure, will typically result in unfavorable cost-to-sales ratios and in reducing profits from operation.

6 **Underpouring.** This technique sometimes is adopted by those who selectively overpour, in an effort to prevent detection of the overpouring. Too, the bartender who keeps mental records of the extent of his underpouring may later use the reserved amounts to prepare drinks. These drinks may then be given to friends or sold to customers with the sales revenue being pocketed by the bartender.

7 **Diluting bottle contents.** This practice involves pouring off some of a bottle's contents to reserve for later use, and replacing it with an equal amount of water. The latter use is typically a sale of a drink for which the money is pocketed.

8 **Bringing own bottles into the bar.** This practice permits a bartender to become a "silent partner" in the operation. He can prepare drinks using his own bottle(s) and pocket the sales revenue without his performance being detected through changes in cost and sales figures.

9 **Charging for drinks not served.** This technique enables a bartender to sell for his own benefit a drink previously paid for by a customer who did not receive it.

10 **Drinking on the job.** In addition to the unprofessional appearance and performance caused by this practice, it must be noted that a drinking employee is more likely to make mistakes in pouring, mixing, and properly recording sales than one who does not drink on the job.

In an effort to reduce these to a minimum, management frequently introduces certain procedures and sophisticated equipment into bar operations.

SALES CONTROL PROCEDURES AT SMALL BARS

Sales control techniques in smaller bars involve strict adherence to operating procedures established by management. One possible procedure is to require that the bartender collect cash for each drink as it is served. However, the bartender can still record in the cash register an inaccurate or insufficient amount, which can lead to theft from the customer, from the bar owner, or both. In the absence of written records on guest checks, an audit of the daily sales is impossible. In the absence of written sales records, no effective control can exist.

With the introduction of the guest check, further control is established. Each drink the bartender makes is recorded on the check, thus enabling one to determine the number of drinks sold each day, as well as the number of each type. It must be pointed out that there are some drawbacks to this requirement. During periods of peak activity, it will slow down the bartender and may lead to lost sales. In an effort to circumvent this problem, some managers eliminate the guest check and require the bartender to collect cash for each drink as it is served, and to record each sale immediately in a special register that dispenses a cash receipt. This receipt is turned over to the customer with his or her change. Any efforts by the bartender to record incorrect amounts may then be noted either by the customer or by a spotter hired by management to observe and report on the bartender's adherence to management's established procedures.

Ring-in, Ring-out Registers

Many bar operations find it undesirable to require patrons to pay for each drink when it is served, particularly where charge sales are involved. Cash registers are available that enable the bartender to record each sale as the drink is served and to accumulate these sales on guest checks for all customers. Such registers make it possible to require that a guest check be placed in front of each customer. When the customer is ready to leave, the check would be rung up in the register as either a cash sale or a charge sale, and at the end of the day's operation, the total of the drink sales recorded in the register, plus any taxes, would be equal to the total of cash and charge sales. Readings taken from such a register at the end of a day would resemble those in figure 16.10. The void key would be used in such cases as drinks rejected by customers, or unserved because of a customer walking out. In any case, each void entry would be investigated by the beverage controller. The accountant or bookkeeper would adjust sales figures to reflect voids before making entries in the accounting records for the day's sales.

FIGURE 16.10

Cash Register Reconciliation

Liquor	$375.00	
Beer	45.00	
Wine	30.00	
Tax	18.00	
Tip	5.00	
Total		$473.00
Cash	$420.00	
Charge	42.00	
Voids	11.00	
Total		$473.00

Automated Bars

Another approach increasingly used, particularly where close supervision by management is impractical, is the so-called automated bar. These systems, many of them quite expensive, are designed so that the alcoholic beverages are out of the bartender's reach, usually in a locked room accessible only to management. Liquor is dispensed from tubes at the bar where a sales check is inserted in a specially designed register and the appropriate key on the register is depressed.

As the liquor is dispensed, the machine automatically records the selling price on the check and maintains a record of the number of drinks sold.

SALES CONTROL PROCEDURES IN LARGER OPERATIONS

In many larger operations where table service only is offered, particularly in major metropolitan hotels, sales control procedures may be easier to institute because of the existence of additional employees, including the full-time cashier and the service bartender. Whenever such division of labor exists, and effective controls have been instituted, cheating becomes more difficult. While any effective control system must be designed to meet a particular establishment's needs, one possible control system is the following.

The waiter takes orders for drinks from customers at tables, records the items on a check, and then proceeds to the service bar and orders the drinks from the service bartender. When the drinks are made and placed on a tray, the waiter goes to a beverage checker, who records on the guest check through a register the price of each drink. After serving the drinks, the waiter leaves the check with the customer at the table. A separate cashier is stationed near the door of the lounge, and the customer presents the check to this cashier on leaving. The casher either collects cash or prepares an appropriate charge voucher and rings the values into a register. At the end of the day, the readings from both the checker's and the cashier's machines are compared and any discrepancies investigated. Any missing checks can be traced to the waiters responsible, provided that checks are distributed according to serial numbers, and waiters are required to sign for checks issued, as well as to return unused checks. Other systems for larger operations typically are variations of these procedures.

Although the above procedures do not eliminate the many possibilities for dishonest employees to cheat, they do make it more difficult to do so, and thus serve the function of keeping the basically honest employees honest.

EDP APPLICATIONS

At the end of each accounting period, management can obtain from the computer a print-out of the book inventory of beverages, as discussed in Chapter 14. This may be compared with an actual inventory, adjusted for inventory differential at the front bar, and a beverage cost for the month can be calculated. If management has also provided for the input of transfers, mixers, and any other adjustments, then a more accurate beverage cost percent may be calculated. Further, this may be done for the establishment as a whole, or for each of the three basic categories: spirits, wines, and beers. A more sophisticated program might be written to provide daily and cumulative cost, sales, and cost percent data as illustrated in figure 16.4.

The various methods of measuring the effectiveness of production controls may readily be adapted for computerized establishments. Some methods, including the ounce control method and potential sales value method, neither of which are currently in wide use, may become commonly accepted as computer-assisted control becomes more common in restaurants. Many larger establishments already find computers and other EDP devices almost indispensable in establishing appropriate levels of control, and a substantial number already use electonic sales terminals, often in systems including microprocessors, as well as some of the more complex automated bars. It should be noted, by the way, that automated bars have received much wider acceptance in service bars than in front bars.

CHAPTER ESSENTIALS

In this chapter, we explained procedures for calculating end-of-month beverage cost and cost percent, both wihout adjustments and, alternately, with adjustments for mixers, transfers, special promotions, and others. We described the manner in which beverage cost figures may be prepared by category, including adjustments.

We explained the techniques for calculating beverage cost and cost percent on both the daily and the cumulative basis. We illustrated and described several methods for measuring the effectiveness of production controls, including ounce control, potential sales value, adjusted on the basis of detailed sales records, average potential sales value, and standard deviation based on a test period. Some possible problems faced by those who attempt to institute beverage sales controls were identified, and we described some of the techniques and procedures that managers commonly use to attempt control. Finally, we described several possible ways to use computers for controlling beverage operations.

QUESTIONS AND PROBLEMS

1 Given the following information, compute the cost of liquor sold in each case.

Storeroom Inventory Information

	Opening Inventory	*Purchases During Month*	*Closing Inventory*
a	$5,000	$ 8,000	$7,000
b	8,325	10,666	9,327
c	4,872	7,454	3,856

Bar Information

	Opening Inventory	*Closing Inventory*
a	$1,000	$1,000
b	2,325	2,050
c	1,867	1,988

2 From the information obtained in Problem #1, compute the cost-to-sales ratio if:

- **a** sales are $20,000
- **b** sales are $41,412.50
- **c** sales are $29,817.85

3 Using the figures from problems 1 and 2 as well as the adjustments given below, calculate adjusted cost of beverages sold following the format of figure 16.1, then calculate cost-to-sales ratio based on adjusted cost.

a	Food to bar (Directs)	$200
	Storeroom issues	150
	Mixers	475
	Cooking liquor	110
	Officers' drinks	120
	Special promotions	160
b	Mixers	$925
	Food to bar (Directs)	500
	Cooking liquor	335
	Special promotions	320
c	Special promotions	$285
	Storeroom issues	235
	Officers' drinks	165
	Mixers	695
	Cooking liquor	185

4 Use the information given below to prepare a report in the form illustrated in figure 16.2, showing costs, sales, and adjustments by category.

Total Beverage Sales—$42,320, of which 10% represents beer sales, 18% represents wine sales, and the balance, spirits sales.

Total Adjustments to Sales—$424, of which 8% is allocated to beer sales, 12% to wine sales, and the balance to spirits sales.

Total Cost of Issues—$10,500, of which 55% is allocated to spirits, 35% to wines, and the balance to beer.

Mixers	$865
Food to bar (Directs)	305
Bar to kitchen	440
Special promotions	520

Mixers and food to bar (Directs) are all adjustments to spirits alone, but bar to kitchen and special promotions must be allocated as follows:

Bar to kitchen: 70% to wines, 10% to beer, and the balance to spirits.

Special promotions: 60% to wines and 40% to spirits.

5 Using figure 16.3 as a guide, prepare a cumulative and daily cost-to-sales ratio chart given the following information.

Date	*Cost*	*Sales*
10/1	$250	$ 910
10/2	225	850
10/3	270	920
10/4	290	1,070
10/5	240	900

6 Using the figures in problem #5, prepare a chart like that illustrated in figure 16.4 if the following additional information is given.

Date	*Food Transferred to Bar*	*Liquor Transferred to Kitchen*
10/1	$15	$25
10/2	10	30
10/3	12	45
10/4	20	10
10/5	8	18

7 Determine the potential sales value of the following issues assuming only one-ounce shots were poured, liter bottles were issued, and all straight shots sell for $1.30.

Liquor	*Number of Bottles Issued*
Gin	5
Scotch whiskey	3
Canadian whiskey	4
Blended whiskey	3
Vodka	4
Bourbon whiskey	2

8 During the period of time in problem 7, the following mixed drinks were served.

Gin martinis: 20
Vodka martinis: 10
Manhattan cocktails (prepared with blended whiskey): 25
Whiskey sours: 18
Rob roys: 16

The price for each mixed drink is $3.00. However, each martini and manhattan contains three ounces of liquor, and each whiskey sour and rob roy contains two ounces of liquor. Use this information and needed data from question 7 above to prepare a chart like the one in figure 16.6.

9 Prepare a chart similar to that illustrated in Figure 16.7. Using the average potential sales value method, determine the potential sales value of twelve liter bottles of gin given the following information from a test period.

Drinks Prepared	*Number Sold*	*Oz./Drink*	*Drink Price*
Martinis	20	2	$1.40
Straight shots	120	1½	1.10

10 **a** Compute the deviation from potential as suggested in the text given the following information.

Test Period
Actual Sales for period = $1,200
Potential Sales based on straight shots = $1,250

b What should actual sales be if the potential sales based on straight shots in 10(*a*) above were $900?

11 Compare and contrast the advantages and disadvantages of the average potential sales value method and the standard deviation method for measuring the effectiveness of production controls.

12 Why are sales controls needed in beverage operations? What measures may large bar operations take to institute sales control?

13 Why is it necessary to determine beverage inventory differential before calculating monthly cost of beverages sold?

14 Define each of the following terms:

Inventory differential	Mixed drink differential
Full bottle sales slip	Secondary ingredients
Ounce control	Automated bar
Potential sales value	Ring-in, ring-out register
Primary ingredient	

15 Two months ago Fred Sneed became the owner of a small bar in Springfield. When he assumed ownership, beverage cost percent was 24.5%. Since Fred assumed ownership, beverage cost percent has increased to 29.5%, although increases in purchase prices have been negligible, as have been changes in the sales mix. The bartender has been employed in the establishment for the last eight years. Fred has concluded that the increase is somehow related to the bartender's work and has decided to observe his performance closely. Rank in order the five most important work habits that he should observe.

16 Describe how computers may be used to aid the manager who attempts to establish effective control over bar operations.

part four

Labor Control

Anyone who visits restaurants has witnessed situations that suggest the need for labor control. Sometimes it seems nearly impossible to get any service; the few waiters in sight clearly have more customers to serve than they can possibly handle, and even when a customer has successfully managed to place an order, it seems an eternity before the food is served. At other times, there seem to be more waiters on duty than there are customers in the dining room, and one wonders how the management can afford to have all that help around when there appears to be no business to support it.

In the first example, one can readily imagine the number of customers who walk out in disgust without ordering at all, as well as those who silently resolve never to return after waiting perhaps fifteen minutes to order and perhaps another forty-five minutes to be served. The gross sales for the day are clearly less than they might have been if adequate service staff had been provided; gross sales for future days may be affected because of a number of customers who have taken their business elsewhere.

From the second example, where there is more staff on duty than is warranted by current business, the wages paid to unneeded staff escalate payroll costs. At the very least, this will lead to owner dissatisfaction on the one hand, and on the other, dissatisfaction among those employees whose incomes depend largely on the tips they receive from customers.

In either case, one certain effect will be the reduction of net profit from current operations, from lower sales in the first instance, and from increased costs in the second. Clearly there is a need to control labor in such a way as to maximize sales while at the same time minimizing costs.

Labor control represents an attempt to obtain maximum efficiency from all employees without compromising standards of operating performance. We shall see that it is most difficult to achieve because of the relative unpredictability of the number of customers in a restaurant at any given time, and to other factors. These will be discussed in the following chapters.

chapter 17

Labor Cost Determinants

Learning Objectives

After reading and studying this chapter, the student should be able to:

1 Explain why labor costs and labor cost percentages vary from one establishment to another.

2 Define labor cost control.

3 Explain why the minimizing of dollar wages is not necessarily synonymous with labor cost control.

4 Explain why each of the following is a determinant of labor cost:

- a weather
- b labor legislation
- c labor contracts
- d labor turnover
- e sales volume
- f location
- g equipment
- h layout
- i preparation
- j service
- k menu
- l hours of operation
- m management ability

In all food and beverage establishments, including hotels and restaurants, the cost of labor accounts for the expenditure of considerable sums of money. Taken as a percentage of sales, the cost of labor typically ranges from 15% to 45%. In some special instances, labor cost percentages have been noted as high as 60%, but only in establishments operated on a not-for-profit basis.

It will be worthwhile, at this point, to restate an important point made in the first section of this text, namely that the three basic categories of cost—fixed, directly variable, and semivariable—taken together must add up to a figure that is less than total sales if the operation is to show a profit. As percentages of sales, these costs must total less than 100%. Therefore, the proportion of total sales that must be allocated to cover each of the three types of costs will partly depend on the proportion required to cover the other two. If fixed and directly variable costs account for a high percentage of the income dollar, semivariable costs (primarily labor costs) must be kept down. By the same token, if fixed and directly variable costs are comparatively low, labor costs may be proportionally higher. Stated another way, assuming fixed costs as a constant 30% of sales in a particular restaurant that seeks to show a profit of 10% of sales, 60% of the sales dollars remain to cover directly variable and semivariable costs. If directly variable costs run regularly in the 20% range, then labor costs may be as high as 40% without disturbing the profit picture. On the other hand, if food and beverage costs are in the 45% range, then labor costs must be held to 15% of the sales dollar in order that the 10% desired profit be maintained. Figure 17.1 comparatively illustrates this point.

It should be obvious that an increase in the percentage of sales attributable to any cost category will have an effect on the remaining cost categories, on profit, or on both. If the semivariable cost of labor increases from 20% to 25%, then management must somehow reduce the percentages for the remaining costs or be prepared to accept a decreased percentage of profit. Similarly, if percentage for variable costs increases, then management must be prepared to exercise some restraining influence on fixed or semivariable cost percentages if percentage of profit is to be held constant.

The objective in this section of the text is to acquaint the student with accepted procedures and techniques for controlling the semivariable cost of labor in foodservice establishments. We will begin by defining labor cost control.

FIGURE 17.1

	Restaurant A		*Restaurant B*	
	Dollars	*Percentage*	*Dollars*	*Percentage*
Sales	$300,000	100%	$300,000	100%
Fixed Costs	90,000	30%	90,000	30%
Semivariable Costs	60,000	20%	105,000	35%
Directly Variable Costs	120,000	40%	75,000	25%
Profit	30,000	10%	30,000	10%

LABOR COST CONTROL DEFINED

Labor cost control is a process by means of which management attempts to direct, regulate, and restrain people's actions in order to obtain a desired level of employee performance at an appropriate level of cost. To the inexperienced, labor cost control is sometimes taken to suggest the mere reduction of payroll costs to their irreducible minimum, a state that might be achieved by employing a bare minimum number of people paid the minimum legal wage. But there is more to labor cost control than just minimizing dollar wages—a mistake sometimes made by owners and managers who take the short-term view of operations, thinking only of immediate profits, and not taking into account the long-term effects of their policies and actions.

Short-term policies geared strictly to minimizing immediate costs may have long-term effects that lead to future undesirable results, including decreased dollar sales, increased and excessive operating costs, and even business failure. For example, hiring a full staff of employees at minimum wage may minimize immediate labor costs but lead to poor quality products, high labor turnover, customer dissatisfaction, decreasing sales volume, and a host of other long-term problems. This is not intended to mean that management should pay beyond the wages necessary to attract and retain qualified personnel. But to overpay, in this sense, may make for a high-volume operation that cannot show a profit.

Appropriate performance levels will and should differ from establishment to establishment. For some—fast food restaurants serving frozen, portioned product that need only be heated and served by comparatively unskilled labor—desired levels of performance may be such that minimum-wage employees are appropriate; for others—fine restaurants attempting to offer the finest in products and services available in their areas—appropriate levels of performance may be such that wages considerably above those prevailing in the area may be required.

But level of performance is not simply a function of wage rates. Unskilled employees in fast food establishments cannot perform at appropriate levels unless they are provided with appropriate equipment, given suitable training, placed in a working environment conducive to working, supervised in a manner that will inspire them to work and remain on the staff. This is also true for those highly skilled employees in the finest restaurants. Wage levels suitable for particular establishments are not guarantors of appropriate performance. Many other factors are involved in ensuring suitable levels of performance.

In the authors' view, the discussion of techniques and procedures for controlling labor cost must be prefaced by an examination of some of the many determinants of labor cost. Some of them are essentially not controllable by a manager, but many—the majority certainly—can be controlled to a greater or lesser extent. Although the following discussion treats each briefly and singly, one must keep in mind that the determinants of labor cost are typically so interdependent and intertwined in practice that managers do not normally have the luxury of dealing with them one at a time in this fashion.

LABOR COST DETERMINANTS

Weather

Of all the determinants of labor cost, weather is surely the least controllable. Nonetheless, it is a factor in determining labor cost. Weather often affects sales volume, which in turn affects staffing levels in our industry. Bad weather, such as snowstorms or heavy rain, will deter potential customers from venturing out to restaurants. Interestingly, identical weather conditions typically increase sales volume in hotel restaurants for the very same reason—those who might have gone out to other restaurants will remain in the hotel to avoid the weather. To the extent one can obtain accurate weather forecasts, one can plan staffing levels suitable for anticipated demand. The problem, of course, is that weather forecasts are not always accurate, and unforeseen weather changes may render planned staffing levels inappropriate. When this occurs, it is often too late to modify the employee schedule. Sometimes employees can be sent home early if the restaurant is overstaffed, although this may have negative consequences, particularly on employee morale, turnover, and performance. On the other hand, weather changes that render planned staffing levels inadequate may cause other types of problems including poor service and even lost sales, as well as an overworked staff. These consequences can sometimes be avoided by maintaining a list of employees willing to come to work on call.

Labor Legislation

Labor legislation differs considerably from state to state, and thus the net effect of legislation on labor cost for any particular food operation must be discussed in terms of the legislation in effect in the particular state where the operation is located. However, it is possible to generalize a discussion of a significant area covered by legislation in all states: minimum wages and provision for overtime.

A minimum wage is the gross dollar wage before deductions that an employer must pay each employee in covered categories. It is usually expressed as a dollar figure per hour. Minimum wage legislation normally defines a maximum number of hours per day for work beyond which overtime must be paid, and a maximum number of consecutive working days per week beyond which overtime must also be paid. As a labor intensive industry, the foodservice industry has traditionally employed for jobs requiring little ability or training a large number of unskilled persons, many of whom have been paid the prevailing minimum wage. Thus, as state legislatures have steadily increased minimum wages, labor cost in the restaurant industry has been significantly affected.

In addition, some states meet the cost of unemployment insurance by levying a tax on an employer's gross dollar payroll. This usually takes the form of a percentage of that payroll, and the percentage is governed by an experience factor such that the higher the employee turnover rate, the higher the percentage that must be paid. Because the foodservice traditionally experiences a higher rate of employee turnover than almost any other industry, this extra expense, categorized as wage expense, has been of considerable importance in calculating overall labor cost. In an effort to reduce the percentage levied against gross payroll, some restaurant employers have made special efforts to reduce the rate of employee turnover and thus reduce at least one aspect of labor cost.

Labor Contracts

The presence or absence of labor contracts will always be an important factor affecting labor cost. Where employees are organized and labor contracts exist, wages for each category of employee tend to be higher than they might have been if the organizations and contracts did not exist. For purposes of this discussion, such fringe benefits as vacation pay, sick pay, employees meals, and health insurance are included in the term *wages*. These fringe benefits are most likely to be found where union organizations and contracts exist.

Although the effects of wages and fringe benefits on labor cost are apparent, in situations where labor contracts exist there are often other factors that also have a significant effect. Of primary concern are provisions in labor contracts that limit management's freedom to change work rules. Such contracts typically restrict management's ability to alter the duties of an employee in a particular job category. An effect of this may be to force the employer to hire someone for a job when existing employees have the time and ability to do it. This would have the obvious effect of increasing the overall labor cost in general, and the labor cost per unit in particular. In one hotel in a certain large city, the work rules mandate that every station in the main kitchen be manned whenever the kitchen is open, regardless of business volume and menu changes. Such a restrictive rule has great impact on the overall labor cost.

Labor Turnover

Labor turnover, a ratio relating the number of departing employees to the total number of employees on the staff and usually expressed as a percentage, is unfortunately high in the foodservice. It has been commonly measured at 100% per year across the industry with some specific establishments showing rates as high as 300%. This does not compare favorably with typical turnover rates in American industry in general, which tend to range between 19% and 20%.

The effect of high labor turnover on labor cost is often enormous, for it places managers in positions of facing two interdependent problems:

1 vacant positions must be filled, and then

2 newly hired employees need training.

When jobs in an organization become vacant and management deems it desirable to fill those jobs, it is typically the responsibility of management itself to see to the recruiting, interviewing, selecting, and hiring of the replacement personnel.

Larger organizations may employ a personnel department or a single personnel officer who is assigned to much of this work; but the smaller, perhaps more typical restaurant has no personnel department, and the work falls to the restaurant manager and possibly to various department heads. It can be time-consuming, depending in part on the nature and extent of the skills sought in a new employee, and to the degree that a manager or department head is engaged in recruiting and hiring, that manager must defer some other tasks. If turnover is so great that it becomes necessary to hire someone full-time to fill vacancies, the additional cost is obvious. If such work consumes a great portion of the manager's time, it may become necessary to hire some assistance for the manager, also at some considerable cost.

The need for the same degree of training exists in all foodservice establishments. Managers, after all, are not typically able to hire employees with a thorough knowledge of the job for which they are hired without some amount of explanation, even if only cursory. On the most elementary level, training may entail merely showing a new dishwasher the location of the machine and explaining the operation of the controls, or it may involve a meeting with a new chef who needs to be familiarized with the nature of the menu or the restaurant's clientele. On another level, training may include daily meetings with sales personnel to make sure that each understands the menu fully and is aware of the items management is most anxious to sell. Then again, training may mean taking completely inexperienced persons and teaching them everything they need to know to perform some particular job, either completely on premises, or partly with the aid of some outside agencies, including public, private, and proprietary schools. For a waiter, this complete training might include instruction in procedures for waiting on customers; methods of serving and removing dishes, flatware, and glassware from tables; standard setups for tables; napkin folding techniques; methods for presenting and pouring wines; and so on.

Training should be conducted on an ongoing basis and need not be restricted to the new employee. Management should maintain certain standards for the performance of all jobs in the establishment, and to the extent that employees are not performing up to these levels, management may effectively use many opportunities for training to improve overall performance. In addition, if management plans change in some aspect of operations, such as introducing a new item on the menu that requires special presentation to the customer, the best interests of the establishment are well served by training the staff to deal wih the change.

Training, even in its simplest form, is not accomplished without cost, however. Both trainer and trainee are being paid while the training process is being carried out, and frequently neither is as productive as a completely trained individual would be. Viewed as an investment in time or in money, or in both of these, training will over the long term provide a more efficient, more effective, and more knowledgeable staff. As a result, customers will probably be better satisfied, and revenue is likely to be higher.

Some establishments do little training, sometimes because managers do not realize its importance, and sometimes because managers are unwilling to incur costs that do not provide immediate return in higher revenue. In such places, it may be apparent to customers that employees are not performing their jobs in the most satisfactory manner. Service may be slow, personnel may be impolite, the quality of food and beverage items may be below customers' expectations, and the overall impression may be entirely unsatisfactory. For these reasons revenue is likely to decrease or at least remain lower than it might be under better conditions.

Establishments that neglect training frequently develop other problems. Managers who are not particularly understanding or articulate tend to become angry with employees who are not performing satisfactorily, often without realizing that the poor performance is largely the result of never having explained the employee's job to him or her in sufficient detail. Employees quit or are fired, and are replaced by others with whom the entire cycle is repeated. Not only do such establishments suffer for failing adequately to satisfy customers, but they must bear the often hidden costs of high employee turnover rates, including advertising costs in classified sections of newspapers, sometimes employment agency fees, higher contribution rates for state unemployment insurance costs based on experience factors, and possibly revenue lost while some position was vacant.

From a labor control viewpoint, it is apparent that employees will be operating at greater efficiency and with greater effectiveness if they are suitably trained for their work. In the long run, this will lead to lower labor costs and potentially higher gross receipts for the foodservice establishment. The extent of training carried on in any particular establishment is an important determinant in the overall cost of labor.

Sales Volume

For a restaurant of any given size, up to its maximum capacity, increases in sales volume will result in increased productivity per employee up to his or her maximum capacity to perform. For example, in a certain restaurant selling only hamburgers and employing only one cook, 100 hamburgers are typically prepared and sold during one busy hour of the lunch period. During the slack period of the afternoon following the lunch hour, the same cook prepares only 10 hamburgers during a one-hour period. If the cook is being paid $5 per hour, the labor cost per unit produced during the peak period is equal to his hourly wage of $5 divided by the 100 hamburgers produced during that period, or $.05 per unit. On the other hand, the labor cost per unit for hamburgers prepared during the slow period is equal to his $5 wage divided by the 10 hamburgers sold, or $.50.

It is clear from the foregoing that the cook in question was working at less than his proven capacity during the slack hour, obviously because of the absence of customers. We can see that as the sales volume increased, the cook's labor was used more efficiently. At the same time, as his efficiency increased, the cost of labor per unit produced decreased. Therefore, it is apparent that an increase in sales volume in the present case has resulted in greater employee efficiency at lower labor cost per unit.

In the previous example, one employee is the minimum number that can be hired for that particular job. However, in larger establishments that require greater numbers of employees as the minimum, it is possible to better schedule employees for greater efficiency. Thus, each of them could be kept busier more of the time. It would be desirable to schedule fewer employees during slack periods and more during busy periods, thus increasing individual efficiency.

In addition, large restaurants are often able to take advantage of the economies of large-scale production. In simplest terms, this also might be identified as the division of labor, assigning individuals to the tasks that they are best qualified to complete, and paying each of them a wage commensurate with his or her level of ability and training. For example, the single cook cited above might be required as part of his job to wash dishes, keep the counter clear, or act as cashier, all for the single wage of $5 per hour. In effect, the jobs of cook, dishwasher, counterman, and cashier are all being paid $5 per hour. Furthermore, the particular individual in the job may not be very good at the side jobs assigned, and his or her performance at those tasks may be less efficient than that of someone hired perhaps at a lower hourly wage, but specifically trained for the job. The small restaurant can usually do nothing about this, but the large restaurant frequently can hire dishwashers and countermen at considerably lower wages.

In larger establishments where there is enough work to keep a specialist in any category busy most of the time, it is usually cheaper to hire the specialist at the prevailing wage for his or her job category, thus reducing the labor cost per unit produced. As an illustration, if the hamburger restaurant cited above were large enough, it could hire cooks at $5 per hour, dishwashers at $3.00 per hour, and a counterman at $3.50 per hour, thus resulting in a reduction of the overall labor cost per unit produced. As an additional benefit, each of the specialists should be more efficient at his job and capable of performing higher quality work. In the long run, this should reduce the labor cost per unit still further.

Location

It is well known that the cost of labor varies from one part of the country to another. In many rural areas, particularly those where jobs are scarce and competition for those few jobs is severe, employers can often pay comparatively low hourly rates, and so keep labor costs down. This same condition often can be noted outside rural areas, particularly in depressed areas and in areas where living costs tend to be low. However, while such conditions as these may result in lower labor costs in dollars, labor costs as percentages of sales may not be lower at all. The reason for this may be the lower menu prices in effect in such areas.

On the other hand, the opposite effect often can be noted in metropolitan areas where living costs are greater and wage scales higher. Under such conditions, labor costs in dollars may be quite high by some standards, but as percentages of sales, may actually run parallel to those found in rural and depressed areas. To illustrate, one might consider a certain item produced in a kitchen in one area at a labor cost of $1.50 and sold at a menu price of $5, contrasted with that same item produced in another area at a labor cost of $3 and sold for $10. In the second instance, the labor cost in dollars is twice what it is in the first, but in both cases the relationship between labor cost and selling price is identical.

Equipment

Assuming that certain tasks such as peeling potatoes, washing dishes, and slicing meats must be accomplished in a particular kitchen, lower labor costs will result from accomplishing those tasks with modern equipment rather than by traditional hand methods. For example, a machine can peel 100 pounds of potatoes in less than twenty minutes, while the same job done by hand might require many hours. Slicing a round of beef with modern slicing equipment may take less than five minutes, while doing the same job manually could require more than fifteen minutes. Chopping cabbage for cole slaw by hand might require four to six times the amount of time needed to do the job with up-to-date machinery. In addition, old equipment in poor condition will often require more time to accomplish a given job than will equipment that is newer, or in better condition, or both. In general, from the point of view of labor cost, doing work by machine is cheaper than doing it by hand, and doing a job with good equipment is cheaper than doing it with poor equipment. The amount of equipment in use, as well as its variety and condition, will have considerable effect on labor cost.

Layout

Labor cost is directly affected by the manner in which space is used. Within the space, equipment must be arranged to facilitate, rather than impede, employees as they go about their various tasks. In new establishments, equipment and facilities can be suitably arranged during construction; in converted properties, arrangement is often less than satisfactory because of the existence of walls that cannot be moved, plumbing that is not readily moved, and room sizes that are less than ideal for a given purpose. If equipment is poorly arranged, employees may have to walk excessive distances. In extreme cases, it may even be necessary to hire employees who might not have been required had the equipment and facilities been better arranged. For example, if the individual working at the broiler does not have ready access to a reach-in refrigerator, he may have to walk a considerable distance each time a broiler order is placed. If the broiler were extremely busy, it might conceivably be necessary to assign one person to bring items from a refrigerator when they are required at the broiler station. In some hotels, the kitchen is so far removed from the dining room that a larger than necessary staff of waiters and waitresses is required.

In all of the above instances, equipment and facilities have been so arranged that labor costs must be higher than they might have been. It is not a question of the workers being inefficient; the poor layout of the restaurant virtually forces them to be so.

Preparation

Theoretically one could rate all foodservice operations on a scale of zero to 100 to reflect the amount of preparation required on the premises. At the zero end of the scale would be any establishment that purchased all items precooked, fully prepared and preportioned, thus requiring minimal preparation beyond reheating prior to sale. At the opposite end would appear those establishments that prepared everything on the premises, including such basic ingredients as mayonnaise and catsup. In places falling near the zero end of the scale, labor costs could clearly be kept minimal. Foods could be served in the disposable packages in which they were purchased, thus eliminating even the need for dishwashing. Clearly, this type of establishment would require largely unskilled personnel in the kitchen. "Cooking" would merely be a matter of reheating. The services of a traditional chef would not be required. Conversely, restaurants at the other end of the scale would require kitchen personnel with special talents for comparatively complex and conceivably elaborate preparations, probably under the expert guidance of a highly trained and comparatively highly paid executive chef. In addition, such an establishment would require additional personnel to take charge of the many responsibilities inolved in the purchasing, receiving, storing, and issuing of the comparatively expensive and highly perishable basic ingredients required for many of the preparations.

While few, if any, restaurants would appear at either absolute end of such a scale, a reasonable number would be near either end. Typical fast food restaurants would tend to appear at the lower end, and traditional restaurants offering haute cuisine would appear at the higher end. Clearly those of the fast food variety would have a considerably lower labor cost than those offering continental dishes to customers with gourmet tastes.

Service

Foodservice establishments could also be charted on a scale of zero to 100, based on the amount of service offered to the customer. At the lower end of the scale might appear vending machine operations offering no service. At the other end are continental establishments that offer French service involving the completion of the cooking of food in the dining room on a gueridon. In the middle range, one could find typical American restaurants where food is plated in the kitchen and served by a waiter or waitress, whose station would include a number of tables.

For those establishments appearing at the lower end of the scale, labor costs for service tend to be minimal. On the other hand, establishments appearing near the opposite end of the scale require not only considerable numbers of service personnel, but also personnel who may be required to demonstrate considerable skill in certain preparations and all service. Clearly, labor costs will tend to be lower in restaurants in the former category and higher in those in the latter category.

Menu

From the point of view of labor cost, it is less costly to prepare 300 portions of some one item than it is to prepare 30 portions each of some 10 different items, especially if those 10 items require several types of preparation, such as braising, broiling, baking, roasting, and boiling. This is because one employee could conceivably prepare all 300 portions of the single item, but the preparation of 10 different items by several different methods would probably require employees in several different job categories, particularly if all portions were needed at one time, as in the case of a banquet. This is one of the primary reasons that many kinds of establishments restrict their menu to a very few items. In the case of certain fast food operations, the menu may even be restricted to one basic entree: the hamburger. Clearly, the limiting of numbers and varieties of menu items is one factor of considerable importance in the control of labor cost.

Hours of Operation

Obviously, the number of hours a restaurant operates will have significant impact on labor cost. A restaurant open only for dinner will have labor costs less than that same operation open for three meals each day. However, decisions concerning numbers of hours of operation involve more considerations than the mere cost of labor.

Every operation has overhead costs that exist regardless of whether the restaurant is open or closed. These would typically include rent or mortgage payments, salaries not based on hours of work (managers' salaries as distinguished from those of service personnel paid hourly wages), insurance premiums, depreciation, property taxes, and so on. These fixed costs are independent of business volume. As a general rule, as long as additional revenue gained by staying open is greater than the additional cost incurred during that period of time, remaining open would be advisable from a financial viewpoint.

For example, assume a restaurateur is trying to determine whether to extend the dinner hours from 9:00 P.M. to 10:00 P.M. He calculates that additional wages for that hour will be $148; heat and light are estimated at $11. These additional costs can be considered fixed once the decision to remain open for the extra hour is made. Variable costs—including food, beverages, linen, and miscellaneous—are estimated at 38% of each dollar of sale. Thus, from the formulas in Chapter 3:

$$\text{Breakeven for the additional hour} = \frac{\text{FC}}{\text{CR (which is } 1 - \text{VR)}}$$

$$\text{BE} = \frac{\$159}{.62}$$

$$\text{BE} = \$256.45$$

If management can project sales volume in excess of $256.45, it would be financially advantageous to remain open. Thus, assume a sales volume of $350 for the additional hour. Costs for that period would include the $159 previously cited plus 38% of $350, or $133. Total costs for the additional hour at the projected sales level would be $292, leaving a net revenue of $58 ($350 − $292) that would be available to cover overhead costs of the restaurant, or additional profit. Management must decide if the $58 additional profit is worth the time and effort required. Assessment of employee morale and long-term effects on overall sales volume must also be considered.

Management Ability

The cost of labor is greatly determined by management's ability to plan, organize, control, direct, and lead the organization in such a way that the desired level of employee performance is obtained at an appropriate level of cost. This requires, among other things, that the manager understand what work is to be done, the number and types of employees required to do it, what constitutes suitable employee performance, how employees should be scheduled to optimize performance level, what training, facilities, equipment, and other materials will be required, and how and when these are to be obtained and in what quantities. The manager's ability to motivate, direct, and effectively lead will determine the quality of work and level of performance.

This might be summed by saying that good management will have positive effects on labor costs while poor management will have negative effects. A good manager, merely by being a good manager, will create a work environment conducive to optimal performance at minimal cost. The student who has studied management methods and leadership styles will recognize that appropriate discussion is really quite beyond the scope of a control text and would require a separate course.

In the light of the foregoing, it is apparent that each of these many and varied factors must be taken into account in any intelligent analysis of labor cost. Moreover, because of the many differences that exist among establishments within this variegated industry—which includes operations ranging from hotdog stands to the finest hotels, and from fast-food chains to award-winning gourmet-style restaurants—it is impossible to arrive at industry-wide standards or averages for a particular manager to use as guides for his or her own establishment.

Each owner or manager must base the desired and optimal labor cost and labor cost percentage for his particular operation on a host of factors and must recognize that labor cost in a particular operation will be affected to a greater or lesser extent by the various determinants discussed above (weather, labor legislation, labor contracts, labor turnover, training, sales volume, location, equipment, layout, preparation, service, menu, hours of operation, as well as his or her own ability). Clearly, the effect of each of these factors will vary considerably from restaurant to restaurant. Indeed, two identical restaurants located in different areas do not, and probably should not, have the same labor costs or the same labor cost percentages. In fact, two such restaurants will normally be found to have significantly different cost structures for food, beverages, and overhead, as well as for labor.

In the final analysis, every restaurant owner or manager must maintain combined food, beverage, and labor costs to the point where the operation earns a satisfactory profit. That combined figure typically should not exceed 60% to 70% of sales, depending on overhead, if overhead is to be met and profits are to result.

Having discussed the determinants of labor cost, it will now be appropriate to examine those specific techniques and procedures that managers employ in attempting to control labor costs. These will be the subjects of the next two chapters.

CHAPTER ESSENTIALS

In this chapter, we explained why labor costs and labor cost percentages vary from one establishment to another, by illustrating the comparative cost structures of two common types of restaurants. We defined labor cost control and explained why minimal labor costs are not necessarily optimal labor costs. Finally, we listed and explained thirteen major determinants of labor cost, including weather, labor legislation, labor contracts, labor turnover, sales volume, location, equipment, layout, preparation, service, menu, hours of operation, and management ability.

QUESTIONS AND PROBLEMS

1 A restaurant's income statement shows the following cost and sales structure:

Sales	$450,000
Costs:Fixed	$135,000
Directly Variable	120,000

What must the semivariable cost figure be if the restaurant is to show a profit of $30,000?

2 A restaurant's cost structure, expressed as a percentage of sales, is as follows:

Fixed costs	30.0%
Directly variable costs	25.0%

As a percentage of sales, what must the semivariable costs be if the restaurant is to show a 10.0% profit?

3 Rank the type of restaurants listed below in order by percentage of labor cost, from low to high. In each case, discuss the effect of preparation on labor cost.

a an industrial cafeteria using primarily convenience foods
b a seafood restaurant advertising "strictly fresh fish"
c a diner specializing in hot meals served to truck drivers
d an elaborate French restaurant

4 A restaurant that employs one cook sells only hamburgers. During the peak lunch hour, he is able to produce 120 hamburgers per hour. During the slack afternoon period, he produces only 30 hamburgers per hour. If each hamburger sells for $.60 and the cook is paid $5.00 per hour, calculate the labor cost per dollar per hamburger for one hour during each period.

5 In a paragraph of at least fifty words, discuss the possible effect on labor cost of a newly negotiated labor contract.

6 Select and describe a reasonably well-known restaurant in your area. Then, in an appropriate number of paragraphs, discuss the effect of at least five of the factors analyzed in this chapter on that particular restaurant's labor cost.

7 Many restaurants that do little training experience high labor turnover. What are some of the hidden costs of high labor turnover?

8 Research the various types of dining room service (American, French, Russian, English, and cafeteria); then rank them according to the labor costs they create. Justify the order in which you have ranked them.

9 Under what circumstances might it be cheaper to use employees to perform certain kitchen work typically performed by machine?

10 What labor legislation exists in your area, and what effect does it have on labor cost? Include in your answer federal minimum wage and overtime provisions.

11 The Aliby Restaurant is normally open for business until 8:00 P.M. Recently business has been getting better during the time period just before closing, and the manager is attempting to determine the viability of remaining open until 9:00 P.M. He estimates his additional costs for the extra hour as follows:

Labor = $75
Heat, light, and gas = $12
Variable cost of food, beverage, etc. = 40% of sales

a What additional sales are necessary for the manager to break even exactly on the extra hour of opening?

b If the manager were able to obtain $280 in sales volume for the extra hour, what income could be applied to normal overhead expenses?

chapter 18

Controlling Labor Costs I

Learning Objectives

After reading and studying this chapter, the student should be able to:

1 Identify the purposes of labor control.
2 Distinguish between variable cost personnel and fixed cost personnel.
3 Explain the nature of demand for restaurant products, and differentiate it from the demand for other manufactured products.
4 List the preliminary steps necessary for work organization.
5 Prepare an organization chart.
6 Write a job description.
7 Develop an analysis of business volume.
8 Distinguish between the scheduling of variable cost personnel and that of fixed cost personnel.
9 Prepare a table of manpower requirements and an hourly schedule for variable cost personnel from an analysis of business volume.
10 Identify the means by which the cost of fixed cost employees may be adjusted on a temporary or on a permanent basis.
11 Explain how the computer can aid management in analyzing business volume and in determining manpower requirements.

Our discussion of the factors affecting labor cost in the previous chapter has shown that job categories, and numbers of personnel involved in each, vary greatly from restaurant to restaurant. As the extent of preparation increases, the numbers of job categories and the degrees of specialization in each are likely to increase as well. In addition, as the service becomes more complicated, going from self-service to elaborate French service, the number of personnel required to perform the service and the degree of expertise necessary to the performance will both increase. Regardless of the extent of preparation and the type and extent of service, however, managers should work to ensure that the labor in their establishments are performing as effectively as possible.

THE PURPOSES OF LABOR CONTROL

One purpose of labor control is to maximize the efficiency of the labor force in a manner consistent with the established standards of quality and service. Ideally, each employee's services will be fully utilized as effectively as possible. There should be a sufficient number of dishwashers working to ensure that dishes will be washed as efficiently as possible; but there should be no time when dishwashers stand around with nothing to do. Similarly, a sufficient number of waiters and waitresses on the premises should ensure that all customers are served as quickly as possible while standards of service are maintained; but at no time should there be more than a sufficient number on hand to serve the customers then in the restaurant.

NATURE OF DEMAND FOR RESTAURANT PRODUCTS

In all efforts to maximize efficiency and control labor cost, management must recognize that a basic difference between the food business and other manufacturing industries makes it more difficult to control labor costs.

The manufacturer and the restaurant operator can anticipate demand for their products at future times. The restaurant operator knows with some degree of certainty that the busy season will bring significantly more business than slow periods. Similarly, the manufacturer will have busy and slow times. However, the manufacturer can utilize labor now in preparing products for sale at a later time. The restaurant operator *cannot* utilize labor now for a future demand, except to a very limited degree. For example, salad dressings can be prepared in quantity so that sufficient amounts are on hand to last a week or so, and possibly certain meat items can be precut and stored for future use, depending on standards. However, because of the perishability of the products, there is virtually no way they can be prepared for demand six months hence. The furniture manufacturer, on the other hand, can gear the production of his present labor to demand six months in the future.

Thus, production in a restaurant must be geared for immediate sale of the items produced, and labor must be hired and available to meet that demand. Further, the demand for the items produced will fluctuate not only daily, but also hourly, so that to achieve ultimate efficiency in the utilization of labor, it is necessary to predict and prepare for the hourly demand for products and schedule accordingly—a difficult task at best.

LABOR CLASSIFICATIONS FOR CONTROL PURPOSES

It is important for any manager attempting to maximize efficiency and to control the labor cost percentage, to recognize the existence of two classifications of employees:

1 Variable cost personnel
2 Fixed cost personnel

Taken as a whole, labor cost becomes a semivariable cost, increasing with increasing volume of business and decreasing with decreasing volume of business, but not in direct proportion to changes in volume.

Because the treatment of each category of employees will be significantly different in the establishment of a labor control system, they will be discussed separately.

Variable Cost Personnel

Variable cost personnel are those whose numbers are related to the volume of business. As business volume increases, hiring more personnel in this category becomes necessary; consequently, the labor cost in dollars increases for this classification of employee. The reverse also should be true: as business volume decreases, it is possible to decrease the number of employees in this category and thus to decrease the dollar cost of labor.

Typical examples of these kinds of employees are waiters, waitresses, and busboys. When business volume reaches a peak, as it typically does during normal meal hours, comparatively large numbers of these personnel must be available to work. During nonpeak times, such as the middle of the afternoon, reduced business volume can be handled with comparatively fewer employees in these categories. Clearly, for employees in these categories the dollar cost of labor is higher during peak hours than it is during nonpeak hours.

Other examples of employees who typically fall into the variable cost category are dishwashers and certain food preparation personnel. As business volume increases, so will the work for these employees; but their hours of work will not necessarily coincide with the hours of peak sales. Preparation personnel, for example, will be needed in comparatively large numbers prior to the hours of anticipated peak sales so that food will be ready when needed.

A time lapse normally exists between the onset of peak sales in the dining room and the beginning of peak dishwashing needs in the kitchen. In addition, the period of peak dishwashing usually continues for some period of time after peak food sales have ended. Thus, an increase or decrease in business volume will dictate the need for an increase or decrease in the number of variable cost personnel; but their hours of work need not necessarily coincide with the hours of peak business volume.

It is important to recognize that the points made in the foregoing discussion also apply to periodic or seasonal changes in business volume. During slower periods, fewer variable cost personnel are needed to handle reduced business volume, and as that volume increases during busier periods, more of these employees must be hired. One typical example would be a restaurant at a well-known eastern seashore resort, which does comparatively little business during the winter months but operates at near capacity during the summer. The number of variable cost personnel is kept at a minimum during the slow season and greatly expanded to deal with the increased volume during the busy summer season.

Fixed Cost Personnel

Fixed cost personnel are those whose numbers normally have little relation to the volume of business. As business volume increases and decreases, the number of these employees remains relatively constant. Because of this, the cost of their services in dollars also remains relatively constant. Typical examples would include the manager, the bookkeeper, the chef, and the steward, as well as maintenance personnel and cashiers. Regardless of the increases and decreases in business volume, there will be only one manager. The same is true for the chef. As business volume changes, it will obviously be necessary to vary the number of personnel working under the cook's jurisdiction, but the chef, whose job as a result will vary in difficulty, will be the single constant factor in the kitchen. The same will usually be true of the bookkeeper. During a slow period, the sales figure entered in the accounting records of the business may be only $1,000 for a given day, but it takes neither more nor less time to make that entry than it does to enter a sales figure of $10,000 for a single day during a busy period. Depending on the particular duties assigned to the bookeeper, preparation for making the bookkeeping entry may take longer in the case of $10,000 in sales, but it is highly unlikely that any additional bookkeeping help would be hired during the busy period.

WORK ORGANIZATION

For the manager to have labor efficiency, the work of his or her employees must be organized. To do that properly, the following preliminary steps are advisable:

1 establish an operational plan
2 prepare job descriptions for all positions in the organizational plan
3 prepare an analysis of business volume

ESTABLISHMENT OF AN OPERATIONAL PLAN

Establishing an operational plan requires the owner or manager first to develop a clear idea of the nature of his or her operation, including the type of clientele, as well as the nature of the products offered, and the extent and type of service rendered the clientele. In addition, he or she must anticipate with some accuracy the number of meals to be prepared and served.

Once the owner or manager has formulated an idea of the nature and scope of the operation, he or she can begin to think in terms of specific jobs that must be performed for the restaurant operation to take shape.

As an illustration, consider the case of a comparatively small establishment serving fast foods from a limited menu and offering counter service rather than table service to a working clientele. The manager could order the comparatively small selection of frozen, portioned foods, and oversee the simple cooking of these items by a small number of cooks of limited ability, who would also serve as counter help. If the items were all served in disposable containers, the services of any dishwasher might not be needed. And if the manager were also able to handle the cash register, a cashier would not be necessary. The restaurant could exist with only two categories of employees—manager and cook/counter help—and with that idea clearly in mind, the manager could begin to think of hiring a staff.

In contrast to the small, fast-food establishment, a larger restaurant offering continental cuisine prepared from basic raw materials by highly skilled kitchen personnel, and highly professional French service, would require a larger staff, consisting of a number of specialists. The kitchen staff might consist of skilled professionals, carefully trained in the arts of butchering meats, preparing soups and sauces, decorating cold platters, and doing other jobs appropriate to such a restaurant. Typically, the manager could not handle any of the other tasks in addition to his own job and hence would require the services of receiving clerks, stewards, storeroom clerks, hosts, cashiers, and a bookkeeper.

In addition to establishing the categories of employees needed to operate an establishment as he or she sees it, any manager must also think in terms of the relationships that should exist between and among employees in various job classifications. Briefly stated, the manager must decide which employees will be responsible for seeing to it that other employees do certain work. The manager must decide, for example, that the chef will have complete jurisdiction over the production of food items, and that to carry out this responsibility, the chef must be placed in charge of the work of the various categories of specialists who will serve under his or her direction and guidance, such as the sous chef, the saucier, the legumier, and the garde manger, among others. In reality, the chef will supervise these other individuals, and it is important that they know this and fully understand all the implications of it. In turn, the chef must know that he or she is responsible to the manager and under the manager's direction. The chef must also realize that a certain special working relationship must exist between him or her and the steward; that while they are equals in the organizational structure, they must be fully cooperating equals if the best interests of the restaurant and the customers are to be served.

So that all of these distinctions and relationships may be seen in their proper perspectives, the owner or manager of a restaurant is usually advised to set them down on paper in the form of a functional organization chart, such as that illustrated in figure 18.1. A functional organization chart shows the positions according to function within the operation. The lines drawn from one position to another signify the lines of authority and cooperation. An unbroken line from one position to another indicates that the person below reports to and takes direction from the person immediately above him on the chart. The dotted lines show communication and cooperation between the two positions, but one does not have authority over or the responsibility for the actions of the other. Thus, on the chart in figure 18.1, the unbroken connecting line shows that the position of executive chef is next above that of sous chef. This, of course, means that the sous chef reports to the executive chef and takes direction from him. On the other hand, the lateral dotted line between the executive chef and the chief steward shows that the two are expected to cooperate in every possible way in accomplishing their respective tasks, but that neither takes direction from the other.

Once the functional organization chart is complete and accurately reflects the operational plan of the owner or manager, particularly with respect to indicating the job titles necessary for successful operation of the plan, it is then desirable to prepare an appropriate job description for each job title on the chart.

JOB DESCRIPTIONS

A primary purpose in creating a job description for each position on the organizational chart is to list in detail the duties each employee with any given title will be expected to perform. The writing of job descriptions forces management to determine in advance which jobs are to be done by which employees. This predetermination of responsibilities ensures that each task is assigned to some position. In addition, by reviewing the completed job descriptions, management has the opportunity to see that an appropriate collection of tasks has been grouped under one job title in such a way that no employee will be asked to perform a series of unrelated tasks requiring very different skills.

In some instances, job descriptions go one step further by specifying particular methods for performing particular tasks. The job description illustrated in figure 18.2, for example, includes instructions on how certain jobs are to be done. In

FIGURE 18.1
Table of Organization

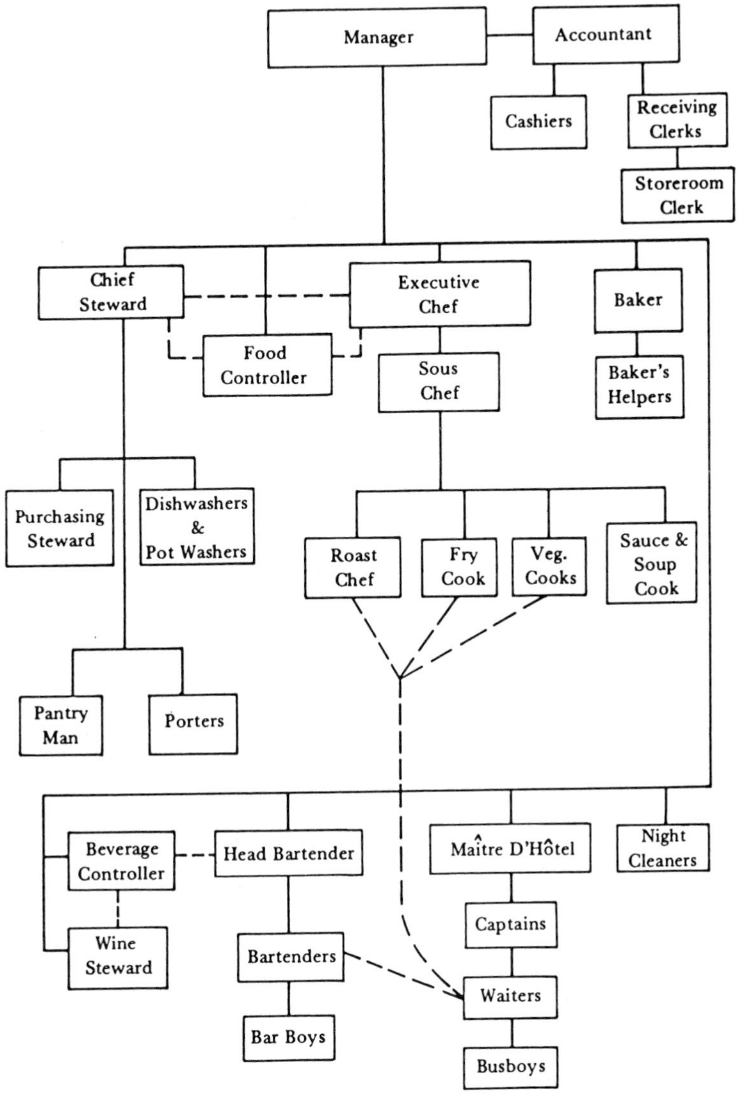

this particular case, the job description not only shows the dishwasher's duties and responsibilities in a general way but also gives instructions on the operation of the dishwashing machine, including a full explanation of the washing and rinsing temperature requirements. It also includes a detailed discussion of which items are to be washed by machine and which are to be done by hand.

FIGURE 18.2

Job Description

Title: Dishwasher

Summary of Work Performed: Washes all dishes, glassware, and silver. Maintains dishwashing machine cleanliness. Keeps dishwashing area clean.

Duties:

1. Washes all dishes, silver, and glassware in automatic dishwasher as follows:
   a. Wash hands and put on clean apron before starting work.
   b. Scrape all dishes into garbage can.
   c. Stack dishes, silver and glassware in separate containers, making sure no container is overloaded.
   d. Obtain instructions for operating dishwasher from steward, taking care that following temperatures are maintained.
      (1) Wash cycle: 140 degrees.
      (2) Rinse cycle: 180 degrees.
   e. Change wash water after each hour of use.
   f. Check each item for cleanliness. Wipe dry with clean dishcloth if necessary and stack in proper place.
2. Keep area immediately around dishwasher clean and dry.
3. Empty garbage at dishwasher after each meal.
4. Clean out dishwasher after each meal.
5. Perform other duties that are required from time to time.

Once the job descriptions are complete—once management has completely reviewed all tasks and assigned each to a particular job title in an orderly and logical way—a copy of the appropriate job description can be given to each employee in each job category. By this means, every employee on the staff can have a complete and thorough understanding of the nature of his or her job, as well as complete instructions for performing it. With these specifications for each job set down in writing, there can be no question of who is responsible for doing what within the framework of the organization.

Once a complete job description has been placed in the hands of each employee, management has a means for holding each employee accountable for performing a particular job in a particular way. One cannot hold the employee responsible for successfully completing a job unless he or she has been assigned it by management. The written job description furnishes an important and useful technique for the assigning of specific work. In addition, when work is well organized in this manner, it is more likely that cost will be kept to a minimum.

ANALYSIS OF BUSINESS VOLUME

The third important step that the manager must take before scheduling employees in such a way that labor costs are effectively controlled involves preparing an analysis of business volume. This analysis of volume typically takes the form of tallies of numbers of covers served. These tallies can and should be made on both a daily and an hourly basis.

Daily Analysis

Several techniques are commonly used for determining the number of covers served daily. Perhaps the simplest is to take the information from records being prepared for a sales history, as discussed in the earlier section on food control. If a cashier, for example, is developing records of the number of portions of each entree served in the dining room, then by simply totaling the number of portions of all items served, one could determine the total number of covers served during the day. In some smaller restaurants, where sales histories are not developed, but where guest checks are used, it would be a reasonably simple matter to record from the checks the number of persons served, after the close of business for the day. A third approach may be found in some establishments, particularly fast-food establishments, which makes use of modern electronic registers for the recording of sales. Several available models of these registers will give readings at the end of the day on the number of persons or covers served. In the last analysis, each restaurant manager must find a technique appropriate to his or her operation to determine the number of covers served daily.

With the development of the figures, business volume can be accurately forecasted in terms of the number of anticipated customers. It will be found in many restaurants, for example, that volume of customers served will vary from day to day during the week, with some days being typically more busy than others. As an illustration, many managers have found that Monday is slow compared to Friday. Knowing this in advance enables a manager to schedule an appropriate number of employees for each of the days, with a lesser number on a Monday and a higher number on a Friday.

In addition to helping forecast the appropriate numbers of employees needed to meet anticipated sales volume on various days of the week, such records also enable a careful manager to spot such things as seasonal variations in business volume, which should be taken into account in scheduling staff. Obviously nontypical days and weeks resulting from such unforeseen circumstances as bad weather, strikes, and gas shortages must be dealt with as they occur. A graphic illustration of the analysis of business volume by day of the week appears in figure 18.3.

Hourly Analysis

The daily analysis of business volume described above helps in controlling labor cost by permitting the manager to schedule employees' workdays and days off in accordance with anticipated needs, but it does not help at all in dealing with very real problems posed by the hourly fluctuation of demand in the restaurant business. Many establishments, for example, find that the middle of the afternoon is a very slack period between two periods of peak volume—the luncheon and dinner hours. In such cases the maximum number of dining room personnel on duty would clearly be necessary during the luncheon and dinner hours. However,

FIGURE 18.3
Analysis of Number of Covers Served per Day

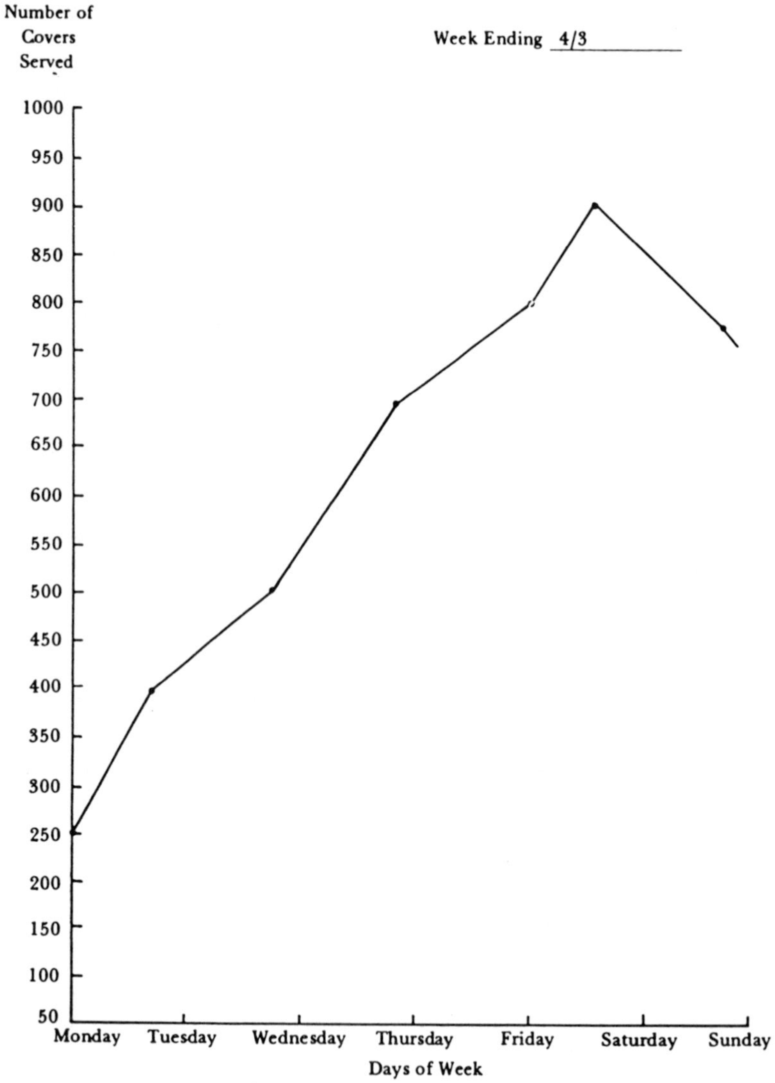

from the standpoint of keeping labor cost at the optimum level, it would normally be undesirable for the dining room personnel who were on duty during the busy lunch hour to stand around idly through the slack afternoon in anticipation of the busy dinner hour. Appropriate scheduling frequently eliminates the resulting excessive labor cost if management knows in advance which are the busy times and which are comparatively slow. In instances that are not as clear-cut as the example given, management can prepare an hourly analysis of business volume, which can be an important aid in establishing proper employee schedules designed to maximize employee efficiency and minimize excessive labor cost.

There are several ways to develop hourly analyses of business volume. Many managers will find that one of the suggested techniques will provide an adequate means for developing such an analysis. Others with special problems will find techniques appropriate for doing the same job under the conditions peculiar to their operations.

One common way for determining hourly volume of business is to require that the host or hostess count and record the number of customers seated in the dining room every hour on the hour. While this is by far the simplest system, it is not the most accurate. After all, a number of customers in some dining rooms order several cocktails before ordering food, and others may linger over coffee after eating. In either case, the hourly count will not accurately reflect the number of covers served during any particular period. To the extent that this count is used to schedule preparation personnel as well as dining room personnel, it may well present a misleading picture and consequently cause the manager to prepare work schedules that are not designed to deal with the volume at appropriate times.

To offset the inadequacy of this hourly counting procedure, some managers have instituted a system that involves time-stamping either guest checks or dupes in the kitchen as orders are given to the cooks. The checks or dupes are then analyzed at the end of the day; these results more accurately reflect when service personnel take orders, as well as when preparation personnel receive them.

A third system for analyzing hourly volume of business requires that the cashier in the dining room record the number of covers served as customers pay or charge guest checks. Each guest check, after all, must reach the cashier as the customer is about to leave the restaurant. Therefore a simple system can be instituted whereby the cashier merely makes marks on a form like the one illustrated in figure 18.4. When the guest check has been paid or charged, and the transaction is completed, the cashier merely determines how many covers are reflected on the check, and records that number in the space on the form for the one-hour period then current. This system is not as completely accurate with respect to preparation and service as is the one involving time stamps in the kitchen, but it has the advantage of being relatively simple and inexpensive.

By one or another of these means, the owner or manager can accumulate in a relatively short period a useful set of figures reflecting the hourly volume of business. By developing and maintaining this information on a regular and ongoing basis, the manager can better schedule variable cost employees, and thus control labor cost more effectively.

The first step in using the information developed above will be to tabulate the hourly volume of business for a given day, as has been done in figure 18.4. These tabulated figures are shown on the graph in figure 18.5. In this graph, the degree of fluctuation in hourly volume of business for this particular restaurant is readily apparent. However, this graph represents only one day, a certain Friday in April, and as yet we have no way of knowing whether or not this day is typical.

FIGURE 18.4
Hourly Volume of Business

Weather Clear Date 4/1

External Conditions Affecting Sales Strong Breeze

Hourly Period		Number of Covers
11:00-Noon	𝍸 𝍸 𝍸 𝍸 𝍸 𝍸 111	33
Noon-1 PM	𝍸 𝍸 𝍸 𝍸 𝍸 𝍸 1111 𝍸 𝍸 𝍸 𝍸 𝍸 𝍸 𝍸 𝍸 𝍸 𝍸 𝍸	90
1PM-2PM	𝍸 𝍸 𝍸 𝍸 𝍸 𝍸 𝍸 𝍸 𝍸 𝍸 𝍸 𝍸 𝍸 𝍸 𝍸 𝍸 𝍸 1111	89
2PM-3PM	𝍸 𝍸 𝍸 𝍸 𝍸 𝍸 𝍸 𝍸 𝍸 𝍸 1	51
3PM-4PM	𝍸 1	6
4PM-5PM	𝍸 11	7
5PM-6PM	𝍸 𝍸 𝍸 𝍸 𝍸 𝍸 𝍸 𝍸 𝍸	45
6PM-7PM	𝍸 𝍸 𝍸 𝍸 𝍸 𝍸 𝍸 𝍸 𝍸 𝍸 𝍸 𝍸 𝍸 𝍸 𝍸 111	78
7PM-8PM	𝍸 𝍸 𝍸 𝍸 𝍸 𝍸 𝍸 𝍸 𝍸 𝍸 𝍸 𝍸 𝍸 𝍸 𝍸 𝍸 𝍸 𝍸 𝍸	95
8PM-9PM	𝍸 𝍸 𝍸 𝍸 𝍸 𝍸 𝍸 𝍸 𝍸 𝍸 𝍸 𝍸 𝍸 𝍸 𝍸 𝍸 𝍸 𝍸 𝍸	95
9PM-10PM	𝍸 𝍸 𝍸 𝍸 𝍸 𝍸 𝍸 𝍸 𝍸 𝍸 𝍸 𝍸 𝍸 𝍸 111	73
10PM-11PM	𝍸 𝍸 𝍸 𝍸 𝍸 𝍸 𝍸 𝍸 𝍸 111	48

Clearly, it would be unwise to base general scheduling on the information reflecting only one day's operation. Therefore, it will be necessary to accumulate similar data for additional Fridays, and for other days of the week as well, because results of one day's operation may be atypical. A broader picture of operations will form a better basis for making these decisions.

A second step in scheduling is to tabulate the hourly volume data for a series of Fridays, for example, in a form similar to that shown in figure 18.6.

FIGURE 18.5
Hourly Analysis of Business Volume

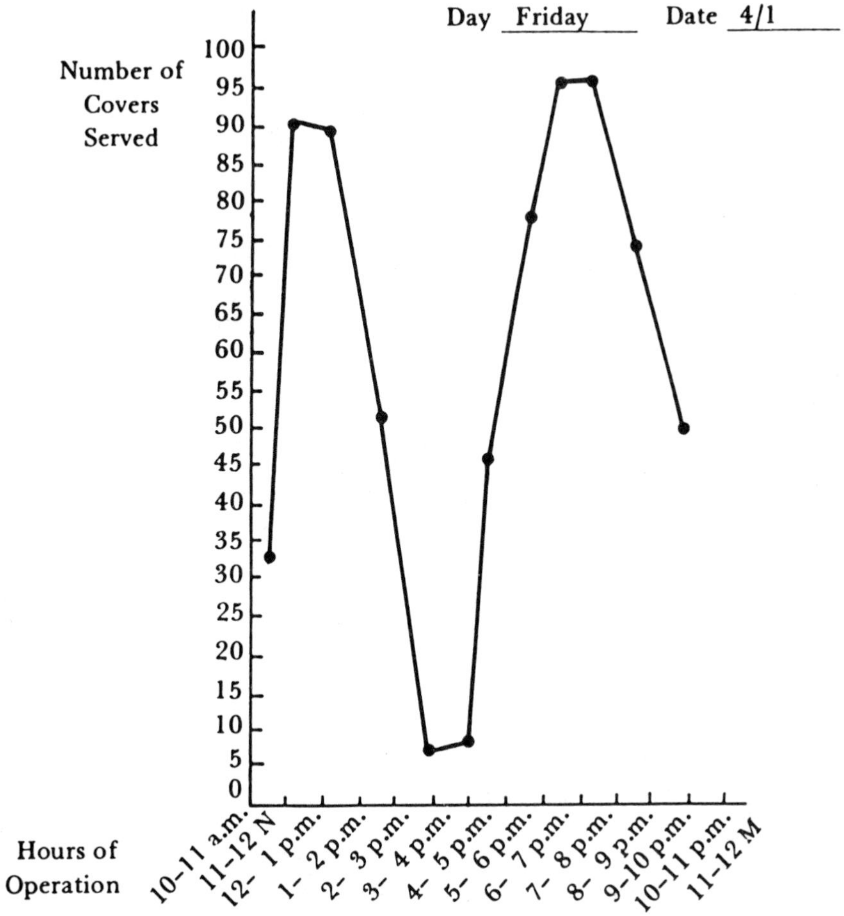

Charts of this nature may be prepared for each day of the business week. Taken together, they present a history of the hourly volume of business, which management can use in planning work activity in such a way that the cost of labor is controlled. One of the keys to labor cost control is effective manpower planning, and it is vital that the manager institute this control by scheduling labor according to anticipated requirements based on experience.

An important third step in the scheduling process is to translate the raw numbers such as those in figure 18.6 into a graphic presentation that will reflect the experienced hourly volume of business over a reasonable period of time. The graph shown in figure 18.7 presents a picture of this experienced hourly volume of business for the month of April in a certain restaurant on a given day. With the figures on the vertical axis showing volume of business and those along the

FIGURE 18.6

Hourly Volume of Business (number of covers): Fridays

Hourly Time Periods	Dates				
	4/1/8–	4/8/8–	4/15/8–	4/22/8–	4/29/8–
11 a.m. to Noon	33	30	50	40	60
Noon to 1 p.m.	90	85	105	100	107
1 p.m. to 2 p.m.	89	85	105	100	105
2 p.m. to 3 p.m.	51	50	63	60	65
3 p.m. to 4 p.m.	6	5	15	10	18
4 p.m. to 5 p.m.	7	5	12	10	18
5 p.m. to 6 p.m.	45	45	55	50	60
6 p.m. to 7 p.m.	78	75	96	90	100
7 p.m. to 8 p.m.	95	95	100	100	105
8 p.m. to 9 p.m.	95	85	95	95	100
9 p.m. to 10 p.m.	73	70	77	75	85
10 p.m. to 11 p.m.	48	45	55	50	60

horizontal axis showing hourly periods of the operating day, three lines are plotted on the graph to show volume at particular times. The upper dotted line shows the maximum volume of business experienced at each hour during the period covered by the graph. The lower dotted line shows the minimum volume. These are the extremes to which the hourly volume has gone during the hours shown. The solid middle line shows the median.

The median is the value of the middle item in a group. It is not an average, but a middle point. Figure 18.7 shows that business volume on the five successive Fridays between the hours of noon and 1 P.M. has ranged from 85 to 107 covers. The number of covers for the five days, taken in ascending order, have been 85, 90, 100, 105, and 107. From this list of five, those two with the highest values have been the days when it reached 105 and 107 covers per hour. The two days when volume was at its lowest were those on which the volume was only 85 and 90 covers per hour. By eliminating the two at the higher and lower ends of the scale, one is left with the value in the middle, the median. If the list of values had included hourly volume for fifteen days, eliminating the seven highest and seven lowest values would leave the middle value, the median hourly volume of business during the period.

The advantage of determining the median number of covers served during an hour rather than the arithmetic mean, commonly known as the average, is

FIGURE 18.7

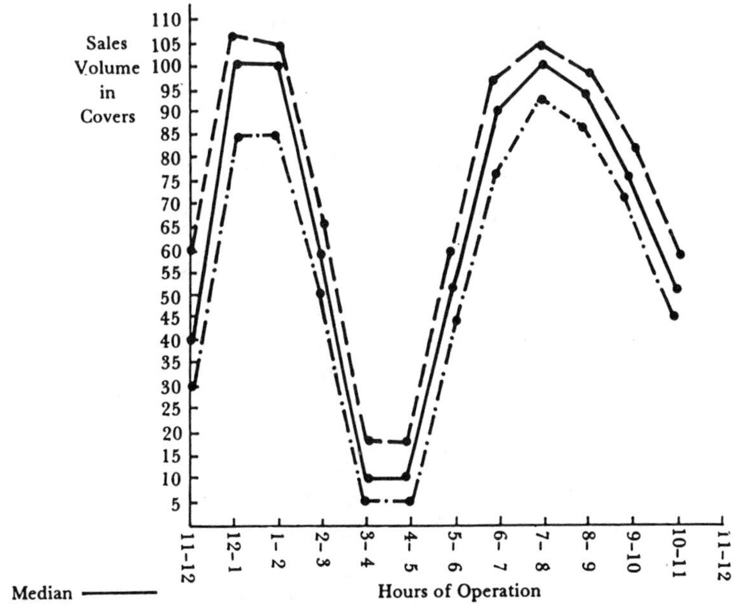

Median, Maximum & Minimum Hourly Sales Volume for Fridays.
1 Month Period Ending 4/31/-

that the median shows the central tendency unaffected by either high or low extremes. For example, if the number of covers served between 1 and 2 P.M. on five successive Fridays were 65, 66, 68, 71, and 25, the arithmetic mean, or average number, would be the total of 295 divided by the 5 periods represented, or 59 covers. The median number would be 66, which would clearly be more representative of the typical number of covers served. The average number has been weighed too heavily by the one extremely low number of covers served durıng one hour on one particular day. Since these figures are to be used for staff scheduling, it would be far safer to plan on the basis of the median number of covers served, rather than on the average. The median number offers a better idea of the typical number of covers to be served. In addition, by adding to the graph both the maximum and minimum numbers that have been served, as discussed above, the manager has a rather complete picture of the hourly volume of sales, including the typical number of covers served, as well as both the maximum and minimum extremes that have occurred.

SCHEDULING

With appropriate information available from the formal analysis of the daily and hourly volume of business, a manager is then prepared to address the next step in the process of controlling labor costs—scheduling employees.

Earlier in this chapter, employees were divided into two categories: variable cost employees and fixed cost employees. Because of marked differences in the scheduling of these two categories, particularly with reference to the use of daily and hourly analysis of business volume, scheduling techniques and procedures for employees in these groups will be discussed separately.

Scheduling Variable Cost Employees

With the completion of the daily and hourly analyses of business volume, a manager is in a highly favorable position to schedule variable cost employees, the need for whom varies directly with business volume. A first step will be to forecast total volume of business on a daily basis for each day in an upcoming period for which employees are to be scheduled, typically a work week. Because of conditions peculiar to a certain estalishment or to a certain geographical area, or to both, this scheduling may be done on a biweekly basis instead, but the same principles will apply.

Any manager or owner is in a better business position if he or she can determine today what conditions and sales volume are likely to be encountered in a future period. For this reason forecasts are made. Since experience has shown that history generally tends to repeat itself in food and beverage service businesses, an owner or manager can successfully use historical records to predict what is likely to occur at some time in the near future. In the area of food and beverage purchasing and production, such forecasts enable the manager to exercise a greater degree of control over costs. Similarly, a manager can better control labor cost if he or she is able to predict with reasonable accuracy the restaurant's manpower requirements for a certain volume of business, and then schedule an appropriate number of variable cost personnel on those days and times when they are needed. Looking back to figure 18.3, one sees a greater daily volume of business on Fridays and Saturdays than on Mondays and Tuesdays. Assuming that the graph represents the historical record of median business volume over an appropriate period, and also that similar conditions are expected for the week to be scheduled, it would be advisable to plan a schedule for variable cost employees that would be geared to the experiences graphed in figure 18.3. A manager should also use, to the extent possible, the recorded analysis of hourly volume of business so that all variable cost employees would not necessarily be working the same schedule. Their working hours should be staggered in a way that meets anticipated hourly demand. However, before this anticipated hourly volume can be of the fullest use in scheduling, the manager must judge the number of employees needed in each affected job classification of variable cost employees related to hourly volume. For waiters, he or she must determine how many covers each can serve in a given hour and still maintain the established service standards. For dishwashers, he or she must determine how many dishes each can wash per hour. Similar judgments must be made for each job category.

Manpower requirements are typically determined by intuitive judgments based on the manager's experience. (A more sophisticated approach used by many

FIGURE 18.8
Table of Manpower Requirements for Waiters for Friday, September 2, 19—, Based on Median Sales

Hours of Operation	*Anticipated Sales Volume in Covers*	*Manpower Requirements for Waiters*
10 a.m. to 11 a.m.	—	2
11 a.m. to Noon	40	2
Noon to 1 p.m.	100	5
1 p.m. to 2 p.m.	100	5
2 p.m. to 3 p.m.	60	3
3 p.m. to 4 p.m.	10	1
4 p.m. to 5 p.m.	10	1
5 p.m. to 6 p.m.	50	3
6 p.m. to 7 p.m.	90	5
7 p.m. to 8 p.m.	100	5
8 p.m. to 9 p.m.	95	5
9 p.m. to 10 p.m.	75	4
10 p.m. to 11 p.m.	50	3
11 p.m. to 12 p.m.	—	2

large operations will be discussed in the next chapter.) In the manpower requirement chart (figure 18.8), the manager judged that each waiter could serve twenty covers per hour, and referred to figure 18.3 showing the number of covers served per week, and to figure 18.7 showing the median number of covers served per hour on a particular day. For purposes of this discussion, we are assuming that the median figures given are those that are expected to occur in the future. Obviously, the manpower requirements would vary if conditions on the date forecasted more nearly approximated the maximum or minimum figure shown. Referring to figure 18.7, it can be seen that 100 covers are expected between 12:00 and 1:00 P.M. If one waiter can serve twenty covers per hour, five waiters are needed for that time period. Similar calculations are made for the other hours of the business day.

The manager can then prepare a schedule showing the total number of waiters needed for the day and the time periods they will work. In figure 18.9, the manager has scheduled waiters one hour before opening and one hour after closing for purposes of preparation and cleanup. To increase efficiency, he has also taken advantage of part-time employees. It is apparent that seven waiters are needed, three of them part-time and four full-time, of whom three are working split shifts. There are other possible working schedules that one could devise. For example, employee B could become a full-time employee by assuming his or her normal shift and taking on the shift of employee G. This would reduce the number of waiters from seven to six.

By following this procedure for all days and hours of operation during the work week being planned, while keeping in mind the number of days and hours that each employee could or would work, one can arrive at a work schedule that

FIGURE 18.9

Hourly Schedule for Waiters

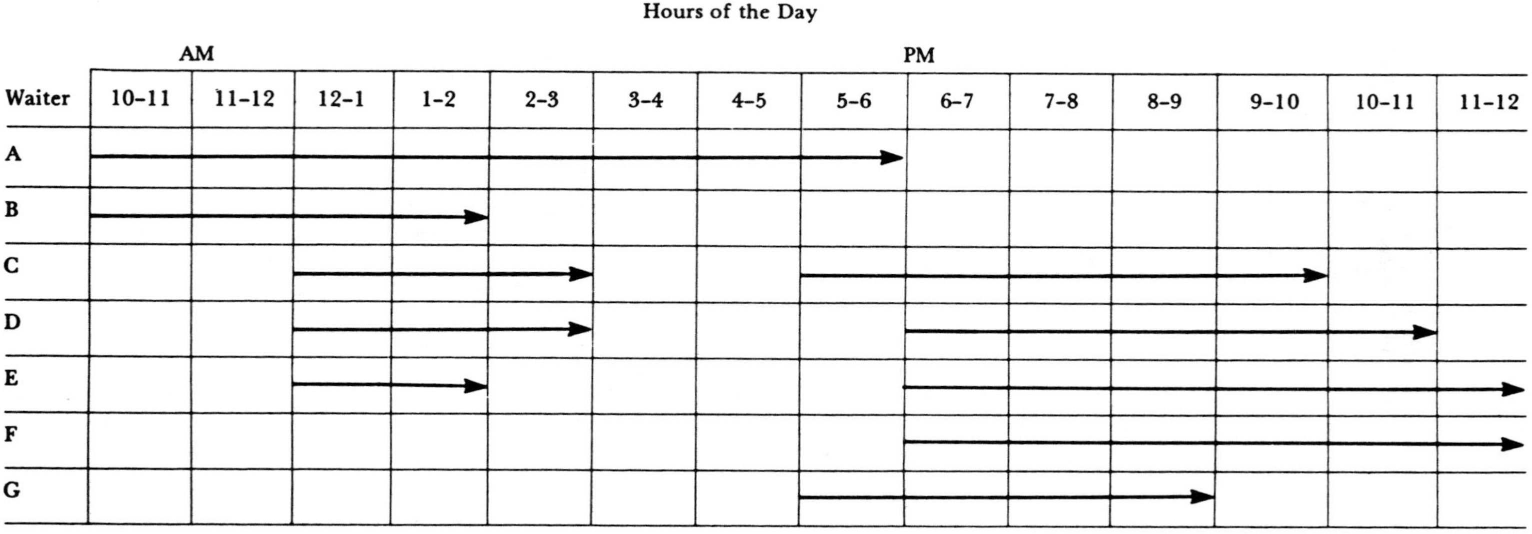

would be based both on anticipated sales volume by the day and hour, and on the manager's judgments concerning waiters' ability to meet these anticipated sales wihout sacrificing the standard of service. In addition, because the schedule would be based on these realistically anticipated needs, it could be set up in such a manner that labor costs would be maintained at the minimum level needed for forecasted sales. Once complete, a schedule like the one shown in figure 18.10 might be made up and posted in an appropriate location so that each employee would know his or her scheduled work hours sufficiently in advance.

FIGURE 18.10

Waiter	*Mon.*	*Tues.*	*Wed.*	*Thurs.*	*Fri.*	*Sat.*	*Sun.*
A	Off	Off	10–6	10–6	10–6	10–6	10–6
B	Off	10–6	10–2	10–2	10–2	10–2	10–2
C	Off	Off	12–3 5–10	12–3 5–10	12–3 5–10	12–3 5–10	12–3 5–10
D	12–3 6–11	Off	Off	12–3 6–11	12–3 6–11	12–3 6–11	12–3 6–11
E	10–2 5–9	10–2 5–9	Off	Off	12–2 6–12	12–2 6–12	12–2 6–12
F	10–6	6–12	Off	Off	6–12	6–12 6–12	
G	Off	5–9	5–12	5–12	5–9	5–9	Off
H						6–10	
I							

Scheduling Fixed Cost Employees

While the scheduling of variable cost employees may be considered as being tied directly to the daily and hourly analysis of business volume, the scheduling of fixed cost employees is related to such an analysis only in the most indirect way, and usually only in extreme circumstances. The fact of this difference is inherent in the very definitions of the terms *variable cost* and *fixed cost* employees.

Numbers of variable cost employees like waiters can be increased or decreased in direct proportion to business volume, but the same cannot be done with such fixed cost employees as the chef, the receiving clerk, and the cashier. For example, the receiving clerk's working schedule will be related to the anticipated delivery times of the food and beverage items. On the other hand, the cashier's working schedule will be closely related to the hours of the restaurant's operation and will not vary with volume of business.

Before fixed cost personnel can be scheduled with any degree of certainty, the manager must determine those factors of operation that affect each job and take all such factors into account in the scheduling process. In the case of the storeroom clerk, such factors as the need to have the storeroom open so that commodities can be issued to the productions staff during hours of preparation, and the need to have the storeroom clerk available to accept commodities taken in by the receiving clerk, both must be considered before establishing the work schedule for the job. When all such factors have been considered, a manager can establish a schedule for fixed cost personnel that would resemble that shown in figure 18.11. This schedule could then be posted for the information of all concerned. While these schedules for fixed cost employees tend to be relatively permanent, changes in business volume extended over a considerable period may cause the manager to reassess both schedules and costs for fixed cost personnel. Substantial decreases in business, for example, may suggest the need for a substantial decrease in labor cost generally, including a reduction in the cost of fixed cost personnel. In such instances, means must be found for instituting appropriate cost reductions without substantial reduction in the efficiency of the operation.

FIGURE 18.11

Employee	*Mon.*	*Tues.*	*Wed.*	*Thurs.*	*Fri.*	*Sat.*	*Sun.*
Purchasing Steward	9–5	9–5	9–5	9–5	9–5	9–5	Off
Storeroom Clerk	Off	8–4	8–4	8–4	8–4	8–4	8–4
Receiving Clerk	7–3	7–3	7–3	7–3	7–3	7–3	Off
Porter	Off	12–8	12–8	12–8	12–8	12–8	12–8
Vegetable Man	Off	8–4	8–4	8–4	8–4	8–4	8–4
Cashier 1	Off	5–12	10–5	10–5	10–5	10–5	10–5
Cashier 2	5–12	Off	5–12	5–12	5–12	5–12	5–12

Adjusting Costs of Fixed Cost Employees

The need for adjusting the costs of fixed cost employees is usually the result of a substantial reduction in business volume, particularly as this volume is reflected in overall dollar sales. As dollar sales decrease, especially for an appreciable period, management must uncover appropriate means for reducing the dollar cost of labor if the predetermined ratio of labor costs to total sales is to be held at a relatively constant level. In certain resort areas, for example, volume of business fluctuates seasonally, and during the slack period when dollar sales volume is substantially reduced, management must take appropriate steps to reduce labor costs as well. This is comparatively simple in the case of variable cost employees, whose presence or absence is governed to such a great extent by the sales volume. In the case of fixed cost employees, however, the solution to the problem of reducing labor cost may not always be quite so simple.

One means for lowering this cost is to take advantage of the many useful possibilities presented by part-time help. During a slow period, a manager might employ a receiving clerk to work fewer than thirty-five hours per week, and accordingly reduce the payroll. In fact, in some areas of the country, certain fixed cost employees look forward to certain slow periods so that they may reduce their work weeks and devote more time to other outside interests; they may even take jobs in other industries for what they regard as a change of pace. Such arrangements are clearly to the advantage of the manager who must bear full responsibility for keeping overall labor costs in line.

During slow periods in some establishments, the manager reduces the work weeks for such employees as cashiers to part-time status and personally fills the position during the other hours of the week. When business is slow enough, managers can often effectively perform two jobs at one time without diminishing their effectiveness as managers, thereby effecting a labor cost saving, or payroll saving, of the dollar cost of the cashier.

A related technique employed by managers whose payroll costs must be reduced during slack periods involves combining jobs. If, for example, a manager determined that a period of reduced business volume dictated reducing by half the hours of both the receiving clerk and the steward, he or she might eliminate one of them from the payroll entirely and retain the other to perform the needed work in both job categories, serving half the time as receiving clerk and the other half as steward. The manager not only will substantially reduce payroll costs at the appropriate time and for the appropriate duration, but will also be able to retain the more able of the two employees, thus effectively strengthening the staff.

In some instances, although management may be determined to reduce the cost of labor in proportion to the reduction in sales, turning some jobs into part-time positions or reducing the size of the fixed cost staff by combining jobs becomes impractical. In these cases, the normal work routines of fixed cost employees can be added to the work that would ordinarily be done by variable cost employees. Under these circumstances, certain positions would carry augmented duties for the duration of the slack period; but duties would revert to normal when the volume of business returned to normal. While this approach would not reduce the dollar cost of the fixed cost employees involved, it would reduce the number of dollars expended for variable cost employees, and the net effect on overall labor cost would be the same.

A fourth method for reducing the cost of certain fixed cost personnel has become feasible in recent years with the increasing popularity of convenience foods of all sorts. Many establishments substantially reduce the payroll expense for fixed cost employees, particularly specialized food preparation staff, by using a variety of items that require little or no preparation other than heating or chilling in the restaurant kitchen. While both advantages and disadvantages accompany the use of such products (which need not be discussed here), it should be apparent that in many instances their use does simplify certain of the purchasing, receiving, and preparation tasks in the restaurant. This simplification frequently enables a manager to reduce the size of the fixed cost work force, or to employ persons with less skill at lower wages, or both. For example, purchasing frozen, portioned meat might result in the elimination of a butcher from the kitchen staff, as well as make possible the hiring at a lower salary of a receiving clerk whose knowledge of meats could be greatly limited.

It must be pointed out that deciding whether to keep a butcher on the staff or to buy frozen, portioned meats is not always simple. When a manager decides to purchase frozen, portioned meats, he or she is deciding, wittingly or unwittingly, to reduce the cost for fixed labor in exchange for an increase in food cost. After all, any item purchased already prepared must include the cost of the producer's labor so that, in effect, the higher food cost to the restaurateur includes a certain labor cost. Assuming qualities to be equal, which may or may not be true, one factor in the "make-or-buy" decision must be a determination of the extent to which the increased food cost will be offset by the reduction in labor cost. A rule of thumb in the industry has been that it is normally cheaper to employ a butcher as long as there is sufficient work to keep one busy for the full number of working hours. However, this does not take into account such varying factors as labor contracts in different parts of the country or how butchering or not butchering on the premises may affect other steps in kitchen production.

A manager can use one or more of these techniques to reduce the payroll expenditure for fixed cost personnel for a limited period. With a return of business volume to a more normal pattern, decisions can be reversed, and the staff of fixed cost personnel returned to former size. However, in the light of changing conditions of various kinds, permanent changes in staffing sometimes become necessary. In effect, the manager must address himself to the problem of total reorganization—a process that may involve changing not only the size and quality of the staff of fixed cost personnel, but also number and calibre of variable cost personnel, and even the entire character of the operation. In the face of drastic problems, drastic measures are often required if the operation is to remain in business profitably. Total reorganization is often the sum of the drastic measures required.

REORGANIZATION

It would be impossible to compose a complete list of the conditions that have led restaurant owners and managers to decide to reorganize their establishments. However, in most cases, the conditions include either increases in costs or decreases in sales or both.

Increases in costs may be noted in any of the three areas discussed in previous chapters: fixed, directly variable, or semivariable.

Fixed costs, which are normally noncontrollable, may be increased when a new lease is negotiated with a landlord. In the case of a restaurant occupying a building owned by the restaurant owner, local government may dramatically increase real estate taxes.

Directly variable costs, primarily those for food and beverage items, may increase to such an extent that a manager cannot maintain a stable cost-to-sales ratio without raising selling prices beyond the amounts that customers are willing to pay. Labor costs may go up because of general economic conditions, or because of a new labor contract negotiated by some management organization to which the restaurant owner belongs, and this cost increase might be greater than what could be offset by an increase in selling prices. On the other hand, the same kinds of effects—increases in cost-to-sales ratios—might result from decreases in dollar sales.

Despite the reasons for these increases in costs or decreases in sales, because of an increase in the cost-to-sales ratio for fixed, semivariable or directly variable costs, or any combination of these three, the owner or manager must take drastic action to ensure favorable cost-to-sales ratios for each cost area, and consequently for the entire operation. While it is frequently possible to affect the food and beverage cost ratios, and thereby ensure profit, and sometimes possible to take a variety of steps to affect fixed costs in the long run, neither of these possibilities need concern us in a discussion of labor control. Rather, we will address ourselves to a need for total reorganization, and consequent restructuring of the labor force, on the assumption that all possibilities have been ruled out in the case in question. This will enable us to make certain points about reorganization in general, as well as to continue pertinent discussion of labor cost control.

Any manager who proposes to undertake a reorganization must remember two principal points:

1. Any resulting increase in cost-to-sales ratio for any cost category must be more than offset by a decrease in the ratio for another.
2. Any resulting increase or decrease in overall dollar sales volume must result in increased profit to the operation.

With these two points in mind, the manager planning reorganization has certain basic objectives against which to measure and judge any plans for change. Assuming that changes in fixed and directly variable costs have been ruled out, the manager will address himself to the subject of possible changes in the area of semivariable costs—labor costs.

The techniques for reducing labor costs as part of a reorganization program do not differ markedly from those employed by managers seeking temporarily to reduce cost. As discussed previously, they include combining jobs, hiring part-time rather than full-time employees where possible, adding duties of variable cost employees to the normal work routines of fixed cost personnel, and making appropriate use of various preprepared food and beverage items to reduce the labor cost for preparation.

The chief differences between a temporary reduction of labor cost and a permanent reduction through reorganization typically involve degree of change, as well as impact on the labor force as a whole and on particular jobs. Clearly, the manager who decides in favor of reorganization is reacting to a situation that has become untenable, one that dictates the need for a steady and reasoned reversal from insupportable financial statements to an acceptable profit picture. The manager knows what he or she must do: reduce the cost of labor to the extent necessary to ensure profit, particularly in instances where there can be no increase in either directly variable or fixed costs. To the extent to which the manager can do this, each dollar reduction in the labor cost should be a dollar increase in profit, assuming no change in overall dollar sales.

As an example of what might be done, figure 18.12 shows the effect of studied change on the organization chart of that hypothetical restaurant first presented in figure 18.1. It will be noted that reorganization has had major impact on a number of positions in the kitchen. For example, the sous chef has been eliminated, and the executive chef is now a working chef. In addition, the work of the purchasing steward has been taken over by the chief steward. Both the fry cook and the vegetable cook have been eliminated and replaced by a new worker whose duties include those of both the former job titles. The entire baking department has been eliminated, probably because of a decision to buy rather than make bakery products. These and other changes have resulted in a net reduction of five fixed cost employees, as well as an indeterminable number of variable cost employees. This reorganization represents an annual payroll saving of thousands of dollars, by which amount net profits should be increased.

It will be noted in the foregoing that management decided to eliminate the jobs of both the fry cook and the vegetable cook in favor of creating a new position for a combination vegetable/fry cook. This new worker could probably not perform all the duties of the former employees, so management would need to undertake another important facet in reorganizing: writing new job descriptions. As a result of the reorganization and the consequent eliminating of some jobs and the combining of others, new areas of responsibility have been created, and it is important that each be clearly and concisely covered by an appropriate job description.

Having completed major reorganization in the operation, it is to be assumed that maximum efficiency has been achieved, with every dollar of labor cost having a positive impact on the profit dollar.

END NOTE

It should be noted that all the procedures previously discussed for controlling labor cost are followed and found particularly useful by many establishments that are able to predict consumer demand with reasonable accuracy. Industrial, college,

FIGURE 18.12
Organization Chart After Reorganization

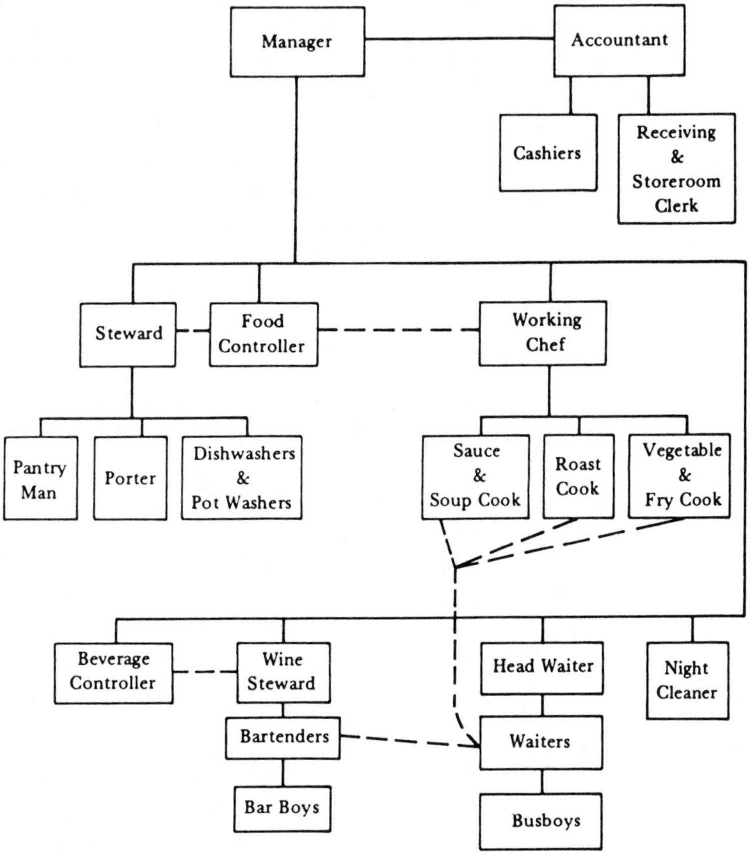

school, and institutional foodservice operations have this definite advantage. However, many operations do not enjoy the luxury of being able to forecast demand. Among them are numerous owner-operated and other commercial restaurants. Although they maintain sales histories, attempt to discern patterns in sales, and continue to strive for accurate forecasting, they find it impossible to predict what their customers are likely to do on any given day. Some have found it possible to predict likely sales for a week, but have not been able to forecast for any one particular day in that week with any high degree of accuracy. Such factors as weather, holidays, long weekends, and other events in the neighboring area all appear to affect sales, but not in a manner sufficiently consistent enough to facilitate a forecast. These operators must, and often do, recognize that they are at some disadvantage in attempting to devise systems and procedures for the strict control of labor cost, and must be prepared to modify accepted control systems to their special conditions.

In general, such operators must be prepared to accept some degree of inefficiency in order to be able to meet customer demand when it occurs. Some are able to offset their disadvantage partially by keeping some personnel on call for possible part-time work if demand develops on some particular day. Others typically staff their operations at levels suitable for meeting minimum demand and stand ready to work alongside their employees when business warrants. Any student planning to own or manage a smaller commercial operation should be aware of the possible limitations on the use of labor cost control techniques, and should keep in mind any possibilities for maintaining a list of willing part-time workers or for becoming a working manager when conditions demand it.

EDP APPLICATIONS

In Chapter 13 we described terminals that waiters and waitresses use at side stands in a dining room for a number of purposes including placing orders in the kitchen. These terminals are employed in conjunction with a CPU that includes a real-time clock. This clock notes the time at which any order is placed. Additional possibilities include determining both the time at which any party placed its first order and the time at which it settled the check. With all of this information stored in the computer, an analysis of business volume by day, meal, or hour is merely a matter of requesting a print-out of the requisite data. This data can be used to prepare a table of manpower requirements that would aid management in the appropriate schedule of variable cost personnel.

CHAPTER ESSENTIALS

In this chapter, we identified the purposes of labor control. We described those special characteristics of the restaurant industry that prevent implementation of labor cost controls to the extent found in other industries. For purposes of labor cost control we distinguished between variable cost personnel and fixed cost personnel. We listed and discussed three preliminary steps in scheduling employees and showed how both variable and fixed cost employees may be scheduled. We discussed how adjustments or reorganization can reduce excessive costs of fixed cost personnel. Finally, we suggested how computers could assist managers in analyzing business volume to determine manpower requirements.

QUESTIONS AND PROBLEMS

1 What are the purposes of labor control?

2 What are the differences between fixed cost personnel and variable cost personnel?

3 In what respects does the demand for restaurant products differ from the demand for most other manufactured products?

4 What preliminary steps should be taken before work can be organized?

5 Prepare a job description for a receiving clerk.

6 A certain restaurant has 100 seats; its business volume as illustrated in the chart below. Prepare a schedule of waiters similar to that illustrated in figure 18.9 (a) each waiter can take care of twenty-five covers per hour, (b) each waiter works an eight-hour shift (insofar as possible). However, part-time employees can be used.

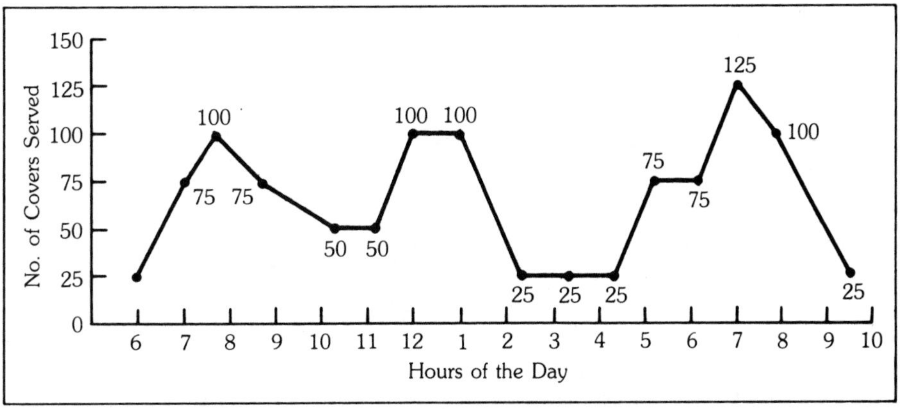

7 Using the same pattern of business volume as in problem 6, prepare a weekly schedule of waiters as in figure 18.10 for the restaurant if the number of covers served was the same each day, except for Monday and Tuesday, on which covers were half the number of the other days. Each full-time waiter works a five-day week.

8 In what ways do the schedules for fixed cost personnel differ from the schedules for variable cost personnel?

9 What conditions would necessitate temporary changes in staffing levels and costs of fixed cost personnel? What conditons might make permanent changes necessary?

10 Identify each of the following terms:

Variable cost personnel	Fixed cost personnel
Job description	Organization chart
Work schedule	Manpower requirements
Reorganization	Median

11 How can the computer aid management in analyzing business volume and determining manpower requirements?

chapter 19

Controlling Labor Costs II

Learning Objectives

After reading and studying this chapter, the student should be able to:

1. Explain the significance of quality and quantity standards in labor control.
2. Explain why foodservice operators cannot normally adopt typical industrial procedures for controlling labor cost.
3. List and describe three methods for establishing performance standards.
4. Prepare a table of standard man-hour requirements, and forecast staffing requirements for a given level of sales.
5. Prepare a reconciliation of standard and actual man-hours based on the number of covers served.
6. Explain how the computer can assist management in developing standard manpower requirements.

The last chapter showed how management could determine manpower requirements for variable cost personnel, based on the number of covers anticipated, taking into account the number of employees in each category needed to service a given number of customers. Daily schedules were then prepared that took advantage of part-time employees and split shifts to create maximum efficiency. Manpower requirements for fixed cost personnel were based on factors other than the number of covers anticipated, and schedules were prepared to best meet the needs of the establishment. Maximum efficiency was achieved through reevaluation of needs using the techniques of combining jobs, part-time employees, adding to work routines the jobs of variable cost employees, and using preportioned or precooked foods to eliminate jobs.

This approach to labor control is useful and widespread throughout the industry. However, many larger restaurants and chain operations have found it desirable to take the process one step further; they try to determine on an ongoing basis how well department heads and individual restaurants are scheduling employees to maintain maximum efficiency. Standards of performance for departments and units have been determined and means have been found to compare these standards with actual performance. That is the subject of this concluding chapter.

STANDARDS OF PERFORMANCE

In Chapter 2 we defined standards as rules or measures established for making comparisons of judgments. Management sets standards to determine the extent to which the results of activity meet preliminary expectations or plans. Other chapters illustrated the importance of the standards in judging the effectiveness of procedures set up to control food and beverage costs. Now it will be appropriate to discuss and illustrate the importance of setting up and using standards to control and measure labor costs.

Previous chapters showed that standards can be divided into two primary categories: *quality* standards and *quantity* standards. Standards for the control of labor cost fall into these same two classifications.

THE DEVELOPMENT OF QUALITY STANDARDS

Before attempting to develop any quality standards for employee performance, the manager must first have in mind a clear and detailed image of the restaurant, which includes an understanding of the quality standards for food and beverage items offered, as well as the nature of the clientele. Only then can quality standards for employee performance be set. For example, a manager would be in a better position to establish quality standards if he or she knew that the restaurant would be serving sandwiches to a hurried clientele of business people and shoppers, rather than steak Diane to a relaxed group of corporate executives celebrating the conclusion of a multimillion-dollar business deal. The quality standards for performance in the first instance need not be quite so exacting as those in the second. Sandwich service need not be so polished as the French service appropriate to serving steak Diane.

THE DEVELOPMENT OF QUANTITY STANDARDS

Once appropriate quality standards have been established, correspondingly appropriate quantity standards must be developed. The manager must determine the number of times that a task of a given level of quality should be performed within a certain time period. The typical time period is the same as that used for payroll purposes, the hour. In effect, the manager must determine the quantity of performance to be expected per hour, per meal, per day from employees in each job classification.

In the business world generally, a number of sophisticated techniques have been developed for the establishment of these standards. These approaches have been successful in setting up performance standards for a variety of factory and office jobs that are essentially repetitive in nature. On an assembly line, for example, one individual is typically responsible for one task and can reasonably be expected to perform that task a certain number of times per hour. Each job may be analyzed by such techniques as a time and motion study, which involves breaking a job down into component parts and particular body movements. Each job may be reevaluated from time to time, and the most efficient means for performance must be clearly defined and taught to the workers. The key to this approach lies in the repetitive nature of the tasks to be performed, as well as in the essentially nonperishable nature of the typical manufactured product.

In a typical manufacturing business, production is tied to demand in the long run, but need not be tied to demand on a day-by-day basis. A factory can turn out items that can be stored in inventory for appreciable periods. In the long run, management must schedule production in such a way that the supply of an item produced does not exceed demand, and this can be done by increasing and decreasing—or even by ceasing—production for a period of time.

Some of the fast-food chains have made significant progress in so defining jobs and scheduling production that they come close to approaching the efficiency found in many manufacturing operations. For example, several of the nationally known hamburger chains produce various kinds of sandwiches for anticipated demand based on ongoing business volume analysis. The sandwiches are stored in inventory for a very short period, usually not more than ten minutes, after which the products are discarded.

While these industrial techniques could possibly be used in the restaurant business, it has not been widely done. For example, a time and motion study might be performed to determine appropriate techniques for a cook to use in making omelets of acceptable quality at peak efficiency for one hour. Such a study might result in a determination that the cook could produce thirty per hour by following certain carefully specified procedures. However, this would be of little use unless the cook actually had to produce thirty per hour for each hour of work. Generally, this is not the case.

In the restaurant business, production must be closely related to immediate customer demand, not to projected demand as in other manufacturing businesses. In part, this is due to the essentially perishable nature of the product. In most instances, there are limits to which produced items can be stored for eventual sale. Many items, such as omelets, cannot be stored at all.

The products of the restaurant kitchen are among the most highly perishable imaginable. In addition, the tasks involved in their production must be governed to a great extent by this perishable nature of the product and also by the fluctuating nature of customer demand. Further, unlike typical factory workers, restaurant personnel do not usually repeat the same specific tasks hour after hour, day after day. The cook who makes omelets one minute may be called on to produce some other item the next. If and when the menu changes, the tasks assigned to the cook may change as well; if omelets are not on the menu, the cook will certainly not be producing omelets.

Some fast-food operators, and a number of food processors catering to fast-food restaurants, have been able to take advantage of certain production techniques used in typical manufacturing enterprises, and have thus been able to employ such techniques as time and motion studies in establishing quantity standards for production. Certain preportioned fast-food items can be produced, frozen, and stored for projected sale, either by the processor or by the fast-food operator. In some instances, such items as hamburgers can be produced by employees doing repetitive assembly-line jobs, and stored in their cooked state for limited periods until sold. However, most restaurants are not able to use these assembly-line techniques. Even those that do use them to a limited extent find that they are applicable only to a limited number of personnel, many of them fixed cost personnel. Therefore, food and beverage service operations must find other ways to establish quantity standards for employee performance.

ESTABLISHING PERFORMANCE STANDARDS

While many disagree about what constitutes the best method for establishing realistic quantity standards for performance and scheduling, several methods have received acceptance in the restaurant industry. Because of their differing emphases, they must be discussed separately.

One popular approach is commonly found in restaurants whose menus seldom vary and whose sales change little from week to week. Managers of these establishments routinely review the staffing of the restaurant in the most recent weeks. Purely on the basis of recollection, they decide whether sufficient staff was on duty to meet customer needs. Then, to the extent to which previous schedules were adequate, they are repeated, thus becoming standards of sorts. If recollection suggests that staffing was excessive or inadequate, seemingly appropriate changes are made and an amended schedule is prepared. It should be noted that the entire scheduling process depends on remembering the details of past performance; pure guesswork is the essential factor in determining increases or decreases in scheduled work hours. Because this approach fails to make use of any recorded data on sales volume, it is usually not a reliable way to maximize efficiency and thus control labor cost.

A second method attempts to set realistic standards by approaching the problem in a pragmatic but orderly manner. A test period of a particular number of days or weeks is established for gathering data. During this period, sales volume records are kept, detailing the number of covers sold per day or per meal, depending on the type of restaurant under analysis. Management also records the number of persons on duty in each fixed and variable cost job category, and reviews each, making intuitive judgments about the sufficiency of the numbers and the efficiency of employee performance in each category.

Variable Cost Personnel

Figure 19.1 relates numbers of variable cost personnel to sales volume in covers for a particular test period, and indicates one manager's judgments about staffing during that period. As the chart shows, with sales of 300 covers and seven waiters

FIGURE 19.1

Employee Performance

NOON MEAL 11:00 A.M.–2:00 P.M.

Date	5/1	5/2	5/3	5/4	5/5	5/6	5/7
No. of Covers Served	275	450	400	350	400	425	500
Waiters Scheduled	7	7	7	7	7	7	7
Efficiency of Performance	Poor—Only 5 Waiters Needed	Excellent	Very Good	Poor—Only 6 Waiters Needed	Very Good	Excel-lent	Poor—8 Waiters Needed
Warewashers Scheduled	3	3	3	3	3	3	3
Efficiency of Performance	Poor—Only 2 Needed	Excellent	Good—Some Ineffi-ciency	Poor—Only 2 Needed	Good—Some Ineffi-ciency	Excel-lent	Poor—Overtime Required
Preparation Personnel Scheduled	4	4	4	4	4	4	4
Efficiency of Performance	Poor—Only 3 Needed	Excellent	Good—1 Less Needed	Not Good—1 Less Needed	Good	Excel-lent	Excellent

scheduled for the luncheon on May 1, the manager judged performance to be highly inefficient because of overstaffing, and recorded his observations for future reference. As the one-week period progressed, he continued to note his estimates of labor efficiency, relating the number of waiters working to the total number of covers served. While figure 19.1 has been set up to record estimates of labor efficiency for an entire meal period, it would be possible to do this on an hourly basis, if a more complete and detailed view were required.

Fixed Cost Personnel

It also is feasible to prepare a similar chart that relates numbers of fixed cost personnel to numbers of covers sold for a period and provides for the manager to estimate employee efficiency by the day or meal, or even by the hour. However, as has been noted, the nature of the work of fixed cost personnel is such that the numbers on duty in any category cannot be varied in normal circumstances. Under extraordinary conditions—for example, when sales increase or decrease abnormally for protracted periods—such charts could reflect the need for either augmenting staff or laying off staff and combining jobs. However, such volume/staffing review charts are normally prepared only for variable cost personnel.

MANPOWER REQUIREMENTS

Once these charts have been prepared for the test period and the manager has a record of sales volume, numbers of variable cost employees working, and personal estimates of the employees' efficiency, he or she can begin to take the next logical step: to develop a table of manpower requirements for variable cost personnel at several levels of business volume. Figure 19.2, a typical example, shows manpower requirements for variable cost personnel in each category. It is apparent from a comparison of figures 19.1 and 19.2 that this particular manager judged seven waiters excessive for serving 300 covers on May 1, and therefore set five as a more appropriate number. Similarly, he judged seven as insufficient for serving 500 covers on May 7, and determined that this number of covers could be satisfactorily served by eight waiters. Thus, by judging performance carefully and recording these judgments over a period of time, a manager can set standards for staffing. Referring to both of these tables of standard manpower requirements and forecasts of anticipated sales for a coming week enables the

FIGURE 19.2
Standard Manpower Requirements—Luncheon

Covers	200–299	300–399	400–499	500–599
Waiters	5	6	7	8
Warewashers	2	2	3	4
Preparation Personnel	3	3	4	4

manager to better control labor cost by more accurately scheduling only that amount of manpower necessary to meet the preparation and service standard of the establishment. This technique can be refined to reflect hourly standards for manpower performance. When hourly tables are used, the manager can achieve an even greater degree of control over labor cost. Clearly, hourly analysis and appropriate tables abstracted from them, as discussed in the previous chapter, would present a more complete and detailed view of labor efficiency.

Although this second approach to developing quantity standards for labor performance is an improvement over the first, particularly in providing a useful approach to the scheduling of variable cost employees for forecasted sales, it does not provide a means for measuring either how well scheduling has been done based on established standards or how efficient labor actually was. If a way could be found to compare actual performance with the standards for performance set by management, differences could be noted, particularly those that reflect inefficiencies in labor productivity. Once these differences, or variances, have been noted, it would be possible for management to make efforts to eliminate them in future planning, bringing labor productivity up to the standards set and potentially reducing labor inefficiencies to the lowest possible point.

In order to accomplish this goal, it is necessary to discuss another way of looking at standards for labor productivity. We will discuss standard man-hours: the number of employee work hours necessary in each job category to perform a given volume of forecasted work.

If, for example, eight waiters are needed to serve 500 covers in a given three-hour luncheon period, the standard man-hours required would be calculated as follows: eight waiters × three hours = twenty-four man-hours of waiters' work. The twenty-four man-hours would become the standard for serving 500 covers over the luncheon period, and any excess of man-hours scheduled would indicate to the manager that some degree of inefficiency exists in the scheduling of waiters. Any number of hours less than the twenty-four would indicate that less than satisfactory service (quality standards) was being given to the customers. A different number of standard man-hours would be required for different levels of sales volume, and it would be up to management to determine what these should be. The increased or decreased number of standard man-hours required to serve more or less than 500 covers would not necessarily increase in direct proportion to the increased or decreased volume of business. In the previous example, twenty-four man-hours of waiters' work was the standard for serving 500 covers during the luncheon period. For the three-hour time period, this works out to 20.83 covers per standard man-hour. At a lesser volume—300 covers, for example—seven waiters representing twenty-one standard man-hours may be necessary because of the accepted relative inefficiency at lower volume. During low-volume periods, a waiter at his station would not have as many customers to wait on but would be kept busy. At the lower volume, this works out to 14.3 covers per standard man-hour. Thus, the number of man-hours required for 300 covers is twenty-one, based on management's judgment of quality service, and twenty-four waiters' man-hours for 500 covers during the three-hour period. To the extent that more man-hours than the standard number required are utilized, management will see that greater efficiency is both possible and desirable. If fewer than the standard are utilized, management might judge that the quality of service was not up to standard. By employing the techniques previously discussed, management can develop tables of standard man-hour requirements for various levels of business activity (see figure 19.3).

FIGURE 19.3
Standard Man-Hour Requirements—Variable Cost Personnel: Luncheon

Number of Covers	*Service Personnel*	*Warewashing Personnel*	*Preparation Personnel*
200	15	6	8
300	17	6	8
400	19	8	11
500	21	10	11
600	23	10	11

Figure 19.3 is one example of a table of standard man-hour requirements for variable cost personnel for one particular restaurant. Used in conjunction with forecasts of sales volume, these figures are helpful in both forecasting manpower and scheduling employees as efficiently as possible.

In a given restaurant, 450 covers for a given luncheon period have been forecast based on the sales history. Schedules are prepared, and at the conclusion of the meal a report like the one in figure 19.4 is written up.

FIGURE 19.4
Daily Comparison of Forecast and Actual Man-Hours Scheduled

Day 6/2/— Date Tuesday Meal Luncheon
Number of Covers:
Forecast 450

Personnel	*Standard Man-Hours*	*Actual Man-Hours*	*Difference*	*Explanation*
Service	19	19	- 0 -	
Warewashers	8	8	- 0 -	
Preparation	11	14	3	training new cook

It should be noted that the scheduling of the service personnel and the warewashers was done well, and that proper explanation was given for the excess over standard man-hours for the preparation personnel. This provides the owner or manager with a report indicating how well or how efficiently the variable cost personnel were scheduled. However, it does not indicate to the manager how efficient his personnel were during actual service because the report does not take into account the actual numbers of covers served. More than the forecasted number of customers might have appeared at the restaurant, in which case the service might not be up to standard quality. Or, on the other hand, if fewer than the forecasted number of covers were served, it can be assumed that labor was not used to its maximum efficiency. Therefore, an additional report, like the one shown in figure 19.5, is necessary so that the manager can determine with some degree of accuracy the efficiency of his or her labor force.

FIGURE 19.5
Daily Reconciliation of Standard and Actual Man-Hours, Based on Actual Covers Served

Day Tuesday Date 6/2/— Meal Luncheon

Number of Covers: Sold 360 Weather fair

Personnel	*Standard Man-Hours*	*Actual Man-Hours*	*Difference*	*Explanation*
Service	17	19	2	covers fewer than forecast
Warewashers	6	8	2	covers fewer than forecast
Preparation	8	14	6	covers fewer than forecast

Although it is readily apparent that while the scheduling has been efficiently accomplished on the basis of the forecasted information, a degree of inefficiency resulted from the overscheduling of too many personnel. If the above result were repeated frequently, the owner or manager might have to find ways to forecast with greater accuracy. Other possible reasons for differences to occur might be found in unforeseen variations in weather and in other conditions affecting sales, such as the street in front of the restaurant being torn up, improper attention to standard man-hour charts resulting in poor scheduling, and absenteeism. The important point is that management now has some means of determining the efficiency of labor, and thus can better pinpoint inefficiency and take remedial action to improve future performance.

EDP APPLICATIONS

Many fast-food chains are using the computer to estabish suitable production rates based on extensive ongoing analysis of sales volume. From the data developed, they have been able to establish standard manpower requirements for all personnel classifications and for all levels of sales volume. This enables the manager of such an establishment to obtain information from the computer to schedule personnel efficiently.

CHAPTER ESSENTIALS

In this chapter we discussed the importance of developing performance standards, both as guides for efficient scheduling and as means for judging performance. We distinguished between quality standards and quantity standards for performance, and explained how performance standards may be implemented and expressed as standard manpower requirements. We showed how standard man-hour and actual hours worked may be compared and analyzed. Finally, we showed how computers may be used to forecast standard manpower requirements for given levels of sales volume and can assist in controlling labor cost.

QUESTIONS AND PROBLEMS

1 Of what significance are established quality and quantity performance standards in controlling labor costs?

2 List and describe the methods for establishing performance standards.

3 Which of the methods for establishing performance standards would be most practical for most foodservice establishments? Why? Which would be the least practical for smaller operations? Why?

4 Why would managers of some smaller restaurants decide not to attempt the standard man-hour approach to control labor cost?

5 Many object to the standard man-hour approach to labor cost control on the grounds that it completely ignores the human relations element in the workplace. What do you believe they mean by this? What possible drawbacks are inherent in this approach?

6 Assume that the figures in figure 19.3 are applicable to a restaurant you are managing. Prepare a list of staffing requirements for the five days forecasted below:

Monday, June 7—200 covers
Tuesday, June 8—350 covers
Wednesday, June 9—450 covers
Thursday, June 10—600 covers
Friday, June 11—800 covers

7 What characteristics of the foodservice industry make it difficult, or impossible, to pursue the industrial approaches to standard man-hour labor control?

8 In a certain restaurant the manager has determined that six waiters are needed for 320 to 380 covers over a three-hour luncheon period; seven waiters are needed for 381 to 440 covers; eight waiters are needed for 441 to 520 covers; and nine waiters are needed for 521 to 600 covers. Prepare a table of standard man-hours using figure 19.3 as a guide.

9 Using the chart developed in question 8 above, prepare a report similar to figure 19.4 for waiters only, if 460 covers are forecasted and twenty-six hours were scheduled on Tuesday, June 4.

10 Using the data from questions 8 and 9 above, prepare a report similar to figure 19.5 for waiters only, if 420 covers were actually served during the three-hour luncheon period Tuesday, June 4.

11 How can the computer assist management in developing standard manpower requirements?

Afterword

Throughout the text the authors have attempted to provide a structured introduction to food, beverage, and labor controls for the student planning a career in some part of the hospitality service industry. We believe, and believe quite strongly, that anyone planning a career on any level of management in this industry should be familiar with the principles of control as they apply to this field. Moreover, anyone planning such a career should be prepared to translate these principles into judicious practice whenever and wherever conditions warrant. The operative phrase here is, of course, judicious practice.

In our teaching experience we have both encountered students who planned to become managers and impose some prefabricated control system on whatever operations they were hired to manage. They have been warned, by us and by others, of the impossibility of doing so. Most have heeded our warning; some have not, and they have been the ones to reconfirm, through their own hard experiences, the problems inherent in installing preconceived control systems where none have previously been used, or, alternatively, of changing existing systems to suit some preconceived ideas of what control systems should be used. Some have even been surprised to discover that most establishments have no food controller and no beverage controller and that, in fact, any control procedures put into effect in the average foodservice operation must be both instituted and supervised by the manager, who, in effect, becomes food controller, or beverage controller, or both.

Those entering the field should be aware, right from the outset of their careers, that comparatively few of the many thousands of foodservice operations maintain anything like complete control systems. Many of the larger establishments, including chains, do have reasonably complex systems. Some individually owned and managed operations attempt to control some aspects of their businesses, and a substantial number have no conception of the principles or techniques of control. This last may help to explain why the business failure rate among restaurants continues to be so very high.

To attempt to impose complex control techniques and procedures on all foodservice operations is probably not the answer. To do so would doubtless be costly, and probably uneconomical. On the other hand, carefully and judiciously selected techniques used in certain phases of the operation would probably benefit many.

This is what we hope the student entering the industry will recognize and be able to implement. We hope, for example, that he or she will see the importance of reasonable portion control measures in most situations, and will be able to suggest or mandate portion control in some particular kitchen setting without feeling obligated to insist on a complete pre-cost, pre-control system. We truly hope that each will be able and feel free to modify and adapt the principles, techniques, procedures, forms, devices, and suggestions from this text to suitable use in particular industry settings. If our student-readers across the years are able to do this, the industry will have been well served.

Index

abacus, 65
actual cost, 6, 193–204
actual hours worked, 342–344
actual inventory, 152–155
actual purchase price method, 127, 129
adding machine, 65
arithmetic ability, 67
automated bar, 254, 287–288
average check price, 56
average cost, 6
average cover, 51
average dollar sale, 14
average number of sales per hour, 15
average sale per seat, 15
average sale per serving person, 14–15
average sales price, 51
average unit cost, 6
average variable cost, 51
average variable rate, 53–58

BE. *See* Break-even point
bar control, 269–289
beginning inventory. *See* Opening inventory
beverage control, 231–292
beverages, 234-235
bin cards, 86–87, 242–243
book inventory, 152–155
break-even point, 45–47, 52–53, 55–58
budgeted costs, 7
budgets, 30–35
Burger King, 209, 210, 217
business location, 208–209, 302–303
business volume, 207–213, 316–323
butcher test, 166–169

CM. *See* Contribution margin
CPU. *See* Central processing unit
CR. *See* Contribution rate
calculating machine, 65
calculator, 65
call brands, 236
cash registers, 65, 287
cashiers, 226–227
central processing unit, 68, 70
centralized purchasing, 93–94
China, 65
cleanliness, 109–110
closing inventory, 126–127
cocktails, 257, 263–265
coding, 242–245
competitive prices, 92–93, 218
computers, 66–73 *See also* Electronic data processing
contracts, 299
contribution margin, 45–47, 218, 219–220
contribution rate, 45–47
control, 20–37, 64–73
controllable costs, 5–6
cooking loss test, 170–172
cost, 3–17, 42–47
cost card, 164–166, 263
cost control, 22, 48–50
cost factors, 169–170
cost of food consumed, 132–134
cost of food sold, 131–132, 134–135
cost per dollar sale, 8
cost percentages, 8–12, 146, 196–203, 270–278
cost-benefit ratio, 36–37

cost-to-sales ratio, 8–12, 218–219
cost/volume/profit relationships, 35, 41–59
cumulative cost percentage, 146, 196–203
customer purchases, 213–227
customers, 207–213

DP. *See* Data processing
data processing, 65–66 *See also* Electronic data processing
dating, 111–112
decor, 210
demand, 209–210, 310–311
desired ending inventory, 87, 89
differentiated product, 209
directly variable costs, 5
Directs, 102–104, 112, 145–148
dollar calculations, 50–51
dupe system, 225

EDP. *See* Electronic data processing
electronic data processing, 64–73, 95, 104–105, 118–119, 139, 155, 174, 190, 203, 227–228, 249, 267, 288–289, 334, 344
employees' meals, 133–134
ending inventory. *See* Closing inventory
end-of-month beverage cost, 270–275
equipment, 98, 108–110, 216, 303
excessive costs, 194–203

FC. *See* Fixed costs
FIFO. *See* First-in, first-out
first-in, first-out, 110, 127, 129
fixed costs, 4, 43–47, 312
flexible budget, 31–32
food checker, 223–225
food control, 75–230
food cost determinations, 124–140, 144–156
food/beverage transfer memo, 116
Foods in Process, 130
forecasting, 161, 177–191
free pouring, 254
front bars, 247
full bottle sales, 248–249

glassware, 254–257
goals, 21–22
gratis to bars, 132
grease sales, 132
gross profit, 203
guest checks, 222–223

hard copy, 68–69
hardware, 69
historical costs, 7–8
homogeneous product, 209
hours of operation, 305–306

IO. *See* Input/output devices
inefficiencies, 201–203
input, 67, 68–69
input/output devices, 68–69
Internal Revenue Service, 129
interunit transfers, 117–118
intraunit transfers, 115–117
inventories, 87–91, 124–140, 152–155, 187–190, 243–245, 271
inventory differential, 271
inventory valuation, 126–129
invoice stamp, 100
invoices, 99
issuing, 102, 107–119, 233–250

jigger, 253
job descriptions, 314–316

labeling, 84, 86
labor control, 293–346
labor cost control, 297, 309–334, 336–345
labor cost determinants, 295–307
last-in, first-out method, 128–129
latest purchase price method, 128, 129
layout, 110, 111, 303
legislation, 298–299
Leibniz, Gottfried Wilhelm, 65
line printer, 68–70
logic, 67
loss, 43

management ability, 26–31, 306–307
management information systems, 29, 102–104, 135–137, 148–152, 186–187, 226, 239–240, 338–339
management reports, 129–131, 135–137
manpower requirements, 324–325, 341–344
matching principle, 16, 115–118
McDonald's, 209, 210, 217
meat tags, 101–102, 112, 114
media, 69
median number, 322–323
Menu Pre-Cost and Abstract form, 189, 194–201, 219
menus, 212, 213–220, 305
metric conversion, 260
minimum wage, 298
mixed drink differential, 280–282
mixed drinks, 257, 263–265, 279–282
mixers, 234
monthly food cost report, 129–131

monthly income statement, 135–137
monthly inventory, 124–140

nanosecond, 66
National Restaurant Association, 15
net profit, 204
New York City, 208
noncontrollable costs, 5–6
nonperishables, 79, 84–85, 93

opening inventory, 126–129
operating budget, 30–35
operational plan, 313–314
optimum purchase price, 92–93
optimum temperatures, 108–109
ordering, 85–87
organization chart, 314
ounce control method, 278
output, 66, 68–69
overproduction, 182
overpurchasing, 81–91, 199
overtime, 298

P. *See* Profits
PSTS. *See* Proportional shares of total sales
par stock, 89–91, 185–186
Pascal, Blaise, 65
payroll costs, 5
performance standards, 337–341
periodic order method, 85–87
perishables, 78–79, 81–84, 92
perpetual inventory method, 87–91, 243–245
physical inventory, 125–127, 138–139
picosecond, 66
planned costs, 7–8
popularity index, 181–182
portion costs, 159–174, 259–265
portion inventory, 187–190
potential sales, 50–51
potential sales value method, 278–285
potential savings, 193–204
pourers, 253–254
pouring brands, 236
precost, precontrol method, 161, 163
preparation, 304
preportioning, 164, 170, 185–186
prices, 111–112, 114–115, 125–129, 209–210, 217–220
prime cost, 7
procedures, 26–27
product differentiation, 209
production control, 177–191, 251–267
production sheet, 183–185
production standards, 159–174
profits, 43–47, 193–204
programs, 69
promotion expense, 132, 276
proportional shares of total sales, 55
purchase order, 238
purchase quantities, 173, 235–236
purchasing control, 77–95, 233–250

quality standards, 25, 79–81, 211, 236–237, 337–338
quantity sold, 15
quantity standards, 25–26, 81–91, 252–257, 338–339

receiving clerk, 98–105
receiving clerk's daily report, 102–104, 239–240
receiving control, 97–105, 233–250
receiving equipment, 98
receiving supplies, 98
recipe detail, 164–166, 263
reconciliation form, 187–190
reorder point, 88–89, 91
reorder quantity, 88, 90
reorganization, 330–332
requisitions, 113–115, 245–248
responsibility, 23, 78, 235
restaurant sales control sheet, 226
revenue, 207, 221–227
ring-in, ring-out register, 287

S. *See* Sales
SP. *See* Sales price
sales, 3–17, 42–47
sales control, 22–23, 206–228, 285–288
sales history, 160–161, 178–182
sales level, 50
sales mix, 15–16
sales per serving person, 14
sales price, 11, 14, 45–47, 217–220, 265–266
sales volume, 301–302
scheduling, 323–330
seat turnover. *See* Turnover (customer)
Second World War, 65–66
secondary ingredients, 234, 263, 280
security, 111, 241
selling, 220–221
semi-variable costs, 5
service bars, 247
service standards, 211–212, 304
shelving, 109
shot glass, 253
signature book, 223
simple formula, 163–164

soft copy, 68–69
software, 69
special purpose bars, 247
standard cost, 26, 160–161, 163–172, 193–204
standard deviation method, 283–285
standard drink, 257–258
standard man-hour, 342–343
standard portion size, 161–162, 210–211
standard procedure, 26–27
standard purchase specifications, 79–81
standard recipe, 161, 162–163, 257–259
standard sales price, 265–266
standards, 25–26
standing order, 94
staples, 112, 114–115
static budget, 31
stemware. *See* Glassware
steward sales, 132
Steward's Market Quotation List, 81–84, 92, 100
Steward's Staple List, 100
stock rotation, 110, 127, 128–129
storage capability, 66
storage containers, 109
storage facilities, 108–111, 241–243
Stores, 102–104, 112–113, 145–148
storing, 107–119, 233–250
straight drinks, 257, 259–262
Sundries, 103
suppliers, 91–92

tagged items, 112, 114
temperatures, 108–109, 241
terminal, 68
test period, 198, 201–202, 282–285
time and motion studies, 338–339
total costs, 6–7
total dollar sales, 14
total sales, 194–203
training, 27–28, 300–301
transfer memo. *See* Food/beverage transfer memo
transfers, 107–119, 131–132, 272
turnover (customer), 15
turnover (labor), 299–301
turnover (stock), 137–139

unit costs, 6–7, 51–53
United States, 65
United States Department of Agriculture, 25, 36

VC. *See* Variable costs
VDT. *See* Visual display terminal
VR. *See* Variable rate
valuations, 126–129, 279–280
variable costs, 4–5, 43–47, 57–58, 311–312
variable rate, 45–47, 53–58
visual display terminal, 68–70
void sheet, 186–187

wages, 298–299
weather, 298
weighted average purchase price method, 128, 129
work organization, 312–313

yield percentages, 165, 166–167, 173